CALIFORNIA

REAL ESTATE ESCROW AND TITLE

George W. Lawrence

President: Dr. Andrew Temte
Chief Learning Officer: Dr. Tim Smaby
Executive Director, Real Estate Education: Melissa Kleeman-Moy
Development Editor: Adam Bissen

CALIFORNIA REAL ESTATE ESCROW AND TITLE
©2014 Kaplan, Inc.
Published by DF Institute, Inc., d/b/a Dearborn Real Estate Education
332 Front St. S., Suite 501
La Crosse, WI 54601

Printed in the United States of America

First revision, June 2018

ISBN: 978-1-4277-9093-4 / 1-4277-9093-0
PPN: 1609-0420

CONTENTS

ACKNOWLEDGMENTS

I dedicate this book to my wife, Regina, who devoted countless hours of technical advice and assistance in helping to make this book a reality. Sharing her twenty-five years' experience in the title and escrow industry, she helped to provide invaluable insight into the practices and ever present challenges of the title and escrow professional. And to my daughter, Tera (who followed her mother into the business), contributing her administrative skills and technical knowledge from start to finish, with the laborious and tedious task of proofreading, especially the technical content and terminology that "spell-check" simply cannot do.

I would also like to thank the following title and escrow professionals, who helped me navigate through and explain much of the technical material:

- Darth Eliopulos, Vice President, Fidelity National Financial

- Don Overton, Chicago Title Company

- Steven A. Sokol, Esq., Hastings & Sokol, LLP, Lawyers

INTRODUCTION

With homeownership rates in the United States reaching 64% in 2013 (down from its all-time high of nearly 70% in 2004), most Americans have been introduced to "escrow." Yet many may not have a clear understanding of the escrow process or why an escrow was used.

The term *escrow*, when used in the context of a transaction involving the sale or hypothecation (offering an asset as collateral for a loan) of real or personal property, refers either to the process of handling and accounting for documents and monies involved in the transaction or to the provider of such services. Escrow may also refer to monies belonging to a borrower that are held by the lender to be used for paying the borrower's property taxes and hazard (homeowner's) insurance when they become due.

Simply put, an escrow exists when a neutral third party depository holds property belonging to another for its disposition.

Title insurance is another matter. The purchaser of a piece of real estate who is required or encouraged to obtain title insurance may find it difficult to understand the need for such insurance and the protection it offers. Whereas escrow provides an immediate service, title insurance offers protection against a future event that may never occur. Few people really want to buy any type of insurance. Many people would not buy auto insurance if not required to do so by state law, and then oftentimes they purchase only the minimum amount of coverage required by the law. While term life insurance provides for the beneficiaries of the policy, it offers no financial benefit to the insured. The prospective property owner, therefore, must be informed about the benefits of title insurance, why it may be required, the coverage and protection it offers, who it protects, and who pays for it.

This book provides an in-depth explanation of the escrow, title, and related real estate services and the specific duties of the professionals who perform these services. It is directed toward those who work in any of the variety of occupations of the real estate industry, including escrow, title insurance, real estate brokerage, appraisal, and lending, and especially those new to their respective professions and careers.

The subjects covered provide the reader with a comprehensive overview of the responsibilities of the escrow and title insurance professional and offers an introduction to the activities, qualifications, and practices of the real estate and loan professionals and the services they deliver.

■ TERMINOLOGY

The following terms are used interchangeably throughout the book:

- *Real estate agents.* When referring to a real estate agent, unless specifically otherwise defined within the context of the subject matter, the terms *agent, real estate agent, broker, real estate broker, salesperson, real estate salesperson,* and *licensee* are all used interchangeably in this text.

- *Escrow holder.* Reference to the escrow holder may also mean the escrow officer, whereas referring to simply "escrow" will usually mean the escrow process itself.

- *Title insurance company.* The title insurance company may simply be called the title company. A reference to the insurer or the insurance company will be identified by the context in which it appears, such as either the title insurance company or a hazard insurance company—or simply homeowner's insurance company.

- *Title officer.* The title officer may also be called the title examiner.

- *REALTOR®.* Not all real estate agents are REALTORS®. Only those real estate professionals who are members of the National Association of REALTORS® may call themselves REALTORS® and use the logo identifying themselves as such. Since 1908, the National Association of REALTORS® and its membership have not only helped make the dream of homeownership a reality, they have adopted the mission of building better communities by helping to shape and promote community values and strengthen community bonds. The objectives of the National Association of REALTORS®, its members, and their collective commitment to the consumer in providing the highest standards of honest and ethical real estate practices are described in Chapter 7.

The real estate business, including escrow, title, and lending services, is often in a state of change. New laws and regulations require changes in the way business practices and procedures are executed. Innovations in technology cause change as well, typically providing greater efficiency and oftentimes with less cost. Some things, on the other hand, never change, such as the fundamental concepts of acquisition and protection of land, title, ownership interests, and property rights. The reader may find the information regarding those subjects covered in this book to be an interesting refresher, perhaps even forgotten or never clearly understood in the first place. The book revisits the past and shares the historical significance of events that contributed to the evolution of the title insurance and escrow industry. By looking at the times when the nation entered and emerged from financial crisis, history can provide a better understanding of the customs and laws that direct today's real estate and financial services practices.

CHAPTER ONE

1

PROPERTY RIGHTS

■ KEY TERMS

absolute ownership	metes and bounds	state lands
estates	property	submerged lands
government lots	Public Land Survey	tidelands
land descriptions	System	Treaty of Guadalupe
legal descriptions	public lands	Hidalgo
meridian and base line	qualified ownership	

■ LEARNING OBJECTIVES

Upon completing this chapter, you will be able to

■ explain the significance of the Treaty of Guadalupe Hidalgo;

■ identify basic land divisions, descriptions, and measurements;

■ explain the legal description of and the difference between personal and real property;

■ identify and explain types of real property ownership; and

■ identify the different estates in property.

■ A HISTORY OF CALIFORNIA REAL PROPERTY TITLE

Following the American War of Independence, each state adopted statutes that, for the most part, accepted English common law. California's system of law is founded in this English common law.

However, the characteristics of property interests and private property rights in California (then called Alta California, an area that included all or parts of Arizona, Utah, Nevada, Colorado, Wyoming, and California) actually come from the Spanish. In 1769, Spanish missions began appearing along the California coast. Among the first major property owners were those who received sizable land grants from California's Spanish governors. Two of the largest consisted of nearly all of what is now Los Angeles County.

The Spanish established forts called "presidios" to provide protection for settlers. Four in all, these eventually became some of California's largest and most beautiful cities: San Diego, San Francisco, Santa Barbara, and Monterey.

After the development of the presidios, the Spanish government created "pueblos," which provided resources such as food and other supplies for the presidios. Three of these pueblos evolved into the cities of San Jose, Los Angeles, and Sonoma.

After the end of the Mexican War of Independence from Spain in 1821, California was part of Mexico. Californians who agreed to become citizens of the new Mexican government received land grants. Known as Californios, they turned their lands into large cattle ranches, called ranchos. One of the largest, Tejon Ranch, was founded in 1843 and contained 270,000 acres. It still operates today as a working cattle ranch about 75 miles north of the city of Los Angeles. Other evidence of the former ranchos appears throughout California. Many cities stand on land once home to these ranchos: Pasadena, San Clemente, and Oakland, to name a few.

Other settlers began emigrating from Canada and the United States to California (remember, California was not part of the United States at this time). In 1846, a group of these settlers rebelled against the oppressive rule of Mexico. Rallying behind the newly adopted California Republic's "Bear Flag" (which would become the basis for the state flag of California), these Americans fought against General Antonio Lopez de Santa Anna and Mexico's rule.

The California Republic, which had been established on June 14, 1846, was short-lived. During the Mexican-American War, the U.S. government gained possession of the republic, and at war's end, California was admitted into the Union as a state. Note that unlike many of the future states that had been part of Alta California—such as Nevada, Arizona, Colorado and Utah—California never became a territory before obtaining statehood. The Mexican-American War ended in 1848 with the **Treaty of Guadalupe Hidalgo**. Under that treaty, Alta California (except for California) and Santa Fé de Nuevo México became territories of the United States.

The title officer will frequently find reference to the historical significance of the Treaty of Guadalupe Hidalgo, as well as ranchos established by Mexican land grants. The title professional will find the names and places founded in California's history sprinkled throughout many legal descriptions. Properties located on former ranchos are legally described using the following format as suggested by California law:

> That portion of the Rancho _____, in the City of _____, County of _____, State of California, as shown on map filed for record in Book____, page_____ of Patents, in the office of the County Recorder of said county, described as follows . . .

The Treaty of Guadalupe Hidalgo

The Treaty of Guadalupe Hidalgo was initially signed on February 2, 1848; ratified by Congress on March 10, 1848; and finalized on May 30, 1848. The treaty led to California's establishment as the 31st state in 1850 and served as the underlying authority for establishing title to property. The treaty is an important part of California's real estate history, having established the fundamental principles of title to property.

The following is an excerpt from the treaty. The title professional may recognize the importance of the treaty as it relates to certain elements of property rights and the protection afforded some parties.

The Treaty of Guadalupe Hidalgo (excerpts)

Article VIII

Mexicans now established in territories previously belonging to Mexico, and which remain for the future within the limits of the United States, as defined by the present treaty, shall be free to continue where they now reside, or to remove at any time to the Mexican Republic, retaining the property which they possess in the said territories, or disposing thereof, and removing the proceeds wherever they please, without their being subjected, on this account, to any contribution, tax, or charge whatever. Those who shall prefer to remain in the said territories may either retain the title and rights of Mexican citizens, or acquire those of citizens of the United States. But they shall be under the obligation to make their election within one year from the date of the exchange of ratifications of this treaty; and those who shall remain in the said territories after the expiration of that year, without having declared their intention to retain the character of Mexicans, shall be considered to have elected to become citizens of the United States. In the said territories, property of every kind, now belonging to Mexicans not established there, shall be inviolably respected. The present owners, the heirs of these, and all Mexicans who may hereafter acquire said property by contract, shall enjoy with respect to it guarantees equally ample as if the same belonged to citizens of the United States.

Article IX

The Mexicans who, in the territories aforesaid, shall not preserve the character of citizens of the Mexican Republic, conformably with what is stipulated in the preceding article, shall be incorporated into the Union of the United States, and be admitted at the proper time (to be judged of by the Congress of the United States) to the enjoyment of all the rights of citizens of the United States, according to the principles of the Constitution; and in the mean time, shall be maintained and protected in the free enjoyment of their liberty and property, and secured in the free exercise of their religion without; restriction.

Under the Treaty of Guadalupe Hidalgo, title to properties was established as follows:

Mexican Land Grants Ranchos and public grants delivered by Spain and Mexico were confirmed to be valid.

State Lands State lands were granted by the U.S. Congress to the State of California

Tidelands and Submerged Lands The federal Submerged Lands Act of 1953 granted ownership of **tidelands** and **submerged lands** and resources to coastal states such as California. The Outer Continental Shelf Lands Act of 1953, legislation passed along with Submerged Lands Act, validated and guaranteed that the U.S. government possessed control and jurisdiction over lands, waters, and other resources beyond three nautical miles from the shore.

Under a 1988 proclamation issued by President Ronald Reagan, the United States has complete and sovereign rights over the lands and waters out to 12 nautical miles from shore (from the original 3 miles).

Public Lands All other lands became property of the United States and are identified as **public lands**.

■ LAND DIVISIONS AND DESCRIPTIONS

Land divisions range from vast areas including townships to sections and fractional sections and individual lots. Title officers and, to a lesser degree, escrow officers must have a thorough understanding of the process of both dividing and describing real property. Real property is identified in a number of ways.

Land Descriptions and Legal Descriptions

Land may be described in several ways, some of which may not be its "legal description." The **legal description** is how a property is recorded in title records and on all deeds—including deeds of trust (or mortgages, although these are seldom used in California)—involved in real estate lending. A legal description may be recorded as a lot and tract, a metes and bounds, or a section and township. Other descriptions, which are not considered legal descriptions, would include the street address and the assessor's parcel number.

Land Descriptions are often dependent on land surveying and the subdividing of properties based on the **Public Land Survey System** (PLSS). The PLSS is called a "rectangular" system and dates back to the original 13 colonies.

Today's survey methods are much more precise than those used in early California, when sophisticated surveying equipment did not exist. The practices employed in measuring distances were often crude and inaccurate. The equipment included chains, ropes, and steel-rimmed wheels.

The crude methods and instruments used often resulted in inaccurate property descriptions. The sizes of wheels, for example, may not have been uniform, resulting in completely inaccurate measurements. Accurate measurements depend on fixed standards. Using today's equipment, the surveyor relies on standard and uniform units of measure (one foot, one yard, one mile, etc.) and knows the conversion factor for each. The conversion of units of measure, such as from the Spanish-language description, requires translation. Title companies depend on experienced title officers and engineers, who have the expertise to prepare accurate and insurable legal descriptions and understand the meaning of centuries-old descriptions.

Public Land Survey System

The Public Land Survey System is the recognized method of subdividing and describing land in the United States. The PLSS is used to divide lands owned by the federal government, including all land granted to the federal government by the original colonies. Most of those lands are now in private ownership.

Division of Lands

Townships are 6 miles square, totaling 36 square miles. Townships are then subdivided into 36 sections, each 1 mile square. Sections can be further subdivided into smaller sections called "aliquots parts." These consist of half-sections or smaller. They also include what are known as government lots, parcels smaller than one-quarter section or irregular in shape.

Survey Process

The surveyor places a permanent marker, called a "monument," at the corner of each section, which enables it to be easily located. Monuments are also placed at the corners of each quarter-section.

Early surveyors often used objects such as a distinctive tree, a rock formation or other natural feature as monuments, or failing any of these being available, they would simply drive a stake into the ground. The result was that with the elements or the passing of time, these monuments oftentimes simply eroded away or disappeared. Today's contemporary monuments are typically inscribed markers placed in concrete or mounted on iron or steel posts, certainly more permanent.

In order to complete the survey of a given parcel, surveyors begin at an arbitrary initial point and measure "to the winds," going north, south, east, and west. The process is repeated from each destination point. While many early surveys were inaccurate because of the more primitive methods employed by the surveyor, today's survey practices are considerably more reliable. Keep in mind, however, that because of these early survey methods, some sections are not square and actually may be greater or less than the standard uniform acreage.

Principal Meridian and Base Line

The line that extends from north to south and runs through the initial point is called the principal **meridian**.

The principal meridian has what is called a **base line**, the east to west line that runs through the initial point.

Townships represent the land's location north or south of the base line. Ranges represent the land's location east or west of the principal meridian.

In forming the township, base lines are horizontal and meridians are vertical, creating a grid. The lines are six miles apart. A box is created at the intersections. The box is six miles long and six miles wide (36 square miles) and forms the township.

Because the earth is not completely round, additional meridians are included to adjust for the discrepancy and are called correction lines, usually located every 24 miles north and south of the base line.

In basic land descriptions, townships extend north or south from a principal base line, whereas ranges extend east or west from a principal meridian.

Basic land measurements and comparative conversions include the following:

- One mile: 5,280 feet in length
- One square mile: 27,878,400 square feet
- One acre: 43,560 square feet
- One township: 6 miles on each side and containing 36 sections
- One section in a township: a square, one mile on each side and containing 640 acres
- One-half section: 320 acres
- One-quarter section: 160 acres

California's Base Lines and Meridians

California has three sets of base lines and meridians: the Humboldt Base Line and Meridian (northern California), the Mt. Diablo Base Line and Meridian (central California), and the San Bernardino Base Line and Meridian (southern California). Comparative land measurements under the system include **metes and bounds** and **government lots**.

Metes and Bounds

Metes are specific units of measure: feet, yards, etc.

Bounds identify the borders of the property. They may be natural—such as rivers, streams, and even unique rock formations—or man-made, such as roads, trails, and highways.

The title professional may be required to rely on a metes-and-bounds description of a property that is not identified by a parcel number as found in a recorded map or, because of its physical shape, is difficult to describe, as are sections and townships. Some metes-and-bounds descriptions are so complex that only a civil engineer or surveyor is likely to understand them. Many title officers, however, are experienced in writing and interpreting an accurate description from readily available information.

A metes-and-bounds description starts at a fixed point and then continues describing the boundaries of the land, from one point or place to another and finishing at the original beginning point. While all land description elements are important in establishing these measurements, the one that is clearly more important than any other is the point of beginning (POB). If the surveyor or engineer errs in determining the point of beginning, the rest of the measurements, as well as the description, is meaningless.

Government Lots

In the original government survey system, waterways and other natural elements created parcels of land that were less than a quarter-section in size, and they were called government lots. Government lots also contain land lost as a result of adjustments made by correction lines. A title officer involved in a land development project might be faced with such a parcel. The developer is certainly interested in knowing, for example, that a government lot does not necessarily contain a standard number of acres and relies on the surveyor to determine the actual size of the property. The surveyor places markers at the corner of each government lot.

■ INTERESTS IN PROPERTY

Property is considered either "real" (immovable) or "personal" (capable of being moved).

Real Property

Real property consists of land and all objects that are "affixed" to and immovable on the land, such as buildings and other structures, walls and fences, and even trees and shrubs. It also includes rights that are "appurtenant" to the land, which means accompanying or belonging to it. An example of an appurtenance would be an easement. An appurtenance is right to use or enjoy the land or a part of it, but it may not actually be part of the land itself. When a property is sold to another person, the title to it also transfers that which is appurtenant.

Land Land consists of the earth and includes the air above it to the heavens and all that is below it to the core of the earth. One's interest in the land may be restricted or limited by government regulation. It also may be subject to the rights of another party who owns the interest in other elements in or under the land, such as oil, gas, or minerals. In fact, seldom will the title officer discover that an interest in land also includes the rights to minerals, oil, and gas—especially in oil-producing states such as California.

Fixtures Fixtures are those items that were originally personal property but are now attached to the land. These may be natural fixtures such as trees, vines, or shrubs. Prior to being planted, these are personal property. Once planted, they are considered part of the real property. Fixtures may also be man-made, such as buildings permanently placed on the land, or components attached by fastening devices such as nail, bolts, or screws.

Title

The transfer deed, such as a grant deed, conveys title. Citizenship is not a requirement under California law to take title to real property. Issues of citizenship that arise from time to time in a real estate transaction may require the escrow officer to perform certain acts or to prepare specific documents, especially regarding income taxes. Acquiring title, however, in itself requires no extraordinary action by the escrow or title professional.

Vesting

Vesting refers to the manner in which title is held, such as "John J. Jones and Mary K. Jones, Husband and Wife as Community Property with the Right of Survivorship."

Absolute Ownership

Absolute ownership is one's complete control over property, with the right to use or dispose of it as the holder sees fit, is absolute ownership.

Qualified Ownership

Ownership of property with another person is considered to be qualified if the use of the property is limited or restricted. **Qualified ownership**, when owned with others, allows title to be held in several ways, as follows:

- *Joint tenants.* A joint tenancy interest exists when a property is owned by two or more persons with equal rights, and that upon the death of one joint tenant, the deceased's share passes to the other survivor(s). Joint tenants do not need to be married to each another, or domestic partners with each another. Joint tenants cannot sell or transfer their interest without the consent of the others.

- *Tenants in common.* Also referred to as a TIC, tenants-in-common property is one owned by several persons having equal or common rights, but each owner holds a separate individual interest. Unlike joint tenancy, these separate interests may be sold, transferred, and willed freely without the consent of the others. Additionally, they may be encumbered as collateral for financing. Pragmatically speaking, however, it would be difficult to find an institutional lender willing to loan to one tenant in common without requiring all owners to be equally liable for repayment.

- *Partnership interest (tenants in partnership).* A partnership interest is interest in a property by an association or entity consisting of two or more persons. It is assumed to be an association formed for the purpose of running a for-profit organization.

- *Community property.* Community property may held either with or without the right of survivorship, as in the vesting example described earlier. However, unlike joint tenants, it is restricted to either a married couple or domestic partners. Note that in California domestic partners need not be of the same sex. If title is held as community property without specifying the right of survivorship, the co-owners are allowed to separately place their half in a will and may provide for the property to go to someone other than the surviving spouse. If, however, vesting includes "community property with the right of survivorship" upon the death of a spouse, the property would pass to the survivor just as it does in joint tenancy. Certain tax benefits may be available to a surviving spouse who has taken title as community property and which may not be available under joint tenancy.

■ *Trust.* Property may be held in a trust by a trustee for the benefit of the actual owners who are called beneficiaries. It is important for the escrow officer to understand that the trust cannot take title itself, but rather the trustee receives title on behalf of the trust. An example of vesting would be "John Jones as Trustee of the Jones Family Trust."

Pro-Tip: Do Not Offer Advice on Vesting!

It is important for the escrow officer not to assume title is going to be taken in one form or another. If principals have not specified how they wish to take title the escrow officer must ask them! It is not unusual for persons who are acquiring real estate for the first time to question the escrow officer about the best way to take title, and to explain the differences, advantages, and disadvantages of each method. The only correct response to these queries is "please seek legal advice."

■ ESTATES IN REAL PROPERTY

Estate is one of those words that is often industry-specific, part of the terminology of a specific profession. We mention this because a person new to the real estate profession, including title and escrow services, upon hearing the word *estate* might envision a grand mansion in the country. Or perhaps one has been involved in the probate of a decedent's estate, which refers to all the property and possessions belonging to the decedent. Neither, however, refers to our discussion of the term. Rather **estate** within the context of this section refers to the degree or extent of one's interest in land. Estates in real property can be either freehold or less-than-freehold.

Freehold Estate

The concept of freehold estates comes from medieval England, which allowed commoners to acquire real property—but subject to the interest of the king. Today, the term *freehold estate* refers to an interest in real property that is of an unspecified period.

Freehold estates include fee simple and life estates.

Fee Simple Estate   A fee simple estate is the highest form of ownership in real estate. Its characteristics are as follows:

- Inheritable by either one's will or by intestate succession, if no will exists

- Transferable, capable of being freely conveyed by a property owner to another

- Perpetual and unlimited in holding term with no termination date on the owner's right to continue to own, possess, and enjoy it

Fee Simple Absolute   A fee simple absolute estate generally has no restrictions placed on it, other than by the government through its powers and regulations. This is the most common form of interest in real property the escrow and title professional may encounter in a typical transaction.

Fee Simple Defeasible   Specific conditions or restrictions are placed on the transferability of the property. It provides for the conveyance of title back to the transferor if the titleholder violates the terms of the agreement. However, under California's Marketable Record Title Act of 1982, court action is necessary for the original transferor to seek the return of title. Seldom will escrow or title professionals find themselves in a transaction such as this.

Life Estate   This is an estate in which ownership exists only during the term of the life of a named person. The person whose life determines the holding term may be either the person who possesses the life estate (called a life tenant) or some other named individual.

■   **EXAMPLE**   John Jones grants title to his property, Lonesome Oak, to Jim James for the Life of Paul Smith. When Paul Smith dies, title to Lonesome Oak reverts to John Jones.

Estate in Reversion   Estate in reversion occurs, for example, when a person named under a life estate dies. In this case, title reverts to the grantor. Reversion is not limited to only life estates. For example, it may apply to a transfer of title that provides that if a certain act specified in the transfer agreement is performed by the grantee, title automatically reverts to the grantor.

■   **EXAMPLE**   John Jones grants title to his property, Lonesome Oak, to Jim James, which includes an agreement that James may hold title as long as he does not change the name of Lonesome Oak. The property would revert to Jones in the event James actually changed the name of Lonesome Oak.

Estate in Remainder   A life estate may be created for the life of the title-holder, with the right to occupy and enjoy the property during the titleholder's life. Upon the death of the titleholder, the estate transfers to the named heir as an estate in remainder.

■   **EXAMPLE**   John Jones grants title to his property, Lonesome Oak, to Jim James for life (the life of James). The agreement also provides that upon the death of James, title is granted to Paul Smith. Smith, therefore, has an estate in remainder.

Less Than Freehold Estate

Simply put, a "less than freehold estate" refers to a tenant's leasehold interest in the property. The interest is considered personal, not real, property. There are four types:

- *Estate for years.* A lease with a specified termination date. All leases in California greater in term than one year must be in writing, with the termination date identified in the lease agreement.

- *Estate from period to period.* Essentially a month-to-month rental. Month-to-month rental agreements in California are not required to be in writing, sometimes creating problems for a purchaser of income property.

- *Estate at will.* No specified term and with no rental agreement. This differs from the meaning of estate from period to period in that the estate at will does not include even the verbal, nonwritten understanding of a specific term that is assumed in the estate from period to period. It allows for the termination of the tenancy by the landowner at any time.

- *Estate at sufferance.* A tenant who fails to vacate the property at the end of a lease and who has neither a month-to-month agreement, which would continue the tenancy, or permission expressly granted by the landlord is considered to have an estate at sufferance. It is not uncommon for an escrow transaction to include a contingency clause addressing a tenant's possession of a property in such cases and a resolution requirement.

■ CHAPTER 1 QUIZ

1. California's property ownership concepts have their roots in

   a. French common law.

   b. Spanish common law.

   c. English common law.

   d. none of these.

2. The character of property interests and private property rights in California can be traced back to

   a. the French.

   b. the Spanish.

   c. the English.

   d. none of these.

3. Spanish missions began sprouting up along the California coast, known at the time as part of

   a. Lower California.

   b. Baja California.

   c. Alta California.

   d. Alta Mexico.

4. Following the Mexican-American War, title to properties was established under

   a. the Treaty of Guadalupe Hidalgo.

   b. the Treaty of Juan Valdez.

   c. the provisions of the Bear Flag Agreement.

   d. John C. Fremont.

5. Property is considered

    a. either real, not capable of being moved, or personal, that which may be moved.

    b. real, whether movable or not, and personal.

    c. immovable.

    d. none of these.

6. Estates in real property are

    a. either free or not.

    b. either freehold or less than freehold.

    c. founded in French law.

    d. founded in Spanish law.

7. An estate for years

    a. is a lease with a specified termination date.

    b. is a month-to-month rental agreement.

    c. must always be for one year.

    d. both a and c.

8. An estate at will

    a. has no specified term.

    b. is always in writing.

    c. is for a specified term.

    d. is for greater than one year.

9. Fee simple estates are

    a. transferable.

    b. perpetual.

    c. inheritable.

    d. all of these.

10.   A common interest or tenant's property is one

a.   with joint tenants.

b.   with community property with right of survivorship.

c.   with tenants in common.

d.   none of these.

TRANSFER OF INTERESTS

■ KEY TERMS

accession   constructive notice   succession
acquisition of property due-on-sale clause   transfer
actual notice   grant deed   trust deed
alienation clause   occupancy   warranty deed
all-inclusive trust deed quitclaim deed   will

■ LEARNING OBJECTIVES

Upon completing this chapter, you will be able to

- ■ identify the five ways that property may be acquired in California,

- ■ explain the concepts of transferring title to property,

- ■ explain the difference between actual notice and constructive notice of delivery of title to property,

- ■ identify the basic transfer deeds used to convey title, and

- ■ explain the use of the trust deed and the all-inclusive trust deed.

■ ACQUISITION OF PROPERTY

Section 1000 of California Civil Code (*Cal. Civ. Code*) specifies that **acquisition of property** in the state of California may be accomplished in one of five ways: occupancy, accession, transfer, will, and succession. Escrow and title professionals are usually involved in a transfer only, taking place through a purchase transaction.

Occupancy

Title to property may be acquired by a person who has been occupying it without permission of the owner of record. Such possession is considered "hostile." Title may be acquired after five years of the occupant's use when such use has been open and notorious (transparent but not in the interest of the titleholder). However, the occupant should not assume that title will automatically be acquired. Another person may be able prove or document a previously acquired title by other legal means as allowed under California law. In such a case, the title officer may have a transaction in which the title is "clouded" (not capable of being transferred) until the issue has been resolved.

A provision of California Civil Code Section 1008, however, restricts a person's ability to exercise the hostile **occupancy** rule to acquire title. The law says that if the property owner has posted a sign at each place of entry to the property, and at intervals no longer than 200 feet each along its boundary, such hostile occupancy is without effect and cannot be enforced. The sign should read, "Right to pass by permission, and subject to control of owner. Sec. 1008, Civil Code." (It is advisable to quote the California Civil Code verbatim as shown.)

Accession

The process whereby land becomes attached to another piece of real property is called **accession**. This is true whether it occurs by annexation, with contiguous (adjoining) land attached through a legal process and reflected on recorded documents, or by the action of natural forces. For example, over the years, a property owner's land may increase in size through deposits of earth added to it from another property. This can happen as a result of accumulation of material from it or the recession of a stream. A fixture attached to the land (see personal versus real property in Chapter 1) becomes part of the land and the property of the landowner unless an existing agreement allows for its removal (*Cal. Civ. Code* § 1014).

Transfer

Transfer may also be performed by several other deeds.

Will

Property owners may **will** their interest in a property to another person by transferring title upon their death. Transferring a decedent's property may or may not require probate. Probate is generally not required if title to the property was held by joint tenants or as community property with the right of survivorship. This would include property held in the name of the deceased only but which is left by will or intestate succession to the surviving spouse. California provides for a fast-track probate, called "summary probate" or the "small estate" probate. Under the summary probate provisions, probate is not required if the value of the property is less than $150,000 and 40 days have lapsed since the death of the decedent. Property held in a living trust or in a life estate is also exempt from probate.

Succession

Under the California Civil Code, intestate **succession** (transfer of title to property of one who dies without a will) is as follows:

- If not married, or the property owner has no surviving spouse, passes to the decedent's children equally if they are of the same generation

- If no children or grandchildren (including all generations of grandchildren), then to parents

- If no parents, then to siblings

- If no siblings, then to grandparents

- If no grandparents, then to aunts and uncles

- If no aunts or uncles, then to cousins

- If no cousins, then to any distant cousins

- If a surviving spouse, decedent's separate property distributed first to surviving spouse, who receives all the separate property, with the following exceptions:

  — If the decedent had one child, the surviving spouse receives one-half of the separate property.

  — If the decedent left parent(s) but no children, the surviving spouse receives one-half of the separate property.

  — If the decedent left more than one child, the surviving spouse receives only one-third of the separate property.

— If the decedent left one child, as well as heirs of one or more deceased children, the surviving spouse receives only one-third of the separate property.

— If the decedent left the issue of two or more deceased children, the surviving spouse receives only one-third of the separate property.

■ TRANSFER OF TITLE

Ownership of real property may be voluntarily and involuntarily transferred in a number of ways; this is called alienation. Quite understandably, the escrow and title professional will typically be involved only in a voluntary transfer of title. An exception would be a title officer working on behalf of a lender client that is foreclosing against a borrower and is preparing a Trustee Sale Guarantee policy (TSG). The two types of transfers are further explained as follows:

■ *Voluntary transfers.* Title may be voluntarily transferred by deed or will. A property owner may sell to another, transferring title by executing a grant deed. Title may also be transferred by quitclaim deed (which carries no protection as to claims by others against the property, unlike grant deed and title insurance coverage). Upon the property owner's death, title may be voluntarily transferred by will. If no will exists, transfer of title requires a court action through probate.

■ *Involuntary transfers.* In the case of foreclosure or adverse possession, title may be involuntarily transferred.

Delivery of a Deed Transferring Title and Actual Notice

Actual notice of transfer of title is accomplished by the "delivery" of the deed into the hands of the grantee, such as to a real estate buyer at escrow closing.

Recordation and Constructive Notice

Constructive notice of transfer of title is accomplished by recording the transfer document with the county recorder's office. What does constructive notice actually mean? It simply means that the world at large may learn that the agreement exists because it is available for any person to see; it is found in recorded and, now public, documents. Any legal document that transfers title to real property should (not must—an important distinction) be recorded as provided for by California Civil Code, Section 1169. If recording is to be performed, the document must be recorded at the county recorder's office in which the property is located. After recording, the document is returned to the requesting party, such as the buyer or the borrower of real property. Documents that are typically recorded include grant deeds, quitclaim deeds, easements, trust deeds or mortgages, installment sales contracts (also known as land contracts), long-term leases, and reconveyances (removal of a security instrument lien on the title of a property) of deeds of trust (or mortgages and land contracts). Recording is intended to protect buyers and lenders of real property. The law specifies that grant deeds are to be recorded in one set of books and mortgages, including deeds of trust, in another.

■ DEEDS AND TRUST DEEDS

Title insurance is offered by the title insurance company following its review and approval of recorded documents, public records, files and other instruments. One of the most common of these documents is the transfer deed.

Specific types of deeds will be discussed in detail later. The following requirements must be met for any deed to be valid:

- *Written.* A valid deed must be in writing.

- *Conveyance.* The deed must include language that specifically conveys title, such as "the grantors do hereby grant title to . . ."

- *Property description.* A deed must include an accurate and complete description of the property.

- *Signed by competent grantor.* A valid deed must be signed by a competent grantor, which means being mentally competent and of legal age. A person of legal age must be 18 or older or be an emancipated minor. In California, an emancipated minor is one who is married, serving on active duty in the U.S. armed forces, or possesses an emancipation decree from the court. Also, if the grantor took title under a different name, the deed must reflect that fact (i.e., "Jane Smith, Seller, who acquired title as Jane Adams, Buyer").

- *Grantee.* The deed must name the grantee. The only requirement under the law is that the grantee be living and clearly identifiable. A misconception exists among some who believe the grantee cannot be a minor or insane. A minor may receive title but cannot give it.

Various types of deeds are used for title conveyance. The following paragraphs briefly describe the most common of these.

Grant Deed

Grant deeds are the most commonly used deeds to transfer title in California. A grant deed conveys fee simple title with absolute ownership unless it expressly indicates otherwise.

The grant deed (Figure 2.1) transfers all the interest in the property that the grantor has as well as "after acquired title," meaning any future interest in title the grantor may acquire. The following deeds are used for specific transactions:

- *Joint tenancy grant deed.* The joint tenancy grant deed (Figure 2.2) conveys title to those who are acquiring title to property and who desire a surviving spouse upon the death of the other to receive the interest of the decedent (and without the need for a full probate).

- *Interspousal deed.* An interspousal grant deed is commonly used for the transfer of an interest in real property from one spouse to another, instead of using a traditional grant deed, to avoid the possibility that a documentary transfer tax may be imposed. It is used especially if no consideration is involved.

- *Community property with right of survivorship deed.* This deed (Figure 2.3) is used when tax considerations of the surviving spouse are important to the parties.

Quitclaim Deed

The **quitclaim deed** conveys any possible interest of the grantor in the property. However, unlike a grant deed, a quitclaim deed, while valid, carries no warranties or guarantees of title protection. It simply conveys whatever title the grantor possesses, or inherently could possess, to the grantee. For example, a spouse may be asked to sign a quitclaim deed (Figure 2.4) to release any potential interest in a property that the other spouse is acquiring or encumbering.

Warranty Deed

The title officer new to California may discover that warranty deeds, used in some states, are seldom used in California. Instead, title insurance typically provides protection against defects in the title. **Warranty deeds**, when used, usually only contain certain title covenants offering limited protection to the titleholder.

Trust Deed

The deeds described previously, except for a quitclaim deed, all transfer "fee title" to the land.

A **trust deed** (or deed of trust) is a debt or security instrument used by a lender to identify and secure the collateral (real property) being pledged by a borrower for obtaining a loan. It does contain a provision in which the borrower conveys the "dormant title" or "bare legal title" to land to another person or company as a "trustee" in order to secure debts it identifies and as evidenced by a promissory note (Figure 2.5).

The note, as the promissory note is commonly called, is the evidence of the debt. It is signed but neither notarized nor recorded.

The deed of trust is the security instrument used almost exclusively by lenders in California (Figure 2.6). It is signed, notarized, and recorded.

FIGURE 2.1

**Grant Deed for
Community Property**

RECORDING REQUESTED BY:

WHEN RECORDED MAIL THIS DEED AND, UNLESS
OTHERWISE SHOWN BELOW, MAIL TAX STATEMENT TO:

Name:

Street
Address:

City
State
& Zip

Title Order No.: _____ Escrow No.: _____

SPACE ABOVE THIS LINE FOR RECORDER'S USE

Grant Deed

The undersigned Grantor(s) declare(s)
    DOCUMENTARY TRANSFER TAX IS $_____

        ☐ Computed on Full Value of the interest or property conveyed, or

        ☐ Computed on full value less value of liens or encumbrances remaining at time of sale,

        ☐ Unincorporated Area   City of _____

        Parcel No.: _____

FOR A VALUABLE CONSIDERATION, receipt of which is hereby acknowledged,

Hereby GRANT(s) to:

The following described real property in the County of _____ , State of California

Dated: _____

STATE OF CALIFORNIA
COUNTY OF _____

On _____ before me, _____
_____, A Notary Public, personally
appeared _____
_____
who proved to me on the basis of satisfactory evidence to be the
person(s) whose name(s) is/are subscribed to the within instrument
and acknowledged to me that he/she/they executed the same in
his/their/her authorized capacity(ies), and that by his/her/their
signature(s) on the instrument the person(s), or the entity upon behalf
of which the person(s) acted, executed the instrument.

I certify under PENALTY OF PERJURY under the laws of the State of
California that the foregoing paragraph is true and correct.

WITNESS my hand and official seal.

Signature _____

(This area for official notarial seal)

MAIL TAX STATEMENTS TO PARTY SHOWN ON FOLLOWING LINE; IF NO PARTY SHOWN, MAIL AS DIRECTED ABOVE.

Name   Street Address   City & State

Source: Fidelity Title Insurance Co.

FIGURE 2.2

Joint Tenancy Grant Deed

RECORDING REQUESTED BY

WHEN RECORDED MAIL TO

AND MAIL TAX STATEMENTS TO

NAME _____

ADDRESS _____

CITY _____

STATE & ZIP _____

Title Order No. _____ Escrow No. _____

JOINT TENANCY GRANT DEED

THE UNDERSIGNED GRANTOR(s) DECLARE(s)

DOCUMENTARY TRANSFER TAX is $_____ CITY TAX $_____

☐   computed on full value of property conveyed, or

☐   computed on full value less value of liens or encumbrances remaining at time of sale,

☐   Unincorporated area:

☐   City of _____, and

FOR A VALUABLE CONSIDERATION, receipt of which is hereby acknowledged,

hereby GRANT(s) to

_____, as Joint Tenants

the following described real property in the City of _____ County of:_____, State of California:

APN _____

Dated: _____

State of California

County of _____

On _____before me, (here insert name and title of the officer), personally appeared _____, who proved to me on the basis of satisfactory evidence to be the person(s) whose name(s) is/are subscribed to the within instrument and acknowledged to me that he/she/they executed the same in his/her/their authorized capacity(ies), and that by his/her/their signature(s) on the instrument the person(s), or the entity upon behalf of which the person(s) acted, executed the instrument.

I certify under PENALTY OF PERJURY under the laws of the State of California that the foregoing paragraph is true and correct.

WITNESS my hand and official seal.

Signature _____ (Seal)

Source: Fidelity Title Insurance Co.

FIGURE 2.3

**Grant Deed for Right of
Survivorship**

RECORDING REQUESTED BY:

WHEN RECORDED MAIL TO
AND MAIL TAX STATEMENTS TO:

NAME:

ADDRESS:

CITY:
STATE/ZIP:

Title Order No.: _____   Space Above This Line For Recorder's Use   Escrow No.: _____

GRANT DEED
(COMMUNITY PROPERTY WITH RIGHT OF SURVIVORSHIP)

THE UNDERSIGNED GRANTOR(s) DECLARE(s):
DOCUMENTARY TRANSFER TAX is $ _____ . CITY TAX $ _____ .
☐ Computed on full value of property conveyed, or ☐ Computed on full value less value of liens or encumbrances remaining at time of sale or transfer.
☐ Unincorporated area: ☐ City of _____ , and
☐ Check when grantees are expressly declaring that the transfer of the property is to be community property with right of survivorship.

FOR A VALUABLE CONSIDERATION, receipt of which is hereby acknowledged,

hereby GRANT(s) to

                        ,Husband and Wife, as Community Property with Right of Survivorship,

the following described real property in the County of _____ , State of California
(Assessor's Parcel No. _____):

Dated: _____   _____
                               (Grantor)

Dated: _____   _____
                               (Grantor)

Source: Chicago Title Insurance Company

FIGURE 2.3
Grant Deed for Right of
Survivorship (continued)

"GRANTEES HEREBY EXPRESSLY DECLARE AND ACCEPT THE TRANSFER OF THE HEREIN DESCRIBED PROPERTY AS COMMUNITY PROPERTY WITH RIGHT OF SURVIVORSHIP."

Dated: _____   _____
                                                                    (Grantee)

Dated: _____   _____
                                                                    (Grantee)

STATE OF CALIFORNIA   }
COUNTY OF _____} SS

On _____ before me, _____
_____ (here insert name and title of the officer),
personally appeared _____
_____,
personally known to me (or proved to me on the basis of satisfactory evidence) to be the person(s) whose name(s) is/are subscribed to the within instrument and acknowledged to me that he/she/they executed the same in his/her/their authorized capacity(ies), and that by his/her/their signature(s) on the instrument the person(s), or the entity upon behalf of which the person(s) acted, executed the instrument.

WITNESS my hand and official seal.

Signature _____

FIGURE 2.4
Quitclaim Deed

RECORDING REQUESTED BY:

WHEN RECORDED MAIL THIS DEED AND, UNLESS
OTHERWISE SHOWN BELOW, MAIL TAX STATEMENT TO:

Name:

Street
Address:

City
State
& Zip

Title Order No.: _____   Escrow No.: _____

SPACE ABOVE THIS LINE FOR RECORDER'S USE

Quitclaim Deed

The undersigned Grantor(s) declare(s)
    DOCUMENTARY TRANSFER TAX IS $_____
        ☐ Computed on Full Value of the interest or property conveyed, or
        ☐ Computed on full value less value of liens or encumbrances remaining at time of sale,
        ☐ Unincorporated Area   City of _____
        Parcel No.: _____

FOR A VALUABLE CONSIDERATION, receipt of which is hereby acknowledged,

Do (does) hereby REMISE, RELEASE AND FOREVER QUITCLAIM to:

The following described property in the County of _____ , State of California

Dated: _____

STATE OF CALIFORNIA
COUNTY OF _____

On _____ before me, _____
_____, A Notary Public, personally
appeared _____
_____
who proved to me on the basis of satisfactory evidence to be the
person(s) whose name(s) is/are subscribed to the within instrument
and acknowledged to me that he/she/they executed the same in
his/their/her authorized capacity(ies), and that by his/her/their
signature(s) on the instrument the person(s), or the entity upon behalf
of which the person(s) acted, executed the instrument.

I certify under PENALTY OF PERJURY under the laws of the State of
California that the foregoing paragraph is true and correct.

WITNESS my hand and official seal.

Signature _____

(This area for official notarial seal)

MAIL TAX STATEMENTS TO PARTY SHOWN ON FOLLOWING LINE; IF NO PARTY SHOWN, MAIL AS DIRECTED ABOVE.

Name _____   Street Address _____   City & State _____

Source: Fidelity Title Insurance Co.

FIGURE 2.5

Promissory Note Secured by Deed of Trust

DO NOT DESTROY THIS NOTE: When paid, this note, with Deed of Trust securing same, must be surrendered to Trustee for cancellation before reconveyance will be made.

NOTE SECURED BY DEED OF TRUST
(INSTALLMENT - INTEREST INCLUDED)

$ _ _ _ _ _ _ _ _ _ _ _ _ _ _ _ _ _ _ _ , California _ _ _ _ _ _ _ _ _ _
In installments as herein stated, for value received, I promise to pay to _ _

_ _
_ _
_ _
_ or order
at _
the principal sum of _

_ _
_ _ _ _ _ _ dollars with interest from _ _ _ _ _ _ _ _ _ _ _ _ _ on unpaid
principal at the rate of _ _ _ _ _ _ _ _ _ _ _ _ _ percent per annum;
principal and interest payable in installments of _ _ _ _ _ _ _ _ _ _ _ _

_ dollars or more on the _ _ _ _
_ _ _ _ _ _ _ _ _ _ _ _ day of each _ _ _ _ _ _ _ _ _ _ _ _ _ _ _ _ _
month, beginning on the _ _ _ _ _ _ _ _ _ _ _ _ _ day of _ _ _ _ _ _ _ _ _ _
and continuing until

Each payment shall be credited first on interest then due; and the remainder on principal; and the interest shall thereupon cease upon the principal so credited. Should default be made in payment of any installment of principal and interest, the whole sum of principal and interest shall, at the option of the holder of this note, become immediately due. Principal and interest payable in lawful money of the United States. If action be instituted on this note, the undersigned promise_ _ _ to pay such sum as the Court may adjudge as attorney's fees. This note is secured by a DEED OF TRUST to **CHICAGO TITLE COMPANY, a California corporation, as Trustee.**

_ _

_ _

Source: Chicago Title Insurance Company

FIGURE 2.6

Trust Deed

When recorded mail to:

Title No.
Escrow No.

DEED OF TRUST WITH ASSIGNMENT OF RENTS

This DEED OF TRUST, made this   day of   ,   between

herein called TRUSTOR

whose address is

CHICAGO TITLE COMPANY, a California corporation, herein called TRUSTEE, and

herein called BENEFICIARY

Trustor irrevocably grants, transfers and assigns to Trustee in Trust, with Power of Sale that property in the County of _____, State of California, described as follows:

A.P.N.

Together with the rents, issues and profits thereof, subject, however, to the right, power and authority hereinafter given to and conferred upon Beneficiary to collect and apply such rents, issues and profits.

FOR THE PURPOSE OF SECURING (1) payment of the sum of ($)_____
Dollars with interest thereon according to the terms of a promissory note or notes of even date herewith made by TRUSTOR, payable to order of BENEFICIARY, and extensions or renewals thereof; (2) the performance of each agreement of TRUSTOR incorporated by reference or contained herein or reciting it is so secured; (3) payment of additional sums and interest thereon which may hereafter be loaned to Trustor, or his or her successors or assigns, when evidenced by a promissory note or notes reciting that they are secured by this Deed of Trust.

A.   To protect the security of this Deed of Trust, and with respect to the property above described, Trustor agrees:

Source: Chicago Title Insurance Company

FIGURE 2.6
Trust Deed (continued)

(1)   To keep said property in good condition and repair; not to remove or demolish any building thereon; to complete or restore promptly and in good and workmanlike manner any building which may be constructed, damaged or destroyed thereon and to pay when due all claims for labor performed and materials furnished therefor; to comply with all laws affecting said property or requiring any alterations or improvements to be made thereon; not to commit or permit waste thereof; not to commit, suffer or permit any act upon said property in violation of the law; to cultivate, irrigate, fertilize, fumigate, prune and do all other acts which from the character or use of said property may be reasonably necessary, the specific enumerations herein not excluding the general.

(2)   To provide, maintain and deliver to Beneficiary fire insurance satisfactory to and with loss payable to Beneficiary. The amount collected under any fire or other insurance policy may be applied by Beneficiary upon any indebtedness secured hereby and in such order as beneficiary may determine, or at option of Beneficiary the entire amount so collected or any part thereof may be released to Trustor. Such application or release shall not cure or waive any default or notice of default hereunder or invalidate any act done pursuant to such notice.

(3)   To appear in and defend any action or proceeding purporting to affect the security hereof or the rights or powers of Beneficiary or Trustee; and to pay all costs and expenses, including cost of evidence of title and attorney's fees in a reasonable sum, in any action or proceeding in which Beneficiary or Trustee may appear, and in any suit brought by Beneficiary to foreclose this Deed of Trust.

(4)   To pay: at least ten days before delinquency all taxes and assessments affecting said property, including assessments on appurtenant water stock; when due, all encumbrances, charges and liens, with interest, on said property or any part thereof, which appear to be prior or superior hereto; all costs, fees and expenses of this Trust.

Should Trustor fail to make any payment or to do any act as herein provided, then Beneficiary or Trustee, but without obligation so to do and without notice to or demand upon Trustor and without releasing Trustor from any obligation hereof, may: make or do the same in such manner and to such extent as either may deem necessary to protect the security hereof, Beneficiary or Trustee being authorized to enter upon said property for such purposes; appear in and defend any action or proceeding purporting to affect the security hereof or the rights or powers of Beneficiary or Trustee; pay, purchase, contest or compromise any encumbrance, charge, or lien which in the judgment of either appears to be prior or superior hereto; and, in exercising any such powers, pay necessary expenses, employ counsel and pay his or her reasonable fees.

(5)   To pay immediately and without demand all sums so expended by Beneficiary or Trustee, with interest from date of expenditure at the amount allowed by law in effect at the date hereof, and to pay for any statement provided for by law in effect at the date hereof regarding the obligation secured hereby, any amount demanded by the Beneficiary not to exceed the maximum allowed by law at the time when said statement is demanded.

B.   It is mutually agreed:

(1)   That any award of damages in connection with any condemnation for public use of or injury to said property or any part thereof is hereby assigned and shall be paid to Beneficiary who may apply or release such moneys received by him or her in the same manner and with the same effect as above provided for disposition or proceeds of fire or other insurance.

(2)   That by accepting payment of any sum secured hereby after its due date, Beneficiary does not waive his or her right either to require prompt payment when due of all other sums so secured or to declare default for failure so to pay.

(3)   That at any time or from time to time, without liability therefor and without notice, upon written request of Beneficiary and presentation of this Deed and said note for endorsement, and without affecting the personal liability or any person for payment of the indebtedness secured hereby, Trustee may: reconvey any part of said property; consent
to making of any map or plat thereof; join in granting any easement thereon; or join in any extension agreement or any agreement subordinating the lien or charge hereof.

(4)   That upon written request of beneficiary stating that all sums secured hereby have been paid, and upon surrender of this Deed and said note to Trustee for cancellation and retention or other disposition as Trustee in its sole discretion may choose and upon payment of its fees, Trustee shall reconvey, without warranty, the property then held hereunder. The recitals in such reconveyance of any matters or facts shall be conclusive proof of the truthfulness thereof. The Grantee in such reconveyance may be described as "the person or persons legally entitled thereto."

2

FIGURE 2.6

Trust Deed (continued)

(5)   That as additional security, Trustor hereby gives to and confers upon Beneficiary the right, power and authority, during the continuance of these Trusts, to collect the rents, issues and profits of said property, reserving unto Trustor the right, prior to any default by Trustor in payment of any indebtedness secured hereby or in performance of any agreement hereunder, to collect and retain such rents, issues and profits as they become due and payable. Upon any such default, Beneficiary may at any time without notice, either in person, by agent, or by a receiver to be appointed by a court, and without regard to the adequacy of any security for the indebtedness hereby secured, enter upon and take possession of said property or any part thereof, in his or her own name sue for or otherwise collect such rents, issues, and profits, including those past due and unpaid, and apply the same, less costs and expenses of operation and collection, including reasonable attorney's fees, upon any indebtedness secured hereby, and in such order as Beneficiary may determine. The entering upon and taking possession of said property, the collection of such rents, issues and profits and the application thereof as aforesaid, shall not cure or waive any default or notice of default hereunder or invalidate any act done pursuant to such notice.

(6)   That upon default by Trustor in payment of any indebtedness secured hereby or in performance of any agreement hereunder, Beneficiary may declare all sums secured hereby immediately due and payable by delivery to Trustee of written declaration of default and demand for sale and of written notice of default and of election to cause to be sold said property, which notice Trustee shall cause to be filed for record. Beneficiary also shall deposit with Trustee this Deed, said note and all documents evidencing expenditures secured hereby.

After the lapse of such time as may then be required by law following the recordation of said notice of default, and notice of sale having been given as then required by law, Trustee without demand on Trustor, shall sell said property at the time and place fixed by it in said notice of sale, either as a whole or in separate parcels, and in such order as it may determine, at public auction to the highest bidder for cash in lawful money of the United States, payable at time of sale. Trustee may postpone sale of all or any portion of said property by public announcement at such time and place of sale, and from time to time thereafter may postpone such sale by public announcement at the time fixed by the preceding postponement. Trustee shall deliver to such purchaser its deed conveying the property so sold, but without any convenant or warranty, express or implied. The recitals in such deed of any matters or facts shall be conclusive proof of the truthfulness thereof. Any person, including Trustor, Trustee, or Beneficiary as hereinafter defined, may purchase at such sale.

After deducting all costs, fees and expenses of Trustee and of this Trust, including cost of evidence of title in connection with sale, Trustee shall apply the proceeds of sale to payment of: all sums expended under the terms hereof, not then repaid, with accrued interest at the amount allowed by law in effect at the date hereof; all other sums then secured hereby; and the remainder, if any, to the person or persons legally entitled thereto.

(7)   Beneficiary, or any successor in ownership of any indebtedness secured hereby, may from time to time, by instrument in writing, substitute a successor of successors to any Trustee named herein or acting hereunder, which instrument, executed by the Beneficiary and duly acknowledged and recorded in the office of the recorder of the county or counties where said property is situated, shall be conclusive proof of proper substitution of such successor Trustee or Trustees, who shall, without conveyance from the Trustee predecessor, succeed to all its title, estate, rights, powers and duties. Said instrument must contain the name of the original Trustor, Trustee and Beneficiary hereunder, the book and page where this Deed is recorded and the name and address of the new Trustee.

(8)   That this Deed applies to, inures to the benefit of, and binds all parties hereto, their heirs, legatees, devisees, administrators, executors, successors, and assigns. The term Beneficiary shall mean the owner and holder , including pledgees, of the note secured hereby, whether or not named as Beneficiary herein. In this Deed, whenever the context so requires, the masculine gender includes the feminine and/or the neuter, and the singular number includes the plural.

(9)   The Trustee accepts this Trust when this Deed, duly executed and acknowledged, is made a public record as provided by law. Trustee is not obliged to notify any party hereto of pending sale under any other Deed of Trust or of any action or proceeding in which Trustor, Beneficiary or Trustee shall be a party unless brought by Trustee.

Beneficiary may charge for a statement regarding the obligation secured hereby, provided the charge thereof does not exceed the maximum allowed by laws.

3

FIGURE 2.6
Trust Deed (continued)

The undersigned Trustor, requests that a copy of any notice of default and any notice of sale hereunder be mailed to him or her at his or her address hereinbefore set forth.

_____
Trustor signature

_____
Trustor signature

_____
Trustor signature

_____
Trustor signature

State of_____

County of_____

On _____ before me, _____, (here insert name and title of the officer), personally appeared _____, who proved to me on the basis of satisfactory evidence to be the person(s) whose name(s) is/are subscribed to the within instrument and acknowledged to me that he/she/they executed the same in his/her/their authorized capacity(ies), and that by his/her/their signature(s) on the instrument the person(s), or the entity upon behalf of which the person(s) acted, executed the instrument.

I certify under PENALTY OF PERJURY under the laws of the State of California that the foregoing paragraph is true and correct.

WITNESS my hand and official seal.

Signature _____ (Seal)

4

FIGURE **2.6**
Trust Deed (continued)

DO NOT RECORD
REQUEST FOR FULL RECONVEYANCE

To Chicago Title Company

      The undersigned is the legal owner and holder of the note or notes, and of all other indebtedness secured by the foregoing Deed of Trust. Said note or notes, together with all other indebtedness secured by said Deed of Trust have been fully paid and satisfied; and you are hereby requested and directed, on payment to you of any sums owning to you under the terms of said Deed of Trust, to cancel said note or notes above mentioned, and all other evidence of indebtedness secured by said Deed of Trust delivered to you herewith, together with the said Deed of Trust, and to reconvey, without warranty, to the parties designated by the terms of said Deed of Trust, all the estate now held by you under the same.

Dated_____

_____

_____

Please mail Deed of Trust, Note(s) and Reconveyance to:

_____

Do not lose or destroy this Deed of Trust OR THE NOTE which it secures. Both must be delivered to the Trustee for cancellation before reconveyance will be made.

5

General Provisions of the Deed of Trust   The following provisions cover most primary and basic rights and obligations of the three parties to a deed of trust; they are identified as described:

- *Beneficiary.* This term is used to identify the lender under a deed of trust. In a mortgage, a lender is sometimes called the mortgagee, though this term is seldom if ever used in California.

- *Trustor.* This term is used to identify the borrower under a deed of trust. In a mortgage, the borrower is called the mortgagor.

- *Trustee.* The trustor transfers, as previously described, the bare legal title to the land to a trustee on behalf of a beneficiary (lender) in order to secure a debt using the property as collateral. The escrow holder or title officer shouldn't become confused as to this legal and technical element of trust deeds. It does not impact or affect the transfer of title such as that which takes place in a grant deed, conveying fee title from a seller to a buyer in a purchase transaction. As a point of interest, under a deed of trust, the borrower conveys bare legal title to a lender (and then to the trustee) providing financing of the property. In the event of the borrower's default, it is this provision contained in the deed of trust that allows the lender to proceed with foreclosure without seeking a court order. This is not the case with a mortgage in which the borrower retains bare legal title, therefore requiring a lender, upon the borrower's default, to foreclose "judicially" through the court system. Typically, the trustee is a title company, a law firm, or even a subsidiary firm of the lender. The trustee also serves to facilitate the reconveyance of the lender's lien against the title upon the satisfactory payoff of the borrower's loan.

- *Loan terms.* The deed of trust will spell out all the terms of the loan, including the interest, rate, loan amount, the amount of principal and interest payment and its frequency (monthly, quarterly, etc), the term of the loan, any balloon balance that may occur and, in the case of adjustable-rate mortgages, the potential for a future adjustment to the interest rate and the amount of the payment. An adjustable-rate rider will be included in the loan documents for the escrow holder or notary to provide to the borrowers for their signatures, along with all the other loan documents.

- *Impound account or escrow account.* The loan terms may require an impound account (also known as escrow account) to be established at closing for the future payment of property taxes and hazard insurance when they come due and payable. Depending on the month of the year in which escrow closes, the amount of property taxes to be deposited into escrow and sent to the lender at closing might be need to be enough to cover nine months' property taxes. Hazard insurance premiums to be impounded are usually two additional months' beyond the amount required to be paid in advance.

Most residential loan programs that allow less than a 10% down payment require the borrower to include impounds in the monthly loan payment.

■ *Default or delinquency.* The deed of trust will indicate all possible charges, along with an explanation of the lender's recourse in the event of the borrower's default. Note that an action by the lender for a borrower's default may be initiated for reasons other than late loan payments. Property taxes that remain unpaid, or even the borrower's lack of maintaining the property, may allow the lender to take action including foreclosure. Usually, a borrower is given a 15-day grace period before a late charge will be assessed; however, the lender may still be entitled to initial a foreclosure proceeding even if the borrower is one day late.

■ *Property insurance.* Hazard and fire insurance requirements are established, requiring the borrower to pay at least one year's insurance premiums at closing.

■ *Inspection of the property.* The lender has the right to visit and inspect the property.

■ *Concessions.* The borrower is informed that any concessions or forbearance granted by the lender during the term of the loan will not automatically entitle the borrower to future concessions.

■ *Successors.* The issue of successors (those who may legally receive title from the borrower) and assigns (those whom the borrower may assign the obligation of the loan to) to the trustor are obligated to the same provisions as the trustor.

■ *Address for notice of legal service.* This is the legal mailing address for both the borrower and the lender.

■ *Due-on-sale clause.* Technically called an **alienation clause**, the **due-on-sale clause** is a form of an acceleration provision in the loan that, as the word implies, "accelerates" the required payoff date of the loan under the lender's right to call the loan due and payable in full upon the unauthorized transfer of title by the borrower.

The escrow holder may be involved in a transaction in which the buyer and the seller agree that the buyer can assume the seller's existing loan without the buyer actually applying to or being approved by the seller's lender. Called "taking title subject to" the existing note and deed of trust, this practice carries potential risk to both the buyer and the seller. In this type of transaction, the seller's lender is not asked to approve the transaction, as it would if the buyer were "formally" assuming the loan.

The major risk to the parties is that the lender may eventually discover the title transfer and enforce the note's due-on-sale clause. The due-on-sale clause is a provision in the note that gives the lender the ability to call the loan due and payable if the borrower transfers title, or any part of it (such as quitclaiming a partial interest to another person), and does not pay off the loan at the time of transfer. Such a transfer takes place without the lender's approval, and the escrow officer is usually instructed by the parties not to notify the lender about the transaction.

When a buyer wants to take over a seller's existing loan and both parties want to avoid the possibility of the seller's loan being called due by the lender, they typically will ask the lender to approve the process (called a formal assumption and substitution of liability, which releases the seller from the legal responsibility of repayment). In such a transaction, the escrow officer would be asked by the seller to send a "request for beneficiary statement" to the lender. The beneficiary statement provides the parties and the escrow officer with the terms of the loan, including the unpaid balance, enabling the officer to accurately determine and account for the closing funds required from the buyer and to calculate amounts to be prorated between the buyer and the seller. Since obviously such a statement is not going to be requested the escrow holder must obtain the information directly from the seller, referred to as an "offset statement," and the buyer is expected to rely upon the information provided. The escrow holder will certainly want to prepare appropriate disclaimer documentation for the parties to sign that relieves the escrow company from erroneous information provided by the seller.

Pro-Tip: The Risk of "Taking Title Subject To"

A seller and a buyer who plan to enter into a "taking title subject to" transaction would be wise to first seek legal advice before proceeding. However, even armed with such advice, both should have a plan of action, including how to pay off the loan in the event the lender calls the loan due. A lender who has discovered the title transfer and who chooses to execute its right to call the loan due and payable will send a letter to the trustor of record (the former seller) demanding payment in full within 30 days. The seller naturally would inform the homeowner (the former buyer) of the lender's demand, expecting the homeowner to make arrangements to pay off the loan. The difficulty arises when the homeowner is unable to obtain payoff funds in a timely manner. Typically, the homeowner will attempt to refinance the property to accommodate the payoff. The homeowner's refinancing lender and the escrow holder need to be made aware of the urgency of the transaction. Providing copies of the refinancing loan escrow instructions to the "calling" lender with a request for a payoff demand may result in the lender's cooperation even if the refinance will take longer than the 30 days. The real difficulty arises when the homeowner is unable to obtain refinancing and has no access to funds. Unless the trustor is able to help, the lender will file foreclosure, affecting both the homeowner and the trustor. While the homeowner's credit will not be affected by the foreclosure, the homeowner loses the property and all the monies invested, and is forced to vacate. The trustor's credit standing is damaged by having a foreclosure listed on the trustor's credit report.

- *Right to reinstate the loan.* This explains the borrower's rights and the procedures required to bring the loan current in the event of a default. In California, the right to reinstatement terminates after the following have lapsed: notice-of-default period, three months, and the first 15 days of the 20-day-notice-of-sale period. During the last five business days of the notice-of-sale period the borrower can retain the home by paying the entire loan balance in full, along with all late charges and foreclosure fees. The escrow officer in a transaction in which the "clock" has been ticking in the foreclosure process should closely monitor the timing.

- *Assignment of rents.* When the borrower is in default on property that has tenants, the lender has the right to appoint a receiver to collect rents from the tenant occupants.

Reconveyance provisions are covered. It is not uncommon for the title officer to discover a lien on the title from a loan that has long since been paid off. In such a case, the trustee must be contacted to facilitate the reconveyance. If the lender cannot be located, court action might be necessary.

A substitute trustee provision gives the lender the right to replace the trustee with another if the lender chooses. This is a logical and sometimes necessary event because companies go out of business, people pass away, and relationships change.

■ *Riders*. These are additional loan documents that cover additional provisions such as adjustable-rate loans, condominiums, and other matters.

■ *Junior lenders*. A junior lender (subordinate lienholder) under California law must be notified by the senior lender in the event the borrower becomes four or more months delinquent. A Notice of Request for Default may be filed the junior lender to be informed when the senior lender actually begins the foreclosure process.

■ *Fictitious deed of trust*. California CC Section 2952 governs and specifies the standard provisions to be contained in a legal deed of trust to be used in California. It is quite lengthy therefore the law allows a deed of trust normally used in actual transactions to contain only certain portions, and to make reference to all others as contained in a document called a "fictitious deed of trust", This document, described in and considered to have be pre-recorded by CC 2952, contains all the legal terms and conditions referred to in the actual deed of trust signed by the borrower, and which is referred to as a "short form" deed of trust. The short form includes the recording information on its front page and all the "boilerplate" on the back page. The escrow officer will note that not only is it not necessary to record the "back page" since it has inherently already been recorded but it may contain specific instructions such as "Do Not Record." The actual reason for the use of the short form deed of trust is to reduce the recording fees that would otherwise have to be paid to the county if all the pages contained in the fictitious deed would have to be included and recorded. By signing the deed of trust, the borrower agrees that the beneficiary has the indirect right to foreclose and sell the property (and this may be executed without court action, as indicated above) as allowed and through the process described under "Non-uniform Covenants" and "acceleration."

All-Inclusive Deed of Trust

The **all-inclusive trust deed** (AITD) (Figure 2.7), or "wraparound," is the security instrument used when a seller is carrying back financing in which an underlying senior lien is included in the note, along with the seller's equity position being carried. In the AITD transaction, the buyer (borrower) "takes title subject to" the seller's existing note and trust deed (with the same risks as previously described), and typically neither the seller nor the buyer informs the underlying note holder of the transaction. The new note, drawn by the escrow holder, includes the senior underlying note but is junior.

Both the buyer and the seller should seek legal counsel before entering into a wraparound transaction. One benefit to the buyer is the ability to obtain financing at an attractive rate with greater principal buildup than that offered by a new loan at even the same rate. (As each payment is made, the amount attributed to interest decreases and the amount attributed to principal increases.) The buyer also saves considerable costs by not having to pay loan fees and other costs associated with obtaining new financing. The risk factor, of course, is the due-on-sale provision. Only by discussing their particular situations with a real estate attorney may the buyer and the seller comfortably proceed.

FIGURE 2.7

All-Inclusive Deed of
Trust (AITD)

RECORDING REQUESTED BY

AND WHEN RECORDED MAIL TO

SPACE ABOVE THIS LINE FOR RECORDER'S USE

ALL-INCLUSIVE DEED OF TRUST AND ASSIGNMENT OF RENTS

BY THIS DEED OF TRUST, made this   day of   ,   ,
between

herein called "TRUSTOR", whose address is
                                        (Number and Street)   (City)
                                        (State)   (zip),
CHICAGO TITLE COMPANY, a California Corporation, herein called "TRUSTEE" and

                                                        herein called "BENEFICIARY."
Trustor IRREVOCABLY GRANTS, TRANSFERS AND ASSIGNS TO TRUSTEE IN TRUST, WITH
POWER OF SALE, that property in
                                                        County, California described as:

Trustor ALSO ASSIGNS to Beneficiary, all rents issues and profits from said real property RESERVING,
HOWEVER, the right to collect and use the same as long as there is no existing default hereunder, AND
DOES HEREBY AUTHORIZE Beneficiary to collect and recover the same in the name of Trustor or his
successor in interest by use of any lawful means.

FOR THE PURPOSE OF SECURING:

(1)   Payment of indebtedness evidenced by one promissory note of even date herewith in the principal
sum of
                                                                ($)
payable to Beneficiary or order hereinafter referred to as "the Note";
(2)   Payment of any additional sums and advances hereafter made by Beneficiary or his assignee to or
for the benefit of Trustor or his successor in ownership of the real property encumbered hereby;
(3)   Performance of each agreement of Trustor incorporated by reference or contained herein.
This is an All-Inclusive Deed of Trust and is subject and subordinate to the following Deed(s) of Trust now
of record securing certain notes (hereinafter called "Underlying Notes") the unpaid principal balance of
which is included in the Note and which the Beneficiary herein has agreed to pay as per the terms thereof
PROVIDING Trustor is not in default in the payment of the Note secured by this Deed of Trust:
a.   Deed of Trust dated   and recorded in the Office of the Recorder of
                                        County, California on
        at   (Book and Page or Serial Number) executed by

Source: Chicago Title Insurance Company

FIGURE **2.7**

All-Inclusive Deed of
Trust (AITD) (continued)

as Trustor in which
is named as Beneficiary
and   as Trustee securing a promissory note in the original principal sum
of   Dollars ($)
in favor of said Beneficiary as payee; and
b.   Deed of Trust dated   and recorded in the Office of the Recorder of
County, California on
at   (Book and Page or Serial Number) executed by
as Trustor in which
is named as Beneficiary
and   as Trustee securing a promissory note in the original principal sum
of   Dollars ($)
in favor of said Beneficiary as payee.

TRUSTOR AND BENEFICIARY MUTUALLY AGREE:

1. In the event of default by Beneficiary:

Should the within Beneficiary default in payment of any installments due under any said prior Deed of Trust the Trustor herein may make said payments , including late charges, penalties and/or advances, direct to the Beneficiary of said prior Deed of Trust and any and all payments so made shall be credited against the installments due on the Note secured by this Deed of Trust.

2. In the event of default by Trustor:

Any demand hereunder delivered by Beneficiary to Trustee for the foreclosure of the lien of this Deed of Trust may be not more than the sum of the following amounts:

a.   The difference between the then unpaid balance of principal and interest on the Note secured hereby and the then unpaid balance of principal and interest on the Underlying Note(s); and

b.   The aggregate of all amounts theretofore paid by Beneficiary pursuant to the terms of this Deed of Trust prior to the date of such foreclosure sale, for taxes and assessments, insurance premiums, delinquency charges, foreclosure costs, and any other sums advanced by Beneficiary pursuant to the terms of this Deed of Trust, to the extent the same were not previously repaid by Trustor to Beneficiary; and

c.   The costs of foreclosure hereunder; plus attorneys fees and costs incurred by Beneficiary in enforcing this Deed of Trust or the Note secured hereby as permitted by law.

Notwithstanding any provision to the contrary herein contained, in the event of a Trustee's sale in furtherance of the foreclosure of this Deed of Trust the balance then due on the Note secured hereby, for the purposes of Beneficiary's demand, shall be reduced by the unpaid balance, if any, of principal and interest then due on the Note(s) secured by the prior Deeds of Trust, satisfactory evidence of which unpaid balances must be submitted to Trustee prior to such sale. The Trustee may rely on any statements received from Beneficiary in this regard and such statements shall be deemed binding and conclusive as between Beneficiary and Trustor on the one a hand and the Trustee on the other hand, to the extent of such reliance. The undersigned Trustor requests that a copy of any Notice of Default and any Notice of Sale hereunder and under any underlying Deed of Trust be mailed to him or her at the address set forth above.

Should Beneficiary incur any penalties, charges, or other expenses under the "Underlying Notes" as a result of any delinquency or default of Trustor the amount of such penalties, charges, and expenses shall be immediately added to the principal amount of the Note secured by this Deed of Trust, and become immediately payable to Beneficiary.

3.   Provided Trustor is not in default under the terms of the Note secured by the within Deed of Trust, Beneficiary shall pay all installments of principal and interest under the "Underlying Notes" when said Notes become due and payable.

4.   Any reduction in the unpaid principal amount of the "Underlying Notes" by proceeds of a casualty insurance award for destruction of improvements, or condemnation award or settlement in lieu thereof, shall reduce in equivalent the unpaid principal balance of the Note secured hereby and be applied to the last sums due under said Note.

5.   At such times as the Note secured hereby becomes all due and payable, the amount of principal and interest then payable to Beneficiary thereunder shall be reduced by the then unpaid balance of principal and interest due on the Underlying Note(s).

FIGURE 2.7

**All-Inclusive Deed of
Trust (AITD) (continued)**

6.   Termination of Beneficiary's obligations: The obligation of Beneficiary hereunder shall terminate upon the earliest of (1) foreclosure of the lien of this All-Inclusive Deed of Trust, or (2) cancellation of the note secured hereby and reconveyance of this All-Inclusive Deed of Trust.

If at any time the unpaid balance of the Note secured hereby, accrued interest thereon, and all other sums due pursuant to the terms thereof and all sums advanced by Beneficiary pursuant to the terms of this Deed of Trust, is equal to or less than the unpaid principal balance of the Underlying Note(s) and accrued interest thereon, the Note secured hereby at the request of Trustor, shall be cancelled and said property shall be reconveyed from the lien of this Deed of Trust. Five years after issuance of a reconveyance hereunder, Trustee may destroy said Note and this Deed of Trust. TO PROTECT THE SECURITY OF THIS DEED OF TRUST TRUSTOR AGREES: (1) To perform the obligations secured by such prior Deeds of Trust other than the payments to be made by Beneficiary as set forth in the Note secured by this Deed of Trust. As between parties hereto and their successors and assigns no assumption or guarantee executed by Trustor(s) for the benefit of the holders of the underlying Notes shall be deemed to affect this obligation of Beneficiary; (2) All of the provisions of Section A Paragraphs 1 through 5, AND IT IS MUTUALLY AGREED that all of the provisions of Section B Paragraphs 1 through 10, both of that certain Fictitious Deed of Trust recorded on the date and in the Book and at the Page of Official Records in the Office of the County Recorder of the county where said property is located, noted below opposite the name of such county, viz:

COUNTY	BOOK	PAGE	COUNTY	BOOK	PAGE	COUNTY	BOOK	PAGE	COUNTY	BOOK	PAGE
Alameda	1288	556	Kings	858	713	Placer	1028	379	Sierra	38	187
Alpine	3	130-31	Lake	437	110	Plumas	166	1307	Siskiyou	506	762
Amador	133	438	Lassen	192	367	Riverside	3778	347	Solano	1287	621
Butte	1330	513	Los Angeles	T-3878	874	Sacramento	71-10-26	615	Sonoma	2067	427
Calaveras	185	338	Madera	911	136	San Benito	300	405	Stanislaus	1970	56
Colusa	323	391	Marin	1849	122	San Bernardino	6213	768	Sutter	655	585
Contra Costa	4684	1	Mariposa	90	453	San Francisco	A-804	596	Tehama	457	183
Del Norte	101	549	Mendocino	667	99	San Joaquin	2855	283	Trinity	108	595
El Dorado	704	635	Merced	1660	753	San Luis Obispo	1311	137	Tulare	2530	108
Fresno	5052	623	Modoc	191	93	San Mateo	4778	175	Tuolumne	177	160
Glenn	469	76	Mono	69	302	Santa Barbara	2065	881	Ventura	2607	237
Humboldt	801	83	Monterey	357	239	Santa Clara	6626	664	Yolo	769	16
Imperial	1189	701	Napa	704	742	Santa Cruz	1638	607	Yuba	398	693
Inyo	165	672	Nevada	363	94	Shasta	800	633			
Kern	3756	690	Orange	7182	18	San Diego	SERIES 5 Book 1964, Pg. 149774				

(which provisions, identical in all counties, are printed on the following page hereof) are hereby incorporated herein, and the parties hereto agree to be bound thereby as though fully set forth herein. All references to property, obligations and parties in the provisions of said Fictitious Deed of Trust are the property, obligations and parties set forth in this Deed of Trust.

_____

_____

_____

_____

FIGURE 2.7
_____

**All-Inclusive Deed of
Trust (AITD) (continued)**

CERTIFICATE OF ACKNOWLEDGEMENT OF NOTARY PUBLIC

STATE OF CALIFORNIA,   )
COUNTY OF _____)

On _____ before me, _____,
(here insert name and title of the officer), personally appeared
_____, who proved to me on the basis of
satisfactory evidence to be the person(s) whose name(s) is/are subscribed to the within
instrument and acknowledged to me that he/she/they executed the same in his/her/their
authorized capacity(ies), and that by his/her/their signature(s) on the instrument the
person(s), or the entity upon behalf of which the person(s) acted, executed the instrument.

I certify under PENALTY OF PERJURY under the laws of the State of California that
the foregoing paragraph is true and correct.

WITNESS my hand and official seal.

Signature _____ (Seal)

**NOTE: Legal rights and duties are created upon the execution of this document. The parties are
advised to consult with their attorneys prior to signing this document.**

FIGURE 2.7
**All-Inclusive Deed of
Trust (AITD) (continued)**

DO NOT RECORD

The following is a copy of Subdivisions A and B of the fictitious Deed of Trust recorded in each county in California as stated in the foregoing Deed of Trust and incorporated by reference in said Deed of Trust as being a part thereof as if set forth at length therein.

A. To protect the security of this Deed of Trust, Trustor agrees:
  (1) To keep said property in good condition and repair; not to remove or demolish any building thereon; to complete or restore promptly and in good and workmanlike manner any building which may be constructed, damaged or destroyed thereon and to pay when due all claims for labor performed and materials furnished therefor; to comply with all laws affecting said property or requiring any alterations or improvements to be made thereon; not to commit or permit waste thereof; not to commit, suffer or permit any act upon said property in violation of law; to cultivate, irrigate, fertilize, fumigate, prune and do all other acts which from the character or use of said property may be reasonably necessary, the specific enumerations herein not excluding the general.
  (2) To provide, maintain and deliver to Beneficiary fire insurance satisfactory to and with loss payable to Beneficiary. The amount collected under any fire or other insurance policy may be applied by Beneficiary upon any indebtedness secured hereby and in such order as Beneficiary may determine, or at option of Beneficiary the entire amount so collected or any part thereof my be released to Trustor. Such application or release shall not cure or waive any default or notice of default hereunder or invalidate any act done pursuant to such notice.
  (3) To appear in and defend any action or proceeding purporting to affect the security hereof or the rights or powers of Beneficiary or Trustee; and to pay all costs and expenses, including cost of evidence of title and attorney's fees in a reasonable sum, in any such action or proceeding in which Beneficiary or Trustee may appear, and in any suit brought by Beneficiary to foreclose this Deed.
  (4) To pay: at least ten days before delinquency all taxes and assessments affecting said property, including assessments on appurtenant water stock; when due, all incumbrances, charges and liens, with interest, on said property or any part thereof, which appear to be prior or superior hereto; all costs, fees and expenses of this Trust.

  Should Trustor fail to make any payment or to do any act as herein provided, then Beneficiary or Trustee, but without obligation so to do and without notice to or demand upon Trustor and without releasing Trustor from any obligation hereof, may: make or do the same in such manner and to such extent as either may deem necessary to protect the security hereof, Beneficiary or Trustee being authorized to enter upon said property for such purposes; appear in and defend any action or proceeding purporting to affect the security hereof or the rights or powers of Beneficiary or Trustee; pay, purchase, contest or compromise any incumbrance,

FIGURE 2.7

**All-Inclusive Deed of
Trust (AITD) (continued)**

charge or lien which in the judgment of either appears to be prior or superior hereto; and, in exercising any such powers, pay necessary expenses, employ counsel and pay his reasonable fees.

(5) To pay immediately and without demand all sums so expended by Beneficiary or Trustee, with interest from date of expenditure at the amount allowed by law in effect at the date hereof, and to pay for any statement provided for by law in effect at the date hereof regarding the obligation secured hereby any amount demanded by the Beneficiary not to exceed the maximum allowed by law at the time when said statement is demanded.

B. It is mutually agreed:

(1) That any award of damages in connection with any condemnation for public use of or injury to said property or any part thereof is hereby assigned and shall be paid to Beneficiary who may apply or release such moneys received by him in the same manner and with the same effect as above provided for disposition of proceeds of fire or other insurance.

(2) That by accepting payment of any sum secured hereby after its due date, Beneficiary does not waive his right either to require prompt payment when due of all other sums so secured or to declare default for failure so to pay.

(3) That at any time or from time to time, without liability therefor and without notice, upon written request of Beneficiary and presentation of this Deed and said note for endorsement, and without affecting the personal liability of any person for payment of the indebtedness secured hereby, Trustee may: recovery any part of said property; consent to the making of any map or plat thereof; join in granting any easement thereon; or join in any extension agreement or any agreement subordinating the lien or charge hereof.

(4) That upon written request of beneficiary stating that all sums secured hereby have been paid, and upon surrender of this Deed and said note to Trustee for cancellation and retention or other disposition as Trustee in its sole discretion may choose and upon payment of its fees, Trustee shall reconvey, without warranty, the property then held hereunder. The recitals in such reconveyance of any matters or facts shall be conclusive proof of the truthfulness thereof. The Grantee in such reconveyance may be described as "the person or persons legally entitled thereto."

(5) That as additional security, Trustor hereby gives to and confers upon Beneficiary the right, power and authority, during the continuance of these Trusts, to collect the rents, issues and profits of said property, reserving unto Trustor the right, prior to any default by Trustor in payment of any indebtedness secured hereby or in performance of any agreement hereunder, to collect and retain such rents, issues and profits as they become due and payable. Upon any such default, Beneficiary may at any time without notice, either in person, by agent, or by a receiver to be appointed by a court, and without regard to the adequacy of any security for the indebtedness hereby secured, enter upon and take possession of said property or any part thereof, in his own name sue for or otherwise collect such rents, issues, and profits,

FIGURE 2.7
**All-Inclusive Deed of
Trust (AITD) (continued)**

including those past due and unpaid, and apply the same, less costs and expenses of operation and collection, including reasonable attorney's fees, upon any indebtedness secured hereby, and in such order as Beneficiary may determine. The entering upon and taking possession of said property, the collection of such rents, issues and profits and the application thereof as aforesaid, shall not cure or waive any default or notice of default hereunder or invalidate any act done pursuant to such notice.

(6) That upon default by Trustor in payment of any indebtedness secured hereby or in performance of any agreement hereunder, Beneficiary may declare all sums secured hereby immediately due and payable by delivery to Trustee of written declaration of default and demand for sale and of written notice of default and of election to cause to be sold said property, which notice Trustee shall cause to be filed for record. Beneficiary also shall deposit with Trustee this Deed, said note and all documents evidencing expenditures secured hereby.

After the lapse of such time as may then be required by law following the recordation of said notice of default, and notice of sale having been given as then required by law, Trustee, without demand on Trustor, shall sell said property at the time and place fixed by it in said notice of sale, either as a whole or in separate parcels, and in such order as it may determine, at public auction to the highest bidder for cash in lawful money of the United States, payable at time of sale. Trustee may postpone sale of all or any portion of said property by public announcement at such time and place of sale, and from time to time thereafter may postpone such sale by public announcement at the time fixed by the preceding postponement. Trustee shall deliver to such purchaser its deed conveying the property so sold, but without any covenant or warranty, express or implied. The recitals in such deed of any matters of facts shall be conclusive proof of the truthfulness thereof. Any person, including Trustor, Trustee, or Beneficiary as hereinafter defined, may purchase at such sale.

After deducting all costs, fees and expenses of Trustee and of this Trust, including cost of evidence of title in connection with sale, Trustee shall apply the proceeds of sale to payment of: all sums expended under the terms hereof, not then repaid, with accrued interest at the amount allowed by law in effect at the date hereof; all other sums then secured hereby; and the remainder, if any, to the person or persons legally entitled thereto.

(7) Beneficiary, or any successor in ownership of any indebtedness secured hereby, may from time to time, by instrument in writing, substitute a successor or successors to any Trustee named herein or acting hereunder, which instrument, executed by the Beneficiary and duly acknowledged and recorded in the office of the recorder of the county or counties where said property is situated, shall be conclusive proof of proper substitution of such successor

FIGURE 2.7

**All-Inclusive Deed of
Trust (AITD) (continued)**

Trustee or Trustees, who shall, without conveyance from the Trustee predecessor, succeed to all its title, estate, rights, powers and duties. Said instrument must contain the name of the original Trustor, Trustee and Beneficiary hereunder, the book and page where this Deed is recorded and the name and address of the new Trustee.

(8) That this Deed applies to, inures to the benefit of, and binds all parties hereto, their heirs, legatees, devisees, administrators, executors, successors and assigns. The term Beneficiary shall mean the owner and holder, including pledgees, of the note secured hereby, whether or not named as Beneficiary herein. In this Deed, whenever the context so requires, the masculine gender includes the feminine and /or neuter, and the singular number includes the plural.

(9) That Trustee accepts this Trust when this Deed, duly executed and acknowledged, is made a public record as provided by law. Trustee is not obligated to notify any party hereto of pending sale under any other Deed of Trust or of any action or proceeding in which Trustor, Beneficiary or Trustee shall be a party unless brought by Trustee.

<u>DO NOT RECORD</u>   REQUEST FOR FULL RECONVEYANCE

TO CHICAGO TITLE COMPANY, TRUSTEE:

The Undersigned is the legal owner and holder of the note or notes, and of all other indebtedness secured by the foregoing Deed of Trust. Said note or notes, together with all other indebtedness secured by said Deed of Trust, have been fully paid and satisfied; and you are hereby requested and directed, on payment to you of any sums owing to you under the terms of said Deed of Trust, to cancel said note or notes above mentioned, and all other evidence of indebtedness secured by said Deed of Trust delivered to you herewith, together with the said Deed of Trust, and to reconvey, without warranty, to the parties designated by the terms of said Deed of Trust, all the estate now held by you under the same.

Dated _____

_____

Please mail Deed of Trust,
Note and Reconveyance to _____

<u>Do not lose or destroy this Deed of Trust OR THE NOTE which it secures. Both must be delivered to the Trustee for cancellation before reconveyance will be made.</u>

Mortgage

In some states, a mortgage is used as the security instrument. In a mortgage, only two parties are involved; there is no trustee, only the lender (referred to as the mortgagee) and the borrower (referred to as the mortgagor). The borrower retains bare legal title, requiring the lender to seek court action to foreclose in the event of default.

Land Contract

Another security instrument is the land contract, also called contract of sale or agreement of sale. It actually may be the written purchase agreement (the written "meeting of the minds"), as well as the security instrument. Fee title is not delivered in a land contract; therefore, no grant deed is used. The following three parties participate in a land contract:

- *Vendor.* The seller under a land contract is called the vendor.

- *Vendee.* The buyer is called the vendee (and receives what is known as equitable title).

- *Trustee.* A trustee exists, just as in a deed of trust, and performs essentially the same services under a land contract.

Performing an escrow involving a land contract may be complex and not clearly understood by the novice escrow officer or technician. It is recommended that only an escrow officer experienced in land contracts handle such a transaction.

■ CHAPTER 2 QUIZ

1. California CC Section 1000 specifies that property in the state of California may be acquired in which of the following five ways?

   a. Occupancy, Accession, Transfer, Will, and Procession

   b. Occupancy, Recession, Transfer, Will, and Succession

   c. Occupancy, Accession, Transfer, Will, and Succession

   d. Accession, Transfer, Will, Succession, and Prevision

2. Trust deeds transfer only

   a. dormant title.

   b. dominant title.

   c. both fee title and dominant title.

   d. both fee title and dormant title.

3. Probate is NOT required if title was held as

   a. tenants in common.

   b. partnership.

   c. joint tenants.

   d. joint partners.

4. Intestate succession applies to one

   a. who died without a will.

   b. who only resided outside California.

   c. who was only unmarried.

   d. all of these.

5. Transfer of title to real property is called

    a. alienation.

    b. accession.

    c. annexation.

    d. none of these.

6. Recording a document provides

    a. destructive notice.

    b. actual notice.

    c. constructive notice.

    d. requested notice.

7. In order to be valid, deeds must be in writing, include the property description, contain conveying language, identify a grantee, and

    a. be signed by a competent grantor.

    b. be signed by a competent grantee.

    c. both a and b.

    d. no other condition.

8. Grant deed forms include

    a. joint tenancy grant deeds.

    b. community property with no right of survivorship.

    c. interspousal grant deeds.

    d. both a and c.

9. A quitclaim deed

    a. guarantees title protection.

    b. is not valid.

    c. conveys title from the grantor to the grantee with no warranty or guaranty.

    d. may not convey less than the entire interest of the grantor.

10. An all-inclusive deed of trust is

    a. typically acceptable to existing lenders.

    b. called a wrap-in deed.

    c. illegal.

    d. a new first deed of trust.

CHAPTER THREE

ELEMENTS OF ESCROW

■ KEY TERMS

abstract of title	certificate of title	Escrow Law
American Escrow	Civil Code Section 1057	fidelity bond
Association	depository	surety bond
California Escrow		trust
Association		

■ LEARNING OBJECTIVES

Upon completing this chapter, you will be able to

- ■ explain the provisions of California Civil Code Section 1057,

- ■ explain Escrow Law as outlined in the California Financial Code,

- ■ define the responsibilities under the law of the escrow agent,

- ■ explain the history and concepts of real property title protection, and

- ■ explain the role of the various escrow practitioners.

■ CALIFORNIA LAW AND THE ESCROW AGENT

California **Civil Code Section 1057** states that "a grant may be deposited by the grantor with a third person, to be delivered on performance of a condition, and, on delivery by the depositary, it will take effect. While in the possession of the third person, and subject to condition, it is called an escrow." The "third parties" referenced in the California Civil Code are escrow companies and are subject to the Escrow Law.

The **Escrow Law** under the California Financial Code (CFC) is intended to protect members of the public who entrust their money or other assets to independent escrow agents in California. Escrow agents are subject to the provisions of the Escrow Law and its licensing requirements. People or companies performing escrow services over the Internet in California, or performing escrow services over the Internet for consumers in California, are also subject to the licensing requirements of the Escrow Law.

California FC Section 17003 states that

> "escrow" means any transaction in which one person, for the purpose of effecting the sale, transfer, encumbering, or leasing of real or personal property to another person, delivers any written instrument, money, evidence of title to real or personal property, or other thing of value to a third person to be held by that third person [escrow holder] until the happening of a specified event or the performance of a prescribed condition, when it is then to be delivered by that third person to a grantee [remember, a buyer would be the grantee], grantor [the seller is the grantor], promisee, promisor, obligee, obligor, bailee, bailor, or any agent or employee of any of the latter.

According to California FC Section 17004, "escrow agent means any person engaged in the business of receiving escrows for deposit or delivery." An escrow holder works to ensure that all parties involved in a transaction comply with the conditions and terms of the agreement, as stipulated in the escrow instructions. California Civil Code Section 1057.7 states,

> All written escrow instructions executed by a buyer and seller ... shall contain a statement in not less than 10-point type which shall include the license name and the name of the department issuing the license or authority under which the person is operating.

Additionally, the escrow holder may coordinate all the activities and services involved in a transaction, including the actions of the lender or title company, as well the activities of the seller, the buyer or the broker.

Escrow Law

The California Department of Corporations (DOC) has established guidelines and regulations that govern escrow practices and agents. The Escrow Law (Section 17000 of the CFC) determines who is subject to the licensing requirements of the law, defining *escrow agent* as "any person engaged in the business of receiving escrows for deposit or delivery." The following provisions apply to escrow agents—the owners and operators of the escrow company and not its employees, unless specifically stated. An escrow agent may also be considered a joint control agent, defined under the Escrow Law as "any person engaging in the business of receiving money or other property for disbursal or use in payment of the cost of labor, material, services, permits, fees, or other items of expense incurred in the construction of improvements upon real property."

- *License required for escrow holders.* The Escrow Law requires any person engaged in the escrow business or joint control business in California to be a corporation organized for that purpose and to be licensed by the commissioner of the Department of Corporations. However, the law exempts certain individuals from the licensure requirements, including the following:

  - Any person doing business under any California law or the United States relating to banks, trust companies, building and loan or savings and loan associations, or insurance companies

  - Any person licensed to practice law in California who has a bona fide client-attorney relationship with a principal in a real estate or personal property transaction and who is not actively engaged in the business of an escrow agent

  - Any person whose principal business is that of preparing abstracts or making searches of title that are used as a basis for the issuance of a policy of title insurance by a company doing business under any law of this state relating to insurance companies

  - Any real estate broker licensed by the real estate commissioner while performing acts in the course of or incidental to a real estate transaction in which the broker is an agent or a party to the transaction and in which the broker is performing an act for which a real estate license is required

- *Obtaining the escrow license.* An application and filing fee are required, plus $625 for the first office or location and $425 for each additional office or location, along with an investigation fee of $100 for each location. The fees are nonrefundable.

■ *Membership in Escrow Agents' Fidelity Corporation (EAFC).* An escrow agent must be a member of EAFC if engaging in the following types of escrows:

— Real property escrows, including, but not limited to, the sale, lease, exchange, or transfer of title, and loans or other obligations to be secured by a lien upon real property

— Bulk sale escrows, including, but not limited to, the sale or transfer of title to a business entity and the transfer of liquor licenses or other types of business licenses or permits

— Fund or joint control escrows, including funds held for the performance of contractors under Section 10263 of the Public Contract Code

— The sale, transfer of title, or refinance escrows for manufactured homes or mobile homes

— Reservation deposits for new home sales under the Subdivided Lands Act as required by the Business and Professions Code or by regulation of the Department of Real Estate

— Escrows for sale, transfer, modification, assignment, or hypothecation of promissory notes secured by deeds of trust

■ *Fidelity bonds.* A **fidelity bond**, a sort of insurance protection that pays for losses to principals of monies held in trust for them, must be filed with the DOC if the transactions to be processed are a type not listed previously. The fidelity bond must provide coverage for each officer, director, trustee, and employee of not less than $125,000. Fidelity coverage is provided for indemnifying the escrow agent for loss of trust funds held by the escrow agent as a result of fraudulent or dishonest actions or embezzlement of trust obligations by any officer, director, trustee, or employee. Although the fidelity bond may contain a deductible, the escrow must deposit a surety bond with the commissioner of the DOC in the amount of the deductible. The amount of the surety bond must be maintained in the amount of the deductible of the fidelity bond for any loss of trust monies incurred that exceeds the amount of the fidelity bond's deductible.

■ *Minimum financial requirements.* The company must document that it has liquid assets in excess of current liabilities by $25,000 and tangible assets in excess of total liabilities by $50,000. If branch offices are maintained by the escrow agent, the tangible net worth requirement increases by 50% of the requirement for the first branch office and 25% for each additional branch office. Any losses projected by the applicant during the first few months of operation as shown in the applicant's proposed budget must be considered when calculating the tangible net worth and liquid assets.

- *Surety bonding.* An escrow agent must file a **surety bond** of at least $25,000 with the commissioner, intended to be used to pay to the state or any person any amount due to the state or such person under the provisions of the Escrow Law. The amount of the bond required may increase up to a maximum of $50,000, depending on the escrow liability of the company, and must be increased by $5,000 for each additional licensed branch office. In lieu of the surety bond, a licensee may deposit a cash bond in the amount required with the commissioner.

- *Background checks.* All stockholders, officers, directors, managers, and employees must have background checks performed by the department. These background checks include, among other things, obtaining criminal history information through the Department of Justice (DOJ) and conducting civil court checks for activities that would indicate previous involvement in fraud, embezzlement, fraudulent conversion, or misappropriation of property. Each stockholder, officer, director, manager, and employee is required to file fingerprints cards, which must be cleared through the DOJ. Applicants may use the Live Scan program to submit fingerprints electronically to the DOJ for clearance. The fee for each clearance is $10 plus any fee charged by the DOJ or the live scan operator.

■ PURPOSE OF ESCROW

Escrow may mean different things depending upon the context in which it is used. A mortgage lender, for example, may have an escrow account for maintaining funds for the renewal of a borrower's property taxes and hazard insurance. In the context of this book, however, escrow refers to the neutral or disinterested third-party holder of documents and funds to facilitate a transfer of title between a buyer and a seller of real property or business opportunity, or the processing of a loan for a property owner on behalf of the property owner and the lender originating the loan. The escrow holder, while representing all principals in the transaction, does not have a fiduciary relationship with them as do real estate agents and their principals.

Depository

The escrow holder serves as a neutral **depository** for both documents and money received from principals of a transaction to hold on their behalf.

Trust

Trust is defined in *Black's Law Dictionary* as the right of property, real or personal, held by one party for the benefit of another. Simply put, trust monies are those that belong to someone else. Trust is placed in the escrow holder, who represents and is the closing agent for all principals in the transaction, which might be a buyer, a seller, a lender, a borrower, a lessee (tenant), a lessor (landlord), a vendee (a buyer under a land contract), or a vendor (a seller under a land contract).

Consumer Protection

The California laws that govern escrow holders, and the law that requires an escrow in some circumstances (escrow for most sales transactions is not a requirement under California law), are designed to protect the consumer from unethical, fraudulent, and negligent practices by other individuals and third-party service providers upon whom they rely to perform the services necessary to accomplish their transactions.

Accounting and Accountability

Escrow provides an accounting of all monies received from and delivered to all principals. A more detailed discussion of the final accounting of the file and the preparation of the closing statement can be found in Chapter 12.

Compliance with Agreement and Terms of Escrow

The escrow holder guarantees that all conditions required per the escrow instructions before a final disposition (closing) occurs are met. The escrow officer uses a checklist for each transaction, identifies all conditions spelled out in the contract, and indicates any forms or documents that may be required to satisfy them. During the escrow, the officer will audit the file to ascertain compliance with its conditions. Until all documents requiring action have been approved and signed by the appropriate parties and other conditions have been met, including the deposit into escrow of the buyer's "good" funds (e.g., all checks have cleared) necessary to close escrow (including funds from the buyer's lender), the escrow holder will not allow the escrow to close.

Unlawful Escrow Practices

California Civil Code Section 1057.5 warns escrow agents that they may not compensate any individual "for referring, soliciting, handling, or servicing escrow customers or accounts." The California Department of Real Estate reference manual stipulates that it is illegal for an escrow holder to pay a real estate agent fees for the referral of services, and it is illegal for the real estate agent to receive such fees.[1] The DRE does not limit such a prohibition to controlled escrow holders such as real estate brokers and title insurance companies.

Fees include gifts, merchandise, and other things of value. Section 1057.5 clearly states that

> no escrow agent shall enter into any arrangement, either of his own making or of a subsidiary nature, or through any persona having a direct or indirect interest in the escrow, or other device, permitting any fee, commission or compensation which is contingent upon the performance of any act, condition or instruction set forth in an escrow, to be drawn or paid, either in whole or in part, or in kind or its equivalent prior to the actual closing and completion of the escrow.

A detailed list of allowable and prohibited activities is covered in Chapter 4 of this book.

California Civil Code Section 2995 also prohibits a developer from requiring a purchaser to use an escrow company in which the developer has an interest. Seemingly innocent and common practices among many escrow and title insurance providers fall into the category of unlawful practices. For example, an escrow officer or marketing representative who provides snacks or other food and beverages at a real estate agent's open house has violated the law. Escrow companies may not provide food or beverages at real estate agents' open houses. Escrow companies may not provide real estate agents with free gifts having a value of $10 or more in exchange for business. The same is true if an escrow officer offers tickets to a sporting event. Anything of value provided as a referral for a current or future transaction is illegal. A detailed list of allowable and prohibited activities is covered in Chapter 4.

■ ESCROW AND TITLE SERVICES IN EARLY AMERICA

Escrow is a practice born in the western United States. As expansion westward accelerated because of the discovery of gold in California (leading to the Gold Rush of 1849), many who came seeking fortunes sought to obtain land grants or purchase properties on which to farm or raise livestock. Even those who failed to achieve riches in gold often sought to obtain land grants or buy properties on

---

1   California Department of Real Estate, *Reference Book: Information Relating to Real Estate Practice, Licensing and Examinations* (Sacramento, Calif.: State of California, Dept. of Real Estate, 2010), p. 126, www.dre.ca.gov/Publications/ReferenceBook.html (accessed May 3, 2013), also available in print.

to achieve riches in gold often sought to obtain land grants or buy properties on which to farm or raise livestock. This real estate boom led to escalating land transfers, which required some professional services to accommodate buyers and sellers. The third-party companies offering these services also provided some level of protection for both buyers and sellers in handling monies and transferring deeds. Before the turn of the 19th century and the California land boom, real estate was transferred directly from the seller to the buyer without escrow services to facilitate the process. The seller simply gave the buyer the deed in exchange for the buyer's check or cash payment.

A common problem was counterfeiting, with the buyer's check's not being good. Until the National Currency Act of 1863 established a central and secure U.S. currency, (followed by the National Bank Act of 1864), banking was regulated, to the extent any regulation existed, by the individual states, with each issuing its own currency. As the nation grew, with rural settlements becoming villages and villages growing into cities and cities expanding into metropolises, buyers and sellers became unknown to one another. This called for a system to overcome the weaknesses inherent in land transfers, such as fraudulent parties and errors in land descriptions. Even before 1850, when California became the 31st state, buyers relied on attorney services to search the public records to verify that the seller actually owned the land. Although of some benefit to buyers, an attorney review offered no guarantee to the buyer concerning errors or fraud. The abstract of title was the first step in providing the land buyer protection.

Abstract of Title

The newly formed abstract companies offered the **abstract of title**, similar to today's preliminary title report, which provided the buyer with a written history of all recorded documents concerning a property. It carried with it an attorney's legal opinion but still offered no protection for damages from a defective title.

Certificate of Title

In the mid- to late-1800s, these abstract companies began issuing a report that was simply a brief history of the property. This report was called a **certificate of title** and was intended to help assure a buyer that the title to the property was valid and the transfer legitimate. But the assurance was meaningless because the courts soon declared that in the event of mistakes or errors, the principals to the transaction had no recourse to the abstract company. Some type of guarantee or form of insurance was needed to protect consumers.

Title Insurance and the Escrow Industry

One of the earliest title insurance companies was established in 1848 in San Francisco. Western Title Insurance Company (now Fidelity National Title Insurance Company of California) was founded by C. V. Gillespie, a notary public and searcher of records in San Francisco. In 1887, California Title Insurance and Trust Company (now TICOR) was incorporated, also in San Francisco, issuing its first policy of title insurance on March 17, 1887. Title insurance companies were among the first to establish escrow services as a logical addition to their business. Then, the demands and volume of California's growing real estate industry and its expanding market led to the development and growth of independent escrow companies (i.e., not part of any title company).

■ ESCROW PRACTITIONERS

A number of entities provide escrow services. Because much of the escrow process involves title insurance services, title companies offer escrow services as well. However, others play a key role in providing escrow services, including independent escrow companies, banks, attorneys, and real estate brokers. In the terminology of the escrow industry, all escrow agents performing escrow services in California are either "licensed" or "controlled" escrow companies.

A licensed escrow company, also known as an independent escrow company, is licensed by the Department of Corporations. This license can only be obtained after the escrow company has met and satisfied all the licensing requirements set forth by the Escrow Law, which are enforced by the Department of Corporations.

According to the Department of Corporations, a controlled escrow, which may be known as a nonindependent escrow, is not licensed by the department. A controlled escrow might be owned and operated by, but not limited to, an attorney, a real estate broker, or a title insurance company, among others. The licensing and regulation of controlled escrows depends on the jurisdiction of the licensing and regulatory authority; therefore, the licensing requirements, laws, and regulations governing them vary widely.

The Escrow Law (Division 6 of the CFC) provides that independent escrow agents must be licensed by the commissioner of Corporations; however, banks, savings and loan associations, title insurance companies, trust companies, attorneys, and real estate brokers are exempt from the licensing requirements of the Escrow Law. They may be regulated by other agencies, such as the California Department of Insurance, which governs the actions of title insurance companies. The California Department of Real Estate governs the practices of broker-owned escrow companies. The California State Bar regulates the practices of attorneys acting as escrow holders.

Independent Escrow Companies

An individual cannot be licensed as an escrow agent; a corporation, duly organized for the purpose of conducting an escrow business, must hold the license. Applicants for escrow licenses must be financially solvent and furnish a surety bond in the amount of $25,000 or more, based on their yearly average trust fund obligations. All officers, directors, trustees, and employees having access to money or negotiable securities in the possession of the corporate licensee must furnish a bond of indemnification against loss. All money deposited in escrow must be placed in a trust account, which is exempt from execution or attachment.

Independent Escrow Company Regulations and Requirements

Escrow companies, other than broker-owned companies and title companies, are regulated by the commissioner of the DOC under provisions of Division 6 of the CFC and Subchapter 9 of the Code of Regulations. The commissioner's office is responsible for overseeing the escrow companies' procedures and practices, insuring that they comply with ethical, financial, and bonding requirements. The DOC may conduct periodic audits with the escrow company paying the cost. Obviously, the escrow company must maintain complete, accurate, and orderly files and records. Independent escrow companies may provide services other than traditional escrow services, including mobile-home transactions, bulk sales, liquor license transfers, acting as corporate trustee on outstanding deeds of trust, and collections.

Experience   DOC regulations require that

> within the organization of each escrow agent corporation, either as owner, officer or employee, there shall be one or more persons possessing a minimum of five years of responsible escrow … experience. … At least one such qualified person shall be stationed on duty at each business location licensed by [the DOC] during the time the location is open for business.

Liquidity and Net Worth   Independent escrow agents are required to possess liquid assets in the amount of $25,000 and have a tangible net worth of $50,000.

Escrow Law Advisory Committee for California Department of Corporations

The purpose of the Escrow Law Advisory Committee is to assist the commissioner in the implementation of his duties under the Escrow Law. The Committee is comprised of 11 members, including the commissioner or his designee. Its members, who are appointed by the commissioner, serve for a period of two years without compensation or reimbursement for expenses. All committee positions are designated in Section 17214 of the CFC. The Escrow Law Advisory Committee also consists of representatives from a medium-size licensed escrow company, an escrow company that handles a different type of business specialization, and an attorney specializing in escrow matters.

Title Insurance Companies

The convenience of using a title company as the escrow holder made sense. The functions of title and escrow are closely related and require considerable interaction with each another. The expansion of title companies as escrow holders also accelerated because state regulation appeared to offer greater protection against loss to the parties in the event they filed a claim against the title company. The DOC requires independent escrow companies, however, to have sufficient financial resources to offer protection to principals, something not explicitly required of title insurance companies. As a practical matter, the nature of the title insurance business and the interaction between title and escrow functions allows them to adequately represent the interests of principals in a transaction.

Real Estate Brokers as Escrow Agents

According to Section 17006 (a)(4) of the CFC, exemption from the licensing requirements for escrow agents applies to

> any broker licensed by the Real Estate Commissioner while performing acts in the course of or incidental to a real estate transaction in which the broker is a party or in which the broker is an agent performing an act for which a real estate license is required.

The DOC has interpreted this section of the CFC to mean that this exemption is limited and applies only to transactions in which the broker is personally involved as a principal or as the selling or listing broker of a principal in the transaction. The exemption also is "not available

- for any association … with other brokers for the purpose of conducting escrows; and

- when the broker's escrow business is a substantial factor in the utilization of the broker's services, the escrow business is not "incidental to a real estate transaction."[2]

---

2   Ibid., p. 125.

Brokers cannot advertise that they conduct escrows without specifying in the advertisement that such services are only in connection with the broker's real estate brokerage business. A broker may not use a fictitious name or a corporate name containing the word "escrow" or advertise in any other manner that would be misleading to the public. A real estate broker who conducts an escrow under the exemption must maintain all escrowed funds in a trust account and keep proper records, and is subject to other provisions of the Commissioner's Regulations.[3]

Commercial Banks

Early in the 20th century, commercial banks began providing buyers and sellers of real property, oftentimes customers of the bank, a logical and convenient location in which to conduct real estate closing services. The bilateral escrow agreement or instructions, used almost exclusively in Southern California (unlike unilateral escrow instructions frequently used in Northern California) was deemed the best form for the escrow process because both buyer and seller were usually present, as a matter of regional practice.

■ NORTHERN CALIFORNIA VERSUS SOUTHERN CALIFORNIA ESCROW COMPANIES

Acting as the escrow holder likely seemed a natural extension of the services offered by the title companies being formed in San Francisco. As the real estate title insurance and escrow business expanded, title companies operating in Northern California seemed best suited to represent both buyers and sellers in real estate transactions and, in keeping with customary title practices, handled the processing of information and documents of buyers and sellers separately, even taking orders independent of each another.

In Southern California, however, local and regional banks led the way for escrow providers other than title insurers to provide those services. New competition entered the market in the form of independent companies, including law firms and. Eventually. real estate brokers operating broker-owned escrow companies. Escrow companies owned by real estate brokers, however, are limited to handling escrow transactions involving only the broker (unless the company is actually operated as a DOC-licensed independent escrow company).

In the cities of Central and Coastal California, we find a combination of both Northern California and Southern California practices and customs. Escrow is predominantly the business of title companies in most Central California cities,

---

3   Ibid., p. 125.

but some customs and procedures may reflect a hybrid of north and south. In fact, the fees, proration, and division of closing costs between buyers and sellers differ in some cases from county to county.

■ THE ROLE OF THE ESCROW HOLDER

The escrow holder is more reactive than proactive; the principals direct the transaction and its processing. The escrow holder takes orders and requests from principals, either directly or through their agents, and reacts.

Duties and Limitations of the Escrow Practitioner

Escrow agents (officers) are limited and restricted as to what they may do under the law. Escrow agents are not arbitrators to resolve disputes; they are limited to receiving instructions from their principals and performing their duties as instructed. Conflicting instructions would require that the escrow holder do nothing until all parties agree to a course of action, after which the escrow holder may proceed accordingly. Escrow agents are not required, nor are they allowed, to eliminate or correct title deficiencies that prevent transfer of title to another party. They are to prepare documentation based solely on the information provided by the principals and others involved in the transaction. They make certain that all documents required for the transaction and for which they are responsible are present and correctly completed. They are responsible for verifying that all funds specified in the transaction instructions are accounted for. If anything is missing or inaccurate, escrow agents cannot allow the transaction to close. It is not the escrow holders' responsibility to resolve the problem; however, it is their duty to inform the appropriate party.

For example, if a buyer or a seller has a federal or state tax lien, it is up to the buyer or the seller to resolve it, not the escrow holder or the title officer. In practice, however, some experienced title officers, usually senior or advisory officers, will assist the principal in communicating with and resolving tax issues.

Escrow agents are to be neutral between principals and act only upon the written instructions from them. Other parties to the transaction, such as the real estate agents representing the principals, are not themselves principals.

Escrow procedures and practices are controlled by state law and include those laws and regulations of the DOC for independent escrow companies and of the Department of Real Estate for broker-owned escrow companies. Escrow companies owned and operated by title insurance companies are regulated by the California Department of Insurance and, like independent escrow companies, may be operated as full-service escrow companies. Broker-owned escrow holders may only represent those buyers and sellers of their own transactions or in which the broker is a principal. Escrow agents are also subject to certain local regulations and those of the California Civil Code.

Principles of Escrow

The State of California has clearly defined the principles and procedures of conduct for escrow holders, including those duties for which they are responsible and those they may not perform. The instructions that escrow holders prepare must be written in a way that provides a clear understanding of the transaction as provided by the principals to the escrow. This clear understanding includes no ambiguity as to the intentions of the parties and the duties of the escrow holder. The instructions must specify that it is the principals and not the escrow holder who must perform the escrow contract by complying fully with the instructions. The escrow holder does not have discretionary authority. As the law states, the escrow holder is not to act as a mediator or advisor, nor participate in any controversy or disputes and attempt to arbitrate them. Instructions must be prepared in a manner that clearly states that it is the principals who make the promises to one another to perform, not the escrow holder to or from the parties. It is the escrow holder's job to carry out the instructions as provided by the principals. The escrow holder is also prohibited from offering legal or tax advice and should suggest that parties seek any such advice from an attorney and/or qualified financial advisor. Any questions regarding continuing negotiations or disputes asked of the escrow holder should be referred to the principals' respective real estate agents.

In summary, escrow holders

- are limited and restricted as to what they may do,

- are not arbitrators to resolve disputes and must remain neutral,

- receive instructions from principals to perform specific duties,

- ensure all documents required are present, and

- must account for all required monies.

Limited Agency   Escrow is a "limited agency" relationship governed by the content and provisions of the escrow. The escrow holder is to act as an agent for both parties during the escrow and only upon the specific written instructions of the principals. Upon the closing of escrow, the escrow holder becomes the agent for each principal relating to the promises and performance of each principal and to which each is entitled, such as conveyance of title in exchange for deposit of consideration. Only when all parties to the escrow have signed mutual (identically conforming) instructions does the escrow become effective. If only one party has signed, that party may terminate the proposed escrow at any time prior to the other party's signing (however the lack of a valid escrow does not in itself cancel the contract). Cancellation of an escrow by a principal may not also cancel a purchase contract and the obligations of the principals to each other. An escrow holder receiving conflicting instructions from the principals must do nothing except notify the principals that escrow will not proceed until the conflict is resolved by the parties.

The escrow holder may only receive instructions, documents, and funds from or authorized in writing by principals or other parties involved in the transaction as authorized by and on behalf of the principals. Monies the escrow holder receives from or for the principals must be accounted for in specific records and maintained in an escrow trust account. Monies that belong to principals are considered trust funds. They are not to be deposited into the general bank account of the escrow holder but into a trust fund bank account. Escrow holders cannot deposit any of their own monies into the trust fund account. Doing so would be considered commingling, which is prohibited under the law. It should go without saying that an overdrawn account is not only serious but also forbidden under trust fund law.

Escrow matters are always confidential between the escrow holder and the principals. The escrow holder may not give out any information provided by one principal to the other principal, or to any third party concerning an escrow matter without approval of the principal(s). Any new fact discovered by the escrow agent and not previously disclosed to the principals should be disclosed to them.

The escrow holder must maintain accurate files during (and after) the escrow procedure. Escrow holders utilize checklists and other forms to ensure the accuracy and complete record of the transaction is maintained. Before closing an escrow, the escrow holder audits the file to account for all items which are addressed by the instructions. These include documents provided to escrow confirming "good funds" (meaning negotiable and readily available) have cleared before disbursing any monies from an escrow trust account.

Following the closing of escrow, settlement must be handled promptly and provided to the principals on appropriate forms and those provided by law. The closing statements required to be provided to principals by the U.S. Department of Housing and Urban Development (HUD) although recently revised for clarity remain somewhat difficult to understand by many principals.

California Requirements for Escrow Managers

California law requires the escrow holder to have a manager who possesses a minimum of five years of responsible escrow experience to be "stationed" at the licensed location during open office hours. *Responsible escrow experience* has been interpreted to mean experience as an escrow officer on a full-time basis for five years. An affidavit that the applicant has read and is familiar with Escrow Law and regulations must be signed.

■ PROFESSIONAL ESCROW ASSOCIATIONS

Escrow services may be provided by title companies, independent escrow companies, broker-owned escrow companies, or in some cases, banks and mortgage lenders. Which service provider is used may depend on the geographical location of the property or the relationship to the escrow agent of the principal or real estate agent.

Escrow professionals in California have two primary professional associations in which membership is offered to all escrow professionals, the **American Escrow Association** (AEA) and the **California Escrow Association** (CEA). Both provide education, guidance and professional standards. The **Escrow Institute of California** (EIC) limits membership to independent escrow practitioners. Additionally, there are numerous local escrow associations in many cities throughout California. Membership in these organizations is accompanied by the escrow officer's pledge to adopt professional standards and ethics in business activities, to principals, to colleagues, and to other related real estate industry professionals.

California Escrow Association

The California Escrow Association, which offers membership to escrow professionals in California, has adopted the following as its mission statement:

> The vision of the California Escrow Association is to both lead and support the escrow settlement services and real estate and financial industries through our commitment to the professional and personal growth of the escrow practitioner.

Members have access to modern training methods, along with other services and benefits.

Education Programs for Escrow Professionals   The California Escrow Association offers convenient and flexible online education programs for students.

Non-CEA Courses   Other course programs are available through local and regional associations. Escrow professionals at every level may find valuable information to enhance their career in the Escrow Handbooks available through CEA.

Professional Designations   The California Escrow Association has created several professional and specialty designations to further the escrow practitioner's abilities and professional growth. Over the years, as communities have experienced growth that includes increased government regulation and more complex real estate transactions and escrows, it has become necessary for escrow professionals to advance their knowledge and skills to adequately perform their duties and responsibilities to their principals. The professional designation program offered by CEA helps in accomplishing those goals. To earn a designation, the escrow practitioner must be a CEA member and pass a comprehensive examination. For complete requirements for all designations, visit the CEA website at www.ceaescrow.org.

Training, Education, and Legislative Advocacy

The AEA, CEA, and EIC offer members continuing education courses, which enhance their ability to provide the highest level of professional services to their principals. Publications, including the *CEA News*, published by the California Escrow Association, and the *AEA News*, published by the American Escrow Association, provide membership with industry trends, technological advances, changing regulations and court decisions, all of which allow escrow professionals to better serve their principals and others with whom they work on a daily basis. Through an aggressive legislative advocacy program, the associations assist in lobbying for the passage of legislation to expedite the escrow process, reduce government intervention, and help maintain local control.

Escrow Personnel

Responsibilities of various personnel may vary and may depend on whether the escrow agent is a title company or an independent escrow company. A career path may lead to a specialty, such as loan escrow, builder services, bulk sales, commercial development, or other business opportunities. The following are representative of typical escrow positions, beginning with entry level.

- *Receptionist.* The receptionist answers the phone, opens and date-stamps incoming mail and deliveries, greets customers upon arrival, and completes other clerical duties as assigned.

  Also may perform in an administrative or assistant capacity, especially in the smaller office, assisting as a "floating" escrow assistant or even as a junior escrow officer.

- *Escrow assistant.* Under the supervision of one or more escrow officers, an escrow assistant communicates by phone and electronic means, obtains information for new escrows, opens title orders and new escrow files, orders demands, orders fire insurance policies, prepares some documents, reviews the preliminary report, delivers settlement statements to the principals for review, completes disbursements and correspondence associated with closing, and manages post-closing issues and shipment of files to permanent storage. While it is a growing practice for escrow companies to outsource notary duties to independent notaries, notary responsibilities may be assigned to the assistant, requiring to the assistant to meet the qualifications required by the State of California.

■ *Junior escrow officer.* The junior escrow officer handles some or all of the escrow assistant/technician duties with a minimum of supervision, as well as the following additional tasks:

— Preparing escrow instructions and amendments

— Recognizing and resolving issues in the preliminary report

— Maintaining a calendar of critical dates

— Completing or delegating completion of requirements

— Preparing buyer and seller estimated statements

— Balancing files for closing

— Obtaining buyers' signatures on loan documents

— Ordering funds on new loans

— Authorizing recording and handling a limited number of files independently under supervision

■ *Escrow officer.* The escrow officer meets with clients, in person or electronically, to open escrow, prepare escrow instructions, prepare complex amendments when needed, prepare estimated settlement statements, and balance the file. The escrow officer also handles telephone calls and customer interaction that are beyond the scope of junior employees. Partnership with the marketing staff or representative is usually part of the escrow officer's client relations and retention responsibilities.

■ *Loan escrow officer.* An escrow company may assign one or more escrow officers for loan refinance escrows, especially in larger companies. Occasionally an escrow company may handle a large "book of business" (a relationship involving exclusivity or near exclusivity and a considerable amount of business) for one lender in particular, in which case, it isn't uncommon to assign an escrow officer exclusively to the account.

An interesting practice of some title insurance companies is to assign a specially trained title officer to perform both title and escrow functions as a loan title-escrow officer.

■ *Escrow manager.* Management of the escrow department or office calls for an experience level and history that includes most types of transactions, including bulk sales, business opportunities, transfer of liquor license, and builder services, among other tasks. The manager should possess people skills, both in managing the company's employees and in dealing with the public, as well as in customer relations with industry participants such as real estate agents, lenders, and builders. The manager should have the ability to teach and train employees.

The escrow manager is typically one of the escrow company's employees who meet the state experience requirement of five years in the industry.

Regulators of Escrow Entities

All companies that provide escrow services are regulated to some extent, whether it is a title company, independent escrow company, mortgage lender, or commercial bank.

Figure 3.1 indicates the regulatory agency or body responsible for the supervision of the ethical, legal, financial oversight, and professional operations of the entity over which they have regulatory control.

FIGURE 3.1
Escrow Entities and Their Regulators

Escrow Entities and Their Regulators	
Entity	**Regulatory Body**
Independent escrow company	Commissioner of Department of Corporations
State-chartered banks	State Banking Commissioner
National banks	Comptroller of the Currency
State-chartered banks as members of the Federal Reserve	Federal Reserve Board
State and national banks	U.S. Federal Deposit Insurance Corporation (FDIC)
State-chartered savings and loan association	Savings and Loan Commissioner
Federally chartered savings and loan association	Office of Thrift Supervision
Real estate brokers	Commissioner of the Department of Real Estate
Builders and developers	Commissioner of Department of Corporations
Mortgage bankers	Commissioner of Department of Corporations
Mortgage brokers, licensed by Department of Real Estate	Commissioner of Department of Real Estate
Mortgage brokers, licensed by Department of Corporations	Commissioner of Department of Corporations
Title insurance companies	Commissioner of Department of Insurance
Attorneys	California State Bar Association
Credit unions	Commissioner of Department of Corporations

Additional Resources For Escrow Practitioners

For title insurance/underwritten title companies performing controlled escrows, contact the California Department of Insurance at (800) 927-HELP, or visit www.insurance.ca.gov.

For real estate broker–controlled escrows, contact the Department of Real Estate at (877) 373-4542, or visit www.DRE.ca.gov.

For attorney-controlled escrows, contact the State Bar of California at (800) 843-9053, or visit www.calbar.ca.gov.

For controlled escrows handled by federally chartered banks or federally chartered savings and loan associations, contact the Office of the Comptroller of the Currency at (800) 613-6743, or visit www.occ.gov.

For controlled escrows handled by state-chartered savings and loan associations or state-chartered savings banks, contact the Department of Financial Institutions at (800) 622-0620, or visit www.dfi.ca.gov.

For independent escrow companies, contact the Department of Corporations at (866) ASK-CORP, or search their licensee listing.

■ CHAPTER 3 QUIZ

1. A grant that may be deposited by the grantor with a third person, to be delivered on performance of a condition and while in the possession of the third person, is

   a. an escrow.

   b. a bailee.

   c. a promisor.

   d. encumbered.

2. Background checks are required of all independent escrow company personnel *EXCEPT*

   a. stockholders.

   b. managers.

   c. employees.

   d. real estate agents.

3. The independent escrow office manager must have

   a. 3 years' experience.

   b. 5 years' experience.

   c. 7 years' experience.

   d. 10 years' experience.

4. The escrow holder holds documents and money as a

   a. neutral depository for only one principal.

   b. neutral depository for both principals.

   c. partial agent for the seller.

   d. partial agent for the buyer.

5. Title policies offer financial protection and recourse to the

   a. escrow company if it commits an error in its search.

   b. seller carrying financing for the buyer if the buyer fails to pay.

   c. buyer who becomes insolvent.

   d. buyer who is financially damaged by the title company's faulty search.

6. Escrow agents may resolve disputes as impartial arbitrators

   a. always.

   b. if the escrow officer manager allows.

   c. if the escrow has the CSEO professional designation.

   d. never.

7. Escrow companies, other than broker-owned companies, are regulated by the

   a. Department of Real Estate.

   b. Department of Justice.

   c. Department of State.

   d. Department of Corporations.

8. Independent escrow agents are required to possess liquid assets in the amount of

   a. $25,000.

   b. $50,000.

   c. $100,000.

   d. $200,000.

9. Which of the following is a position at an escrow company?

   a. Escrow advisor

   b. Junior escrow officer

   c. Escrow facilitator

   d. None of these

10. As the principals direct the transaction, the escrow holder is said to be more

    a. reactive than proactive.

    b. proactive than reactive.

    c. active than reactive.

    d. reactionary than proactive.

TITLE INSURANCE BASICS

■ KEY TERMS

assessor's parcel number
California Recording
    Statutes
chain of title
clear and marketable
    title

cloud on title
date down
defects in title
patents
preliminary title report
premium

quiet title action
title plant
title professionals
title search

■ LEARNING OBJECTIVES

Upon completing this chapter, you will be able to

■ explain the reason for title policies,

■ explain the significance of defects in title,

■ define *clear and marketable title*,

■ recall the provisions of the California Recording Statutes, and

■ recognize the benefits of title plants in the title search process.

■ THE TITLE COMPANY AND THE ESCROW HOLDER

Although the escrow holder interacts with a number of others during the escrow process, it could be said that the title insurance company is the escrow holder's closest partner in performing its task, whether they are related companies or not. The buyer's agent spends considerable time arranging inspections and coordinating financing for the buyer. The seller's agent's focus is directed to facilitating access to the seller's property for the buyer's inspections, the appraisal, and any work to be completed. The loan officer concentrates on gathering documents and necessary information for processing the loan. While all these activities may require communication with the escrow holder, the escrow officer works most frequently with the title officer.

The Reason for Title Policies

Title policies "assure and insure." They assure buyers that the title to the land they are acquiring is marketable, with no existing prior claims against it by others. They insure the buyer against errors or mistakes in the assurances given. Title policies, therefore, insure owners and lenders against possible losses from claims against real property ownership. The preliminary report or commitment provides advance information on matters that will be "excepted" or excluded from coverage. Lenders and owners are thereby given an opportunity to make an informed decision to lend or purchase before proceeding. It is important to remember that a lender's title policy does not insure a borrower against title risks. While certain types of policies pertain to both the owner and the lender, it makes good sense for real estate or **title professionals**, as well as legal counsel, to help protect the borrowers by explaining the limitations of their particular coverage. For the title professional, the underlying objective is to analyze and evaluate conditions affecting the property to be insured in order to both offer the principals the protection they desire and mitigate the potential liability risk for the insurance company.

Title Insurance Protection

Title insurance is a contractual obligation of the title company. It protects the insured against losses from defective title and also insures that statements in the title policy are true. It protects the insured against unknown liens, encumbrances, and defects, as of the date the policy was issued.

Protection for a buyer to acquire **clear and marketable title** to a property with the ability to own, use, enjoy, and convey its title to another dates back to early America and the "certificate of title." That early protection evolved to today's title insurance protection. The covenants provided in the grant deed delivered from a seller to a buyer are expressed in California Civil Code Section 1113:

> That previous to the time of the execution of such conveyance, the grantor has not conveyed the same estate, or any right, title or interest therein, to any person other than the grantee; [and] that such estate is at the time of the execution of such conveyance free from encumbrances done, made or suffered by the grantor, or any person claiming under him.

Simply, it is the purpose of the title insurance company and the policy of insurance it provides to insure that those statements are indeed true. As stated by the California Department of Insurance, title insurance is a contractual obligation that protects against losses that occur when title to a property is not free and clear of defects such as liens, encumbrances, and defects that were unknown when the title policy was issued.

Defects in Title   Title insurance protects the property owner against losses due to **defects in title** that could prevent the property owner from either conveying clear title to another or hypothecate the property (as collateral for a loan). Defects may include some other party's inherent claim to title, which was unknown to the buyer at the time the property was purchased but discovered subsequent to the buyer's ownership of the property. A title insurance policy contains provisions for the payment of losses that result from a such a claim. The title insurance policy may also cover legal fees in defense of a claim against the property. The protection offered by the title insurance policy may benefit either the property owner or the owner's lender. Before issuing a title insurance policy, title companies search and examine—meaning to thoroughly review and analyze—public records. Occasionally the title examiner may order a survey of the property to more accurately identify liens, claims, or encumbrances on the property that may result in possible defects in the title.

Clear and Marketable Title: Covered and Excluded Risks   The title insurance company provides protection to the property owner so that title to the property may be clear and marketable. Protection is not uniform. The terms and conditions of the policy define what risks are covered and what risks are excluded from coverage. The title insurer reimburses the property owner for losses that are covered, up to the face amount of the policy (usually the sales price or loan amount), and any related legal expenses. This protection is effective as of the date the policy was issued, typically the close of escrow, and covers only those defects that occurred before the date when the property owner acquired title. Two types of title insurance policies for real property are common: an owner's policy and a lender's policy.

■ TITLE RECORDS

Title insurance originated in the late 19th century as a way to overcome land ownership problems due to forgeries, as well as errors in searching historical records of the property and its ownership. The nation was expanding at a rapid pace. Farmland vanished as homes, offices, factories, and shopping centers were built in their place. The title company was faced with not having adequate systems and resources to search and discover issues not found in public records. Forgeries, changes in family status, and just plain mistakes in the searches and recording processes called for a better way to protect the buyer and ensure (and insure) that the title to the land was valid and marketable. The answer to the problem was the public recordation system.

Recordation of Documents

After achieving statehood in 1850, California adopted a system by which transfers of title to land would be recorded and maintained by the government as public records, typically by the county. These documents would, and do, provide all the details about the property, such as its legal description, the name of the owner, the nature of the recorded transaction, and other information that may affect a subsequent transfer or encumbering of the property. These records are available to the public without restriction. The obvious intent was to protect the public, lenders, and purchasers of properties against nontransparent and undisclosed conveyances of title or liens against them.

Purpose of Recording Statutes   The general purpose of recording statutes is to permit rather than require the recordation of any instrument that affects the title to or possession of real property. Recording allows purchasers and others, such as lenders, to rely on the ownership and other matters regarding the property as represented by the recorded instruments. While the recording statutes do not specify any particular time within which an instrument must be recorded, priority of recordation will ordinarily determine the rights of the parties, especially if one or more parties have conflicting claims. The instrument affecting real property is to be recorded by the county recorder in the county within which the property is located. If the property—such as larger parcels of land, farms, and ranches—is situated in more than one county, the document must be recorded in each county in order provide constructive notice in all respective counties.

Constructive Notice   Recordation provides constructive notice, which means notice given by the public records, or "notice to the world at large." Anyone may seek to read and review these documents. "Actual" notice, on the other hand, is accomplished by delivery of the deed. Constructive notice is presumed because it allows interested parties to discover, review, and rely on the contents of recorded instruments.

Documents That May Be Recorded   The recording statutes provide that any instrument or document affecting the title to or possession of real property may be recorded. The law does not provide that recording is required, only that it is allowed for certain transactions, documents, and instruments. In fact, the law specifies that only certain documents may be recorded. The word "instrument," as used in the recording statutes, means any document executed (signed and delivered) by one party to another, transferring the title to property, placing a lien on the property, or encumbering the property. While "instrument" does not necessarily include every writing regarding real property, it allows it for "certain transactions and documents." These include deeds, mortgages, leases, land contracts, deeds of trust, and other agreements between a landowner and other landowners.

Title Plants

Instead of visiting the county recorder's office to search public records, title companies have established their own facilities, called **title plants**, storing in them copies of all public records they obtain from the county recorder's office. These plants contain vast computer databases of all public records from the county in which the property is located. Title records dating back to 1850 are available. In larger counties, it is common for several title companies to jointly own and operate a plant, sharing the facilities and costs.

Title Company Operations and Personnel

Title insurance operations include researching and interpreting the facts of title, underwriting, management and administration, legal services, technology, and marketing.

- *Title searchers* perform the "date down" (see under "Searching the Property Records") and title search.

- *Junior title officers* assist the title officer in underwriting activities, and in some larger units, may actually handle the file completely.

- *Title officers* review the search results, investigate, and write an opinion as to items acceptable for coverage in what is called the preliminary title report.

- *Advisory title officers* are consulted on complex matters or high liability transactions and may perform the underwriting and preparation of the preliminary title report on extremely complex cases.

- *Chief title officers* provide guidance and assistance to title officers and advisory title officers. They typically have years of service and experience and the ability to resolve the most complex of matters. They frequently interface with counsel and may in fact be both a longtime title officer and attorney for the company.

■ THE TITLE SEARCH

In today's digitized world, **title searches** are usually efficient and quick. The title process begins with a thorough and diligent search of all title records and public documents related to both the property and the principals, reviewing matters that may affect title and risk to the title insurance company for claims.

Real Property Legal Description

The property's legal description may be represented in one of the following ways, as discussed in Chapter 1 and explained further in Chapter 17.

Lot and Tract   "Lot and tract" or "block and tract" refers to the individual lot and tract numbers located in a specific block or tract as subdivided by the developer and identified by the local government agency, such as the following:

> Lot 1 in Tract 2345 in the City of Palmdale, as per map recorded in Book 1061, pages 50 to 52 inclusive of Maps, in the Officer of the County Recorder of Los Angeles County, California.

Township and Section   Properties not capable of being identified by a lot and tract may be described, if appropriate, by referring to the portions of the section it occupies within the township in which it is located, such as the following:

> Beginning at the NE corner of SW ¼ of Sec. 17, thence southeasterly to the NW corner of the SE ¼ of Section 21, thence southwesterly to the SE corner of the NW ¼ of Sec. 29, thence northwesterly to the SW corner of the NE ¼ of Sec. 19, thence northeasterly to the point of beginning.

Metes and Bounds   Some properties, due to their configurations, may only be logically described by using metes and bounds, such as the following:

> Beginning at a point on the southerly line of "0" Street, 150 feet westerly of the SW corner of the intersection of "0" and 8th Streets; running thence due south 300 feet to the northerly line of "P" Street; thence westerly along the northerly line of "P" Street, 100 feet; thence northerly and parallel to the first course, 300 feet, to the southerly line of "0" Street; thence easterly along the southerly line of "0" Street, 100 feet, to the point or place of beginning.

Other Descriptions

A property may be typically identified by other means, but they are not considered legal descriptions. They are, however, commonly used in both referring to the property and locating it, physically and on recorded maps.

Street Address   Most properties not located in rural locations, especially those with improvements on the land or lot, are typically referred to by street address (1123 Elm Street, San Bernardino, CA). Legal title companies will not ordinarily insure title with such a description; when the escrow holder draws a deed, the legal description referred to consists of lot and tract, township and section, or metes and bounds.

Assessor's Parcel Number (APN)   The county assessor will prepare and file in the assessor's office an accurate map of any land in the county and may number or letter the parcels in a manner approved by the board of supervisors. Section 327 of the Revenue and Taxation Code provides "that land shall not be described in any deed or conveyance by a reference to any such map unless such map has been filed for record in the office of the county recorder of the county in which such land is located." The number assigned to the property is called the **assessor's parcel number**. The APN is not a legal description.

Searching the Property Records

When the document is recorded at the county recorder's office, its contents are placed in the "book of records." The document will include the page on which it is placed in the book. The original document is mailed either to the party who delivered it for recording, such as the title company, or the party indicated on the document, such as the buyer or borrower. The recorder sorts (or indexes) all recorded documents in alphabetical order according to the names of the grantors and grantees or mortgagors (trustors) or mortgagees (beneficiaries) and the name or nature of the document. They are also indexed by date of recording. This is especially important when multiple loans are recorded against a property, such as a loan originally obtained to purchase the property and a later and subsequent loan to retrieve funds through refinancing in the form of a home equity line of credit. The date and time of recording determines the seniority position of each. It is also an important consideration in the foreclosure process.

Search Begins with the "Date Down"   The title searcher begins the search by **dating down** the **chain of title**, a history of all previous property owners in chronological order, beginning with the present, and then searching back in time for any matter that may affect title.

1. The search includes judgments, divorces, tax liens, bankruptcies, probates, those persons declared to be incompetent, and other matters of record.

2. The chain of title lists the type of document (such as a deed of trust or a grant deed), parties involved, and the recording date. The chain includes all reconveyances of previously recorded liens. (Remember that *reconvey* means to remove the lien from title).

3. The search may include a request for information regarding ownership of oil and mineral rights, reversionary rights under a recorded deed of restriction, and leasehold interests.

Searches Begin With the Present and Work Backward in Time

Beginning with the latest title policy, if available, the searcher explores title records from the most recent going backward. A dangerous practice is for the title examiner to only search back to the latest title policy. Relying on the accuracy of another searcher's work may result in financial damage, as was the case in the situation described in "Importance of Accuracy in Title Search."

Pro-Tip: Importance of Accuracy in Title Search

The following account is based on a real transaction; names, places, documents, and details have been changed to allow the parties to remain anonymous.

A new home subdivision named Golden Acres was built near Riverside. The developer purchased the land from the owner, encumbering it with a $1 million loan secured by a blanket deed of trust. A blanket deed of trust typically includes a provision for releasing a portion of the land from the lien upon the payment of a portion of the debts, called partial releases. The developer built and sold the project's 20 single-family homes quickly.

The title company that had performed the original search for the developer (we'll call it A) issued a title policy for the developer. Later a different title insurance company (we'll call it B) searching and issuing policies for the sell-out of the homes insured the 20 "sell-out" transactions.

One day, each house was posted with a foreclosure notice from a lender that none of the homeowners had ever heard of. What happened was that the foreclosing deed of trust had been given years ago by a prior owner of the land. There was no mention in the title policy issued for each of the 20 homes of the old debt, and therefore it was not paid at the close of each of their respective escrows.

The problem began with the fact that there were two tracts involved, described by metes-and- bounds legal descriptions, recorded and stamped with instrument number 90-0140 by the recorder's office.

Later, six partial releases were recorded with the same instrument number 90-0140. Each partial release had a legal description referring to lots shown on a recorded tract known as River Run. Together, the partial releases covered (and therefore released) all the lots in the River Run tract. What does all this have to do the 20 new homes insured by the title company? Nothing—and that was the problem.

Upon first searching and examining the property, A's title examiner apparently thought that both tracts covered by the $1 million deed of trust had been merged and together became River Run. Because all lots in River Run had been sold and released as title records indicated, the examiner would naturally conclude that the old deed of trust was paid (satisfied). The title examiner working on the project, therefore, issued a title policy for the land that would later become Golden Acres without any exception for the unpaid remaining portions of the underlying old deed of trust (meaning that the title examiner was acting under the erroneous assumption that it simply no longer existed).

B's examiner relied on the competitor's work and searched back only to the date of the competitor's last policy. This is a shortcut frequently taken by some title companies and their examiners. B's examiner had no idea that the old deed of trust remained as an encumbrance with an unpaid balance. As a result, when each of the 20 homes were sold, the holder of the underlying deed of trust was not paid!

However, with title to the 20 property owners having been insured by it, B paid $533,000, the amount for full release of the deed of trust, and incurred $37,000 in legal expenses including claims from homeowners for the foreclosure action.

The title search on more than one occasion shows an old deed of trust that is still shown as a lien on the property. Usually, the debt has been long paid, but yet the lien has not been released (reconveyed). The title officer understands that this happens and knows how to proceed and what is necessary to appropriately eliminate it from the policy.

Special Searches Additional and more labor-intensive searches are required for special policy coverage, such as eminent domain, trust deed foreclosure, subdivision, and litigation guarantees. The searcher orders any special maps or property rights necessary to complete the search.

Patents   A **patent**, as defined within the context of land and conveyance of its title, is a deed transferring land from the federal or state government to a private individual, thereby making it private land. A person may mine and remove minerals from a mining claim without a mineral patent. However, a mineral patent gives the owner exclusive title to the locatable minerals. In most cases, a patent also gives the owner title to the surface and other resources.

In geographical areas subject to oil exploration, while most lands in California have long since had mineral or oil rights resting beneath of the land's surface transferred to someone other than the title holder of the surface rights (the land), a prospective buyer or other interested party may still be interested in discovering whether such mineral or oil rights have indeed been conveyed to someone else. The title company may, therefore, be asked to provide information regarding the status of such mineral or oil rights, including patents.

Bureau of Land Management

The Bureau of Land Management (BLM) collects, analyzes, and records information about public lands and resources, ranging from land title and recreational usage to wildlife habitat and mineral rights. A Master Title Plat (MTP) is a graphical depiction of current land status on a drafted map affecting one particular township. Other plats in the MTP plat group include oil, gas, and leasable minerals. Figure 4.1 is a screenshot of the BLM search engine for records in its database.

FIGURE 4.1

BLM Search Engine

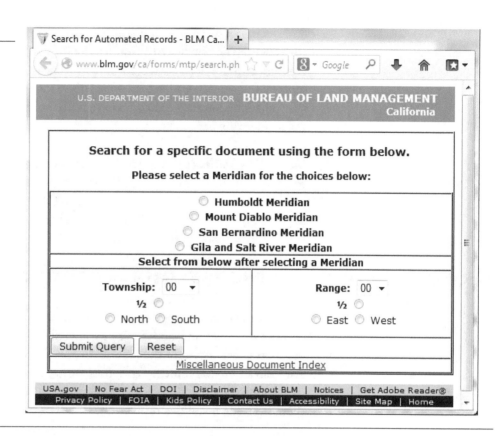

Searching Records Regarding the Principals

Using the Statement of Information (SI), which was provided by escrow to the principals to be completed, the title searcher performs what is called a general index run, or "G.I." This is a search of all databases containing records of outstanding liens against any of the principals for unpaid judgments, unpaid taxes or other liens, divorces, bankruptcies, or other matters that could affect title or prevent the title from being transferred or encumbered. Such matters are called a **cloud on the title.**

Cloud on Title

In most cases, the circumstances that result in a cloud on title are minor and can be easily corrected. For example, the deed may have been filed and recorded containing a minor spelling error in name of the principal or the street address of the property. All that is typically required is for the seller or, in a refinance, the borrower, to sign a corrected deed prepared by the escrow holder. Other issues may become a little more complex requiring considerably more work to resolve. Perhaps the seller or the borrower had paid off a loan, though the deed of trust had not been reconveyed (removed and released from the title). Occasionally a lender may have failed to provide the reconveyance to the county recorder's office for action. Because the lien is still recorded against the property, it is necessary for the seller or the borrower to contact the former lender and have the information contained in the deed corrected. In the event the lender cannot be located, is no longer in business, or fails to respond, the searcher will note the problem for the title officer to determine the action required to resolve the matter, such as initiating a quiet title action.

Quiet Title Action   A **quiet title action** may be used to submit the discrepancy to court for the judge to make a ruling. Unless the issue is complex, the request to have it reconveyed will usually be granted. Once the documents are received and approved by the recorder's office, the cloud on title is eliminated.

■ UNDERWRITING AND THE PRELIMINARY TITLE REPORT

The information obtained from the search is gathered and delivered to the title officer for review and underwriting. The title officer's objective is to be able to ensure the legal right for the grantee to posses, use, and enjoy the property within any restrictions or limiting conditions discovered on or affecting the property, identifying those conditions that the title company will not insure and excluding them from the insurance protection.

Underwriting

Underwriting Defined   Merriam-Webster defines underwriting as "to write under or at the end of something, to set one's name to an (insurance policy) for the purpose of thereby becoming answerable for a designated loss or damage on consideration of receiving a premium percent; insure on life or property; to assume liability as an insurer."

Underwriting Process   The title officer approaches the underwriting assignment with the objective of eliminating information and data obtained during the search that do not affect title; do not involve either of the parties to the transaction; or do not involve any liens on the property, encumbrances, or the rights to ownership or interests in or of the property. Items that cannot be eliminated, meaning they affect title in some capacity, must then be analyzed by the title officer to determine exactly what effect on title, if any, they may have.

Chain of Title Review   The title officer reviews the history of title in chronological order by the date or recordation of events to establish the chain of events or **chain of title**. For example, a lien on the property that was recorded in the past is noted, with the title officer then searching more recent recordings to determine whether the lien has been removed and released. The title officer dismisses a released event as having no affect on title and continues reviewing other findings in the same manner.

Preliminary Title Report

At the conclusion of the review process, a written opinion of title will be prepared by the title officer; this opinion is called a **preliminary title report** (see Appendix 2, "How to Read a Preliminary Title Report"). The report indicates the conditions under which a title insurance policy will be offered to the buyer or borrower, including with any exceptions to coverage. If a loan is involved a "joint coverage" policy, extending protection to the lender will be required by the lender. The title coverage offered will insure the buyer's title rights (and those of a lender) and also ensure that the title company will defend him or her against any claim by another party of a right to the title or an interest in the property which does not already exist and which will remain as agreed to by the buyer as the grantee.

Selecting the Title Insurance Company

As with all third-party services required in a real estate transaction, the principal parties have the right to choose which company to use. Some controversy has arisen in the past regarding lenders that have taken title to properties through the foreclosure process and then selling them as real estate owned (REO). It has been a practice of some of these lenders to require a buyer to used a specific title company. However, just as with selecting the escrow holder, the choice of selecting the title insurance company usually falls to the real estate agent in a sale transaction and to the lender or mortgage broker in a refinance transaction. The title company to use is typically determined by custom and by who will pay for the policy. In Southern California, the seller usually pays, and in Northern California, the buyer usually pays.

Fees and Premiums

The title insurance company's **premium** (the rate an insurer charges for its protection coverage) is a one-time fee payable at the time of escrow closing. When compared with homeowner's insurance, whose premiums must be renewed annually for the owner to be protected under the policy, title insurance coverage and fees are quite reasonable.

Under California law, every title insurer, underwritten title company (a company that provides the actual coverage for one or more title insurance companies), and controlled escrow company must file its schedule of rates and forms with the insurance commissioner at least 30 days before the rates become effective. Rates among insurers vary because of the differing loss histories and which of those histories influence the rates charged.

Premium Comparison   The buyer or the homeowner can compare rates on up to 100 California title insurance companies at http://clta.titlewizard .com/, which delivers up-to-date title rates. In recent years, however, many title companies have merged or consolidated, offering the consumer fewer choices.

Coverage Requirements   Even though there are competitors, the market-place, competition, and required coverage influences the rates that title insurers charge. Sellers, homebuyers, and homeowners seeking to refinance their homes are able to search by ZIP code and other factors to find the most competitive provider in their area. While finding the most competitive rate is important, if financing is to be obtained by the buyer, the coverage the title company offers must meet the lender's standards and guidelines. The premium will be based on the required coverage.

Title Insurance Underwriting Procedures

Policies are written on the basis of a search of public records and other records that provide constructive notice. Remember that a deed does not actually prove that the seller is the owner of the property. The purpose of title insurance is to protect one's interest in the property from unknown encumbrances, legal conflicts, and unforeseen claims. The insured are reimbursed for any losses incurred because of the defects in the title covered under the title policy.

Examination of Title   A title examiner, title officer, or junior title officer will interpret the search results through examination of all the facts, making inquiries as necessary and appropriate from legal counsel or advisory title officers or even the chief title officer to arrive at a written determination of insurance coverage to be provided. This is called a preliminary title report, and it sets forth the insurance coverage and provisions that will apply when the title policy is issued.

■ REGULATION OF TITLE INSURERS

Regulated by the commissioner of the California Department of Insurance (CDI), title insurance companies are prohibited from certain activities, just as the Department of Corporations prohibits the escrow holder from the same or similar practices. For example, insurance companies may not offer unlawful rebates or commissions to persons or entities referring business to them.

Prohibited Acts

Rebates   An unlawful rebate occurs when a lender, real estate broker, or home-builder receives services, property, or money in exchange for steering business to the title company under the theory that such rebates act to inflate title insurance premium rates for all consumers.

Discounted Policy Premiums and Fees   It is also unlawful for a title insurer, underwritten title company, or controlled escrow company to offer the insured party a fee or charge that is less than the currently effective schedule for fees and charges filed with and approved by the Department of Insurance. Because the fee schedule is a tool to be used as a basis for comparison between companies, a title insurer offering a rebate from scheduled fees and charges might be engaging in a discriminatory practice, which is unfair to all consumers.

Referral Fees or Commissions for the Placement of Title Services
It is unlawful to pay a commission to any person as a means of generating a referral or actual placement of title insurance. If either of these activities involves an escrow transaction where a title insurance company is not handling the escrow function, the unfair practice would be regulated by either the Department of Real Estate or the Department of Corporations.

California Insurance Code Section 12404   This law provides that

> it is unlawful for any title insurer, underwritten title company, or controlled escrow company to pay any commission, compensation, or other consideration to any person as an inducement for the placement or referral of title business. The following activities are deemed per se [defined as "in itself," meaning self-evident and no other explanation or fact is necessary] inducements for the placement or referral of title insurance business by any person and are unlawful:
>
> ■ Paying or offering to pay, furnishing or offering to furnish, or providing or offering to provide assistance with the business expenses of any person, including, but not limited to, rent, employee salaries, furniture, copiers, facsimile machines, automobiles, telephone services or equipment, or computers
>
> Providing or offering to provide any form of consideration intended for the benefit of any person, including cash, below-market-rate loans, automobile charges, or merchandise or merchandise credits
>
> ■ Placing or offering to place on behalf of any person, compensating balances

- Advancing or paying, or offering to advance or pay money on behalf of any person into an escrow to facilitate the closing thereof, other than any sum which represents the proceeds of a loan made in the ordinary course of business; or an advance not to exceed 2% of the sales price of the real property being sold or exchanged through the escrow or the amount of any loan secured by real property involved in the escrow, whichever is greater; or the extension of credit or an advance for the costs, fees and expenses of the escrow or of the title insurance issued or to be issued in connection therewith

- Disbursing or offering to disburse on behalf of any person escrow funds held by a title insurer, underwritten title company, or controlled escrow company before the conditions of the escrow applicable to that disbursement have been met, or in a manner which does not conform to Section 12413.1 of the California Insurance Code, including disbursing or offering to disburse before the expiration of the appropriate period established in Section 12413.1

- Furnishing or offering to furnish all or any part of the time or productive effort of any employee of the title insurer, underwritten title company, or controlled escrow company to any person for any service unrelated to the title business

- Advertising or paying for the advertising in any newspaper, newsletter, magazine, or publication that is produced by, or on behalf of, a person, or that results in a direct or indirect subsidy to a person

- Expenditures for food, beverages, and entertainment for a person

Expenditures not deemed unlawful or in violation of this section include the following:

- Promotional items with a permanently affixed company logo of the underwritten title company, title insurer, or controlled-escrow company having a value of not more than $10 each

- "Promotional item" does not include a gift certificates, gift cards, or other items that have a specific monetary value on their face, or that may be exchanged for any other item having a specific monetary value

- Furnishing education or educational materials exclusively related to the business of title insurance for a person if continuing education credits are not provided

Title Company Ancillary Services

In addition to title company personnel performing escrow duties, the services listed in Figure 4.2 are representative of typical title company services and responsibilities. Title companies have ventured into new fields due to technology, offering a variety of information services, including many directed toward the lending community, especially for loss management and mitigation services. Third-party asset management companies, especially those owned by title insurance companies, have become a large part of the lending industry's outsource partners for managing, valuating, and marketing their foreclosed properties (REOs).

FIGURE 4.2
Typical Title Company Services

Escrow and other Ancillary Services Offered by Title Companies or Related Subsidiaries	
Escrow	Collection and trust services
Reconveyances	Trustee sale guarantees
Recording	Real estate tax service
Attorney services	Foreclosure publishing and posting
Flood certification	Exchange intermediary services
Credit reporting	Real estate information and technology services
Auction services	Third-party assistance in marketing properties through on-site, ballroom, and internet auctions

Additional Services for the Lending Industry
Loan origination
Funding
Secondary market purchasing and selling
Information and market research services
Loss mitigation assistance (REO services)
Asset management services (REO services)
Securitizing
Servicing equipment leases

The Future of Title Insurance Companies

As evidenced by the list of ancillary services provided by title companies, it is clear that the future holds much more opportunities for title company owners and professionals than merely title insurance protection. The new direction offered by technological services and vast databases stored with information necessary for the performance of the services offered by a variety of industries, even those unrelated to insurance and escrow, offers numerous possibilities for employment in the years to come.

■ CHAPTER 4 QUIZ

1. Title insurance protects the property against losses due to

    a.   defects in title.

    b.   defects to the property.

    c.   acts of God.

    d.   earthquake.

2. The title insurer reimburses the property owner for covered losses up to

    a. $1,000,000.

    b.   the face amount of the insurance.

    c.   the face amount of the insurance plus legal expenses.

    d.   the face amount of the insurance less the deductible.

3. The title company's primary facility, which stores copies of all public records from the county in which the property is located, is the

    a.   title warehouse.

    b.   record warehouse.

    c.   record and title warehouse.

    d.   title plant.

4. The chain of title lists

    a.   only the names of the parties.

    b.   only the parties subject to grant deeds.

    c.   the parties and documents, such as a trust or grant deed and recording date.

    d.   none of these.

5. A patent is a deed transferring land from

    a. an inventor to the federal government.

    b. an incompetent person to one who is competent.

    c. one spouse to another.

    d. the federal or state government to a private individual.

6. Using the Statement of Information (SI), the title searcher performs a

    a. general index run.

    b. general informational run.

    c. property boundary search.

    d. legal description verification.

7. If a searcher discovers an error in spelling on a previously recorded deed,

    a. the title company must go to court to resolve it.

    b. the escrow company must go to court to resolve it.

    c. escrow may send a corrected deed to the grantor to sign and record.

    d. it can be ignored.

8. *Underwriting* is defined as

    a. writing under or at the end of something.

    b. writing at the beginning of something.

    c. the process of writing a legal description.

    d. the process of writing a will.

9. The preliminary title report indicates

    a. the conditions under which a lender will approval a loan.

    b. the conditions under which a title insurance policy will be offered to
        a buyer.

    c. the conditions under which a title insurance policy will be offered to
        a seller.

    d. none of these.

10. Title policies are written on the basis of a search of public records and other records that impart

    a.   confirmation.

    b.   constructive confirmation.

    c.   constructive notice.

    d.   confirmation notice.

CHAPTER FIVE

TITLE INSURANCE POLICIES

■ KEY TERMS

ALTA extended policies
ALTA lenders' policies
bankruptcy
beneficiary
CLTA extended
  coverage
CLTA standard policies

condemnation
deficiency judgment
eminent domain
encumbrances
endorsements
insuring clause
liens

off-record matters
right of redemption
spurious title
trustee's sale guarantee
  (TSG)

■ LEARNING OBJECTIVES

Upon completing this chapter, you will be able to

■ explain the coverage, exceptions, and exclusions of the standard coverage (or CLTA) and the extended coverage (or ALTA) policies, including lenders' policies, and the differences between them;

■ understand the principles of the "insuring clause" of the title policy;

■ explain the provisions of the trustee sale guarantee (TSG);

- explain the various endorsements available and required for certain title protection; and

- understand the effect of bankruptcy, foreclosure, and liens as they relate to title services.

■ TITLE INSURANCE POLICIES

California Land Title Association (CLTA) Standard Coverage Policy

Title companies offer title insurance policies for property owners and for their lenders. The owner's policy, referred to as a standard policy, provides basic protection through insurance coverage for the policyholder but is mostly limited to matters of public record. For example, **liens** are matters recorded against the property that may prevent a transfer or insurability of title, such as loans, judgments, easements, and taxes. Some off-record items (the term used to refer to those items not of public record), however, are covered under its provisions. What exactly is public record? When we say public record, we are referring to those allowable documents recorded by the county recorder.

In California, the standard policy is the California Land Title Association (CLTA) policy. The property owner's lender is protected by a title insurance policy, usually an American Land Title Association (ALTA) policy that provides even more protection than that offered to the property owner. However a CLTA policy can be used not only as the owner's policy but in some instances also as a joint protection (JP) policy insuring both the owner and the owner's lender.

Endorsements   **Endorsements** are riders or addenda to title policies that offer extra coverage for items not covered in the basic policy. The nature or characteristics of the property, the details of the transaction, or the type and terms of the loan a buyer may be obtaining may require additional protection and coverage but still be available in a CLTA policy. The title company may offer these protections with extra insurance coverage—called endorsements—to **CLTA standard policies**. The ability to add to the basic policy coverage through endorsements make the CLTA one of the most flexible policies available for the cost and therefore the most popular, as compared with paying the price for an extended coverage American Land Title Association (ALTA) policy. Endorsements include protection against forgery and fraud and are included as a part of the overall policy.

CLTA Insuring Clause

The insuring clause of the CLTA standard form is that provision in the policy that obligates the title insurer to pay the insured for a claim, or defend the insured against claims, on or to the title by others for the following:

■ Loss or damage not exceeding the amount of insurance stated in Schedule A and costs, attorneys' fees, and expenses which the company may be obligated to pay hereunder sustained or incurred by said insured by reason of:

— Title to the estate or interest described in the policy being vested other than as stated therein;

■ **EXAMPLE**   Another party claims to have a vested interest in the property but is not listed in the policy. The title company would be responsible for paying to or for the party suffering any financial damage as a result. John and Mary Jones purchased a home from Paul and Jane Smith. The Smiths bought the property 20 years earlier. Ten years later, they added their adult daughter, Sarah Smith, to the title as a tenant in common. Sarah never lived in the property. In examining the records for the title policy, the title examiner overlooked Sarah's vested interest and accordingly did not exclude her from the insurance coverage. Upon discovering her parents' sale of the property Sarah sued the title company, which was found liable to her for damages.

— Any defect in or lien or encumbrance on such title;

■ **EXAMPLE**   Henry James obtained a home equity line of credit. At the time, he had an unpaid balance on the loan he obtained to purchase the property four years earlier. When the title company issued the policy, it failed to disclose the existing senior lien. Two years later Henry sold the home. At closing, only the beneficiary (lender) of the home equity line of credit was paid because there was no record of any other mortgage lien. Subsequently, the original lender discovered the sale of the property and filed a claim against the title company, which was obligated to pay.

— Unmarketability of such title; or

— Any lack of the ordinary right of any abutting owner for access to at least one physically open street or highway if the land, in fact, abuts upon one or more such streets or highways.

■ In addition, the insuring clause provides further coverage to an insured lender for:

— Invalidity of the lien of the insured mortgage (deed of trust) upon said estate or interest except to the extent that such invalidity, or claim thereof, arises out of the transaction evidenced by the insured mortgage and is based upon usury, or any consumer protection or truth in lending law;

— Priority of any lien or encumbrance over the lien of the insured mortgage, said mortgage being shown in Schedule B in order of its priority; or

— Invalidity of any assignment as shown in the policy.

CLTA Standard Coverage Policy Conditions and stipulations describe what claims the title company will pay and the conditions governing payment. The conditions and stipulations of the standard coverage policy contain important provisions and limitations of the coverage to both the insurer and the insured. The main points are as follows:

■ That the principal terms used are defined

■ The circumstances under which the policy will remain in force when the estate or interest in the insured property is acquired by another

■ How and when the claimant must give notice of claim, and the provision for defense and prosecution of actions

■ The insurer's options in removing adverse interest and paying or settling claims

■ How losses are determined and the payment of loss

■ Limitations and reductions of liability; subrogation on payment or settlement, and policy limit liability

■ Provisions for arbitration

CLTA Standard Coverage Exclusions There are some claims the title company will not pay. Coverage under the standard title insurance policy is excluded for the following matters:

■ Any law, ordinance, governmental regulation or police power relating to building, zoning, occupancy, use, or environmental protection

■ Rights of eminent domain (see "Eminent Domain" discussed later)

■ Defects, such as liens, created by the insured

- Defects known to the insured but not specified in writing to the underwriter by the specified date

- Defects, but no loss or damage is suffered by the insured

- Defects created or attached after the policy date (with the exception of mechanic's lien insurance offered elsewhere in the policy)

- If the lien of the insured mortgage is unenforceable because the insured does not comply with "doing business" laws in the state of the insured property

- Any claim arising out of the transaction creating the interest of the mortgagee insured by reason of the operation of federal bankruptcy, state insolvency, or similar creditors' rights laws

CLTA Extended Coverage   A standard title policy provides only limited coverage, but there are additional claims that the title company may honor. This additional protection is limited to items that are not recorded and those the title insurance underwriter would have no way of knowing without additional research or some sort of physical inspection of the property and which represent risks to the title insurance company. The **CLTA extended coverage** specifically states in the policy exactly the deficiencies indicated in the following paragraphs and differs from the protection afforded by the ALTA owner's policy (but carries a higher premium):

- *Building-permit violations.* The homeowner is covered if forced to correct or remove an existing structure, excluding the boundary walls and fences, if it was built by a previous property owner who did not obtain appropriate building permits from the proper governmental agency or authority.

- *Subdivision Map Act.* Coverage is extended to the property owner whose title is restricted (cannot convey title, obtain financing, or obtain a building permit) because the property was incorrectly subdivided.

- *Restrictive covenant violations.* Coverage is extended to the homeowner for violations of restrictions that occurred before the homeowner's purchase of the property.

- *Post-policy adverse possession.* Coverage is provided against others who attempt to claim title by reason of continued sue and dominion.

- *Enhanced access.* Coverage is provided for existing right of access, including both pedestrian and vehicular access.

- *Post-policy encroachment.* Coverage is provided against someone who builds a structure, not including the boundary walls or fences that encroach on the insured property after the present owner purchased it.

- *Post-policy prescriptive rights*. Coverage is offered against attempts by others to claim easement rights by reason of continued use.

- *Structural damage from minerals extractions*. Because the property owner more often than not also owns the mineral rights, this coverage provides protection against damage to the improvements by others in the course of extracting minerals.

- *Map inconsistencies*. Protection is provided against loss when the map attached to the title policy does not show the same location and dimensions as those shown in the public record.

- *Living trust coverage*. Cover is extended to the trustee who receives the deed from the homeowner after the policy date. No new policy or endorsement is required to maintain existing coverage in such transfers.

American Land Title Association (ALTA) Policy

An American Land Title Association (ALTA) policy generally offers extended coverage over and above that provided by CLTA policies. Usually the ALTA extended coverage policy (see Figure 5.1) is the most common policy offering extended coverage. It was originally for the lender's interest only in an **ALTA lender's policy** (see Figure 5.2) but is also available to the homeowner and is called an ALTA owner's policy. These policies offer protection from certain additional "off-record" (not of public record) matters, such as encroachments, unrecorded easements (see Chapter 17), interests of others in possession, and discrepancies in boundaries—matters that may generally be determined by a land inspection or a proper survey. It assures the lender that its lien will take priority over various interest and claims to the subject property.

FIGURE 5.1
ALTA Owner's Policy

OWNER'S POLICY OF TITLE INSURANCE

Issued by

BLANK TITLE INSURANCE COMPANY

Any notice of claim and any other notice or statement in writing required to be given to the Company under this Policy must be given to the Company at the address shown in Section 18 of the Conditions.

COVERED RISKS

SUBJECT TO THE EXCLUSIONS FROM COVERAGE, THE EXCEPTIONS FROM COVERAGE CONTAINED IN SCHEDULE B, AND THE CONDITIONS, BLANK TITLE INSURANCE COMPANY, a Blank corporation (the "Company") insures, as of Date of Policy and, to the extent stated in Covered Risks 9 and 10, after Date of Policy, against loss or damage, not exceeding the Amount of Insurance, sustained or incurred by the Insured by reason of:

1. Title being vested other than as stated in Schedule A.

2. Any defect in or lien or encumbrance on the Title. This Covered Risk includes but is not limited to insurance against loss from

    (a) A defect in the Title caused by

    (i) forgery, fraud, undue influence, duress, incompetency, incapacity, or impersonation;

    (ii) failure of any person or Entity to have authorized a transfer or conveyance;

    (iii) a document affecting Title not properly created, executed, witnessed, sealed, acknowledged, notarized, or delivered;

    (iv) failure to perform those acts necessary to create a document by electronic means authorized by law;

    (v) a document executed under a falsified, expired, or otherwise invalid power of attorney;

    (vi) a document not properly filed, recorded, or indexed in the Public Records including failure to perform those acts by electronic means authorized by law; or

This form is copyrighted and reprinted with permission from American Land Title Association®, 1828 L Street, N.W., Suite 705, Washington, DC 20036.

FIGURE 5.1
**ALTA Owner's Policy
(continued)**

(vii) a defective judicial or administrative proceeding.

(b) The lien of real estate taxes or assessments imposed on the Title by a governmental authority due or payable, but unpaid.

(c) Any encroachment, encumbrance, violation, variation, or adverse circumstance affecting the Title that would be disclosed by an accurate and complete land survey of the Land. The term "encroachment" includes encroachments of existing improvements located on the Land onto adjoining land, and encroachments onto the Land of existing

(d) improvements located on adjoining land.

3. Unmarketable Title.

4. No right of access to and from the Land.

5. The violation or enforcement of any law, ordinance, permit, or governmental regulation (including those relating to building and zoning) restricting, regulating, prohibiting, or relating to

(a) the occupancy, use, or enjoyment of the Land;

(b) the character, dimensions, or location of any improvement erected on the Land;

(c) the subdivision of land; or

(d) environmental protection

if a notice, describing any part of the Land, is recorded in the Public Records setting forth the violation or intention to enforce, but only to the extent of the violation or enforcement referred to in that notice.

6. An enforcement action based on the exercise of a governmental police power not covered by Covered Risk 5 if a notice of the enforcement action, describing any part of the Land, is recorded in the Public Records, but only to the extent of the enforcement referred to in that notice.

7. The exercise of the rights of eminent domain if a notice of the exercise, describing any part of the Land, is recorded in the Public Records.

8. Any taking by a governmental body that has occurred and is binding on the rights of a purchaser for value without Knowledge.

9. Title being vested other than as stated in Schedule A or being defective

(a) as a result of the avoidance in whole or in part, or from a court order providing an alternative remedy, of a transfer of all or any part of the title to or any interest in the Land occurring prior to the transaction vesting Title as shown in Schedule A because that prior transfer constituted a fraudulent or preferential transfer under federal bankruptcy, state insolvency, or similar creditors' rights laws; or

(b) because the instrument of transfer vesting Title as shown in Schedule A constitutes a preferential transfer under federal bankruptcy, state insolvency, or similar creditors' rights laws by reason of the failure of its recording in the Public Records

(i) to be timely, or

(ii) to impart notice of its existence to a purchaser for value or to a judgment or lien creditor.

10. Any defect in or lien or encumbrance on the Title or other matter included in Covered Risks 1 through 9 that has been created or attached or has been filed or recorded in the Public Records subsequent to Date of Policy and prior to the recording of the deed or other instrument of transfer in the Public Records that vests Title as shown in Schedule A.

The Company will also pay the costs, attorneys' fees, and expenses incurred in defense of any matter insured against by this Policy, but only to the extent provided in the Conditions.

[Witness clause optional]

BLANK TITLE INSURANCE COMPANY

BY: **PRESIDENT**

BY: **SECRETARY**

FIGURE 5.1
ALTA Owner's Policy
(continued)

EXCLUSIONS FROM COVERAGE

The following matters are expressly excluded from the coverage of this policy, and the Company will not pay loss or damage, costs, attorneys' fees, or expenses that arise by reason of:

1. (a) Any law, ordinance, permit, or governmental regulation (including those relating to building and zoning) restricting, regulating, prohibiting, or relating to

      (i)   the occupancy, use, or enjoyment of the Land;

      (ii) the character, dimensions, or location of any improvement erected on the Land;

      (iii) the subdivision of land; or

      (iv) environmental protection;

      or the effect of any violation of these laws, ordinances, or governmental regulations. This Exclusion 1(a) does not modify or limit the coverage provided under Covered Risk 5.

    (b) Any governmental police power. This Exclusion 1(b) does not modify or limit the coverage provided under Covered Risk 6.

2. Rights of eminent domain. This Exclusion does not modify or limit the coverage provided under Covered Risk 7 or 8.

3. Defects, liens, encumbrances, adverse claims, or other matters

    (a) created, suffered, assumed, or agreed to by the Insured Claimant;

    (b) not Known to the Company, not recorded in the Public Records at Date of Policy, but Known to the Insured Claimant and not disclosed in writing to the Company by the Insured Claimant prior to the date the Insured Claimant became an Insured under this policy;

    (c) resulting in no loss or damage to the Insured Claimant;

    (d) attaching or created subsequent to Date of Policy (however, this does not modify or limit the coverage provided under Covered Risk 9 and 10); or

    (e) resulting in loss or damage that would not have been sustained if the Insured Claimant had paid value for the Title.

4. Any claim, by reason of the operation of federal bankruptcy, state insolvency, or similar creditors' rights laws, that the transaction vesting the Title as shown in Schedule A, is

    (a) a fraudulent conveyance or fraudulent transfer; or

    (b) a preferential transfer for any reason not stated in Covered Risk 9 of this policy.

5. Any lien on the Title for real estate taxes or assessments imposed by governmental authority and created or attaching between Date of Policy and the date of recording of the deed or other instrument of transfer in the Public Records that vests Title as shown in Schedule A.

SCHEDULE A

Name and Address of Title Insurance Company:

[File No.:   ]   Policy No.:

Address Reference:

Amount of Insurance: $ [Premium: $]

Date of Policy: [at a.m./p.m.]

FIGURE 5.1

**ALTA Owner's Policy
(continued)**

1. Name of Insured:

2. The estate or interest in the Land that is insured by this policy is:

3. Title is vested in:

4. The Land referred to in this policy is described as follows:

SCHEDULE B

[File No.   ] Policy No.

EXCEPTIONS FROM COVERAGE

This policy does not insure against loss or damage, and the Company will not pay costs, attorneys' fees, or expenses that arise by reason of:

1. [Policy may include regional exceptions if so desired by the issuing Company.]

2. [Variable exceptions such as taxes, easements, CC&R's, etc., shown here]

CONDITIONS

1. DEFINITION OF TERMS

The following terms when used in this policy mean:

(a) "Amount of Insurance": The amount stated in Schedule A, as may be increased or decreased by endorsement to this policy, increased by Section 8(b), or decreased by Sections 10 and 11 of these Conditions.

(b) "Date of Policy": The date designated as "Date of Policy" in Schedule A.

(c) "Entity": A corporation, partnership, trust, limited liability company, or other similar legal entity.

(d) "Insured": The Insured named in Schedule A.

  (i) the term "Insured" also includes

   (A) successors to the Title of the Insured by operation of law as distinguished from purchase, including heirs, devisees, survivors, personal representatives, or next of kin;

   (B) successors to an Insured by dissolution, merger, consolidation, distribution, or reorganization;

   (C) successors to an Insured by its conversion to another kind of Entity;

   (D) a grantee of an Insured under a deed delivered without payment of actual valuable consideration conveying the Title

    (1) if the stock, shares, memberships, or other equity interests of the grantee are wholly-owned by the named Insured,

    (2) if the grantee wholly owns the named Insured,

    (3) if the grantee is wholly-owned by an affiliated Entity of the named Insured, provided the affiliated Entity and the named Insured are both wholly-owned by the same person or Entity, or

    (4) if the grantee is a trustee or beneficiary of a trust created by a written instrument established by the Insured named in Schedule A for estate planning purposes.

  (ii) with regard to (A), (B), (C), and (D) reserving, however, all rights and defenses as to any successor that the Company would have had against any predecessor Insured.

FIGURE 5.1

ALTA Owner's Policy
(continued)

(e) "Insured Claimant": An Insured claiming loss or damage.

(f) "Knowledge" or "Known": Actual knowledge, not constructive knowledge or notice that may be imputed to an Insured by reason of the Public Records or any other records that impart constructive notice of matters affecting the Title.

(g) "Land": The land described in Schedule A, and affixed improvements that by law constitute real property. The term "Land" does not include any property beyond the lines of the area described in Schedule A, nor any right, title, interest, estate, or easement in abutting streets, roads, avenues, alleys, lanes, ways, or waterways, but this does not modify or limit the extent that a right of access to and from the Land is insured by this policy.

(h) "Mortgage": Mortgage, deed of trust, trust deed, or other security instrument, including one evidenced by electronic means authorized by law.

(i) "Public Records": Records established under state statutes at Date of Policy for the purpose of imparting constructive notice of matters relating to real property to purchasers for value and without Knowledge. With respect to Covered Risk 5(d), "Public Records" shall also include environmental protection liens filed in the records of the clerk of the United States District Court for the district where the Land is located.

(j) "Title": The estate or interest described in Schedule A.

(k) "Unmarketable Title": Title affected by an alleged or apparent matter that would permit a prospective purchaser or lessee of the Title or lender on the Title to be released from the obligation to purchase, lease, or lend if there is a contractual condition requiring the delivery of marketable title.

2. CONTINUATION OF INSURANCE

The coverage of this policy shall continue in force as of Date of Policy in favor of an Insured, but only so long as the Insured retains an estate or interest in the Land, or holds an obligation secured by a purchase money Mortgage given by a purchaser from the Insured, or only so long as the Insured shall have liability by reason of warranties in any transfer or conveyance of the Title. This policy shall not continue in force in favor of any purchaser from the Insured of either (i) an estate or interest in the Land, or (ii) an obligation secured by a purchase money Mortgage given to the Insured.

3. NOTICE OF CLAIM TO BE GIVEN BY INSURED CLAIMANT

The Insured shall notify the Company promptly in writing (i) in case of any litigation as set forth in Section 5(a) of these Conditions, (ii) in case Knowledge shall come to an Insured hereunder of any claim of title or interest that is adverse to the Title, as insured, and that might cause loss or damage for which the Company may be liable by virtue of this policy, or (iii) if the Title, as insured, is rejected as Unmarketable Title. If the Company is prejudiced by the failure of the Insured Claimant to provide prompt notice, the Company's liability to the Insured Claimant under the policy shall be reduced to the extent of the prejudice.

4. PROOF OF LOSS

In the event the Company is unable to determine the amount of loss or damage, the Company may, at its option, require as a condition of payment that the Insured Claimant furnish a signed proof of loss. The proof of loss must describe the defect, lien, encumbrance, or other matter insured against by this policy that constitutes the basis of loss or damage and shall state, to the extent possible, the basis of calculating the amount of the loss or damage.

5. DEFENSE AND PROSECUTION OF ACTIONS

(a) Upon written request by the Insured, and subject to the options contained in Section 7 of these Conditions, the Company, at its own cost and without unreasonable delay, shall provide for the defense of an Insured in litigation in which any third party asserts a claim covered by this policy adverse to the Insured. This obligation is limited to only those stated causes of action alleging matters insured against by this policy. The Company shall have the right to select counsel of its choice (subject to the right of the Insured to object for reasonable cause) to represent the Insured as to those stated causes of action. It shall not be liable for and will not pay the fees of any other counsel. The Company will not pay any fees, costs, or expenses incurred by the Insured in the defense of those causes of action that allege matters not insured against by this policy.

FIGURE 5.1
ALTA Owner's Policy
(continued)

(b) The Company shall have the right, in addition to the options contained in Section 7 of these Conditions, at its own cost, to institute and prosecute any action or proceeding or to do any other act that in its opinion may be necessary or desirable to establish the Title, as insured, or to prevent or reduce loss or damage to the Insured. The Company may take any appropriate action under the terms of this policy, whether or not it shall be liable to the Insured. The exercise of these rights shall not be an admission of liability or waiver of any provision of this policy. If the Company exercises its rights under this subsection, it must do so diligently.

(c) Whenever the Company brings an action or asserts a defense as required or permitted by this policy, the Company may pursue the litigation to a final determination by a court of competent jurisdiction, and it expressly reserves the right, in its sole discretion, to appeal any adverse judgment or order.

6. DUTY OF INSURED CLAIMANT TO COOPERATE

(a) In all cases where this policy permits or requires the Company to prosecute or provide for the defense of any action or proceeding and any appeals, the Insured shall secure to the Company the right to so prosecute or provide defense in the action or proceeding, including the right to use, at its option, the name of the Insured for this purpose. Whenever requested by the Company, the Insured, at the Company's expense, shall give the Company all reasonable aid (i) in securing evidence, obtaining witnesses, prosecuting or defending the action or proceeding, or effecting settlement, and (ii) in any other lawful act that in the opinion of the Company may be necessary or desirable to establish the Title or any other matter as insured. If the Company is prejudiced by the failure of the Insured to furnish the required cooperation, the Company's obligations to the Insured under the policy shall terminate, including any liability or obligation to defend, prosecute, or continue any litigation, with regard to the matter or matters requiring such cooperation.

(b) The Company may reasonably require the Insured Claimant to submit to examination under oath by any authorized representative of the Company and to produce for examination, inspection, and copying, at such reasonable times and places as may be designated by the authorized representative of the Company, all records, in whatever medium maintained, including books, ledgers, checks, memoranda, correspondence, reports, e-mails, disks, tapes, and videos whether bearing a date before or after Date of Policy, that reasonably pertain to the loss or damage. Further, if requested by any authorized representative of the Company, the Insured Claimant shall grant its permission, in writing, for any authorized representative of the Company to examine, inspect, and copy all of these records in the custody or control of a third party that reasonably pertain to the loss or damage. All information designated as confidential by the Insured Claimant provided to the Company pursuant to this Section shall not be disclosed to others unless, in the reasonable judgment of the Company, it is necessary in the administration of the claim. Failure of the Insured Claimant to submit for examination under oath, produce any reasonably requested information, or grant permission to secure reasonably necessary information from third parties as required in this subsection, unless prohibited by law or governmental regulation, shall terminate any liability of the Company under this policy as to that claim.

7. OPTIONS TO PAY OR OTHERWISE SETTLE CLAIMS; TERMINATION OF LIABILITY

In case of a claim under this policy, the Company shall have the following additional options:

(a) To Pay or Tender Payment of the Amount of Insurance.

To pay or tender payment of the Amount of Insurance under this policy together with any costs, attorneys' fees, and expenses incurred by the Insured Claimant that were authorized by the Company up to the time of payment or tender of payment and that the Company is obligated to pay.

Upon the exercise by the Company of this option, all liability and obligations of the Company to the Insured under this policy, other than to make the payment required in this subsection, shall terminate, including any liability or obligation to defend, prosecute, or continue any litigation.

(b) To Pay or Otherwise Settle With Parties Other Than the Insured or With the Insured Claimant.

(i) to pay or otherwise settle with other parties for or in the name of an Insured Claimant any claim insured against under this policy. In addition, the Company will pay any costs, attorneys' fees, and expenses incurred by the Insured Claimant that were authorized by the Company up to the time of payment and that the Company is obligated to pay; or

FIGURE 5.1
**ALTA Owner's Policy
(continued)**

(ii)   to pay or otherwise settle with the Insured Claimant the loss or damage provided for under this policy, together with any costs, attorneys' fees, and expenses incurred by the Insured Claimant that were authorized by the Company up to the time of payment and that the Company is obligated to pay.

Upon the exercise by the Company of either of the options provided for in subsections (b)(i) or (ii), the Company's obligations to the Insured under this policy for the claimed loss or damage, other than the payments required to be made, shall terminate, including any liability or obligation to defend, prosecute, or continue any litigation.

8.   DETERMINATION AND EXTENT OF LIABILITY

This policy is a contract of indemnity against actual monetary loss or damage sustained or incurred by the Insured Claimant who has suffered loss or damage by reason of matters insured against by this policy.

(a)   The extent of liability of the Company for loss or damage under this policy shall not exceed the lesser of

(i)   the Amount of Insurance; or

(ii)   the difference between the value of the Title as insured and the value of the Title subject to the risk insured against by this policy.

(b)   If the Company pursues its rights under Section 5 of these Conditions and is unsuccessful in establishing the Title, as insured,

(i)   the Amount of Insurance shall be increased by 10%, and

(ii)   the Insured Claimant shall have the right to have the loss or damage determined either as of the date the claim was made by the Insured Claimant or as of the date it is settled and paid.

(c)   In addition to the extent of liability under (a) and (b), the Company will also pay those costs, attorneys' fees, and expenses incurred in accordance with Sections 5 and 7 of these Conditions.

9.   LIMITATION OF LIABILITY

(a)   If the Company establishes the Title, or removes the alleged defect, lien, or encumbrance, or cures the lack of a right of access to or from the Land, or cures the claim of Unmarketable Title, all as insured, in a reasonably diligent manner by any method, including litigation and the completion of any appeals, it shall have fully performed its obligations with respect to that matter and shall not be liable for any loss or damage caused to the Insured.

(b)   In the event of any litigation, including litigation by the Company or with the Company's consent, the Company shall have no liability for loss or damage until there has been a final determination by a court of competent jurisdiction, and disposition of all appeals, adverse to the Title, as insured.

(c)   The Company shall not be liable for loss or damage to the Insured for liability voluntarily assumed by the Insured in settling any claim or suit without the prior written consent of the Company.

10.   REDUCTION OF INSURANCE; REDUCTION OR TERMINATION OF LIABILITY

All payments under this policy, except payments made for costs, attorneys' fees, and expenses, shall reduce the Amount of Insurance by the amount of the payment.

11.   LIABILITY NONCUMULATIVE

The Amount of Insurance shall be reduced by any amount the Company pays under any policy insuring a Mortgage to which exception is taken in Schedule B or to which the Insured has agreed, assumed, or taken subject, or which is executed by an Insured after Date of Policy and which is a charge or lien on the Title, and the amount so paid shall be deemed a payment to the Insured under this policy.

12.   PAYMENT OF LOSS

When liability and the extent of loss or damage have been definitely fixed in accordance with these Conditions, the payment shall be made within 30 days.

FIGURE 5.1

ALTA Owner's Policy
(continued)

13. RIGHTS OF RECOVERY UPON PAYMENT OR SETTLEMENT

(a)   Whenever the Company shall have settled and paid a claim under this policy, it shall be subrogated and entitled to the rights of the Insured Claimant in the Title and all other rights and remedies in respect to the claim that the Insured Claimant has against any person or property, to the extent of the amount of any loss, costs, attorneys' fees, and expenses paid by the Company. If requested by the Company, the Insured Claimant shall execute documents to evidence the transfer to the Company of these rights and remedies. The Insured Claimant shall permit the Company to sue, compromise, or settle in the name of the Insured Claimant and to use the name of the Insured Claimant in any transaction or litigation involving these rights and remedies.

   If a payment on account of a claim does not fully cover the loss of the Insured Claimant, the Company shall defer the exercise of its right to recover until after the Insured Claimant shall have recovered its loss.

(b)   The Company's right of subrogation includes the rights of the Insured to indemnities, guaranties, other policies of insurance, or bonds, notwithstanding any terms or conditions contained in those instruments that address subrogation rights.

14. ARBITRATION

Either the Company or the Insured may demand that the claim or controversy shall be submitted to arbitration pursuant to the Title Insurance Arbitration Rules of the American Land Title Association ("Rules"). Except as provided in the Rules, there shall be no joinder or consolidation with claims or controversies of other persons. Arbitrable matters may include, but are not limited to, any controversy or claim between the Company and the Insured arising out of or relating to this policy, any service in connection with its issuance or the breach of a policy provision, or to any other controversy or claim arising out of the transaction giving rise to this policy. All arbitrable matters when the Amount of Insurance is $2,000,000 or less shall be arbitrated at the option of either the Company or the Insured. All arbitrable matters when the Amount of Insurance is in excess of $2,000,000 shall be arbitrated only when agreed to by both the Company and the Insured. Arbitration pursuant to this policy and under the Rules shall be binding upon the parties. Judgment upon the award rendered by the Arbitrator(s) may be entered in any court of competent jurisdiction.

15. LIABILITY LIMITED TO THIS POLICY; POLICY ENTIRE CONTRACT

(a)   This policy together with all endorsements, if any, attached to it by the Company is the entire policy and contract between the Insured and the Company. In interpreting any provision of this policy, this policy shall be construed as a whole.

(b)   Any claim of loss or damage that arises out of the status of the Title or by any action asserting such claim shall be restricted to this policy.

(c)   Any amendment of or endorsement to this policy must be in writing and authenticated by an authorized person, or expressly incorporated by Schedule A of this policy.

(d)   Each endorsement to this policy issued at any time is made a part of this policy and is subject to all of its terms and provisions. Except as the endorsement expressly states, it does not (i) modify any of the terms and provisions of the policy, (ii) modify any prior endorsement, (iii) extend the Date of Policy, or (iv) increase the Amount of Insurance.

16. SEVERABILITY

In the event any provision of this policy, in whole or in part, is held invalid or unenforceable under applicable law, the policy shall be deemed not to include that provision or such part held to be invalid, but all other provisions shall remain in full force and effect.

17. CHOICE OF LAW; FORUM

(a)   Choice of Law: The Insured acknowledges the Company has underwritten the risks covered by this policy and determined the premium charged therefor in reliance upon the law affecting interests in real property and applicable to the interpretation, rights, remedies, or enforcement of policies of title insurance of the jurisdiction where the Land is located.

   Therefore, the court or an arbitrator shall apply the law of the jurisdiction where the Land is located to determine the validity of claims against the Title that are adverse to the Insured and to interpret and enforce the terms of this policy. In neither case shall the court or arbitrator apply its conflicts of law principles to determine the applicable law.

FIGURE 5.1

ALTA Owner's Policy
(continued)

(b) Choice of Forum: Any litigation or other proceeding brought by the Insured against the Company must be filed only in a state or federal court within the United States of America or its territories having appropriate jurisdiction.

18. NOTICES, WHERE SENT

Any notice of claim and any other notice or statement in writing required to be given to the Company under this policy must be given to the Company at [fill in].

NOTE: Bracketed [ ] material optional

FIGURE 5.2

ALTA Loan Policy

LOAN POLICY OF TITLE INSURANCE
Issued By
BLANK TITLE INSURANCE COMPANY

Any notice of claim and any other notice or statement in writing required to be given to the Company under this Policy must be given to the Company at the address shown in Section 17 of the Conditions.

COVERED RISKS

SUBJECT TO THE EXCLUSIONS FROM COVERAGE, THE EXCEPTIONS FROM COVERAGE CONTAINED IN <u>SCHEDULE B</u>, AND THE <u>CONDITIONS</u>, BLANK TITLE INSURANCE COMPANY, a Blank corporation (the "Company") insures as of Date of Policy and, to the extent stated in Covered Risks 11, 13, and 14, after Date of Policy, against loss or damage, not exceeding the Amount of Insurance, sustained or incurred by the Insured by reason of:

1. Title being vested other than as stated in Schedule A.

2. Any defect in or lien or encumbrance on the Title. This Covered Risk includes but is not limited to insurance against loss from

    (a) A defect in the Title caused by

        (i)   forgery, fraud, undue influence, duress, incompetency, incapacity, or impersonation;

        (ii)   failure of any person or Entity to have authorized a transfer or conveyance;

        (iii) a document affecting Title not properly created, executed, witnessed, sealed, acknowledged, notarized, or delivered;

        (iv) failure to perform those acts necessary to create a document by electronic means authorized by law;

        (v)   a document executed under a falsified, expired, or otherwise invalid power of attorney;

        (vi) a document not properly filed, recorded, or indexed in the Public Records including failure to perform those acts by electronic means authorized by law; or

        (vii) a defective judicial or administrative proceeding.

    (b) The lien of real estate taxes or assessments imposed on the Title by a governmental authority due or payable, but unpaid.

    (c) Any encroachment, encumbrance, violation, variation, or adverse circumstance affecting the Title that would be disclosed by an accurate and complete land survey of the Land. The term "encroachment" includes encroachments of existing improvements located on the Land onto adjoining land, and encroachments onto the Land of existing improvements located on adjoining land.

This form is copyrighted and reprinted with permission from American Land Title Association®, 1828 L Street, N.W., Suite 705, Washington, DC 20036.

FIGURE 5.2

**ALTA Loan Policy
(continued)**

3. Unmarketable Title.

4. No right of access to and from the Land.

5. The violation or enforcement of any law, ordinance, permit, or governmental regulation (including those relating to building and zoning) restricting, regulating, prohibiting, or relating to

    (a) the occupancy, use, or enjoyment of the Land;

    (b) the character, dimensions, or location of any improvement erected on the Land;

    (c) the subdivision of land; or

    (d) environmental protection

    if a notice, describing any part of the Land, is recorded in the Public Records setting forth the violation or intention to enforce, but only to the extent of the violation or enforcement referred to in that notice.

6. An enforcement action based on the exercise of a governmental police power not covered by Covered Risk 5 if a notice of the enforcement action, describing any part of the Land, is recorded in the Public Records, but only to the extent of the enforcement referred to in that notice.

7. The exercise of the rights of eminent domain if a notice of the exercise, describing any part of the Land, is recorded in the Public Records.

8. Any taking by a governmental body that has occurred and is binding on the rights of a purchaser for value without Knowledge.

9. The invalidity or unenforceability of the lien of the Insured Mortgage upon the Title. This Covered Risk includes but is not limited to insurance against loss from any of the following impairing the lien of the Insured Mortgage

    (a) forgery, fraud, undue influence, duress, incompetency, incapacity, or impersonation;

    (b) failure of any person or Entity to have authorized a transfer or conveyance;

    (c) the Insured Mortgage not being properly created, executed, witnessed, sealed, acknowledged, notarized, or delivered;

    (d) failure to perform those acts necessary to create a document by electronic means authorized by law;

    (e) a document executed under a falsified, expired, or otherwise invalid power of attorney;

    (f) a document not properly filed, recorded, or indexed in the Public Records including failure to perform those acts by electronic means authorized by law; or

    (g) a defective judicial or administrative proceeding.

10. The lack of priority of the lien of the Insured Mortgage upon the Title over any other lien or encumbrance.

11. The lack of priority of the lien of the Insured Mortgage upon the Title

    (a) as security for each and every advance of proceeds of the loan secured by the Insured Mortgage over any statutory lien for services, labor, or material arising from construction of an improvement or work related to the Land when the improvement or work is either

        (i) contracted for or commenced on or before Date of Policy; or

        (ii) contracted for, commenced, or continued after Date of Policy if the construction is financed, in whole or in part, by proceeds of the loan secured by the Insured Mortgage that the Insured has advanced or is obligated on Date of Policy to advance; and

    (b) over the lien of any assessments for street improvements under construction or completed at Date of Policy.

12. The invalidity or unenforceability of any assignment of the Insured Mortgage, provided the assignment is shown in Schedule A, or the failure of the assignment shown in Schedule A to vest title to the Insured Mortgage in the named Insured assignee free and clear of all liens.

FIGURE 5.2

ALTA Loan Policy
(continued)

13. The invalidity, unenforceability, lack of priority, or avoidance of the lien of the Insured Mortgage upon the Title

    (a) resulting from the avoidance in whole or in part, or from a court order providing an alternative remedy, of any transfer of all or any part of the title to or any interest in the Land occurring prior to the transaction creating the lien of the Insured Mortgage because that prior transfer constituted a fraudulent or preferential transfer under federal bankruptcy, state insolvency, or similar creditors' rights laws; or

    (b) because the Insured Mortgage constitutes a preferential transfer under federal bankruptcy, state insolvency, or similar creditors' rights laws by reason of the failure of its recording in the Public Records

        (i) to be timely, or

        (ii) to impart notice of its existence to a purchaser for value or to a judgment or lien creditor.

14. Any defect in or lien or encumbrance on the Title or other matter included in Covered Risks 1 through 13 that has been created or attached or has been filed or recorded in the Public Records subsequent to Date of Policy and prior to the recording of the Insured Mortgage in the Public Records.

The Company will also pay the costs, attorneys' fees, and expenses incurred in defense of any matter insured against by this Policy, but only to the extent provided in the Conditions.

[Witness clause optional]

BLANK TITLE INSURANCE COMPANY

BY: **PRESIDENT**

BY: **SECRETARY**

EXCLUSIONS FROM COVERAGE

The following matters are expressly excluded from the coverage of this policy, and the Company will not pay loss or damage, costs, attorneys' fees, or expenses that arise by reason of:

1. (a) Any law, ordinance, permit, or governmental regulation (including those relating to building and zoning) restricting, regulating, prohibiting, or relating to

        (i)   the occupancy, use, or enjoyment of the Land;

        (ii) the character, dimensions, or location of any improvement erected on the Land;

        (iii) the subdivision of land; or

        (iv) environmental protection;

        or the effect of any violation of these laws, ordinances, or governmental regulations. This Exclusion 1(a) does not modify or limit the coverage provided under Covered Risk 5.

    (b) Any governmental police power. This Exclusion 1(b) does not modify or limit the coverage provided under Covered Risk 6.

2. Rights of eminent domain. This Exclusion does not modify or limit the coverage provided under Covered Risk 7 or 8.

3. Defects, liens, encumbrances, adverse claims, or other matters

    (a) created, suffered, assumed, or agreed to by the Insured Claimant;

    (b) not Known to the Company, not recorded in the Public Records at Date of Policy, but Known to the Insured Claimant and not disclosed in writing to the Company by the Insured Claimant prior to the date the Insured Claimant became an Insured under this policy;

FIGURE 5.2

ALTA Loan Policy
(continued)

    (c) resulting in no loss or damage to the Insured Claimant;

    (d) attaching or created subsequent to Date of Policy (however, this does not modify or limit the coverage provided under Covered Risk 11, 13, or 14); or

    (e) resulting in loss or damage that would not have been sustained if the Insured Claimant had paid value for the Insured Mortgage.

4.   Unenforceability of the lien of the Insured Mortgage because of the inability or failure of an Insured to comply with applicable doing-business laws of the state where the Land is situated.

5.   Invalidity or unenforceability in whole or in part of the lien of the Insured Mortgage that arises out of the transaction evidenced by the Insured Mortgage and is based upon usury or any consumer credit protection or truth-in-lending law.

6.   Any claim, by reason of the operation of federal bankruptcy, state insolvency, or similar creditors' rights laws, that the transaction creating the lien of the Insured Mortgage, is

    (a) a fraudulent conveyance or fraudulent transfer, or

    (b) a preferential transfer for any reason not stated in Covered Risk 13(b) of this policy.

7.   Any lien on the Title for real estate taxes or assessments imposed by governmental authority and created or attaching between Date of Policy and the date of recording of the Insured Mortgage in the Public Records. This Exclusion does not modify or limit the coverage provided under Covered Risk 11(b).

SCHEDULE A

Name and Address of Title Insurance Company:
[File No.:   ]   Policy No.:
Loan No.:
Address Reference:
Amount of Insurance: $ [Premium: $]
Date of Policy: [at a.m./p.m.]

1.   Name of Insured:

2.   The estate or interest in the Land that is encumbered by the Insured Mortgage is:

3.   Title is vested in:

4.   The Insured Mortgage and its assignments, if any, are described as follows:

5.   The Land referred to in this policy is described as follows:

[6. This policy incorporates by reference those ALTA endorsements selected below:

4-06	(Condominium)
4.1-06	
5-06	(Planned Unit Development)
5.1-06	
6-06	(Variable Rate)
6.2-06	(Variable Rate--Negative Amortization)
8.1-06	(Environmental Protection Lien) Paragraph b refers to the following state statute(s):
9-06	(Restrictions, Encroachments, Minerals)
13.1-06	(Leasehold Loan)
14-06	(Future Advance-Priority)
14.1-06	(Future Advance-Knowledge)
14.3-06	(Future Advance-Reverse Mortgage)
22-06	(Location) The type of improvement is a _____, and the street address is as shown above.]

FIGURE 5.2
ALTA Loan Policy
(continued)

SCHEDULE B

[File No.   ]   Policy No.

EXCEPTIONS FROM COVERAGE

[Except as provided in Schedule B - Part II,] t[or T]his policy does not insure against loss or damage, and the Company will not pay costs, attorneys› fees, or expenses that arise by reason of:

[PART I

PART II

In addition to the matters set forth in Part I of this Schedule, the Title is subject to the following matters, and the Company insures against loss or damage sustained in the event that they are not subordinate to the lien of the Insured Mortgage:]

CONDITIONS

1.   DEFINITION OF TERMS

The following terms when used in this policy mean:

(a)   "Amount of Insurance": The amount stated in Schedule A, as may be increased or decreased by endorsement to this policy, increased by Section 8(b) or decreased by Section 10 of these Conditions.

(b)   "Date of Policy": The date designated as "Date of Policy" in Schedule A.

(c)   "Entity": A corporation, partnership, trust, limited liability company, or other similar legal entity.

(d)   "Indebtedness": The obligation secured by the Insured Mortgage including one evidenced by electronic means authorized by law, and if that obligation is the payment of a debt, the Indebtedness is the sum of

(i)   the amount of the principal disbursed as of Date of Policy;

(ii)   the amount of the principal disbursed subsequent to Date of Policy;

(iii) the construction loan advances made subsequent to Date of Policy for the purpose of financing in whole or in part the construction of an improvement to the Land or related to the Land that the Insured was and continued to be obligated to advance at Date of Policy and at the date of the advance;

(iv) interest on the loan;

(v)   the prepayment premiums, exit fees, and other similar fees or penalties allowed by law;

FIGURE 5.2
ALTA Loan Policy
(continued)

    (vi) the expenses of foreclosure and any other costs of enforcement;

    (vii) the amounts advanced to assure compliance with laws or to protect the lien or the priority of the lien of the Insured Mortgage before the acquisition of the estate or interest in the Title;

    (viii) the amounts to pay taxes and insurance; and

    (ix) the reasonable amounts expended to prevent deterioration of improvements;

    but the Indebtedness is reduced by the total of all payments and by any amount forgiven by an Insured.

(e) "Insured": The Insured named in Schedule A.

    (i) The term "Insured" also includes

      (A) the owner of the Indebtedness and each successor in ownership of the Indebtedness, whether the owner or successor owns the Indebtedness for its own account or as a trustee or other fiduciary, except a successor who is an obligor under the provisions of Section 12(c) of these Conditions;

      (B) the person or Entity who has "control" of the "transferable record," if the Indebtedness is evidenced by a "transferable record," as these terms are defined by applicable electronic transactions law;

      (C) successors to an Insured by dissolution, merger, consolidation, distribution, or reorganization;

      (D) successors to an Insured by its conversion to another kind of Entity;

      (E) a grantee of an Insured under a deed delivered without payment of actual valuable consideration conveying the Title

        (1) if the stock, shares, memberships, or other equity interests of the grantee are wholly-owned by the named Insured,

        (2) if the grantee wholly owns the named Insured, or

        (3) if the grantee is wholly-owned by an affiliated Entity of the named Insured, provided the affiliated Entity and the named Insured are both wholly-owned by the same person or Entity;

      (F) any government agency or instrumentality that is an insurer or guarantor under an insurance contract or guaranty insuring or guaranteeing the Indebtedness secured by the Insured Mortgage, or any part of it, whether named as an Insured or not;

    (ii) With regard to (A), (B), (C), (D), and (E) reserving, however, all rights and defenses as to any successor that the Company would have had against any predecessor Insured, unless the successor acquired the Indebtedness as a purchaser for value without Knowledge of the asserted defect, lien, encumbrance, or other matter insured against by this policy.

(f) "Insured Claimant": An Insured claiming loss or damage.

(g) "Insured Mortgage": The Mortgage described in paragraph 4 of Schedule A.

(h) "Knowledge" or "Known": Actual knowledge, not constructive knowledge or notice that may be imputed to an Insured by reason of the Public Records or any other records that impart constructive notice of matters affecting the Title.

(i) "Land": The land described in Schedule A, and affixed improvements that by law constitute real property. The term "Land" does not include any property beyond the lines of the area described in Schedule A, nor any right, title, interest, estate, or easement in abutting streets, roads, avenues, alleys, lanes, ways, or waterways, but this does not modify or limit the extent that a right of access to and from the Land is insured by this policy.

(j) "Mortgage": Mortgage, deed of trust, trust deed, or other security instrument, including one evidenced by electronic means authorized by law.

FIGURE 5.2

ALTA Loan Policy
(continued)

(k) "Public Records": Records established under state statutes at Date of Policy for the purpose of imparting constructive notice of matters relating to real property to purchasers for value and without Knowledge. With respect to Covered Risk 5(d), "Public Records" shall also include environmental protection liens filed in the records of the clerk of the United States District Court for the district where the Land is located.

(l) "Title": The estate or interest described in Schedule A.

(m) "Unmarketable Title": Title affected by an alleged or apparent matter that would permit a prospective purchaser or lessee of the Title or lender on the Title or a prospective purchaser of the Insured Mortgage to be released from the obligation to purchase, lease, or lend if there is a contractual condition requiring the delivery of marketable title.

2.   CONTINUATION OF INSURANCE

The coverage of this policy shall continue in force as of Date of Policy in favor of an Insured after acquisition of the Title by an Insured or after conveyance by an Insured, but only so long as the Insured retains an estate or interest in the Land, or holds an obligation secured by a purchase money Mortgage given by a purchaser from the Insured, or only so long as the Insured shall have liability by reason of warranties in any transfer or conveyance of the Title. This policy shall not continue in force in favor of any purchaser from the Insured of either (i) an estate or interest in the Land, or (ii) an obligation secured by a purchase money Mortgage given to the Insured.

3.   NOTICE OF CLAIM TO BE GIVEN BY INSURED CLAIMANT

The Insured shall notify the Company promptly in writing (i) in case of any litigation as set forth in Section 5(a) of these Conditions, (ii) in case Knowledge shall come to an Insured of any claim of title or interest that is adverse to the Title or the lien of the Insured Mortgage, as insured, and that might cause loss or damage for which the Company may be liable by virtue of this policy, or (iii) if the Title or the lien of the Insured Mortgage, as insured, is rejected as Unmarketable Title. If the Company is prejudiced by the failure of the Insured Claimant to provide prompt notice, the Company's liability to the Insured Claimant under the policy shall be reduced to the extent of the prejudice.

4.   PROOF OF LOSS

In the event the Company is unable to determine the amount of loss or damage, the Company may, at its option, require as a condition of payment that the Insured Claimant furnish a signed proof of loss. The proof of loss must describe the defect, lien, encumbrance, or other matter insured against by this policy that constitutes the basis of loss or damage and shall state, to the extent possible, the basis of calculating the amount of the loss or damage.

5.   DEFENSE AND PROSECUTION OF ACTIONS

(a) Upon written request by the Insured, and subject to the options contained in Section 7 of these Conditions, the Company, at its own cost and without unreasonable delay, shall provide for the defense of an Insured in litigation in which any third party asserts a claim covered by this policy adverse to the Insured. This obligation is limited to only those stated causes of action alleging matters insured against by this policy. The Company shall have the right to select counsel of its choice (subject to the right of the Insured to object for reasonable cause) to represent the Insured as to those stated causes of action. It shall not be liable for and will not pay the fees of any other counsel. The Company will not pay any fees, costs, or expenses incurred by the Insured in the defense of those causes of action that allege matters not insured against by this policy.

(b) The Company shall have the right, in addition to the options contained in Section 7 of these Conditions, at its own cost, to institute and prosecute any action or proceeding or to do any other act that in its opinion may be necessary or desirable to establish the Title or the lien of the Insured Mortgage, as insured, or to prevent or reduce loss or damage to the Insured. The Company may take any appropriate action under the terms of this policy, whether or not it shall be liable to the Insured. The exercise of these rights shall not be an admission of liability or waiver of any provision of this policy. If the Company exercises its rights under this subsection, it must do so diligently.

(c) Whenever the Company brings an action or asserts a defense as required or permitted by this policy, the Company may pursue the litigation to a final determination by a court of competent jurisdiction, and it expressly reserves the right, in its sole discretion, to appeal any adverse judgment or order.

FIGURE 5.2

**ALTA Loan Policy
(continued)**

6. DUTY OF INSURED CLAIMANT TO COOPERATE

(a) In all cases where this policy permits or requires the Company to prosecute or provide for the defense of any action or proceeding and any appeals, the Insured shall secure to the

Company the right to so prosecute or provide defense in the action or proceeding, including the right to use, at its option, the name of the Insured for this purpose.

Whenever requested by the Company, the Insured, at the Company's expense, shall give the Company all reasonable aid (i) in securing evidence, obtaining witnesses, prosecuting or defending the action or proceeding, or effecting settlement, and (ii) in any other lawful act that in the opinion of the Company may be necessary or desirable to establish the Title, the lien of the Insured Mortgage, or any other matter as insured. If the Company is prejudiced by the failure of the Insured to furnish the required cooperation, the Company's obligations to the Insured under the policy shall terminate, including any liability or obligation to defend, prosecute, or continue any litigation, with regard to the matter or matters requiring such cooperation.

(b) The Company may reasonably require the Insured Claimant to submit to examination under oath by any authorized representative of the Company and to produce for examination, inspection, and copying, at such reasonable times and places as may be designated by the authorized representative of the Company, all records, in whatever medium maintained, including books, ledgers, checks, memoranda, correspondence, reports, e-mails, disks, tapes, and videos whether bearing a date before or after Date of Policy, that reasonably pertain to the loss or damage. Further, if requested by any authorized representative of the Company, the Insured Claimant shall grant its permission, in writing, for any authorized representative of the Company to examine, inspect, and copy all of these records in the custody or control of a third party that reasonably pertain to the loss or damage. All information designated as confidential by the Insured Claimant provided to the Company pursuant to this Section shall not be disclosed to others unless, in the reasonable judgment of the Company, it is necessary in the administration of the claim. Failure of the Insured Claimant to submit for examination under oath, produce any reasonably requested information, or grant permission to secure reasonably necessary information from third parties as required in this subsection, unless prohibited by law or governmental regulation, shall terminate any liability of the Company under this policy as to that claim.

7. OPTIONS TO PAY OR OTHERWISE SETTLE CLAIMS; TERMINATION OF LIABILITY

In case of a claim under this policy, the Company shall have the following additional options:

(a) To Pay or Tender Payment of the Amount of Insurance or to Purchase the Indebtedness.

   (i) To pay or tender payment of the Amount of Insurance under this policy together with any costs, attorneys' fees, and expenses incurred by the Insured Claimant that were authorized by the Company up to the time of payment or tender of payment and that the Company is obligated to pay; or

   (ii) To purchase the Indebtedness for the amount of the Indebtedness on the date of purchase, together with any costs, attorneys' fees, and expenses incurred by the Insured Claimant that were authorized by the Company up to the time of purchase and that the Company is obligated to pay.

   When the Company purchases the Indebtedness, the Insured shall transfer, assign, and convey to the Company the Indebtedness and the Insured Mortgage, together with any collateral security.

   Upon the exercise by the Company of either of the options provided for in subsections (a)(i) or (ii), all liability and obligations of the Company to the Insured under this policy, other than to make the payment required in those subsections, shall terminate, including any liability or obligation to defend, prosecute, or continue any litigation.

(b) To Pay or Otherwise Settle With Parties Other Than the Insured or With the Insured Claimant.

   (i) to pay or otherwise settle with other parties for or in the name of an Insured Claimant any claim insured against under this policy. In addition, the Company will pay any costs, attorneys' fees, and expenses incurred by the Insured Claimant that were authorized by the Company up to the time of payment and that the Company is obligated to pay; or

   (ii) to pay or otherwise settle with the Insured Claimant the loss or damage provided for under this policy, together with any costs, attorneys' fees, and expenses incurred by the Insured Claimant that were authorized by the Company up to the time of payment and that the Company is obligated to pay.

FIGURE 5.2

ALTA Loan Policy
(continued)

Upon the exercise by the Company of either of the options provided for in subsections (b)(i) or (ii), the Company's obligations to the Insured under this policy for the claimed loss or damage, other than the payments required to be made, shall terminate, including any liability or obligation to defend, prosecute, or continue any litigation.

8. DETERMINATION AND EXTENT OF LIABILITY

This policy is a contract of indemnity against actual monetary loss or damage sustained or incurred by the Insured Claimant who has suffered loss or damage by reason of matters insured against by this policy.

(a) The extent of liability of the Company for loss or damage under this policy shall not exceed the least of

   (i) the Amount of Insurance,

   (ii) the Indebtedness,

   (iii) the difference between the value of the Title as insured and the value of the Title subject to the risk insured against by this policy, or

   (iv) if a government agency or instrumentality is the Insured Claimant, the amount it paid in the acquisition of the Title or the Insured Mortgage in satisfaction of its insurance contract or guaranty.

(b) If the Company pursues its rights under Section 5 of these Conditions and is unsuccessful in establishing the Title or the lien of the Insured Mortgage, as insured,

   (i) the Amount of Insurance shall be increased by 10%, and

   (ii) the Insured Claimant shall have the right to have the loss or damage determined either as of the date the claim was made by the Insured Claimant or as of the date it is settled and paid.

(c) In the event the Insured has acquired the Title in the manner described in Section 2 of these Conditions or has conveyed the Title, then the extent of liability of the Company shall continue as set forth in Section 8(a) of these Conditions.

(d) In addition to the extent of liability under (a), (b), and (c), the Company will also pay those costs, attorneys' fees, and expenses incurred in accordance with Sections 5 and 7 of these Conditions.

9. LIMITATION OF LIABILITY

(a) If the Company establishes the Title, or removes the alleged defect, lien, or encumbrance, or cures the lack of a right of access to or from the Land, or cures the claim of Unmarketable Title, or establishes the lien of the Insured Mortgage, all as insured, in a reasonably diligent manner by any method, including litigation and the completion of any appeals, it shall have fully performed its obligations with respect to that matter and shall not be liable for any loss or damage caused to the Insured.

(b) In the event of any litigation, including litigation by the Company or with the Company's consent, the Company shall have no liability for loss or damage until there has been a final determination by a court of competent jurisdiction, and disposition of all appeals, adverse to the Title or to the lien of the Insured Mortgage, as insured.

(c) The Company shall not be liable for loss or damage to the Insured for liability voluntarily assumed by the Insured in settling any claim or suit without the prior written consent of the Company.

10. REDUCTION OF INSURANCE; REDUCTION OR TERMINATION OF LIABILITY

(a) All payments under this policy, except payments made for costs, attorneys' fees, and expenses, shall reduce the Amount of Insurance by the amount of the payment. However, any payments made prior to the acquisition of Title as provided in Section 2 of these Conditions shall not reduce the Amount of Insurance afforded under this policy except to the extent that the payments reduce the Indebtedness.

(b) The voluntary satisfaction or release of the Insured Mortgage shall terminate all liability of the Company except as provided in Section 2 of these Conditions.

11. PAYMENT OF LOSS

When liability and the extent of loss or damage have been definitely fixed in accordance with these Conditions, the payment shall be made within 30 days.

FIGURE 5.2
**ALTA Loan Policy
(continued)**

12. RIGHTS OF RECOVERY UPON PAYMENT OR SETTLEMENT

(a) The Company's Right to Recover

Whenever the Company shall have settled and paid a claim under this policy, it shall be subrogated and entitled to the rights of the Insured Claimant in the Title or Insured Mortgage and all other rights and remedies in respect to the claim that the Insured Claimant has against any person or property, to the extent of the amount of any loss, costs, attorneys' fees, and expenses paid by the Company. If requested by the Company, the Insured Claimant shall execute documents to evidence the transfer to the Company of these rights and remedies. The Insured Claimant shall permit the Company to sue, compromise, or settle in the name of the Insured Claimant and to use the name of the Insured Claimant in any transaction or litigation involving these rights and remedies.

If a payment on account of a claim does not fully cover the loss of the Insured Claimant, the Company shall defer the exercise of its right to recover until after the Insured Claimant shall have recovered its loss.

(b) The Insured's Rights and Limitations

(i) The owner of the Indebtedness may release or substitute the personal liability of any debtor or guarantor, extend or otherwise modify the terms of payment, release a portion of the Title from the lien of the Insured Mortgage, or release any collateral security for the Indebtedness, if it does not affect the enforceability or priority of the lien of the Insured Mortgage.

(ii) If the Insured exercises a right provided in (b)(i), but has Knowledge of any claim adverse to the Title or the lien of the Insured Mortgage insured against by this policy, the Company shall be required to pay only that part of any losses insured against by this policy that shall exceed the amount, if any, lost to the Company by reason of the impairment by the Insured Claimant of the Company's right of subrogation.

(c) The Company's Rights Against Noninsured Obligors

The Company's right of subrogation includes the Insured's rights against non-insured obligors including the rights of the Insured to indemnities, guaranties, other policies of insurance, or bonds, notwithstanding any terms or conditions contained in those instruments that address subrogation rights.

The Company's right of subrogation shall not be avoided by acquisition of the Insured Mortgage by an obligor (except an obligor described in Section 1(e)(i)(F) of these Conditions) who acquires the Insured Mortgage as a result of an indemnity, guarantee, other policy of insurance, or bond, and the obligor will not be an Insured under this policy.

13. ARBITRATION

Either the Company or the Insured may demand that the claim or controversy shall be submitted to arbitration pursuant to the Title Insurance Arbitration Rules of the American Land Title Association ("Rules"). Except as provided in the Rules, there shall be no joinder or consolidation with claims or controversies of other persons. Arbitrable matters may include, but are not limited to, any controversy or claim between the Company and the Insured arising out of or relating to this policy, any service in connection with its issuance or the breach of a policy provision, or to any other controversy or claim arising out of the transaction giving rise to this policy. All arbitrable matters when the Amount of Insurance is $2,000,000 or less shall be arbitrated at the option of either the Company or the Insured. All arbitrable matters when the Amount of Insurance is in excess of $2,000,000 shall be arbitrated only when agreed to by both the Company and the Insured. Arbitration pursuant to this policy and under the Rules shall be binding upon the parties. Judgment upon the award rendered by the Arbitrator(s) may be entered in any court of competent jurisdiction.

14. LIABILITY LIMITED TO THIS POLICY; POLICY ENTIRE CONTRACT

(a) This policy together with all endorsements, if any, attached to it by the Company is the entire policy and contract between the Insured and the Company. In interpreting any provision of this policy, this policy shall be construed as a whole.

(b) Any claim of loss or damage that arises out of the status of the Title or lien of the Insured Mortgage or by any action asserting such claim shall be restricted to this policy.

(c) Any amendment of or endorsement to this policy must be in writing and authenticated by an authorized person, or expressly incorporated by Schedule A of this policy.

FIGURE 5.2
ALTA Loan Policy
(continued)

(d) Each endorsement to this policy issued at any time is made a part of this policy and is subject to all of its terms and provisions. Except as the endorsement expressly states, it does not (i) modify any of the terms and provisions of the policy, (ii) modify any prior endorsement, (iii) extend the Date of Policy, or (iv) increase the Amount of Insurance.

15. SEVERABILITY

In the event any provision of this policy, in whole or in part, is held invalid or unenforceable under applicable law, the policy shall be deemed not to include that provision or such part held to be invalid, but all other provisions shall remain in full force and effect.

16. CHOICE OF LAW; FORUM

(a) Choice of Law: The Insured acknowledges the Company has underwritten the risks covered by this policy and determined the premium charged therefor in reliance upon the law affecting interests in real property and applicable to the interpretation, rights, remedies, or enforcement of policies of title insurance of the jurisdiction where the Land is located.

Therefore, the court or an arbitrator shall apply the law of the jurisdiction where the Land is located to determine the validity of claims against the Title or the lien of the Insured Mortgage that are adverse to the Insured and to interpret and enforce the terms of this policy. In neither case shall the court or arbitrator apply its conflicts of law principles to determine the applicable law.

(b) Choice of Forum: Any litigation or other proceeding brought by the Insured against the Company must be filed only in a state or federal court within the United States of America or its territories having appropriate jurisdiction.

17. NOTICES, WHERE SENT

Any notice of claim and any other notice or statement in writing required to be given to the Company under this policy must be given to the Company at [fill in].

NOTE: Bracketed [ ] material optional

ALTA provides extended coverage for risks not a matter of public record beyond the protection afforded by a standard coverage (CLTA) policy, though at considerably higher premiums. Institutional lenders often require that an **ALTA extended policy** be obtained for financing. Other homeowners may want the coverage for the additional protection it offers them. Coverage includes the following:

■ Matters disclosed by a physical inspection of the premises not previously disclosed by public record

■ Matters disclosed by inquiry of the occupants of the property that might disclose off-record matters

■ Matters disclosed by a current survey, including

— shortages (or overages) in lot dimensions,

— natural watercourses through the property,

— unrecorded easements, and

— encroachments.

Pro-Tip: The Importance of a Title Survey

The reason a title company would spend the time and expense to perform a survey is evidenced by the following example that actually happened!

An extended coverage title policy was ordered by a major retail department store considering establishing a presence in an expanding and growing business neighborhood in the city of Los Angeles

The title company's survey discovered the following:

A paved, marked and traffic-signaled thoroughfare traversed the middle of the property. It was marked as "one-way" traffic only from south to north during morning hours, and reversed the direction in the evening (One may discovered several such traffic patterns in cities throughout California to accommodate the greatest numbers of vehicles traveling in one particular direction, especially during commute hours. Several cities have such traffic patterns for roadways leading to and from center of attractions, such as sports stadiums, theme parks and others.) The title company engineer doing the investigation discovered the reason for the traffic pattern was the result of a "license" between the land owner and the city. A license differs from an easement by being non-possessory in nature, meaning that it may be removed. It does not "run with the land" but rather is merely an agreement for one to use the land of another's for a particular purpose. Such an agreement typically terminates upon certain events taking place, such as the death of either party or the sale of the property.

The buyer, in the case the department store, certainly would want the license removed to facilitate travel in both directions to the property.

The reason for the license was that workers from a nearby plant had been using the property for parking (which could have served as grounds for establishing a possible easement had it not been for the "posting" of a sign on the property indicating "right to pass by permission only" as provided by California Civil Code Section 1008).

The survey also revealed that a natural watercourse existed across the property. Due to potential drainage problems the store made plans to divert the waters to maintain proper drainage. Both of the issues, left unknown, could have created major problems and considerable delays in constructing, opening and operating the planned new store.

The additional coverage of the ALTA lender's policy differs from the standard coverage policy by offering insurance against matters that cannot be determined by an examination of public records. An ALTA extended loan policy covers the lender only. The homeowner wishing the extended protection purchases an ALTA owner's policy separately. Its advantage to the lender lies in its ability to include matters that are not generally public record. ALTA extended coverage loan policy coverage varies from state to state. In California, an ALTA loan policy will insure the lender against loss if

- the vesting is other than as listed;

- a defect, lien, or encumbrance is not excluded and the underwriter failed to disclose it in the policy;

- there is no right of access to a public street;

- the title is unmarketable as insured;

- the insured mortgage is invalid or unenforceable (unless a claim is based on usury or any consumer credit protection or truth-in-lending law);

- mechanics' liens gain priority over the insured mortgage (unless those liens arise from contractual work started after the policy date and are not financed by the insured loan); and

- an assignment of the insured mortgage is invalid or unenforceable by reason of an error against in the policy.

Conditions and Stipulations   The principal conditions and stipulations of the ALTA extended policy are as follows:

- The principal terms defined

- The circumstances under which the policy remain in force when the estate or interest in the insured property is acquired by another

- How and when the claimant must give notice of claim, and the provision for defense and prosecution of actions

- The insurer's options in paying or settling claims

- How losses are determined and the payment of loss

- Limitations and reductions of liability, noncumulative liability, subrogation on payment or settlement, and policy limit liability

- Provisions for arbitration

ALTA: Lender's Coverage Exclusions   The following claims are not covered by ALTA policies:

- Any law, ordinance, or governmental regulation, or police power relating to building, zoning, occupancy, use, or environmental protection except to the extent that a notice of defect has been recorded

- Rights of eminent domain

- Defects such as liens created by the insured

- Defects known to the insured, but not specified in writing to the underwriter by the specified date

- Defects, but no loss or damage is suffered by the insured

- Defects created or attached after the policy date (with the exception of mechanic's lien insurance offered elsewhere in the policy)

- If the lien of the insured mortgage is unenforceable because the insured does not comply with "doing business" laws in the state of the insured property

- Any claim, which arises out of the transaction creating the interest of the mortgagee insured by reason of the operation of federal bankruptcy, state insolvency, or similar creditors' rights laws

ALTA Standards and Guidelines for Title Insurers   Title insurers offering ALTA policies subscribe to the standards and "best practices" as implemented by the American Land Title Association. See Figure 5.3.

FIGURE 5.3

ALTA Standards and
Guidelines for Title Insurers

American Land Title Association
Title Insurance and Settlement Company Best Practices
Executive Summary

ALTA seeks to guide its membership in best practices to protect consumers, ensure quality service, and meet legal and market requirements. These practices are voluntary and designed to help members illustrate for consumers and clients the practices the industry uses to ensure a positive and compliant real estate settlement experience.

ALTA is publishing these best practices as a benchmark for the mortgage lending and real estate settlement industry. ALTA seeks comments from stakeholders as the Association seeks to continually improve these best practices. A formal committee in ALTA will regularly review and make improvements to these best practices, seeking comment on each revision.

1. Best Practice: Establish and maintain current license(s) as required to conduct the business of title insurance and settlement services.

Purpose: Ensure that the company is fully compliant with all applicable business laws and regulations.

2. Best Practice: Adopt and maintain appropriate written procedures and controls for Escrow Trust Accounts allowing for electronic verification of reconciliation.

Purpose: Appropriate and effective escrow controls and ongoing employee training help title and settlement companies meet client and legal requirements for the safeguarding of client funds. These procedures ensure accuracy and minimize the exposure to loss of client funds. Settlement Companies may engage outside contractors to segregate trust accounting duties.

3. Best Practice: Adopt and maintain a written privacy and information security plan to protect Non-public Personal Information as required by local, state and federal law.

Purpose: Federal and state laws (including the Gramm-Leach-Bliley Act) require title companies to develop a written information security plan that describes their program to protect non-public customer information. The plan must be appropriate to the company's size and complexity, the nature and scope of company's activities, and the sensitivity of the customer information the company handles. A company evaluates and adjusts its program in light of relevant circumstances, including changes in the firm's business or operations, or the results of security testing and monitoring.

4. Best Practice: Adopt standard real estate settlement procedures and policies that ensure compliance with Federal and State Consumer Financial Laws as applicable.

Purpose: Adopting appropriate policies can ensure a real estate settlement company can provide a safe and compliant settlement and meet state, federal and contractual obligations governing the settlement process and provide for ongoing training.

5. Best practice: Adopt and maintain written procedures related to title policy production, delivery, reporting and premium remittance.

Purpose: Appropriate procedures for the production, delivery and remittance of title insurance policies ensure title companies meet their legal and contractual obligations.

6. Best Practice: Maintain appropriate professional liability insurance and fidelity coverage.

Purpose: Appropriate levels of professional liability (errors and omissions insurance) ensure that title agencies and settlement companies have the financial capacity to stand behind their professional services. In addition, state law and contractual obligations may require a company to maintain fidelity bond and surety bond policies with prescribed minimum amounts of coverage.

7. Best Practice: Adopt and maintain procedures for resolving consumer complaints.

Purpose: A process for receiving and addressing consumer complaints is important to ensure that any instances of poor service or non-compliance do not go undiscovered.

Sample Blank ALTA Policies. Samples of ALTA title policies, owners and lenders, are represented on the following pages. Shown first is the ALTA Owners Policy, followed by a standard ALTA Lenders Extended Coverage Policy.

This form is copyrighted and reprinted with permission from American Land Title Association®, 1828 L Street, N.W., Suite 705, Washington, DC 20036.

Trustee's Sale Guarantee (TSG)

In some states, including California, in the event of a borrower's default on a loan secured by real property utilizing a debt or security instrument called a deed of trust, a lender is allowed to foreclose without having to seek court approval. This is called nonjudicial foreclosure. The law prescribes how the foreclosure is to be conducted and the specific notices that must be provided to the parties involved. Parties under a deed of trust include the lender (called the **beneficiary**), the borrower (called the trustor), and the trustee (the party who represents and responds to instructions of the beneficiary). The student who is somewhat familiar with the traditional role of a trustee should understand that the trustee under a deed of trust has a much different relationship with the other parties than that of a traditional trustee. The beneficiary's trustee is not a neutral third party but instead works for and at the direction of the beneficiary. The **trustee's sale guarantee (TSG)** offered by the title insurer addresses the needs of a foreclosing lender through its trustee by providing public record information to individuals and entities who, under state law, must receive notice of the pending foreclosure.

A buyer purchasing a property from a lender that has acquired title through the foreclosure process may be advised to use the title company that issued the TSG because it may qualify for a reduced policy fee.

The Report   The TSG report provides the foreclosing trustee with the information necessary to process the trustee's foreclosure and guarantees the correctness of that information. It sets forth the record owners and lists all exceptions of record against the secured property. It provides the names of those who are to receive notices and the name of the newspaper in which the trustee must publish. The TSG is provided by a title company in the county where the property is located and alerts the trustee to the following matters:

- New owners

- Delinquent real estate taxes

- Notice of default recorded by a senior deed of trust. You should contact the senior beneficiary to determine if their loan is still delinquent

- Federal (IRS) tax liens recorded

- Bankruptcy

- Lis pendens. This provides constructive notice of pending litigation, the outcome of which will not be affected by the foreclosure.

- Notice of substandard dwelling

- Any irregularities noted therein

- The vesting of title to the estate or interest encumbered by the mortgage or deed of trust

- The encumbrances against the land

- The names and addresses of individuals and entities who must, under state law, receive notice of the foreclosure proceedings

- The newspaper qualified to public notice of the foreclosure proceedings

- The city or judicial district in which the land is located

Encumbrances   Encumbrances against a property consist of taxes, assessments and liens as well as building restrictions, encroachments, easements, and pending legal actions.

Off-record matters, those issues not been recorded by the county and therefore not of public record (e.g., zoning restrictions and proposed assessments) are not considered encumbrances.

■ HIGH LIABILITY TRANSACTIONS

Title companies offer a variety of title insurance policies. In some instances, due the type of the transaction or possible extraordinary potential liability to the title insurer, the title insurance company may have a senior title officer investigate and underwrite "high liability" policies. These are transactions that carry additional and higher risk to the title company and are more likely to be subject to claims, such as larger commercial properties and complex or higher-dollar transactions. Guidelines vary from company to company, but an example would be any policy that exceeds a given amount, such as $1 million or $5 million or more.

A search revealing major issues that could significantly increase the title company's risk or complex issues arising during the course of underwriting and that may be outside the experience level of the title officer and even a senior title officer may be referred to an advisory title officer (ATO) or even to the chief title officer (CTO). The ATO and the CTO typically have years of experience and the ability to formulate underwriting decisions that consider the balance of the degree of liability to the title company against the desire to service the needs of the customer, especially one with whom the title company has a long-term relationship. Some title companies may require that the CTO "sign off on" (approve) the policy even with the ATO's personal review of the transaction. Development and construction projects are those typical of high-liability transactions, especially if work has commenced before the title company's search and inspection.

■ SPECIAL TITLE CONSIDERATIONS

Title Needs Relative to Property Owner's Investment and Use

The American Land Title Association, through its Land Title Institute, provides an explanation for the title professional of various special title considerations. The information discussed in this section is in part taken from the ALTA publications, with permission, and offers a wealth of information for the title officer.

Title requirements of the property owner reflect the needs of the party obtaining coverage. A developer seeking to build a major improvement such as a shopping center or mall, for example, would require extended owner's coverage, which in turn would require an extended coverage survey. Most title insurance companies have title officers, including advisory title officers, who handle these types of transactions.

Endorsements   An ALTA policy may have additional protection coverage identified by other forms included with the policy and referred to as endorsements, which may include leaseholds, bankruptcies, eminent domain, Native American lands, tidelands, foreclosure probate, and others. These are available from all major title companies and address the other risks along with the additional protection.

Leaseholds   Some projects involve a buyer leasing the land under a long-term lease and then building an improvement on it. In some cases, an improvement may already exist, and the purchaser buys the improvement yet leases the land. Property may be leased up to 99 years under California law.

ALTA Leasehold Endorsements   ALTA developed a policy form intended to be used for leaseholds. The lessee's financial investment, relying on the lessor's capacity and condition of title to the property, can be protected by the expanded coverage for possible damages listed in the leasehold endorsement. The policy also makes it possible to insure complex transactions where an insured may acquire both fee ownership and leasehold interests in a single project with one policy. The endorsements only add to the coverage and apply only to the leasehold. As the costs of tenant improvements increase, prospective lessees are interested in the protection available to them through title insurance. New lessees usually assume (an always potentially dangerous move) that the owner has no defects in the title and is capable to legally convey a leasehold estate. However, covenants, easements, or other matters regarding the title to the property may exist that could affect the lessee's use of the land, even though the landlord's lease permits such use. If restrictions exist that prevent the lessee from using the property as intended, significant losses may occur unless the lessee has obtained protection from losses.

A title search of the leasehold property provides information about matters that might affect the title, relative to the lessee's intended use of the property and, equally important, the lessee's investment. Obtaining title insurance protection against certain damages provides the lessee with the comfort level to continue. Among the information the lessee would want to discover and that could affect use and investment are the following:

- Verify that the lessor the true owner of the property

- Confirm the lease valid and binding against the landlord

- No defect in the chain of landlord's title exists, except those indicated in a title report

- Also, except as specified in the title report, the leasehold estate is not encumbered by a superior lien or claim

- Approval as may be required by the lender or any party having an estate senior to the tenant have been obtained

- No covenants, conditions, or restrictions that prohibit or limit the tenant's proposed use of the premises, and no easements or other restrictions exist that may limit development or use of the leased premises

- The landlord has the right to grant the lessee legal access to the premises

- The owner's title as well as the lessee's leasehold title are marketable

Special Circumstances   Title issues that are especially unique may call for a title officer experienced in researching, evaluating, and rendering a decision regarding risk and coverage. ALTA and its Land Title Institute advise the title professional regarding the following:

- *Native American lands*. Many legal requirements apply to the leasing or collateralizing or hypothecating (borrowing against) Native American lands. Escrow instructions must provide for the Bureau of Indian Affairs (BIA) fees and approvals involved in the transfer. Lease terms are governed by the BIA and provide for a maximum term of 25 years for residential use with a provision to be renewed by another 25 years (except for the Palm Springs Reservation, Fort Mojave Reservation, and Colorado River Reservation, all of which allow a 99-year term lease).

- *Tidelands*. Tidelands, as discussed earlier, are lands located between the ordinary high-water and ordinary low-water lines of tidal waters. Rights to tideland property are often open to interpretation and quite complex. As such, only a senior title professional, such as an ATO or CTO, with considerable experience and knowledge regarding such rights, should be involved in a transaction involving tidelands.

- *Submerged lands.* Lands whose "shoreward" (against the land) boundaries coincide with the "seaward" (toward the sea) boundaries of tidelands are submerged lands. Since states and the federal government have disputed for years as to who has jurisdiction, even ownership, of these lands knowing who the real owner is of a certain area is critical, for example, to the oil company who wishes to drill or explore for oil. Generally, the United States, through the passage of certain laws, has granted ownership of land extending from and within a three-mile limit from the coast to the affected coastal state.

- *Cemetery lands.* Cemetery lands are perhaps among the most difficult and complex for the title insurer to research, with insurance coverage usually not offered because of the great number of individual owners and the rights of all others.

- *Dedication of lands to a government agency.* One cannot simply deed lands to a public agency, such as a city, county, or state, without the approval and acceptance of the public entity to which title is to be transferred.

- *Spurious title.* **Spurious title** to property, meaning false or erroneously acquired, occasionally is discovered after escrow closing. It could be a prior claim to title from another party, such as through adverse possession, and calls into question who the legitimate owner is. The title insurer may be faced with a claim by its insured against such title. To have a valid claim to title through adverse possession, the party must have enjoyed open and uninterrupted possession of the property for at least five years, in a manner that is hostile to the interests of the true owner, have paid the taxes, and claim title.

- *Eminent domain.* **Eminent domain** is the power of local, state, or federal government agencies to take private property for public use so long as the government pays just compensation. The government can exercise its power of eminent domain, called **condemnation**, even if the property owner does not wish to sell. This governmental power is found in the Fifth Amendment to the U.S. Constitution.

Only the government, and quasi-governmental entities (i.e., utilities), enjoy the power of eminent domain. These entities may use title companies to obtain information regarding owners of record to proceed with eminent domain and to acquire title from them.

The process is not automatic, nor does the condemning agency possess absolute power to merely take the land. As noted here, the property owner has the ability, and right, to challenge and contest the action. The following step-by-step process must be adhered to:

1. The government agency expresses interest in the property

2. A date to appraise the property is set

3. An environmental inspection may be scheduled, depending on the land

4. Appraisal of the property, including improvements, by agency-retained appraiser

5. Offer to purchase the property is made to the owner, together with summary of appraisal upon which offer to purchase is made

6. Notice of public hearing to adopt "resolution of necessity" to acquire property by eminent domain

7. Public hearing held to adopt "resolution of necessity" to acquire the property by eminent domain

8. Eminent domain case filed in court and served on property owner

9. Deposit by agency of the probable amount of just compensation is paid into court and motion by agency for early possession of the property

10. Discovery (i.e., depositions and document production) takes place in eminent domain action, and both the property owner and government hire appraisers to determine "fair market value" of the subject property

11. The property owner and government exchange their respective appraisers' reports

12. Final settlement offers and demands are exchanged (about 20 days before trial)

13. If settlement cannot be reached, trial of the eminent domain action takes place before a jury, whose job it is to determine "fair market value" of the subject property

14. Jury returns verdict and judgment entered

15. Government pays judgment within 30 days following entry of judgment and title to subject property transferred to the government

Bankruptcy

Under the Bankruptcy Reform Act of 1978, and as amended in 2005, title may or may not pass if the owner is in the process of **bankruptcy**. Title insurers examine the bankruptcy file to determine whether proper procedure has been followed for notification and protection of the creditors prior to disposition of the property by the bankrupt estate. A situation that arises quite often in a title insurance investigation is a transaction where an abstract of judgment has been recorded against a seller, and the seller has subsequently received a discharge of the debt in bankruptcy. The discharge of the debt itself does not remove the recorded judgment. It must be removed by a separate bankruptcy court order known as an "order avoiding lien." Therefore, unless removed, the judgment lien recorded prior to the bankruptcy can still be enforced against the real property, even if it has been sold or transferred to a third party. For this reason, a title company will not issue a policy without either a proper order avoiding lien from the bankruptcy court, or a release of the lien by the judgment creditor, which understandably is oftentimes difficult to obtain. The lien, however, will not attach to any property acquired by the debtor after the date the bankruptcy was discharged, and the title company would issue the policy without making an exception for it.

Foreclosure Under a Deed of Trust   In California, since the deed of trust is used almost exclusively by lenders, unless the foreclosing lender is entitled to a deficiency judgment, foreclosure begins with the notice of default filed and recorded. This is a relatively simple process taking about four months from the date the notice of default is filed to the date of the trustee's sale, which is the day on which the beneficiary's (lender's) trustee takes the property to sale.

Specifically, the process begins with the trustee filing and recording the notice of default (NOD). The NOD period lasts three months, after which if the borrower has not brought the loan current, the notice of sale (NOS) is filed by the trustee. The notice-of-sale term is 20 days. The borrower may pay the delinquent amount plus late charges during the first 15 days of the NOS term and reinstate the loan. The foreclosure action is then cancelled. If not brought current, during the final 5 days of the 20 day NOS term, in order to retain the property, the borrower must pay the loan off in its entirety. If not paid completely by the 20th day, the trustee conducts the sale of the property on the 21st day.

The escrow officer must be familiar with this foreclosure process and the time frame involved. If the homeowner in foreclosure has opened escrow late in the foreclosure process, time is definitely of the essence. The foreclosure process is explained further in Chapter 18.

Foreclosure Under a Trust Deed With Deficiency Judgment   If the lender is entitled to a deficiency judgment (see below) and wishes to pursue it, the lender must begin with a judicial foreclosure in superior court in the county where the property is located. A number of issues may affect the ability to transfer title in a timely manner. Judicial foreclosures can take longer to complete, jeopardizing a closing of the escrow. Once the property goes to and completes the foreclosure sale, the property is no longer owned by the seller.

Foreclosure Under a Mortgage   For those states using a mortgage instead of a trust deed as the security instrument, a foreclosing lender must proceed with a judicial foreclosure through the courts. Foreclosure under a mortgage allows for a deficiency judgment, as previously explained.

Deficiency Judgment   A lender who foreclosures judicially may be entitled to seek a **deficiency judgment**. A mortgagee (lender in a mortgage) or a beneficiary (lender in a trust deed) who receives less than the amount of the unpaid loan balance due at the time of the foreclosure sale may obtain a court judgment for the difference. The defaulting borrower in such a case has the **right of redemption** for up to one year after the foreclosure sale to buy the property back from whoever purchased it from the lender, or from the foreclosing lender if it has not resold the property. In most cases, if the property consists of one to four units, one of which is owner-occupied, and providing the loan was obtained to purchase the property, a lender under a deed of trust is prohibited from obtaining a deficiency judgment.

Probate   Probate is the legal process of handling the business affairs of a person who has died. Assets need to be distributed to the heirs, estate debts need to be paid, and any loose ends need to be looked after. Probate establishes whether a will is present. If the decedent left a will, probate determines the validity of it. It describes the identity of the heirs. Those who are named in a will to receive real property are called devisees. Persons who are to receive personal property, which includes monies, are called legatees. One function of probate is to pay creditors and taxes. It also ensures that the property is preserved and even maintained until the process is complete. No probate is required in the following circumstances:

- When one joint tenant dies and there are other living joint tenants, whether spouses or not, title to the property passes to the surviving joint tenant(s), even if another has been named in a will. An actual probate will be required upon the death of the remaining joint tenant.

- Community property (spouses only and domestic partnerships) and community property (original type) passes to the surviving spouse when one spouse dies. Unlike joint tenancy, spouses may will their share to someone other than the spouses who will survive them.

- Community property with right of survivorship passes to the surviving spouse when one spouse dies. As with joint tenancy, a will naming someone other than the surviving spouse is not valid.

■ For property in a small estate, where real property is valued at less than $150,000, a petition to determine succession to real property may be filed under Probate Code Section 13150.

— Separate property may be passed to a surviving spouse.

— If property is held in a living trust, a written agreement should appoint a trustee to manage, control, and distribute property during lifetime and after death. Probate is not required.

Life Estate   The right to use or occupy real property is granted to the person named in the life estate for the duration of that person's life. This is coupled by identifying another person, commonly a family member, who will acquire title upon the death of the person granted the life estate. Title may also return to the person giving or deeding the property (called a reversion) or to any other designated person or persons (e.g., surviving children or descendants [called a remainder]) upon the death of the specified person.

■ **EXAMPLE**   I grant a life estate to my mother for her life. Upon her death the property goes to my daughter.

Rules for probate venue (location where probate proceedings are to take place) are as follows:

■ If the decedent was a resident of California, the proceedings should be commenced in the county of residence at the time of death.

■ If the deceased was a nonresident of this state, the proceedings should be commenced in the county in California where the property was located. This should occur irrespective of the location where the individual died.

■ If the nonresident decedent leaves property in more than one county, the county in which proceedings are first commenced has jurisdiction.

Another form of probate is that which is technically referred to as a conservatorship or guardianship. This is a form of probate that involves minors. It also includes adults who are unable or lack the competency or capacity to make decisions to contract or otherwise manage their affairs.

Endorsements

In addition to the protection afforded by the above policies, additional protection is provided by other endorsements. For example, if there are multiple parcels involved in the transaction, the title company may provide for a contiguity endorsement to protect the buyer against the future possibility that parcels may be found to not be contiguous to one another. Other endorsements may include the following, as listed and as described by the American Land Title Association:

Off-Record Matters (Form 100)   This endorsement offers an explicit extension of coverage to an ALTA Extended Coverage Loan Policy by adding insurance for certain off-record matters. The coverage is extended to covenants, conditions, and restrictions (CC&Rs); encroachments; and the rights to use the land surface for mineral development. Form 100 also assures a lender that existing CC&Rs do not contain any enforceable reverter, right of re-entry, or power of termination. This endorsement is not issued in conjunction with policies covering raw land or construction loans.

Construction and Property Boundaries (Form 102.4)   This foundation endorsement ensures the lender that the foundations of the structure under construction are within the boundaries of the insured land and that the location of these foundations does not violate the CC&Rs.

Construction Encroachment (Form 102.5)   The form is the same as Form 102.4 with the addition of insurance that the foundations do not, at the date of endorsement, encroach upon any easements referred to in the policy.

Reverter, Right of Re-Entry and Power of Termination (Form 100.12)   Also used with ALTA policies, Form 100.12 assures a lender that existing CC&Rs do not contain any enforceable reverter, right of re-entry, or power of termination.

Mechanics' Liens and Construction Loan (Form 101)   A mechanic's lien endorsement issued only with a standard coverage policy insuring a construction loan deed of trust, it insures the lender against loss if a mechanic's lien establishes priority because of the prior commencement of the work on the improvement.

Mechanic's Lien, Construction to Permanent Loan (Form 101.2)   A mechanic's lien endorsement used with either an ALTA extended or standard coverage policy, it is issued after a notice of completion is recorded and is usually requested when a construction loan is exchanged for a permanent loan to the borrower or the loan is designed for sale to another lender.

Blanket Easement Protection (Form 103.1)   This is an encroachment endorsement used with ALTA or standard coverage policies that expands the coverage provided by a Form 100. It is issued when items listed in the preliminary report are "blanket" easements that cannot be precisely located.

Additional Loan Advances (Form 108.7 and 108.8) Both are used to insure the priority of additional advances secured by a deed of trust or mortgage. Form 108.7 is used with standard coverage policies. Form 108.8 is the ALTA version.

Designation of Address and Property Type (Form 116) An address endorsement used with ALTA policies, this form designates the street address of the land insured and specifies the type of improvement on said land.

Condominium Coverage (Form 116.2) This address endorsement, used with either an ALTA extended or standard coverage policy, insures an interest in a condominium.

■ CHAPTER 5 QUIZ

1. An ALTA extended coverage loan policy differs from the standard coverage policy by offering

   a. insurance against matters not of public record.

   b. a smaller deductible.

   c. fire insurance.

   d. flood insurance.

2. A lender who discovers that the borrower's property has no access to a public street would be protected under

   a. a CLTA policy.

   b. a LCTA policy.

   c. an ALTA extended coverage policy.

   d. could not be covered.

3. Conditions that would *NOT* be covered under an ALTA policy include

   a. defects such as liens created by the insured.

   b. defects known to the insured but not specified in writing to the underwriter.

   c. defects, but no loss or damage is suffered by the insured.

   d. all of these.

4. The CLTA standard title policy is

   a. seldom issued.

   b. the least policy issued.

   c. the most frequently type of policy issued.

   d. none of these.

5. The CLTA standard title policy

   a. never includes any coverage for off-record matters.

   b. includes coverage for all off-record matters.

   c. includes coverage for forgery and fraud.

   d. is the most expensive.

6. Conditions that would *NOT* be covered under the CLTA policy include

   a. defects such as liens created by the insured.

   b. defects known to the insured but not specified in writing to the underwriter.

   c. defects, but no loss or damage is suffered by the insured.

   d. all of these.

7. The additional coverage offered by an ALTA policy includes which of the following?

   a. Matters disclosed by a physical inspection of the premises not previously disclosed by public record

   b. Matters disclosed by inquiry of the occupants of the property, which might disclose off-record matters

   c. Matters disclosed by a current survey

   d. All of these

8. Encumbrances against a property consist of

   a. taxes, assessments, and liens, as well as building restrictions, encroachments, easements, and pending legal actions.

   b. off-record matters, such as zoning restrictions and proposed assessments.

   c. both a and b.

   d. neither a nor b.

9. Eminent domain is

    a. the process whereby a citizen claims title to public land.

    b. exercisable by the government only if the land owner agrees.

    c. the power of the government or a quasi-public agency to take private property for a public use upon payment of just compensation.

    d. the ability of a public agency to take private land with no compensation paid.

10. The trust deed is

    a. seldom used by lenders in California.

    b. almost exclusively used by lenders in California.

    c. used to convey title but without representations of encumbrances on title.

    d. used to convey title from one spouse to another.

CHAPTER SIX

CONTRACTS

■ KEY TERMS

bilateral contract
Department of
    Housing and Urban
    Development (HUD)
executory contract
express contract
hazard insurance
high fire hazard
homeowners
    associations

implied contracts
natural hazard reports
ordinances
parties to the contract
Real Estate Settlement
    Procedures Act
    (RESPA)
severity zone
statute of frauds

Truth in Lending Act
    (TILA)
unenforceable contract
unilateral contract
void and voidable
    contract

■ LEARNING OBJECTIVES

Upon completing this chapter, you will be able to

■ understand the essential elements of contracts and the parties involved;

■ understand the difference between bilateral and unilateral contracts, express and implied contracts, executory and executed contracts, void and voidable contracts and unenforceable contracts;

■ understand the essential provisions of the federal Truth in Lending Act (Reg. Z) and Real Estate Settlement Procedures Act;

■ identify and explain the escrow procedures relating to homeowners associations;

■ understand the basic Department of Housing and Urban Development (HUD) disclosures and reports; and

■ identify and explain required government disclosures and reports as they pertain to the escrow holder's responsibilities.

■ CONTRACTUAL RELATIONSHIPS

In order to be valid, an escrow requires a valid contract. As the "holder of the stakes," or "stakeholder," in a sale or loan transaction, the escrow officer, under direction of the principals, must obtain the pertinent information from which the contract of transfer and/or hypothecation in the form of an instruction will be prepared. Existence of a contractual relationship, however, does not necessarily mean the contract is enforceable, a matter with which the escrow officer is often faced during the escrow. Escrow instructions may be prepared but not signed by all the parties, or negotiations may continue during the escrow without a mutual agreement over some aspect of the transaction that surfaced after escrow opened; myriad issues may arise that may dissolve the contract and threaten the escrow. Understanding the basics of contracts is essential so that the escrow holder can provide the necessary level of service to the parties while, at the same time, recognize when the escrow process cannot continue.

What Is a Contract?

Article I, Section 10, of the U.S. Constitution protects the individual right to contract with the words "No State shall . . . pass any . . . law impairing the obligations of Contracts." Many states have similar laws. A contract is an agreement between two or more parties. There must be a "meeting of the minds" to the extent that both parties clearly understand the terms and the contract sets forth the understanding in equally clear terms. The contract may call for the parties to either do or not do something. Generally, the law of contracts does not come from statutes passed by Congress or by state legislatures; it rather is founded in common law, with court decisions dating back to precolonial English courts. The law of contracts is also influenced by the Uniform Commercial Code (UCC), with which the escrow officer will become involved in many transactions, such as those involving bulk sales, liquor stores, and others.

The difficulty the escrow holder encounters relative to **parties to the contract** that is the foundation for the escrow is the fact that it is not uncommon for matters the parties have not agreed upon to remain unresolved at the opening of escrow. Therefore, while the contract exists for those issues the parties have agreed to, there are others that must be resolved and agreement reached before escrow may close.

Express Contracts

An **express contract** is one that has been put into words, whether written or verbal.

Implied Contracts

An **implied contract** is one that has not been verbalized or written but has been implied by the actions of the parties. The act of one party performing an act for the benefit for another party who does not refuse or reject it constitutes an implied contract.

■ **EXAMPLE**   An arriving hotel guest pulls up to the hotel entrance and next to a sign that says "Registration" and another sign saying "Valet Parking, $20." He exits the car, leaving the keys in the car. A bellman takes his luggage from the trunk and hands him a ticket. A parking valet enters the car and drives off. Neither the valet nor the guest said a word. Certainly an implied contract has been created. The sign clearly specified the service offered and the price to be paid for it. By allowing the valet to drive off with the car, the guest agreed to the contract.

Unilateral Contracts

A **unilateral contract** occurs when one party to the contract promises to perform, but the other party or parties do not. Only if the others, in turn, perform as well do the promises form a contract. An example of a unilateral contract would be a person offering to clean a home in exchange for a given price. Until the home owner responds, the contract is unilateral.

Bilateral Contracts

A **bilateral contract** occurs when a promise to perform made by one party is met by an equal promise to perform offered by another party. Typically, most contracts fall into this category. If a seller promises and agrees to sell real property at a specified price, and a buyer promises and agrees to pay the purchase price, the contract is bilateral.

Executory Contracts

A valid contract yet to be performed by one or more of the principals is said to be an **executory contract**. Until the buyer of the real property, having agreed to purchase it at the given price, actually pays the money and completes the purchase and the seller delivers the deed, the contract is an executory contract.

Executed Contracts

A contract that has been performed by all principals is said to have been executed. After the money to purchase the real property has been paid to the seller, and the buyer has received the deed, the contract has been executed.

Enforceability   In order to be enforceable, a contract must comply with the law. The fact that a legal requirement is not present doesn't necessarily make the contract void, however. A contract may be voidable but not void, and a contract may be unenforceable but again not void.

Void Contracts   A **void contract** does not exist; for example, all elements of the contract are present except consideration. Therefore, even if it is in writing, there is no contract. A contract is also void if it involves an illegal act, meaning it cannot be enforced.

Voidable Contracts   A **voidable contract** is one that is valid but not enforceable if it is rejected by one of the parties, typically the party who stands to be damaged as a result of the contract lacking one or more essential elements. For example, one party to the contract violated the promise or condition or has taken advantage of the terms, though the other party may still proceed if desiring to do so.

Unenforceable Contracts   Some contracts are **unenforceable contracts**, even if they are not void or voidable. For example, perhaps the statute of limitations has expired, making an otherwise and previously enforceable contract now unenforceable. Additionally, contracts involving the sale of real estate, or rental or lease agreements for longer than one year must be in writing to be enforceable.

Elements of a Contract

To be valid and effective, four specific elements must be present in any contract:

- Mutual consent—meeting of the minds
- Capacity—of legal age and be competent
- Consideration—something of value to be given
- Lawful purpose—cannot be for an illegal act or purpose

Mutual Consent   There must be a "meeting of the minds." A contract must contain a promise to perform with an offer and acceptance of the promise.

■   **EXAMPLE**   In a land contract, a *vendee* (the term used to describe the buyer under a land contract) promises to pay the *vendor* (the term used to describe the seller under a land contract) a certain amount of money, either over time on a specified basis or at the conclusion of the term of the contract, while the vendor promises to allow the vendee to occupy, enjoy, and use the real property. Of course, the promise to perform must be legal and enforceable.

An offer is not valid or binding until it is accepted.

An offer may be terminated by lapse of time if it includes an expiration date, by the death or incapacity of one of the parties, by revocation by the offeror (effective as soon as the offeree receives the notice), or by rejection by the offeree (and as with revocation, rejection is effective as soon as the offeror receives the notice).

An offer must have definite terms and express the intent to enter into a contract.

Capacity to Contract   The parties must be legally capable and competent of performing the contractual relationship. The following paragraphs describe the elements of capacity.

Competency   The person must be competent. A person must be declared incompetent by a court in order to lack capacity to contract. A mentally ill person may appear to not have the capacity to enter into a contract, though the extent of the person's incapacity may not be easy to determine. Additionally, a person under the influence of alcohol or drugs may be determined to have been incompetent at the time of the agreeing to the contract.

Individuals   The person must be of legal age, typically 18 years or older. A minor may acquire title to real property but may not dispose of it. A contract by a minor to acquire or hypothecate real property is void, for personal property it is voidable. An exception to the age requirement applies if the minor has been emancipated, either by court action or through one of two other actions as specified as noted in the next paragraph, in which case the minor has the legal capacity to buy, sell, lease, encumber exchange, or transfer an interest in real or personal property.

An emancipated minor is one of the following:

- Is or has been married

- Is currently on active duty in the armed forces of the United States. One who has been discharged from military service if under legal age is no longer emancipated.

- Has received a court declaration of emancipation

Emancipated minors must also demonstrate that they are

- living separately and apart from parents or guardian with their consent, and

- managing their own financial affairs with income from lawful sources.

Corporations If the principal is a corporation, the person having legal authority to sign on behalf of the corporation must provide written evidence of that authority, usually in the form of a corporate resolution or contained in the articles of incorporation and typically signed by the secretary of the corporation.

Trusts If the principal is a trust, documentation is required to confirm the authority of the person signing on behalf of the trust.

Partnerships If the principal is a general partnership, a statement of partnership usually must be provided to the title or escrow company. If the principal is a limited partnership, it will have been recorded with the secretary of state of California, and that document will serve as the authority.

Limited Liability Companies (LLC) If the principal is a limited liability company (LLC), a copy of the articles of organization filed with the secretary of state of California will serve as the authority.

Consideration The agreement must include consideration, something of value, usually cash or equity in an asset, such as in an exchange of real property. Contract law requires the consideration to be sufficient to bind the parties. The consideration need not necessarily be tangible, with the promise itself the consideration.

Lawful Purpose The purpose or intent of the contract must be lawful at the time the contract was agreed to. A contract is void if it violates or intends to violate the law. Even if the intention is lawful, any contract that is contrary to what is considered public policy and good morals is void and unenforceable. For example, John owns a property that he agrees to sell to Sam. John's wife is also on the title to the property but is out of the country. She will not return for a considerable period of time, plus she is unaware of the John's intention to sell. John tells Sam that he will sell the property to him, and at a significantly reduced price, but only if Sam agrees have someone forge Martha's signature on all required documents.

Statute of Frauds

The **statute of frauds** specifies which contracts must be in writing and signed. Some unwritten contracts are nonetheless still valid and enforceable. For example, although a listing agreement between a seller and a real estate broker must be in writing, a verbal agreement between two real estate brokers to share a commission is a valid contract. It is always wise to have a written contract, whether required or not by the statute of frauds (because it eliminates confusion or misunderstanding of the agreement between or among the parties). The following contracts used in real estate transactions are among those required to be in writing to be enforceable:

- *Purchase agreement and joint escrow instructions.* Any contract for the sale, exchange, or other transfer of real estate must be in writing.

- *Lease agreement.* A lease for real property that exceeds one year must be in writing.

- *Listing agreement.* Any listing agreement, regardless of the term, must be in writing.

■ PARTIES TO THE TRANSACTION

In addition to the principals involved in a real estate transaction, a number of other persons or entities participate, such as real estate agents, escrow personnel, a loan officer and support staff, title company personnel, insurance agents, pest control operators, homeowners associations, and others, including those who may have liens against the property or judgments against the principals.

Real Estate Agents

Interaction and communication between the real estate agents and the escrow officer should be frequent to assure a proper coordination of the closing. The role of the real estate agent, as discussed in this chapter, reveals the extent to which both the escrow holder and the real estate agent must interact during the escrow and the importance of an understanding of the purchase agreement's provisions as they relate to the escrow.

Escrow and Broker Relations   To help escrow proceed smoothly, efficiently, and effectively, it is necessary to establish the preferences of each party to the transaction and escrow process, including the manner of providing and taking escrow instructions, client relations, the delivery of documents to the respective parties and obtaining signatures, processing the loan and communicating with the lender, closing, and delivery of the principals funds.

Disclosures   The escrow holder should have an understanding of the requirements a real estate agent has to provide a buyer and a seller concerning certain activities and disclosures in which the escrow holder may become indirectly involved. One such requirement that applies to one-to-four unit residential properties is to not only have the seller of a property disclose all known defects but also have the agents perform a diligent visual inspection and disclose any defect the seller has not offered. It has become almost a universal standard of practice to have a home warranty provided to the buyer of the property. As with many fees, a buyer may be charged for services related to the purchase of a property and the vendor may submit the invoice for those services to the escrow holder. While it is the responsibility of the buyer or the agent to secure the home warranty plan and arrange for billing, the escrow holder may be asked to pay the vendor from buyer's funds placed into escrow.

Title Insurance Companies

The title insurance professional works hand in hand with the escrow holder from the beginning to the end of the transaction. It starts with the title company's preliminary title search and report, which is delivered to the escrow holder, and ends with the title company's receipt of the buyers funds, which is forwarded to escrow for disbursement.

Independent Escrow   The independent escrow company may, for example, offer a more convenient location for the real estate agent's or lender's sphere of business. Of course relationships are important, and the agents or loan officers and even some consumers may have a longstanding relationship with a particular escrow officer or marketing representative. As far as fees are concerned, the marketplace is always an equalizer, with fees typically and reasonably within a satisfactory range.

Title Company Escrow   One advantage of using a title company escrow is the obvious: both title and escrow services may occur under the same roof, offering a potentially more efficient coordination between the two services. Relationships may be equally important. Unlike title operations that may not involve much, if any, direct communication between the real estate agent, loan officer, consumer, and the title officer, the title company's escrow officer interacts frequently with them, just as their independent counterparts do.

> ## Pro-Tip: Relationship Is Key
>
> When it comes to deciding whether to use an independent escrow company or a title insurer's or broker's escrow company, no one can say that using one or the other is better. It is usually the relationship or a referral that brings a real estate agent, a loan officer, or a consumer to recommend a service provider to a buyer, a seller, or a borrower. Remember, the real estate licensee is the escrow holder's best customer.

Lenders Communication between the escrow officer and the lender's staff becomes critical as loan processing progresses. The escrow officer must be familiar with lenders' loan processing, document, and funding requirements, as well as state and federal legal requirements. Some escrow companies, and most title companies, have lenders' units, which only do loan escrows, title searching, and underwriting. It is conceivable, in fact, for a title company to have one lender unit staffed by both escrow and title personnel, providing efficiency for both the title company and the lender. Some lenders do their own escrows, with only an outside title company involved (see "Loan Processing" in this chapter).

Loan programs and lenders are regulated by government agencies and are subject to limitations, restrictions, and disclosures, many of which involve the escrow holder. These government guidelines and lender requirements are discussed in length in later chapters as well as in "Government Agencies" in this chapter.

Lien Claimants The title company's search will reveal any outstanding liens against any of the principals personally and against the property. The preliminary title report will exclude these from protection, which means a clear title cannot be delivered until they are resolved and removed. The title and escrow officers may require proof from the courts that they have been removed and released. It is a common practice to allow judgment liens to be paid through escrow, with the escrow officer disbursing the funds. The same would apply to IRS and property tax liens. Note: In practice most escrow and title professionals have discovered that it is usually more likely for an IRS lien to be negotiated for removal, if at all, than one levied by the State of California. Once funds are disbursed and the judgment liens are paid, the escrow officer would record a satisfaction of judgment form or a release of mechanic's lien form.

Structural Pest Control Companies

The escrow process involving especially, but not limited to, one-to-four unit residential properties typically requires a structural pest control inspection—commonly but incorrectly called a termite report. Structural pest control is the control of a variety of household pests, including wood-destroying pests such as termites, rodents, and others. Structural pest control services involve the identification of the presence of these pests and infestations, and preparing reports as required by the state of California. The reports include recommendations to eliminate or mitigate the problems and must provide either estimates or bids for all work to be performed, The reports also indicate exactly which chemicals or other procedures to be employed to accomplish the work required.

A homebuyer may or may not require a pest control inspection; however, if financing is being obtained, the buyer's lender may require one. For example, if the buyer is obtaining an FHA or a VA loan, an inspection is usually required. The escrow holder will not be required to obtain an inspection report unless required by the lender or part of the required inspections as indicated in the purchase agreement and joint escrow instructions. While it is not the responsibility of the escrow holder to provide recommendations to the buyers regarding any part of the purchase terms and agreement, if asked whether a pest control inspection should be performed (e.g., a buyer may believe it's only necessary to order an inspection for older properties), the escrow holder should advise the buyers to ask their agent or to seek legal counsel. As background information for the escrow holder who may not be aware of the nature of certain pests, termites are like most flying insects in that they swarm and easily move from one property to another. Therefore, the age of a property has little to do with the possible presence of certain pests.

The structural pest control company is accountable to both the buyer and the seller, regardless of who orders and pays for the inspection. It must furnish the person who ordered the inspection with a copy of the report within 10 working days. Under Section 1099 of the California Civil Code, the seller usually delivers copies of the inspection reports to the buyer through escrow. If there is any question about the reports, the buyer should contact the company that made the inspection and/or performed the work. It is not the escrow holder's responsibility to order the inspection; it is the duty of the escrow holder in a real estate transaction that requires a termite clearance to deliver the structural pest control report to the appropriate parties for review and approval.

Pest Control Report   The report consists of two parts (see Figure 6.1).

Part I or Section I, Corrective Work   The inspection report will include evidence of any wood-destroying pests (such as termites or wood-boring beetles), fungus, and the resulting structural damage that is visible and accessible on the date of inspection and that require treatment to eradicate, which may involve toxic gas treatment requiring the property to be vacated and "tented," treating affected areas with chemicals or via some other nontoxic method.

Part II or Section II, Preventive Work   Conditions that are not presently affected but which could lead to future infestations, such as excessive moisture, earth-to-wood contact, and faulty grade levels are also identified on the report. Recommendations are made for treatment or repair in the report.

State Filing   When a structural pest control report is completed on residential property, a copy must be filed with the state Structural Pest Control Board in Sacramento.

Second Opinion   Occasionally, the party responsible for the pest control work will seek a second opinion to find a lower bid to perform corrective work. Each report must be delivered to all parties to the transaction, including escrow. The parties must agree which report is to be used and indicate that to escrow.

Notice of Work Completed and Not Completed   After the parties agree to the work to be performed and who will pay the cost, the work is commenced. Usually, it must be performed before escrow closes, though occasionally that's not practical. A lender may allow the escrow to close but require the escrow holder to withhold the cost of the work, plus an additional amount from the proceeds, until the work has been completed. Upon completion of the work, the pest control company will issue a report (Standard Notice of Work Completed and Not Completed; see figure 6.2).

FIGURE 6.1

Structural Pest Control Inspection Report
(California state approved forms)

WOOD DESTROYING PESTS AND ORGANISMS INSPECTION REPORT

Building No.	Street	City	Zip	Date of Inspection	Number of Pages

Ordered by:	Property Owner and/or Party of Interest:	Report sent to:

COMPLETE REPORT ☐   LIMITED REPORT ☐   SUPPLEMENTAL REPORT ☐   REINSPECTION REPORT ☐

General Description:	Inspection Tag Posted:
	Other Tags Posted:

An inspection has been made of the structure(s) shown on the diagram in accordance with the Structural Pest Control Act. Detached porches, detached steps, detached decks and any other structures not on the diagram were not inspected.

Subterranean Termites ☐   Drywood Termites ☐   Fungus / Dryrot ☐   Other Findings ☐   Further Inspection ☐

If any of the above boxes are checked, it indicates that there were visible problems in accessible areas. Read the report for details on checked items.

Inspected by: _____ **State License No.** _____ **Signature**_____

You are entitled to obtain copies of all reports and completion notices on this property reported to the Structural Pest Control Board during the preceding two years. To obtain copies contact: Structural Pest Control Board, 2005 Evergreen Street, Suite 1500, Sacramento, California, 95815.

NOTE: Questions or problems concerning the above report should be directed to the manager of the company. Unresolved questions or problems with services performed may be directed to the Structural Pest Control Board at (916) 561-8708, (800) 737-8188 or www.pestboard.ca.gov.   43M-41 (REV. 10/01)

FIGURE 6.2
Standard Notice of Pest Control Work Completed and Not Completed

STANDARD NOTICE OF WORK COMPLETED AND NOT COMPLETED

NOTICE - All recommendations may not have been completed - See below - Recommendations not completed.
This form is prescribed by the Structural Pest Control Board.

Building No.	Street	City	Zip	Date of Completion

Ordered By:	Property Owner and/or Party of Interest:	Completion Sent To:

The following recommendations on the above designated property, as outlined in Wood Destroying Pests and Organisms Inspection Report dated _____ **have been and/or have not been completed.**

Recommendations completed by this firm that are in accordance with the Structural Pest Control Board's Rules and Regulations:

Recommendations completed by this firm that are considered secondary and substandard measures under Section 1992 of the Structural Pest Control Board's Rules and Regulations including person requesting secondary measure:

Cost of work completed:

Cost: $ _____
Inspection Fee: $ _____
Other: $ _____
Total: $ _____

Recommendations not completed by this firm:

Estimated Cost $ _____

Remarks:

Signature _____

You are entitled to obtain copies of all reports and completion notices on this property reported to the Board during the preceding two years upon payment of a search fee to: Structural Pest Control Board, 2005 Evergreen Street, Suite 1500, Sacramento, California, 95815.
NOTE: Questions or problems concerning the above report should be directed to the manager of this company. Unresolved questions or problems with services performed may be directed to the Structural Pest Control Board at (916) 561-8708, (800) 737-8188 or www.pestboard.ca.gov. 43M-44 (Rev.10/01)

Escrow Responsibility   The escrow officer must be informed as to the corrective work to be completed so an accurate accounting of the allocation of cost between the buyer and the seller may be provided to them.

Hazard Insurance Companies

An integral part of most real estate transactions involves the buyer's securing a **hazard insurance** policy to protect the property, and its contents, from potential loss due to fire or other hazards. If a real property transaction involves financing, the lender will require the buyer to obtain adequate hazard insurance protection. Hazard insurance policies are commonly referred to as fire insurance but actually include more perils than simply fire. They also include liability (see "Insurance Packages or All-inclusive Policies" in this chapter). If the property is a common-interest development (CID), such as a condominium, the buyer will usually not be required to purchase an insurance policy because the property will typically be covered under the association's master policy, a copy of which must be delivered to escrow and the lender (see "Homeowners Association—Master Insurance Policy" in this chapter). The buyer paying in cash would be well advised to voluntarily obtain insurance protection or the investment could literally go up in smoke. Note that some CIDs, such as a planned development (PD; formerly called planned unit development [PUD]), require individual hazard insurance.

Earthquake protection is usually not a requirement of the lender, but the buyer or the refinancing homeowner may want to explore the cost and coverage of obtaining such additional protection. The escrow officer will become involved in the process, communicating with the buyer or the homeowner's insurance agent and company to ensure that the insurance policy meets the lender's requirements and to provide an accurate accounting for payment of any premium due at closing. Communicating with the insurance agent early in the escrow process is important to avoid a delay in closing, especially for purchase transactions (and even more especially if the buyer is a first-time homebuyer).

Insurance Packages or All-Inclusive Policies   Insurance policies available to the buyer or the homeowner are often all-inclusive, providing not only protection against loss from fire and damage but also with extended coverage protection applying to losses due to liability, lost rents, accidents on the property, earthquake, and floods. The Federal Emergency Management Agency (FEMA) has prepared maps indicating flood zones throughout the United States, and a property located within a specified flood zone may be required by the lender to obtain flood insurance, as explained in this chapter under "Government Agencies." A buyer obtaining a rental property will most likely obtain an insurance policy that includes certain additional coverage relating to investment properties, such as loss of rents due to the property being inhabitable as a result of damage caused by some covered hazard.

Exclusions to Coverage   Most insurance policies will include exclusions to coverage, such as earthquakes, flood, and mudslide. Separate policies must be obtained to include protection for these perils. Lenders almost never require earthquake insurance protection as part of the loan conditions.

Homeowners Associations for Common-Interest Developments (CID)

Common interest developments (CID), which include property types such as condominiums, in California require a **homeowners association.** In California, the Davis-Stirling Act is the law that governs common-interest developments. Escrow professionals should possess a basic understanding of Davis-Stirling as it relates to their duties. First, exactly what is a common-interest development? It is important for escrow professionals to understand the difference between the "form of ownership" of a property and the "type of property." One often confusing real estate concept is the CID. It is a form of ownership, not a type of property or construction. A CID may take form as condominium, planned development, community apartment, or stock cooperative.

Example: Town House

A condominium could be of town-house design and construction, which is a multistory dwelling. Not uncommonly, many people, including real estate professionals, think of town houses as always being condominiums or planned developments. While oftentimes, as a form of ownership, it is indeed a CID, the term *town house* refers only to its design and construction. Perhaps the distinction is easier to understand when realizing that apartment buildings are frequently of town-house design and, in fact, commonly referred to as town-house apartments, but they are not CIDs.

In each of these CID cases, a homeowners association (HOA) will exist. In fact Davis-Stirling requires such and regulates its activities, including collecting, disbursing, and accounting for funds that it collects from homeowners. Referred to as membership dues, these funds, which the HOA usually collects monthly from the property owners, are used to pay expenses incurred in maintaining the exterior and common areas of the property. Such maintenance typically includes sweeping and cleaning, landscaping, pool maintenance, and other "housekeeping" activities. The monthly dues do not include funds for the replacement of components that fail. The HOA maintains a separate reserve for these extraordinary expenses or to replace major components of the building, if necessary. Such major expenses include garage gates, elevators, stairways, pool equipment, roofs, and other items.

Escrow's Role   It is the responsibility of the HOA, not the escrow holder, to comply with Davis-Stirling in accommodating a homeowner's request to receive financial documentation and other documents from the HOA, including a sale escrow. Under the law, the HOA has 10 days to provide the requested documentation. When delivered by the HOA, the documentation is placed into the hands of the escrow holder, on behalf of the seller, to deliver to a buyer to review in accordance with the typical terms of a purchase agreement and corresponding escrow instructions. In addition to being the "delivery agent," the escrow holder determines the status of assessment liens or those assessments pending to be imposed, if any, to be certain they are not in arrears and to provide disclosure to the buyers and to the lender. At escrow closing, dues and assessments may be required to be prorated between the parties.

Delivery of Bylaws   Obtaining and delivering a copy of the HOA bylaws and restrictions along with a copy of the current financial statement and annual budget to the buyers may be services requested of the escrow holder, though the actual duty and responsibility rests with the seller. The escrow holder will also request an HOA certification to be completed and delivered. Under the Davis-Stirling Act, the HOA must comply within 10 business days of the date of the request.

Pro-Tip: Escrow Holder Checklist Reminder

Remember, the ten day time limit applies to delivery to the seller, not to the buyer. An HOA is in compliance with Davis-Stirling if documents are delivered by it to the escrow holder on behalf of the seller within the ten day time limit. It is up to the seller to then deliver to the buyer, however the escrow holder may be instructed by the seller to perform delivery.

Disclosure of Assessments   While the disclosure of assessments pending or currently due is the responsibility of the seller, the escrow holder usually communicates with HOA management or a representative to gather all required HOA items. Pending assessments may run into the tens of thousands of dollars, so it's essential to obtain this information as early as possible in the escrow.

Master Insurance Policy   As mentioned, condominiums are subject to a master insurance policy. The condominium HOAs will be asked to provide a copy of the master insurance policy to the seller and, in turn, from the seller to the escrow holder to deliver to the buyer's lender, if any. A buyer is not obligated to obtain a separate hazard insurance policy because the master policy provides the necessary protection required by the lender. The buyer, however, may wish to secure a separate homeowners policy for coverage protection to the interior and contents similar to a renter's policy because these items are excluded from coverage in the association's master policy.

■ GOVERNMENT AGENCIES

The escrow holder interacts either directly or indirectly with a number of government agencies and their requirements, regulations, and restrictions. These agencies may impose fees, require certain disclosures or reports from or to the parties, and require the escrow holder to process these on behalf of the principals.

It is important, therefore, for the escrow holder to be knowledgeable of matters that pertain to a particular transaction. During the escrow process, it may be necessary to prepare additional or supplemental escrow instructions to address these, as well as to account for fees that may be required along with the reports. There are customarily more disclosures and reports required for transactions involving one-to-four unit residential properties, such as those described in the following paragraphs.

Zoning and Building Permits

Many cities have ordinances that require a report to be acknowledged and delivered before the transfer of real property, indicating when the initial building permit was issued and any approved modifications to the structure since then. The primary purpose is to protect the consumer from acquiring a "nonconforming" structure, such as improvements performed without appropriate permits or illegal conversions, including patios, garages, or unpermitted apartment conversions (e.g., converting a four-unit apartment building into five units). Apartment conversions that fail to comply with California's Uniform Housing Code can result in additional problems for both the buyer and the seller. The responsible party for delivery of the report may be either the principals or the escrow holder.

Example: A Warning to the Apartment Buyer

Henry Jackman, a real estate licensee, listed a five-unit apartment building for sale with a list price of $1,500,000. In advertising the property, he indicated that the sales price reflected a value of $300,000 per unit, quite reasonable but yet reflecting fair market value for a five-unit property in that neighborhood. Henry had sold the property to the seller 10 years earlier and was, or should have been, familiar with the property.

Real estate agent Bob Bassett represented a buyer interested in making an offer on the listed property. The property appeared to be in excellent condition, reasonably priced, and, above all else, was fully rented. In reviewing the information provided by the listing agent regarding the property's financial data, Bob discovered that all five units were under leases with no less than one year remaining. The property was unique in that it was located in a neighborhood composed of mostly single-family homes and a scattering of fourplexes. It was the only five-unit property in the area and as such would command greater revenues than all the others.

Bob's buyer paid full price for the property, paying "all cash." During the escrow process, Bob failed to research the existence of any post-original-construction building permits. Plus time was of the essence. The seller had asked for, and had received from the buyer, a short 21-day escrow.

Limiting his research to a visual inspection during which he moved rather quickly from unit to unit, Bob failed to note any matter that could have been a concern to the buyer. Bob's buyer had indicated that he was relying on Bob's knowledge and skills to do whatever was necessary not only to appropriately inspect both the physical and financial aspects of the property but to also do whatever was necessary to close escrow in accordance with the agreement, namely within 21 days.

Two weeks into the escrow, the escrow officer handling the transaction while reviewing the contract between the buyer and the seller—(the California Association of REALTORS® Residential Income Purchase Agreement and Joint Escrow Instructions (RIPA))—noted the omission in paragraph 14 of the "number of legally approved units." He asked the listing agent about this omission, and the agent said to address it by including in the "Supplemental Instructions," to be signed by both buyer and seller, that the property consists of five units.

The buyer, who declined Bob's advice to obtain an appraisal that might have alerted him to the lack of permits, signed the Supplemental Instructions, as did the seller.

After escrow closed, the buyer employed ABC Property Management to manage the units for him. In making the initial inspection of the property, the property manager, a real estate broker long experienced in selling and managing income properties, became concerned about the fifth unit. It clearly was different from the other four units and seemed smaller. As a result of the inspection, the buyer discovered that the unit was not only built without permits but also did not meet the Uniform Housing Code's minimum square feet required of a legal dwelling unit. His five-unit building was legally only four, because of both the permit issue and the housing code.

While mistakes were made by both parties, the results of a subsequent lawsuit brought by the buyer against the seller and both licensees included compensation to the buyer in the amount of $300,000, plus damages, the value of one unit based on the sales price paid.

Natural Hazard Reports

The Natural Hazards Disclosure Act of California requires that the seller of real property and their agent provide any prospective buyer with a Natural Hazard Disclosure Statement (see Figure 6.3) when the property being sold lies within one or more state-mapped hazard areas.

California Civil Code Section 1103 may require the completion and delivery to a buyer of the Natural Hazard Disclosure Statement (NHD) revealing the existence of any natural hazard. The requirement applies to any sale, exchange, land contract, or lease with an option to buy any one-to-four-unit residential property (including manufactured homes), whether the transaction requires the completion and delivery to the buyer of the Natural Hazard Transfer Disclosure Statement (*Cal. Civ. Code* § 1102) and whether the property is located in one of six designated hazard zones.

The State of California has a standardized reporting format for sellers and their agents to use in order to comply with the law. Sellers and their agents may, and are advised to, use an independent company to perform specific services and to prepare required **natural hazard reports** on their behalf, such as a licensed engineer, land surveyor, geologist, or expert in natural hazard discovery to prepare the report for them.

The NHD report must be signed by all parties before the close of escrow. It is illegal for agents to require the seller to use a particular disclosure company. If the company chosen is either affiliated with the real estate company or has a controlled broker agreement with it, that fact must be disclosed to the parties in writing and be reflected in the escrow instructions or supplemental instructions. Figure 6.3 is an example of the required format for the natural hazard disclosure statement (NHDS).

FIGURE 6.3

Sample Natural Hazard Disclosure Statement

California Natural Hazard Disclosure Statement

This statement applies to the following property: _____

The transferor and his or her agent(s) or a third-party consultant disclose the following information with the knowledge that even though this is not a warranty, prospective transferees may rely on this information in deciding whether and on what terms to purchase the subject property. Transferor hereby authorizes any agent(s) representing any principal(s) in this action to provide a copy of this statement to any person or entity in connection with any actual or anticipated sale of the property.

The following are representations made by the transferor and his or her agent(s) based on their knowledge and maps drawn by the state and federal governments. This information is a disclosure and is not intended to be part of any contract between the transferee and transferor.

THIS REAL PROPERTY LIES WITHIN THE FOLLOWING HAZARDOUS AREA(S):

A SPECIAL FLOOD HAZARD AREA (Any type Zone "A" or "V") designated by the Federal Emergency Management Agency.

Yes _____ No _____   Do not know and information not available from local jurisdiction _____

AN AREA OF POTENTIAL FLOODING shown on a dam failure inundation map pursuant to Section 8589.5 of the Government Code.

Yes _____ No _____   Do not know and information not available from local jurisdiction _____

A VERY HIGH FIRE HAZARD SEVERITY ZONE pursuant to Section 51178 or 51179 of the Government Code. The owner of this property is subject to the maintenance requirements of Section 51182 of the Government Code.

Yes _____ No _____

A WILDLAND AREA THAT MAY CONTAIN SUBSTANTIAL FOREST FIRE RISKS AND HAZARDS pursuant to Section 4125 of the Public Resources Code. The owner of this property is subject to the maintenance requirements of Section 4291 of the Public Resources Code. Additionally, it is not the state's responsibility to provide fire protection services to any building or structure located within the wildlands unless the Department of Forestry and Fire Protection has entered into a cooperative agreement with a local agency for those purposes pursuant to Section 4142 of the Public Resources Code.

Yes _____ No _____

AN EARTHQUAKE FAULT ZONE pursuant to Section 2622 of the Public Resources Code.

Yes _____ No _____

A SEISMIC HAZARD ZONE pursuant to Section 2696 of the Public Resources Code.

Yes (Landslide Zone) _____   No _____   Map not yet released by state _____
Yes (Liquefaction Zone) _____   No _____   Map not yet released by state _____

THESE HAZARDS MAY LIMIT YOUR ABILITY TO DEVELOP THE REAL PROPERTY, TO OBTAIN INSURANCE, OR TO RECEIVE ASSISTANCE AFTER A DISASTER.

THE MAPS ON WHICH THESE DISCLOSURES ARE BASED ESTIMATE WHERE NATURAL HAZARDS EXIST. THEY ARE NOT DEFINITIVE INDICATORS OF WHETHER OR NOT A PROPERTY WILL BE AFFECTED BY A NATURAL DISASTER. TRANSFEREE(S) AND TRANSFEROR(S) MAY WISH TO OBTAIN PROFESSIONAL ADVICE REGARDING THOSE HAZARDS AND OTHER HAZARDS THAT MAY AFFECT THE PROPERTY.

Signature of Transferor (s) _____ Date _____

Agent (s) _____ Date _____

Agent(s) _____ Date _____

Check only one of the following:

___ Transferor(s) and their agent(s) represent that the information herein is true and correct to the best of their knowledge as of the date signed by the transferor(s) and agent(s).

___ Transferor(s) and their agent(s) acknowledge that they have exercised good faith in the selection of a third-party report provider as required in Civil Code Section 1103.7, and that the representations made in this Natural Hazard Disclosure Statement are based upon information provided by the independent third-party disclosure provider as a substituted disclosure pursuant to Civil Code Section 1103.4. Neither transferor(s) nor their agent(s) (1) has independently verified the information contained in this statement and report or (2) is personally aware of any errors or inaccuracies in the information contained on the statement. This statement was prepared by the provider below:

Third-Party Disclosure Provider(s) _____ Date _____

Transferee represents that he or she has read and understands this document.

Pursuant to Civil Code Section 1103.8, the representations made in this Natural Hazard Disclosure Statement do not constitute all of the transferor's or agent's disclosure obligations in this transaction.

Signature of Transferee(s) _____ Date _____

Signature of Transferee(s) _____ Date _____

Required disclosures consist of the following:

Special Flood Hazard Area   Any type 100-year flood Zone A (mostly inland areas) or Zone V (coastal areas), which are designated as high-risk areas by the Federal Emergency Management Agency (FEMA), must be disclosed. These zones indicate where flood insurance may be required. A flood hazard area established by FEMA on the Flood Insurance Rate Map is identified as a Special Flood Hazard Area (SFHA), which is defined as an area that will be inundated by a flood event having a 1% chance of being equaled or exceeded in any given year. The 1% annual chance flood is also called the base flood or 100-year flood. A borrower obtaining a loan secured by a property located within such a zone will be required to obtain flood insurance. Lenders look not only at the appraisal of the property in performing its risk assessment but also at other factors that may threaten the value of the collateral. Properties located in a federally designated flood zone present one of these concerns. If a home is swept away because of flooding, lenders realize that many, if not most, homeowners are not protected by insurance for such damage. Insurance is available, however, and the lender will require the buyer to obtain such coverage.

Pro-Tip: Escrow Officer's Role in Flood Insurance

The experienced escrow officer should have a basic understanding regarding flood zones in his or her marketplace as well as lender's requirements. He or she will not be surprised to find a lender's "instructions" for signing loan documents to include the need for flood insurance.

Area of Potential Flooding   Any area as shown on a dam failure inundation map under Section 8589.5 of the California Government Code (CGC) as being an area of potential flooding must be disclosed.

High Fire Hazard Severity Zone   An area designated as being a **high fire hazard severity zone** under Section 51178 or 51179 of the CGC must be disclosed to the buyer.

Earthquake Fault Zone   A property located within a designated earthquake fault zone (Alquist-Priolo Fault Zone) under Section 4142 of the California Public Resources Code (CPRC) must be disclosed. Earthquake insurance is not typically included in the coverage of most homeowners insurance policies and must be purchased separately if the homeowner desires it. Lenders, interestingly, do not require a buyer to obtain earthquake policies in spite of the prolific presence of many fault lines and zones in California. Deductible amounts for earthquake insurance are quite high, usually a minimum of 10% of the property's value (cost of construction), with premiums from about $500 to as high as $3,000. It is not the escrow holder's responsibility to advise or recommend that a buyer obtain earthquake insurance.

Seismic Hazard Zone   A property located within a seismic hazard zone under CPRC Section 2696 identified as a landslide or liquefaction zone must be disclosed to the buyer.

Wildland Forest Fire Risk Area   A property located within an area identified to be at considerable risk of forest fires must be disclosed to the buyer. Hazard insurance for a home located in a Wildland Forest Fire Risk Area may be difficult for a buyer to obtain. However, insurance may be available to such a homeowner through the Fair Access to Insurance Requirements (FAIR) program, established by the federal government in the 1960s and regulated and operated by each state. Rates are higher than most other insurances policies and coverage is less, but the plan provides at least a basic level of protection to the homeowner. The State of California FAIR plan is available through independent insurance agents and brokers. The specific coverage offered by the FAIR plan varies from state to state as determined by the most likely peril that makes other insurance policies difficult to obtain. In California, it assists homeowners in obtaining fire insurance. In Georgia, it includes coverage for high winds. More information is available through the California Fair Plan Association at 213-487-0111.

Ordinances

Other local laws and **ordinances** (city and county rules and regulations that restrict or limit the use of a property) may apply to a transaction, and the escrow officer should become familiar with them.

U.S. Department of Housing and Urban Development (HUD)

The U. S. **Department of Housing and Urban Development (HUD)** and other government agencies play a significant role in real estate lending as it relates to consumer protection and fraud. Real estate professionals must have a thorough knowledge of the requirements for disclosing certain aspects in the lending process to buyers. Escrow officers should also possess a working knowledge of them because they will be guiding the borrowers through the many documents that address some of the disclosures and other requirements. Essentials of loan programs and the escrow officer's role with them are discussed later, though a brief overview of state and federal government involvement in the sales, loan, and escrow processes are noted in the rest of this chapter.

HUD's Mission   The stated mission of HUD is to increase homeownership, support community development, and increase access to affordable housing free from discrimination. HUD traces its roots to the National Housing Act of 1934 and the U.S. Housing Act of 1937. HUD was established in 1965 as a cabinet-level department of the U.S. government. The secretary of HUD is appointed by the president with the approval of the Senate and administers the department. The Housing Act of 1968 established the Government National Mortgage Association (GNMA, or Ginnie Mae) under HUD's authority to expand the availability of mortgage funds for moderate-income families, using government-guaranteed mortgage-backed securities for the Federal Housing Administration (FHA) loan program. Ginnie Mae's role in the lending community is included in Chapter 13 in discussion about the secondary mortgage market.

HUD's Responsibilities HUD is responsible for programs concerned with housing needs, especially fair housing and the enforcement of laws and regulations regarding fair and equal access to housing for all Americans. HUD is also concerned with the improvement and development of urban areas, with research programs in such areas as public housing improvements, housing finance issues, and proposed tax changes. HUD is the primary regulator for lending on one-to-four unit residential housing. HUD replaced the Federal Housing Administration (FHA) as the primary government housing agency and administers the FHA loan program.

HUD's Programs and Functions HUD's functions may be grouped into six major categories. Escrow holders and parties to the escrows become actively involved with them, either as governed by their guidelines and laws or indirectly using their programs and benefits. The categories are as follows:

- *Housing programs.* These include facilitating the production of new and rehabilitated housing, conserving and preserving existing homes, insuring mortgages for single- and multi-family housing and loans for home improvement and the purchase of manufactured (mobile) homes, providing housing subsidies for low and moderate-income families, and making direct loans to construct or rehabilitate housing projects for the elderly and the disabled.

- *Community Development Block Grant Program.* This program provides monetary grants to carry out a wide range of community development activities. This program consolidates a number of earlier programs, such as Model Cities, urban renewal, and sewage treatment.

- *Supplemental Assistance for Facilities to Assist the Homeless.* This and other programs were established to house the indigent.

- *Public and Native American housing programs.* These programs are involved with the financing, production, and maintenance of low-income public housing and with providing housing that meets the requirements of Native American and Alaska Native communities.

■ *Fair housing and equal opportunity programs.* These programs oversee policies affecting civil rights in housing and community development.

■ *Government National Mortgage Association (GNMA).* Called Ginnie Mae, this is a government corporation charged with increasing the money available for mortgage loans. GNMA does this by providing the means to channel funds from the securities and other financial markets into the mortgage market.

California State Usury Laws

State usury law governs the interest rates that may be charged on real estate loans. Usury provisions under Proposition 2, enacted by the California voters on November 7, 1979, provided some major changes in usury.

Usury Exempt Parties Offering Real Estate Loans   The parties to the escrow, including a seller carrying back financing for the buyer, and the escrow holder having transactions involving lending, must be aware of how they may or may not be subject to its provisions. The law exempts from usury most lenders who typically originate residential loans:

■ Commercial banks and savings banks

■ Finance companies

■ Licensed real estate brokers

■ Credit unions

■ Sellers carryback financing

Usury Nonexempt Parties Offering Real Estate Loans   Interest rates on nonpersonal loans made by nonexempt lenders may not exceed the Federal Reserve discount rate plus 5%. If today's Federal Reserve Board discount rate is 0.25%, the ceiling for nonexempt lenders would be 5.25%.

Mortgage Broker Commission Limitations

As prescribed by the California Mortgage Loan Broker's Law (Article 7 of Chapter 3 of the Real Estate Law) in general, the shorter the term of the loan, the less commission the broker may charge as a percentage of the face amount of the loan. These commission limits apply to all real estate brokers originating or brokering loans and their sales persons secured by residential one-to-four unit properties as follows:

First Trust Deeds   On first trust deeds less than $30,000, commissions are limited to

- 5% of the total loan amount if the term is less than 3 years; 10% if for 3 years or longer; and

- for amounts $30,000 and greater, no restriction is placed on the amount of the broker's fee.

Second Trust Deeds   On junior loans of less than $20,000, commissions are limited to

- 5% of the total amount, if drawn for a term of less than 2 years;

- 10% of the total loan amount, if for a term of 2 years but less than 3 years;

- 15%, if drawn for a term of 3 years or longer; and

- the broker may charge as much as the borrower agrees to pay for amounts over $20,000.

Broker-Controlled Funds

If a real estate broker anticipates that the loan to the borrower may be made wholly or in part from broker-controlled funds, the disclosure must include a statement to that effect.

Definition of Broker-Controlled Funds   The law defines broker-controlled funds as those monies owned by the broker; a spouse, child, parent, grandparent, brother, sister, father-in-law, mother-in-law, brother-in-law, or sister-in-law of the broker; or by any entity in which the broker alone or together with any of the above relatives of the broker has an ownership interest of greater than 25%.

The California Loan Broker's Law

Real estate brokers who negotiate loans in any amount, to be secured directly or collaterally by a lien on real property, must, before the borrower becomes obligated to complete the loan, deliver to the borrower a Mortgage Loan Disclosure Statement (MLDS) in prescribed form containing specified information (Sections 10240 and 10241 of the California Business and Professions Code). The law covers any mortgage loan in any amount negotiated by a real estate broker or a salesperson on behalf of a broker.

Certification Requirements The licensee must certify compliance with specified provisions of the law only if the loan is a first trust deed loan under $30,000 or a junior loan under $20,000. Certification of compliance is provided in the Mortgage Loan Disclosure Statement (MLDS) which is delivered to the borrower.

The certification language in the Mortgage Loan Disclosure Statement, which is required by Section 10240, has been amended in Regulation 2840 to read as follows:

> Neither the broker nor the designated representative identified below is the lender in this transaction, either directly or indirectly

and

> If the loan to which this disclosure statement applies is a loan secured by a first trust deed in a principal amount of less than $30,000 or a loan secured by a junior lien of less than $20,000, the undersigned certifies that the loan will be made in compliance with Article 7, Chapter 3 of the Real Estate Law.

Federal Truth in Lending Act (Regulation Z)

Escrow, title insurance, and real estate professionals find themselves frequently in transactions subject to the **Truth in Lending Act (TILA)**, or Regulation Z. Frequently referred to as "Reg Z," it requires real estate licensees acting as creditors to furnish truth-in-lending disclosures to consumers. Creditors as defined by Regulation Z are those who extend credit more than five times a year, which is secured by residential real estate consisting of one to four units. The purpose of this regulation is to promote the informed use of consumer credit by requiring disclosures about its terms and cost. The regulation also gives consumers the right to cancel certain credit transactions that involve a lien on a consumer's principal dwelling, regulates certain credit card practices, and provides a means for fair and timely resolution of credit billing disputes.

> ### Pro-Tip: Borrower's Right to Rescind the Loan Contract and Cancel Escrow
>
> For example in a refinance transaction in which the borrower is obtaining a loan on his or her primary residence the escrow officer needs to be aware that funding cannot take place for three days after the signing of loan documents. It is typically the escrow holder who calls or contacts the buyer's lender to "fund the loan." Accordingly he or she needs to understand funding cannot, and will not, take place until the three day waiting term has lapsed. This restriction is not placed on primary residence purchase loan transactions or for loans on any investment property, whether purchase or refinance.

The regulation does not govern charges for consumer credit (meaning credit granted for non-real estate borrowing, such as automobiles and credit cards). The regulation requires a maximum interest rate to be stated in variable-rate contracts secured by the consumer's dwelling. It also imposes limitations on home equity plans that are subject to the requirements under the law. Regulation Z prohibits certain acts or practices in connection with credit secured by a consumer's principal dwelling. Regulation Z is discussed further in Chapter 11.

Federal Real Estate Settlement Procedures Act (RESPA)

One of the main purposes of the federal **Real Estate Settlement Procedures Act (RESPA)** is to provide purchasers of real property with information to take the mystery out of the settlement (closing) process and assist purchasers in obtaining the best value in settlement services for the money spent. The act covers sales or transfers of one-to-four-family homes, condominiums, and cooperatives financed by federally related loans and include the provisions noted in the following paragraphs. RESPA provisions apply to and must be rigidly adhered to by real estate agents, title insurance companies, escrow companies, hazard insurance agents, real estate appraisers, home warranty protection companies, home inspection companies, and structural pest control inspection companies. The act requires lenders, mortgage brokers, and servicers of home loans to provide borrowers with pertinent and timely disclosures about the nature and costs of the real estate settlement process. It also protects borrowers against certain abusive practices such as kickbacks and places limitations on the use of escrow accounts.

RESPA Revised in 2011   The Frank-Dodd Wall Street Reform and Consumer Protection Act implemented new truth-in-lending rules, effective April 1, 2011. These changes influence the procedures the escrow officer must follow in preparing the Settlement Statement (HUD-1). The revisions include the following (others affecting the escrow holder's services are discussed in Chapter 12):

- Payments to the loan originator that are based on the loan's interest rate or other terms are prohibited.

- Compensation that is based on a fixed percentage of the loan amount is permitted.

- A loan originator that increases the consumer's interest rate to generate a larger yield spread premium, as explained by the Federal Reserve Board, can apply the excess creditor payment to third-party closing costs and thereby reduce the amount of consumer funds needed to cover upfront fees. Yield spread premiums no longer may be shown on the Settlement Statement as paid outside of closing (POC) and in fact will not be identified as yield spread premiums. (This is covered in detail in Chapter 12.)

- The rule, therefore, does not prohibit creditors or loan originators from using the interest rate to cover upfront closing costs, as long as any creditor-paid compensation retained by the originator does not vary based on the transaction's terms or conditions.

- For example, suppose that for a loan with a 5% interest rate, the originator will receive a payment of $1,000 from the creditor as compensation, and for a loan with a 6% interest rate, a yield spread premium of $3,000 will be generated. The originator must apply the additional $2,000 to cover the consumer's other closing costs.

- The revisions also prohibit a mortgage broker or loan officer from receiving payments directly from a consumer while also receiving compensation from the creditor or another person.

- A mortgage broker or loan officer is explicitly prohibited from "steering" a consumer to a lender offering less favorable terms in order to increase the broker's or loan officer's compensation.

Transactions Subject to RESPA RESPA is applicable to all federally related mortgage loans (loans, including refinances, secured by a first or subordinate lien on residential real property) including one-to four-family properties, either existing or to be constructed using proceeds of the loan (including individual units of condominiums and cooperatives), and manufactured homes, either existing or to be constructed using proceeds of the loan.

In addition, the federally related mortgage loan

- must be made by a lender, creditor, or dealer; or

- must be made by or insured by an agency of the federal government or in connection with a housing or urban development program administered by an agency of the federal government; or

- must be made by and intended to be sold by the originating lender or creditor to FNMA, GNMA, or FHLMC (or its successor, an entity that receives the interest in the object from the original holder known as the beneficiary); or

- is the subject of a home equity conversion mortgage or a reverse mortgage issued by a lender or creditor subject to the regulation; or

- must be made by a lender, dealer, or creditor subject to the regulation and used in whole or in part to fund an installment sales contract, land contract, or contract for deed on otherwise qualifying residential property.

Transactions Exempt from RESPA   The following transactions are exempt from RESPA:

- A loan on property of 25 acres or more (whether or not a dwelling is located on the property)

- A loan primarily for business, commercial, or agricultural purposes; and temporary loans, such as a construction loan

  — The exemption does not apply if the loan is used as, or may be converted to, permanent financing by the same financial institution; if the lender issues a commitment for permanent financing, the loan is covered.

- A construction loan with a term of two or more years is covered unless made to a bona fide contractor

- A "bridge" and "swing" loan, loans that provide interim financing for a temporary purpose after which permanent financing will be obtained, as well as loans secured by vacant or unimproved property when no proceeds of the loan will be used to construct a one-to-four-family residential structure

  — However, if the proceeds will be used to locate a manufactured home or construct a structure within two years from the date of settlement, the loan is covered and must comply with RESPA.

- An assumption of an existing loan by the buyer, unless the mortgage instruments require lender approval for the assumption and the lender actually approves the assumption

- A renewal of an original loan still in effect, or a modification of an original loan still in effect.

Pro-Tip: Loan Modifications

Loan modifications were seldom offered to borrowers in the past. However, since the financial crisis that led to the 2007–2009 recession, millions of loan modifications have been executed on behalf of homeowners through various programs, including the federal government's Home Affordable Modification Program (HAMP). These, along with any other modification to an existing loan, are exempt from RESPA. The escrow holder will most likely not be involved with a loan modification because an escrow is not typically used.

Settlement Statements (HUD-1)   The completed HUD-1 or HUD-1A Settlement (closing) Statement (see Figure 12.5) must be mailed or delivered to the borrower, the seller (if there is one), and the lender (if the lender is not the escrow holder), or their agents at or before settlement. However, the borrower may waive the right of delivery by executing a written waiver at or before settlement. If the borrower or the borrower's agent do not attend the closing, as they commonly do not in California, the statement must be mailed or delivered as soon as practical after settlement.

Retention of Settlement Statements   The lender must retain each completed HUD-1 or HUD-1A Settlement Statement and related documents for five years after settlement, unless the institution disposes of its interest in the mortgage and does not service the mortgage. If the loan is transferred, the transferring lender must provide a copy of the statement, as part of the transfer, to the acquiring lender (the investor) or mortgage servicer (the entity that actually administers the loan, collects the payments, and otherwise acts on behalf of the investor), who then must retain it for the remainder of the five year term.

Request for Discharge of IRS Tax Liens

Tax liens against a property being sold are a common occurrence in the life of the escrow holder. If the net proceeds due a seller at closing exceed an IRS lien amount, the IRS may want to be paid in full. However, in such an event, the taxpayer may still ask the IRS to discharge and release the lien from the property's title to accommodate closing. (Only the lien is released; the debt is not discharged, and liability for repayment of the tax due does not go away.) There is no assurance the IRS will comply, but depending on the circumstances, the taxpayer might obtain the government's agreement. In fact, even if the IRS liens are less than the net proceeds, sometimes it may be possible for the IRS to still discharge the lien, allowing the seller to retain a portion of the proceeds. There is no standard IRS request form for the taxpayer to use; the IRS requires only that the request not be handwritten and that it be delivered to the appropriate IRS department. While typically performed for the taxpayer by an attorney, the escrow holder or title officer may assist in the process by providing the required documentation, including a preliminary title report and an estimated HUD-1.

■ CHAPTER 6 QUIZ

1. An express contract is one that has been put into words,

   a. whether written or verbal.

   b. in writing only.

   c. verbally only.

   d. none of these.

2. A bilateral contract occurs when a promise to perform is made by one party,

   a. but an equal promise to perform is not required of the party.

   b. but typically few contracts are bilateral.

   c. and a second party makes an equal promise to perform.

   d. and it carries the same effect as a unilateral contract.

3. A contract that is considered valid but not enforceable if it is rejected by one of the parties is said to be

   a. voidable.

   b. void.

   c. validated.

   d. unvoidable.

4. To be valid, effective, and enforceable, a contract must include

   a. mutual consent, capacity to contract, consideration, and a lawful object.

   b. mutual consent, capacity to contract, and consideration.

   c. capacity to contract, consideration, and a lawful object.

   d. mutual consent, consideration, and a lawful object.

5. Under the statue of frauds, which of the following contracts must be in writing?

    a. A real estate listing agreement

    b. A real estate purchase agreement

    c. An agreement between brokers to share a commission

    d. Both a and b

6. The structural pest control report

    a. consists of four parts.

    b. requires an inspection to only determine live infestation.

    c. includes a Section I and a Section II.

    d. is regulated by the U.S. Department of Agriculture.

7. The Natural Hazard Disclosure Statement is *NOT* required for properties

    a. located in a special flood hazard zone.

    b. located in a seismic hazard zone.

    c. having five units or more.

    d. both a and b.

8. A master insurance policy would be obtained for

    a. a new single-family home.

    b. a condominium.

    c. protection against forgery or fraud.

    d. protection against off-record matters.

9. Under Regulation Z, a creditor is defined as

    a. one who extends credit more than five times a year secured by a dwelling.

    b. one who extends credit one to four times a year secured by a dwelling.

    c. anyone who extends credit.

    d. anyone who obtains credit.

10. The primary regulator for lending on residential housing in the United States is the

    a. Department of Urban Development.

    b. Department of Housing.

    c. Department of Housing and Urban Development.

    d. Department of Housing and Lending.

CHAPTER SEVEN

7

REAL ESTATE PRACTICE

◼ KEY TERMS

allocation of costs
CalHFA
Buyer's Choice Act
contingency removal
dispute resolution

liquidated damages
loan contingency
real estate licensing
selection of escrow
  providers

seller financing
smoke detectors

◼ LEARNING OBJECTIVES

Upon completing this chapter, you will be able to

- ◼ understand the real estate agent's role in the purchase or sale transaction;

- ◼ understand the general guidelines of real estate licensing law in California;

- ◼ understand the real estate agent's primary responsibilities and limitations, both under the law and as a matter of customary practices; and

- ◼ understand and explain the fundamental provisions of the purchase contract and joint escrow instructions typically used by most real estate agents in California, especially as they relate to the interaction with the escrow holder.

■ THE REAL ESTATE AGENT'S ROLE

The escrow and title professional works closely with real estate agents in every purchase transaction, an interaction requiring a keen understanding of the essential roles of each party and the challenges encountered during the process. While it is the principal who will direct the actions of and provide the instructions to the escrow holder, it is the real estate agent who, in most instances, will guide the principal throughout the process.

It could be said, therefore, that the escrow holder has two customers in every purchase escrow—the principal and the agent—and should remain sensitive to both the obligations and the limitations of the agent to the principal. This relationship between the real estate agent and the escrow officer can be summed up in this way: The real estate agent is the de facto principal in practice, although not the true principal as it is defined at Lawyers.com:

> One who engages another to act for him or her subject to his or her general control or instruction; in an agency relationship, the principal is the person who gives authority to another, called an agent, to act on his or her behalf.

The California Department of Real Estate advises and cautions real estate agents to balance guiding and directing the principal, which includes steering the principal toward a specific escrow holder instead of allowing the principal to make the choice. California law specifically states the following: "A real estate broker may not nominate an escrow holder as a condition precedent to a transaction, but may suggest an escrow holder if requested to do so by the parties."

The Real Estate Professional

For those new to the escrow or title insurance industry (including the consumer), learning more about the real estate profession and its practices, laws, customs, and people provides a greater understanding of the escrow process itself. The escrow holder is "reactive" in the escrow transaction, while the real estate agent is "proactive." Putting the agent's responsibilities in proper perspective, the escrow holder relies on the real estate agent to help provide that to which the escrow holder "reacts." Both real estate agent and escrow officer are an integral part of a team equally responsible to their mutual principals, who place trust in them to accomplish a successful closing.

■ CALIFORNIA REAL ESTATE LICENSE REQUIREMENTS

California Real Estate Licensing

Salesperson License   Before a person may act as a real estate agent in California, a real estate license issued by the California Department of Real Estate must be obtained. An individual may be licensed as either a salesperson or a broker.

The California Department of Real Estate (DRE) has established certain requirements for **real estate licensing**. An applicant for a real estate salesperson license must meet those requirements, including certain educational requirements and a written examination. After passing the examination, the prospective licensee must submit an application for approval to the DRE. A license may be obtained by a person who does not immediately intend to be employed by a broker, but a salesperson without an employing broker may not perform acts requiring a real estate license.

General Qualifications   Following are the general qualifications for a real estate license in California:

- The applicant must be at least 18 years of age.

- The applicant must possess proof of legal presence in the United States. Residency in California is not a requirement, though the applicant must complete and submit to DRE a Consent to Service of Process (DRE form 234), as well as a set of fingerprints submitted directly to the DRE.

- The applicant must be honest and truthful; conviction of a crime or failure to disclose any criminal violation may result in denial of a license.

Educational Requirements   The applicant must successfully complete three college-level real estate courses before taking the DRE salesperson exam. The courses include two mandatory courses (Real Estate Principles and Real Estate Practice) and any one elective course from the following list: Real Estate Appraisal, Property Management, Real Estate Finance, Real Estate Economics, Legal Aspects of Real Estate, Real Estate Office Administration, General Accounting, Business Law, Escrows, Mortgage Loan Brokering and Lending, Computer Applications in Real Estate, or Common Interest Developments.

Members of the California State Bar are statutorily exempt from the college-level course requirements. Evidence of admission to practice law in California must be furnished, such as a photocopy of both sides of a California State Bar membership card.

Members of any other state bar, as well as individuals holding a bachelor of laws or a juris doctor degree, who are not members of any state bar, including California, may generally qualify on the basis of education. The applicant is required to submit evidence of a degree from a college or university accredited by the Western Association of Schools and Colleges (or comparable regional accrediting agency recognized by the U.S. Department of Education) for evaluation.

Also, applicants who submit evidence of having completed the eight statutory college-level courses required for the broker examination and license are eligible to take the salesperson examination without submitting further evidence of experience or education.

Continuing education offerings do not satisfy the college-level course requirements for this examination.

Courses must be three semester-units or four quarter-units at the college level. Courses must be completed at an institution of higher learning accredited by the Western Association of Schools and Colleges or by a comparable regional accrediting agency recognized by the U.S. Department of Education, or by a private real estate school that has had its courses approved by the California real estate commissioner.

Courses completed through foreign institutions of higher learning must be evaluated by a foreign credentials evaluation service approved by the Department of Real Estate.

Copies of official transcripts are generally acceptable evidence of completed courses. Transcripts of equivalent courses submitted as substitutes for the college-level courses listed must be supported by an official course or catalog description.

The Real Estate Salesperson Examination

Applicants wishing to take the exam for a California real estate salesperson's license must provide evidence of the satisfactory completion of the following college level courses:

- Real Estate Principles course: mandatory three-semester-unit course

- Real Estate Practices course: mandatory three-semester-unit course

- One elective course: elective three-semester-unit course from the allowable courses described in "Educational Requirements"

Most consumers and possibly some real estate industry professionals other than agents probably are not familiar with the contents, and the public policy concepts that establish the contents, of the examination for the real estate salesperson license. A passing score of 70% or greater is required, with the examinee allowed 3 hours and 15 minutes in which to complete it. Applicants must demonstrate in the examination knowledge of the following subjects and topics, which are specifically identified under the law:

- *Language and mathematical skills.* Appropriate knowledge of the English language, including reading, writing, and spelling and of arithmetical computations common to real estate and business opportunity practices.

- *Real estate principles and concepts.* An understanding of the principles of real estate and business opportunity conveyancing; the general purposes and general legal effect of agency contracts, deposit receipts, deeds, deeds of trust, chattel mortgages, bills of sale, mortgages, land contracts of sale, and leases; and of the principles of business, land economics, and appraisals.

- *Agency laws and principles.* A general and fair understanding of the obligations between principal and agent; the principles of real estate and business opportunity transactions, and the code of business ethics pertaining thereto; as well as of the provisions of the law relating to real estate as administered by the real estate commissioner.

- *Additional topics* contained in the examination may include property ownership and land-use controls and regulations, laws of agency, valuation and market analysis, financing, transfer of property, practice of real estate and mandated disclosures and contracts.

California Real Estate Broker's License

Broker examinees must successfully pass the examination with a passing score of 75% or greater.

Experience   Before being eligible to take the broker's examination, an individual must have a minimum of two years' experience in the last five years as a licensed California real estate salesperson, with certain exceptions. An applicant also may qualify with two years' full-time experience gained within the five-year period immediately prior to the date of application for the broker examination in any of the following areas:

- *Escrow or title officer* or *a loan officer* in a capacity directly related to the financing or conveying of real property

- *Subdivider, contractor, or speculative builder*, during which time the applicant performed comprehensive duties relating to the purchase, finance, development, and sale or lease of real property

- *Real property appraiser*

- *Holder of bachelor's degree, minimum.* An applicant with a four-year degree from an accredited college (Western Association of Schools and Colleges or comparable regional accrediting agency recognized by the U.S. Department of Education) with a major in a real estate discipline may be exempt from the two-year salesperson experience requirement. This may be verified by submitting either a copy of the diploma or transcript showing the degree earned. Regardless of the degree, the applicant must show evidence (transcripts) of having completed eight college-level courses as listed in "Educational Requirements for All Applicants" at the time of filing the application. The eight required courses may be part of the degree requirements, or they may be completed separately from the degree course work.

Members of the California State Bar are statutorily exempt from the college-level course requirements and are also exempt from the two-year experience requirement. Evidence of admission to the practice of law in California must be furnished, such as a photocopy of both sides of a California State Bar membership card.

Members of any other state bar, as well as individuals holding an LL.B or J.D. degree who are not members of any state bar, including California, may generally qualify on the basis of education and be exempt from the two-year experience requirement. These applicants are required to submit evidence of a bachelor of laws or a juris doctor degree from a college or university accredited by the Western Association of Schools and Colleges (or comparable regional accrediting agency recognized by the U.S. Department of Education) for evaluation, as well as proof of successful completion of a three semester-unit or four quarter-unit college-level courses in real estate finance and real estate appraisal.

Educational Requirements for All Applicants   Courses must be three semester-units or four quarter-units at the college level. Courses must be completed prior to being scheduled for an examination. Copies of official transcripts are generally acceptable evidence of completed courses. Transcripts of other courses, submitted as equivalent courses of study in lieu of the statutory courses, must be accompanied by an official course or catalog description.

- Broker qualification courses must be completed at an institution of higher learning accredited by the Western Association of Schools and Colleges, a comparable regional accrediting agency recognized by the U.S. Department of Education, or a private real estate school that has had its courses approved by the California real estate commissioner.

- Courses completed through foreign institutions of higher learning must be evaluated by a foreign credentials evaluation service approved by the Department of Real Estate.

■ THE PURCHASE CONTRACT AND ESCROW

Resources for REALTORS®

How often has one heard someone use the word "REALTOR®" when referring to a real estate agent? Probably most of the time, if not always. It is entirely possible, however, that the person is not a REALTOR® at all. The term "REALTOR®" is a registered collective membership mark that identifies a real estate professional who is a member of the National Association of REALTORS® (NAR) and agrees to abide by its strict Code of Ethics. Only licensed real estate agents who are also members of the National NAR may refer to themselves as REALTORS®.

Founded in 1908, NAR has approximately 1 million members involved in residential and commercial real estate as brokers, salespersons, property managers, appraisers, counselors, and others. An important aspect of NAR membership for the consumer to know is the members' universal commitment and pledge to the Code of Ethics and Standards of Practice, which were originally adopted in 1913. When working with a REALTOR®, consumers know that the agent representing them has agreed to and abides by a specified and verifiable standard of professional behavior.

In guiding and navigating a prospective buyer through California Association of REALTORS® (CAR) purchase agreements, the agent relies on the content of the agreement. These agreements also include joint escrow instructions, which allow the escrow holder to usually prepare only supplemental instructions. These include the basic "boilerplate" disclosures. Many of its clauses may require the escrow agent to monitor the buyer's or the seller's compliance for performance without specific time frames. Contingency clauses may require the seller to contribute toward the buyer's closing costs or provide for seller carryback financing (see the Seller Financing Addendum), inspections. Some considerations of the contract must be addressed in the escrow instructions if the original is prepared by the escrow holder (for transactions for which a standard CAR purchase agreement is not used) and, in either case, which the escrow holder must monitor.

Purchase Price

The agent representing the buyers has the duty to work diligently in trying to secure an acceptance of the buyer's offer at the price and on the terms offered;

however, at the same time, the buyers may be willing to increase the price they are willing to pay if multiple offers are present and a "bidding war" has ensued. The dual agent has a unique challenge in attempting to obtain the lowest price for the buyer and the highest price based on market value for the seller. The challenge is mitigated somewhat if the buyer is willing to pay a reasonable price not exceeding market value and if the property meets the needs of the buyer more than any other, including those that are not the listings of the buyer's agent. The real estate agent can feel comfortable in such a case to have achieved the goals of both the buyer and the seller.

Financing

If financing is part of the purchase transaction, the buyer and the seller both must be cautioned by their respective agents that if the appraised value is less than the offered purchase price, the escrow closing may be jeopardized. In such cases, the sellers must be willing to accept the lower value as the sales price, the buyers must be willing to pay the higher price (if they have the additional funds, and if the buyers' lender will allow the higher sales price), or the escrow must be cancelled.

CalHFA Financing   If the buyers are obtaining California Housing Financing Agency financing (CalHFA) in an offer already accepted by the seller and if the purchase price offered exceeds the maximum allowable **CalHFA** sales price for the area, escrow cannot close.

Loan Contingency   A loan contingency refers to a buyer's responsibility to obtain financing as stated in and under the terms of the contract. If unable to do so, the buyer will be required to either cancel the escrow in order to be free of any penalty or loss of deposit or waive the contingency and proceed with the transaction. The CAR purchase agreement calls for a loan contingency to be removed within 17 days of the seller's acceptance, unless stated otherwise. The escrow officer should carefully note the actual removal date and monitor it. The details of financing should be completely spelled out in the purchase agreement to avoid any confusion or misunderstanding relative to the terms of the loan and the obligations of the parties. It is the loan contingency that causes most delays to escrow or failure to close at all.

Rate and Term   This includes the amount of the loan; the interest rate, including the initial adjustable rate if the buyer is obtaining an adjustable rate along with its maximum rate; the term of the loan; and the amortization of the loan.

The term, for example, may be 15 years, meaning the loan is due and payable in full at the end of 15 years, although the amortization of the loan shows 30 years, the loan payment being based on a 30-year term. A balloon balance will be due because the loan will not have been fully amortized.

A fully amortized loan is one that is completely paid at the end of the amortization term. The financing clause should also indicate whether the seller is paying any points on behalf of the buyer; if not, the agent should indicate so by writing a zero in the space provided. If the loan is to be seller financing, there are additional requirements for both the agent and the escrow holder noted in the next paragraph.

Seller Financing   If the seller is to provide financing in the form of a *carry-back* (a real estate industry term used to describe a seller-originated loan provided from funds otherwise due the seller from equity at closing), this **seller financing** should be indicated in the paragraph under "Additional Financing," and the escrow holder will be requested to prepare the note and trust deed. If seller financing is part of the transaction, the real estate agent will be required under the law to provide the seller with a disclosure regarding recommended terms, conditions, and obligations of the parties when seller financing is involved. The Seller Financing Addendum (CAR form SFA) will be prepared with the seller by the agent and then will be delivered to the escrow holder for presentation to the buyer.

The escrow officer will prepare a note and trust deed based on the terms indicated by the seller in the Seller Financing Addendum.

All-Cash Offer   A seller accepting an all-cash offer may require the buyer to place an additional and more substantial deposit into escrow. The escrow holder should review the instructions to determine whether such a demand has been made.

Closing Date   An experienced escrow officer knows that if a number of inspections are required to be performed, not only must the contingency removal date be noted but also the results of the inspections may impact closing date.

Financing and Closing   If financing is involved, most buyers typically prefer to close escrow as close to the end of the month as possible. Because the borrower's first payment will usually be due on the first day of the second month following the close of escrow and will include only 30 days' interest, the borrower will be charged interest per diem from the date the loan funds (not the recording date) to the end of the calendar month. The fewer days remaining in the month following the close of escrow, therefore, the less interest due at closing.

> **Example: Interest**
>
> Buyer obtains a loan in the amount of $315,000 at 5% interest, with a monthly payment of $1,690.99 principal and interest.
>
> Loan funds January 15, and escrow closes and records January 16 (15 days remaining in the month after funding)—recording in most counties in California will take place the day after funding.
>
> First payment is due March 1.
>
> Amount of interest required to be paid at closing = $656.25 (15 days at $43.75 per day)

REO and Per Diem Penalty   If escrow is allowed to continue after the anticipated closing date has passed and the property is an REO (real estate owned and acquired by a lender foreclosing), the terms of the contract may require the buyer to pay a penalty (per diem fee) each day the escrow continues. The escrow holder must calculate and account for the total amount of per diem fees at closing and charge the buyer accordingly and disbursing the funds to the seller as part of the total proceeds.

> **Example: Per Diem Penalty**
>
> Sales price: $1,000,000
>
> Closing date per escrow instructions: January 31
>
> Per diem penalty: $100 daily for each day beyond the scheduled closing date, including the day of closing
>
> Actual closing date: February 7
>
> Per diem penalty charged buyer at closing: $700

Guidelines for the truth-in-lending (TIL) statement and APR disclosures may delay loan processing and escrow closing. The buyer may not close escrow until seven days after the initial truth-in-lending disclosures have been received by the buyer. If the buyers' interest rate is not locked in or expires before the closing date, any rate increase over the originally disclosed rate of 0.125 or greater requires a new TIL and an additional waiting period of three days before loan signing and possibly past the date of anticipated escrow closing.

Return of Deposit   In the event escrow has not closed by the agreed-upon closing date, a special statutory rule applies to the transaction for a one-to-four-unit property, one unit of which will be occupied by the buyer.

> ### Pro-Tip: One-to-Four Units
>
> Persons new to the real estate business are frequently introduced to terms and phrases which are unique to the industry and part of the technical terminology. One such phrase is "one-to-four units," which refers to residential properties consisting of one unit (single family home or condominium), two units (duplex), three units (triplex) and four units (fourplex).

If one of the parties submits a written request to the escrow holder canceling the escrow and requesting that any funds deposited by the canceling party be returned, the escrow holder must prepare a release of funds and deliver it to the other party to be signed within 30 days. If the party requesting the cancellation does not receive the funds requested within the 30-day term, that party may sue the other party. The court will likely order the reluctant party to release the funds and to pay the other party treble damages (but not more than $1,000 or less than $100). An escrow holder in such a circumstance could interplead the funds into the court.

Tenant-Occupied Properties   If the property is currently tenant occupied, an investor-buyer must be made aware of the following: Under the Protecting Tenants at Foreclosure Act of 2009, all leases will survive foreclosure as follows:

- The tenant may stay in the property until the end of the lease.

- A tenant with a month-to-month rental agreement must be given 90 days' notice to move instead of the 60 days under California law.

Buyers who intend to occupy the property are not subject to the survival of lease regulation, though they must still comply with the 90-day notice provision.

Allocation of Costs   Buyers often ask the seller to pay all or part of their closing costs, though lenders' guidelines restrict the actual amount of the seller's contributions toward the buyers' costs. It's helpful if the escrow officer has an understanding of these restrictions and limitations. The escrow officer should confirm the **allocation of costs**—that the total amount of buyers' costs the seller has agreed to pay does not exceed the maximum amount allowed by the buyers' lender, otherwise escrow will be delayed while the buyer and the seller renegotiate, if possible. A problem arises when a buyer's agent has asked the seller to pay a certain amount, the seller agrees, and later the parties discover that the amount of contributions exceed the maximum allowable by the buyer's lender—the seller is willing to perform but is unable. Chapter 13 discusses the actual maximum allowed seller contributions.

■ PROPERTY REQUIREMENTS

Smoke Detectors

State law requires that residential properties be equipped with **smoke detectors**, and local ordinances may impose more rigid requirements. The specific requirements may vary depending on the type of property, the number of units, and the number of stories of the property. In addition, local climatic conditions give municipalities the opportunity to create more stringent requirements. For example, some municipalities accept battery-operated smoke detectors, but others require hardwired smoke detectors. For that reason, it is imperative to check with the local department of building and safety to determine the local requirements. Summarized in the following paragraphs are the California state law requirements and additional regulations promulgated by the state fire marshal. (Cal. Health and Safety Code § 13113.8)

The smoke detectors must be centrally located outside each sleeping area. For example, a two-story home with bedrooms upstairs and downstairs would need two smoke detectors, one in the hallway outside the bedrooms(s) upstairs and one in the hallway outside the bedroom(s) downstairs. Furthermore, for any new construction or any additions, alterations, or repairs made after August 14, 1992, that exceed $1,000 and for which a permit is required, a smoke detector must be installed in each bedroom, in addition to being centrally located in the corridor or area outside the bedroom.

For new construction only, the smoke detector must be hardwired with a battery backup. For all other homes, the smoke detector may be battery operated. (Cal. Health and Safety Code § 13113.7)

Sellers must check with the local department of building and safety in which the home is located to determine any additional local requirements.

Unless exempt, the seller must provide the buyer with a written statement indicating that the property is in compliance with the law governing smoke detectors. This requirement may be satisfied by using CAR form SDC. Delivery of this written statement of compliance to the spouse of a buyer is considered delivery to the buyer, unless the contract states otherwise. (Cal. Health and Safety Code § 13113.8(c))

Exemptions to a written statement are as follows:

■ Transfers that require a copy of a public report be given to the buyer

■ Transfers pursuant to court order

■ Transfers during foreclosure or trustee's sale or through deed in lieu of fore-closure (REO transfers are not exempted, however)

■ Transfers by a fiduciary of a trust, decedent's estate, guardianship, or conservatorship

■ Transfers between co-owners

■ Transfers to a spouse or to a child, grandchild, parent, grandparent, or other direct ancestor or descendant

■ Transfers between spouses in connection with a dissolution of marriage or similar proceeding

■ Transfers by the state controller pursuant to the unclaimed property law

■ Transfers as a result of failure to pay property taxes

California law requires that every condominium, stock cooperative, time-share project, duplex, and apartment complex have operable smoke detectors that are approved and listed by the state fire marshal and installed in accordance with the state fire marshal's regulations. A written statement of compliance is not required for these types of dwelling units when transferring the property.

The owner or landlord is responsible for testing and maintaining smoke detectors in lodging houses and the common stairwells of apartment complexes and other multiple-dwelling complexes.

The tenant has a duty to notify the manager or the owner of an inoperable smoke detector within the tenant's unit. The owner or authorized agent who has not been notified of the deficiency by the tenant is not in violation.

The location requirements and the type of the smoke detectors to be used are exactly the same as for single-family homes

California law requires that every used mobile home or used manufactured home have an operable smoke detector on the date of transfer of title. A written state-ment of compliance is not required for these types of properties. If within 45 days prior to the date of transfer of title, the transferor signs a declaration stating that each smoke detector in the manufactured home or mobile home is operable on the date that the declaration is signed. "Used manufactured home" or "used mobile home," means a manufactured home or mobile home that was previously sold and registered or titled with the department, appropriate agency, authority, or any other state.

The escrow instructions will reflect the party responsible for payment of any required smoke detector compliance work, with invoices submitted to the escrow holder to be paid at closing.

Carbon Monoxide Detectors

As of July 1, 2011, the Carbon Monoxide Poisoning Prevention Act (SB 183) requires all single-family homes with an attached garage or a fossil fuel source to install carbon monoxide alarms within the home. Thereafter, all owners and landlords of all residential properties having one to four units must comply with the act. These devices must be installed outside each sleeping areas of the home, including the basement. They do not replace smoke alarms. By law, both smoke alarms/detectors and carbon monoxide devices are required to be installed in all dwellings. However, a combination smoke and carbon monoxide alarm/detector will satisfy both requirements.

Water Heater Strapping and Bracing

According to the California Real Estate Inspection Association, California health and safety standards for residential properties were amended by the state legislature in 1989 to include the following: (1) All water heaters sold in California must be braced; (2) manufacturers of water heaters must provide installation instructions for seismic straps with each fixture sold; and (3) the Office of the State Architect must prepare generic installation instructions with standard details illustrating minimum standards for earthquake strapping. The state architect's specifications, published in 1992, stand as the legal criteria for adequate strapping of water heaters in California. Due to bureaucracy and inefficient communication, violations and misapplications remain commonplace. The effective standards are as follows:

- All water heaters must be strapped.

- Two straps are needed, one on the upper one-third and one on the lower one-third of the fixture.

- Straps may consist of either plumbers' tape (at least 24 gauge) or half-inch-diameter metal conduit.

- Straps should wrap all the way around the body of the water heater. (Note that many of the strapping kits available in hardware stores fail to comply with this requirement.)

- Straps should be secured to adjacent walls and from opposing directions.

- Straps should be secured to the wall studs using ¼-inch-diameter-by-3-inch-long lag bolts with washers.

- The requirement that water heaters be properly anchored, strapped, and braced must be disclosed to the buyer. The cost of any work in order to comply is negotiable between buyer and seller. The cost of installation is negotiable between buyer and seller. The escrow officer should note which party is responsible for paying any costs for installing smoke detectors and bracing the water heater, if required.

- The escrow instructions will reflect the party responsible for payment of any required water heater strapping or bracing compliance work, with invoices submitted to the escrow holder to be paid at closing.

■ SELECTION OF ESCROW AND TITLE SERVICES

Buyers and sellers may select any escrow holder or title insurer. California's **Buyer's Choice Act** (AB 957) specifically prohibits the seller who as a beneficiary acquired title by foreclosing on the property from requiring the buyer to use a certain escrow holder or title insurer There is no requirement that a buyer use a particular company selected by the seller. Legislation was introduced in California to strengthen homebuyer protection and rights in **selection of escrow providers** because of a practice among some foreclosing lenders that mandated the buyer use an escrow company chosen by the foreclosing bank.

The act, signed into law in October 2009, specifically prohibits

until January 1, 2015 a mortgagee or beneficiary under a deed of trust who acquired title to residential real property improved by four or fewer dwelling units at a foreclosure sale from requiring, directly or indirectly, as a condition of selling the property, that the buyer purchase title insurance or escrow services in connection with the sale from a particular title insurer or escrow agent.

The law provides that the act does not prohibit a buyer from agreeing to accept a title insurer or an escrow agent recommended by the seller if written notice of the right to make an independent selection is first provided by the seller to the buyer.

A seller who violates these provisions would be liable to the buyer for an amount equal to three times all charges made for the title insurance or escrow services.

Notice Regarding the Advisability of Title Insurance   In an escrow for a sale (or exchange) of real property where no title insurance is to be issued, the buyer (or both parties to an exchange) must receive and sign and acknowledge the following notice in the format (capital letters and bold type) shown and as required by California Civil Code Section 1057.6, as a separate document in the escrow:

> IMPORTANT: IN A PURCHASE OR EXCHANGE OF REAL PROPERTY, IT MAY BE ADVISABLE TO OBTAIN TITLE INSURANCE IN CONNECTION WITH THE CLOSE OF ESCROW SINCE THERE MAY BE PRIOR RECORDED LIENS AND ENCUMBRANCES WHICH AFFECT YOUR INTEREST IN THE PROPERTY BEING ACQUIRED. A NEW POLICY OF TITLE INSURANCE SHOULD BE OBTAINED IN ORDER TO INSURE OUR INTEREST IN THE PROPERTY THAT YOU ARE ACQUIRING.

While the statute does not expressly assign the duty, it is reasonable to assume that delivery of the notice is an obligation of the escrow holder. A real estate broker conducting an escrow pursuant to the exemption set forth in CFC Section 17006(a)(4) would, therefore, be responsible for delivery of the notice. (Cal. Civ. Code § 1057.6.)

Transfer Disclosures: The Transfer Disclosure Statement and Other Statutory Disclosures   Unless exempt, under California Civil Code Section 1102, the seller of a one-to-four unit residential property must provide the buyer with a written statement representing certain characteristics of the property, whether or not any components or features are not in operating condition, and the disclosure of any known defects in the property. Additionally, the seller must disclose the fact of any death occurring on the property within three years from the date that the purchase agreement was entered into, and any known neighborhood nuisance or noise problem. If the property being sold has been acquired by the seller through a foreclosure action, such as an REO, California law provides that the seller is exempt from providing certain disclosure forms to the buyers. The escrow agent must be aware, however, that the sale is not exempt from the required disclosure of certain known defects and hazards. Additionally, agent for the buyer and the seller are required in every transaction to perform a diligent visual inspection of the property and, in accordance with California Civil Code Section 1102, provide a written disclosure of the condition of the property (Transfer Disclosure Statement; CAR form TDS) to the buyer, as well as disclosures regarding earthquake fault zones, seismic hazard zones, state fire responsibility zones, very high fire hazard severity zones, flood hazard zones, and special flood hazard zones.

Lead-Based Paint   If the property was built before 1978, a written statement complying with federal law to disclose known lead-based paint must be provided, along with copies of reports covering lead-based paint and hazards on the property and copies of the pamphlet *Protect Your Family from Lead in Your Home.* Buyers must have 10 days to inspect for lead-based paint and hazards. The buyer's agent will make such disclosure and the buyer's acknowledgment part of the escrow. The required time frames for delivery to the buyer should be monitored by the escrow holder.

Registered Sex Offenders   Under the law the buyer must be provided with a written notice regarding the availability of information about registered sex offenders.

Condominium or PUD   HOA documentation must be presented to the buyer, while the responsibility of the seller, who may ask the listing agent to obtain it, but it often falls to the escrow officer.

Items Included or Excluded from the Sale   If any personal property, such as refrigerators, washers and dryers, free-standing ranges, and microwaves, is present and is to be included in the sale; the escrow officer should reflect each in the instruction or the supplemental instruction (often during the escrow, personal property that was not to be included through on-going negotiation becomes included).

Buyer's Investigation of the Property   Upon the buyers' timely review of all inspections and reports, the buyers should either accept the inspections and reports as being favorable and remove the contingencies or cancel the escrow. The escrow officer should closely monitor removal dates and be prepared for any required action.

Title and Vesting   The escrow officer should match the title and vesting as indicated on the purchase agreement to that provided by the buyer. Any differences should be resolved.

Contingency Sale of Buyer's Property   If escrow closing is contingent on the sale of the buyer's property, the escrow instruction will so state. If such a contingency has a removal date, which usually it does, the escrow officer should note the file.

Time Period for Removal of Contingencies   The CAR purchase agreement provides for a 17-day **contingency removal** term, unless otherwise specified. A purchase agreement may provide for different removal terms for various contingencies. The escrow officer should closely review the instructions to note the file, with the removal date for each, and monitor them accordingly. A buyer's removal in writing to be delivered to escrow and to the seller may be required.

Final Inspection of Premises by the Buyer   The buyers have the right to make a final inspection of the property but must understand that this inspection is not a contingency of the sale. If any controversy occurs and conflicting instructions are presented, the escrow officer should not proceed with either instruction but notify each party in writing that escrow may not proceed until the conflict is resolved.

Dispute Resolution The California Association of REALTORS® standard purchase agreements provide for the parties to first attempt **dispute resolution** through "mediation" before resorting to either "arbitration" or a court action. The purchase agreement offers the parties a choice of arbitration or no arbitration. Neither REALTORS® nor escrow officers should advise buyers or sellers as to the benefit, if any, of agreeing to the dispute resolution clause regarding arbitration as specified in the standard California Association of REALTORS® purchase agreements, except to explain the choices. Only an attorney may advise the buyers.

Liquidated Damages and Buyer's Deposit If the buyer cancels for any reason (other than disapproval of a contingency condition) within the specified time period and the parties have agreed to **liquidated damages** as specified in the purchase agreement, the seller retains the buyer's deposit. If the property is a one-to-four unit building, one of which the buyer had intended to occupy, the amount to be retained by the seller will be no more than 3% of the sales price, with any excess returned to the buyer. Actual release of the funds to the seller requires the buyer's agreement, a court order, or a finding in an arbitration.

Prorations of Property Taxes and Other Items The buyers should understand that they have been, or will be, provided with an estimate of prorated amounts for which they will be responsible, including supplemental property taxes, by the buyer's lender or by the escrow company.

■ CHAPTER 7 QUIZ

1. California law specifically states that a real estate broker may

   a. nominate an escrow holder as a condition to a transaction.

   b. not nominate an escrow holder as a condition to a transaction.

   c. nominate an escrow holder if the agent represents the seller.

   d. nominate an escrow holder if the agent represents the buyer.

2. The general qualifications for obtaining a California real estate license state that

   a. an individual must be 18 years of age or older.

   b. an individual must reside in California.

   c. an individual convicted of a crime may be denied a license.

   d. both a and c.

3. Under the general education requirements for obtaining a California real estate salesperson license, and individual must

   a. complete three college-level courses as specified by the Department of Real Estate.

   b. possess a degree from a four-year university.

   c. possess a high school diploma or GED.

   d. complete eight college-level courses as indicated by the Department of Real Estate.

4. Under California law, members of the state bar who want to obtain a California real estate license are

   a. exempt from the college course requirements.

   b. required to complete the college courses as required.

   c. required to complete only one of the college level courses.

   d. exempt from college course requirements if practicing real estate law.

5. Unless exempted under the law, to take the California real estate broker's license exam, an individual must have experience as a full-time California licensed salesperson

   a. for two of the last five years.

   b. for two years.

   c. for five years.

   d. for 18 months.

6. The California Association of REALTORS® Purchase Agreement and Joint Escrow Instructions calls for a loan contingency to be removed

   a. in 7 days, unless otherwise stated.

   b. in 17 days, unless otherwise stated.

   c. in 30 days, unless otherwise stated.

   d. as specified under specific California law.

7. Under truth-in-lending disclosure laws, a borrower obtaining a loan, subject to its provisions, must obtain a revised TIL from the lender if the originally disclosed rate is increased by 0.125% or greater and must wait an additional

   a. three business days before loan signing.

   b. three calendar days before loan signing.

   c. seven business days before loan signing.

   d. seven calendar days before loan signing.

8. Under California Buyer's Choice Act, a beneficiary who obtained a property through foreclosure and violates the law as a seller may be

   a. subject to damages twice the amount of escrow and title charges.

   b. subject to damages three times the amount of escrow and title charges.

   c. within its legal rights to do so in every instance.

   d. subject to a written order to cease but no financial penalty is imposed.

9. Under California law, a beneficiary acquiring a property through foreclosure and who is the seller in an escrow transaction

   a. is not exempt from delivering a Transfer Disclosure Statement to the buyer.

   b. is not exempt from being required to disclose any known defects to a buyer.

   c. is exempt from being required to disclose any known defects to a buyer.

   d. and is represented by a real estate agent, neither the seller nor the agent is required to deliver a Transfer Disclosure Statement to the buyer.

10. Under federal law, the buyer of a residential one-to-four-unit building constructed before 1978 must be given a booklet prepared by the government regarding the possibility of lead-based paint and

    a. 10 days to inspect the property.

    b. 17 days to inspect the property.

    c. 3 days to inspect the property.

    d. a reasonable amount of time to inspect the property.

CHAPTER EIGHT

8

OPENING ESCROW

■ KEY TERMS

Alcoholic Beverage Control	apportionment of charges	FSBO
joint escrow instructions	prorations	supplemental instructions
transaction outline	commission instructions	hazard insurance
	statement of identity	take sheet

■ LEARNING OBJECTIVES

Upon completing this chapter, you will be able to

- understand the information necessary to prepare the initial escrow instructions;

- understand the concept of instructions, as though written by the principals;

- understand and explain the operative clauses in the standard Purchase Agreement and Joint Escrow Instructions;

- understand and explain the real estate contractual requirements for for-sale-by-owner transactions and the limitations placed on the escrow holder in offering advice;

■ understand and explain the California legal requirement for escrow in a transaction involving the transfer of a liquor license;

■ understand and explain the distinction between escrow instructions and contracts; and

■ understand the fundamental escrow process and the escrow holder's responsibilities.

■ STEPS IN THE ESCROW

Once the title report has been ordered, escrow has been opened, and instructions prepared and delivered to the parties, the escrow holder proceeds through various tasks that conclude with closing and final reporting. The life of an escrow progresses generally as shown in the diagrams in Figure 8.1. After the initial interview, the escrow holder gathers the required information, documents, and forms; prepares the instructions; receives and reviews the title report; and delivers it to the parties. along with the completed instructions. While there may be some differences between the procedures in Northern and Southern California as shown in the flow charts, escrow involves gathering the required information, assembling it, and processing it through the closing to accomplish the principals' objectives: transferring title to or hypothecating (borrowing against) real or personal property and then providing a final accounting to the parties.

Step-by-Step Escrow Procedures

Prepare the Escrow Instructions   Reducing the terms of the contract to written escrow instructions establishes the contractual agreement of the parties. Escrow's agency to the principals is limited in scope, responsible only for carrying out the duties as specified in the escrow instructions. The escrow holder is not held to the same full disclosure requirements as those of a general agent. Copies of the instructions will be delivered to all parties as required, including information copies sent to the lender in the case of a refinance.

FIGURE 8.1

**Life of an Escrow:
Opening to Closing**

Southern California Processing

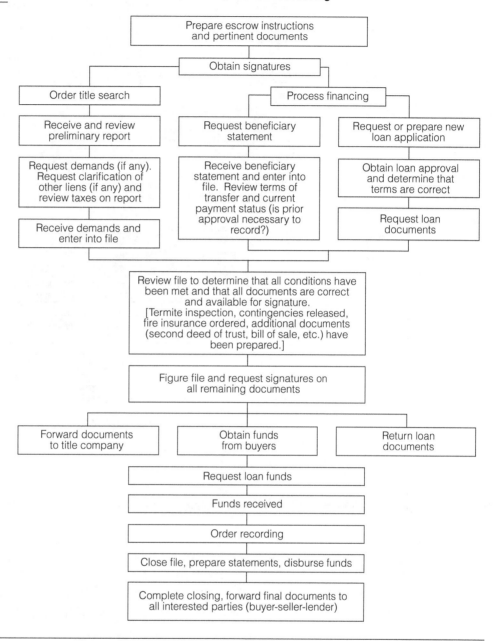

FIGURE 8.1

Life of an Escrow: Opening to Closing (continued)

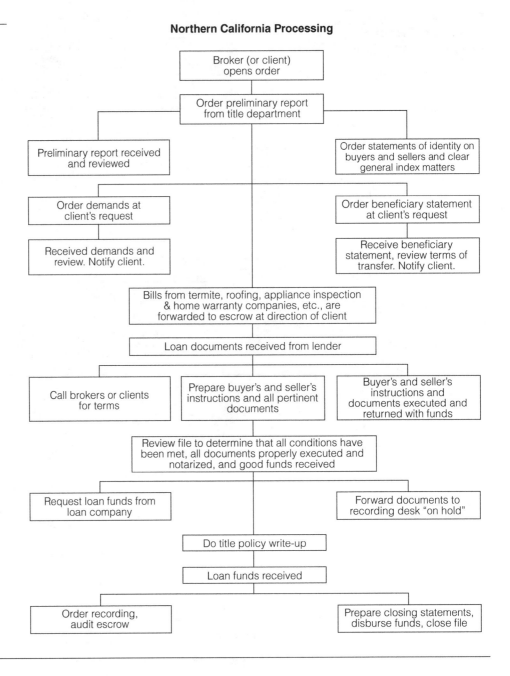

Northern California Processing

Broker (or client) opens order

Order preliminary report from title department

Preliminary report received and reviewed

Order statements of identity on buyers and sellers and clear general index matters

Order demands at client's request

Order beneficiary statement at client's request

Received demands and review. Notify client.

Receive beneficiary statement, review terms of transfer. Notify client.

Bills from termite, roofing, appliance inspection & home warranty companies, etc., are forwarded to escrow at direction of client

Loan documents received from lender

Call brokers or clients for terms

Prepare buyer's and seller's instructions and all pertinent documents

Buyer's and seller's instructions and documents executed and returned with funds

Review file to determine that all conditions have been met, all documents properly executed and notarized, and good funds received

Request loan funds from loan company

Forward documents to recording desk "on hold"

Do title policy write-up

Loan funds received

Order recording, audit escrow

Prepare closing statements, disburse funds, close file

Supplemental Instructions In a purchase transaction, the escrow holder usually only prepares instructions called **supplemental instructions** if the purchase agreement used is one provided by the California Association of REALTORS® (CAR). The CAR form already includes **joint escrow instructions** (*joint* meaning instructions prepared on one form for both the buyer and the seller) and therefore do not need to be prepared once again by the escrow holder. (Refinance loan escrow procedures are discussed in Chapter 12).

Assemble the Documentation   The escrow holder obtains, prepares, and assembles the required documents. These include deeds; notes; bills of sale; trust deeds; security agreements; UCC (Uniform Commercial Code) forms for filing financing statements, if necessary; and requests for information from parties to the transaction, such as payoff demands. A "demand" is a document that will be delivered to the escrow holder from the lender (beneficiary) indicating the total amount that must be deducted from the seller's proceeds to send to the lender to pay off the loan. If the buyer is assuming the seller's existing loan, after the approval process, the lender will send the escrow holder an "assignments of trust deed" document to be included with others for the buyer's signature.

Obtain and Review Title Report   The escrow holder orders the preliminary title report and proceeds to work with the title officer to eliminate items such as existing trust deeds securing loans that will be paid off in closing, unpaid taxes, judgments, tax liens, and any other items that must be resolved before clear title can be provided to the buyer or reported to the lender.

Obtain the Principals' Signatures   The escrow holder obtains signatures from the principals, ensuring they are delivered to escrow in a timely manner. Escrow is not considered open until all signatures have been obtained. If a buyer, for example, has signed and returned escrow instructions but the seller has not, there is technically no escrow until the remaining signatures are obtained.

Send Requests for Demands or Beneficiary Statements   The escrow holder will send a request for payoff information (demand) to the lender of a loan to be paid off or a request for a beneficiary statement to the lender of a loan to be assumed.

Receipt of Demands and Posting the Information   Upon receipt of the lender's payoff demand and any other lien or judgment payoff demand, the escrow officer will post (list) the information for use in accounting at closing when calculating the seller's net proceeds. Judgments, collections, or other liens attached to the buyer will be posted and used in arriving at the total funds the buyer must bring to close escrow.

■ BUYER'S FINANCING PROCEDURES AND ESCROW HOLDER INVOLVEMENT

Buyer's Loan Approval   Upon receipt of the buyer's loan documents, the escrow holder will review them with the loan officer or loan processor to ensure that no errors exist. The loan officer obtains the lender's fees to calculate the total funds due from the buyer, along with any other funds necessary to pay any liens.

Signing the Loan Documents   The loan officer arranges for the signing of the loan documents with the escrow officer or coordinates the signing with the escrow officer and a third-party notary public.

At least one hour should be reserved for signing loan documents.

If a non-escrow notary will be assisting the buyers' in signing their loan documents, the documents must be delivered to escrow first for accounting and processing escrow-related items. Today, most loan documents are delivered to the escrow holder electronically, greatly expediting the process. It is also helpful to have the loan officer present or available during the signing in the event the borrowers have questions regarding any portion of the documents. For example, questions that frequently arise include fees or costs on the settlement statement that differ from the amounts originally provided to the borrowers.

Escrow Officer's Role in the Borrowers' Signing Process   The escrow officer may only answer procedural questions regarding the escrow (i.e., fees, costs, and accounting) and may not interpret the meaning of any information in the loan documents. The escrow officer should instruct the borrowers to carefully read the documents before or as they sign and initial the pages. While all forms, documents, and clauses are important, some deserve special attention. The escrow officer should be certain that the borrowers read these and acknowledge their understanding of them. If they do not completely understand the documents and the loan officer is not present, the escrow officer should stop the signing process and contact the loan officer to offer an explanation. A copy of the loan application will be included with the documents to be signed by the borrower(s).

Borrowers Sign the Acknowledgment on Loan Application

In the loan application, the borrower(s) are advised of the following:

> Intentional or negligent misrepresentation of this information contained in this application may result in civil liability, including monetary damages, to any person who may suffer any loss due to reliance upon any misrepresentation that I have made on this application, and/or in criminal penalties including, but not limited to, fine or imprisonment or both under the provisions of Title 18, United States Code, Sec. 1001, et seq.

Above the spaces whether the borrowers sign are statements that the borrowers acknowledge as they sign the application. The paragraphs state, in part:

> The information provided in this application is true and correct as of the date set forth opposite my signature and *that any intentional or negligent misrepresentation of this information contained in this application may result in civil liability,*

including monetary damages, to any person who may suffer any loss due to reliance upon any misrepresentation that I have made on this application, and/or in criminal penalties including, but not limited to, fine or imprisonment or both under the provisions of Title 18, United States Code, Sec. 1001, et seq.; (emphasis added)

The loan requested pursuant to this application (the "Loan") will be secured by a mortgage or deed of trust on the property described in this application;

The property will not be used for any illegal or prohibited purpose or use;

All statements made in this application are made for the purpose of obtaining a residential mortgage loan;

The Lender, its servicers, successors or assigns may retain the original and/or an electronic record of this application, whether or not the Loan is approved;

The Lender and its agents, brokers, insurers, servicers, successors, and assigns may continuously rely on the information contained in the application, and *I am obligated to amend and/or supplement the information provided in this application if any of the material facts that I have represented herein should change prior to closing of the Loan* (emphasis added);

"In the event that my payments on the Loan become delinquent, the Lender, its servicers, successors or assigns may, in addition to any other rights and remedies that it may have relating to such delinquency, report my name and account information to one or more consumer reporting agencies";

Ownership of the Loan and/or administration of the Loan account may be transferred with such notice as may be required by law;

Neither Lender nor its agents, brokers, insurers, servicers, successors or assigns has made any representation or warranty, express or implied, to me regarding the property or the condition or value of the property; and

"My transmission of this application as an electronic record containing my electronic signature, as those terms are defined in applicable federal and/or state laws (excluding audio and video recordings), or my facsimile transmission of this application containing a facsimile of my signature, shall be as effective, enforceable and valid as if a paper version of this application were delivered containing my original written signature."

Acknowledgement. Each of the undersigned hereby acknowledges that any owner of the Loan, its servicers, successors and assigns, may verify or reverify any information contained in this application or obtain any information or data relating to the Loan, for any legitimate business purpose through any source, including a source named in this application or a consumer reporting agency.

Mistakes or Misstatements in Applications, Documents, or Signing

The major concerns a borrower should have are these: "Are the financial and credit information on the application complete and accurate?" "If the application and the loan documents indicate that the property is to be owner-occupied, is that true?"

Obviously, neither the escrow officer nor the loan officer wants to imply that any inaccurate information was intentionally provided as stated. Both officers should merely ask the borrowers to carefully read the documents for accuracy and verify that they understand the contents.

A report released by the FBI and the U.S. Treasury Financial Crimes Enforcement Network as a result of an investigation into loan fraud in a 2008 report revealed the following regarding borrower fraud:

- *Occupancy fraud.* The greatest percentage of all fraud types committed by borrowers who had made applications for "owner-occupied" loans is "occupancy fraud." These borrowers intentionally did not occupy the properties, renting them to tenants instead. The obvious reason was to obtain the typically lower rate offered by lenders for owner-occupied loans and the somewhat more liberal underwriting standards than for investment properties. Included with the loan documents is an Affidavit of Occupancy form that must be signed by borrowers' obtaining financing for a primary residence.

- *Other fraud.* Other types of fraud cited in the report included escrow holders forging applicants signatures, borrowers forging co-owners' signatures (usually a spouse forging the other's signature), and builder's forging borrowers' signatures on loan documents to expedite the closing process.

Loan Documents Delivered to Title   After the buyers sign the loan documents, the escrow holder returns the signed loan documents to the lender for funding when ready, and the trust deed is forwarded to the title company to be recorded when ready. For refinance loans, if the property is an owner-occupied one-to-four-unit residential, the lender must wait three days before funding the loan (right of rescission); the right of rescission does not apply to commercial or non-owner-occupied loan transactions.

Review File for Conditions   The escrow holder reviews the escrow file, comparing action items against the instructions, sending requests or inquiring with the source for any item not received. Typical conditions include a pest control inspection report with work completed and invoices, hazard insurance, secondary financing (prepare the seller's note and trust deed, if any), and any other action required.

Preclosing   Escrow officer "figures the file," calculating all monies due from or to the parties, and obtains final signatures for any documents remaining unsigned. The estimated settlement statement and the HUD-1 are prepared and forwarded to the parties for review.

Buyers' Funds   When escrow is "complete"—meaning all conditions have been met by both the buyer and the seller, all necessary documents have been signed and delivered to appropriate parties, and closing can be accommodated— the escrow officer calls for the buyers' funds to be delivered to escrow. The buyer may deliver a cashier's or certified check to escrow or have the bank wire the funds to escrow. California's "good funds" law provides for the following:

- Cash or electronically transferred funds delivered to the escrow holder can be disbursed the same day.

- Cashier's, certified, or teller's checks must be deposited one business day before the day of disbursement.

- Personal checks that are local must be held three business days before disbursement and non-local personal checks must be held five business days before disbursement of funds.

Request and Verify Loan Funds   When closing is ready, the escrow officer requests the borrower's loan funds from the lender and verifies the delivery date.

Recording   When all funds have been requested from both the buyer and the lender funding the buyer's loan, the escrow holder arranges for recording through the title company.

Closing and Accounting   Following the receipt of funds and recording of title, the escrow holder performs the final accounting, which includes the final Settlement Statement (HUD-1) and, if applicable, disburses funds to the parties.

Transmittal and Delivery of Final Documents   The last function of the escrow holder is to deliver final documents to all parties entitled to receive them, including buyer, seller, real estate agents, lender, and others.

■ OBTAINING THE INFORMATION

In a purchase transaction, after the purchase contract has been written, presented to, and accepted by the seller, escrow will be "opened." This begins when the real estate agent or principals (if no agent is involved) first select the escrow holder. The agent who actually selects the escrow holder, whether it's the buyer's or the seller's, depends on local custom. (Unless one or both principals frequently buy, sell, or refinance real estate, it is uncommon for them to have an escrow company relationship, deferring the selection to the real estate agent.)

The agent usually emails or faxes the purchase agreement to the escrow holder to begin the process, then calls or visits the escrow holder to provide the additional necessary information the escrow officer needs to prepare escrow instructions. Instructions are prepared as though written by the principals, who "instruct" the escrow holder as to the terms and conditions of the contract, and in which the escrow holder is "instructed" to progress toward a closing of escrow and to affect such a closing when the parties have complied with all the terms and conditions.

Purchase Agreement and Joint Escrow Instructions

The purchase contract usually used will be a CAR form, such as the Purchase Agreement and Joint Escrow Instructions (RPA-CA, for residential one-to-four unit properties). The CAR purchase agreement includes joint escrow instructions, which eliminate the need for the escrow holder to prepare instructions specifying the terms of the contract, using instead the purchase agreement as the fundamental basic escrow instruction. The escrow officer then prepares and issues supplemental escrow instructions, consisting primarily of matters not addressed in the purchase agreement and including boilerplate information such as language releasing the escrow holder from liability or limiting the escrow's responsibility for certain items and activities, such as the disposition of personal property.

The FSBO (For Sale by Owner)

Occasionally, escrow is opened by a principal not represented by a REALTOR®, such as a **FSBO** (pronounced *fiz-boe* and short for *For Sale by Owner*), using some other contract or instrument than the CAR form. In such a case, the escrow officer must prepare the entire escrow instruction, specifying the details as indicated in the contract and including information provided in their usual supplemental instructions. A FSBO seller may not be aware of all the many disclosures required to be provided to a buyer under the law.

The escrow holder may suggest that the principals seek legal advice if they are not represented by legal counsel or other professionals. If not, considerable delays may be encountered during the escrow, possibly even threatening closing.

Pro-Tip: FSBOs

When considering a For-Sale-by-Owner (FSBO) purchase contract, note the following:

■ Real estate purchase contracts in California must be in writing.

■ The escrow instruction is not a contract.

■ If the FSBO parties do not have a purchase contract, the instructions they provide to the escrow holder do not constitute a contract.

■ The escrow holder may not draw the contract but should suggest that the parties seek legal counsel and/or obtain a standard purchase agreement form available at most office supply stores or on the internet.

Once in awhile, principals will have no written contract at all, arriving at escrow and expecting the escrow holder to prepare "the meeting of the minds" in writing. Unless the escrow holder is an attorney and agrees to prepare such a contract as an ancillary and out-of-escrow service, the escrow holder will not prepare the contract. Accordingly, no contract exists and, therefore, no escrow will usually be opened or exist until the principals first prepare and execute a contract. The escrow holder should suggest that the parties seek appropriate legal or professional advice or service to assist them with the preparation of a contract.

Escrow and Transferring Liquor Licenses

The only transaction for which escrow is legally required is for the transfer of any license that comes under the jurisdiction of the Department of **Alcoholic Beverage Control** of the State of California (ABC), including all beer, wine, and liquor licenses issued for both the off-sale purpose (beverages are not to be consumed on the premises, such as for grocery stores, liquor stores, and minimarkets) and the on-sale purpose (to be consumed on the premises, such as bars and restaurants). These transactions require that a notice of the transfer be recorded and published, giving creditors of the seller the opportunity to file any claims with the escrow holder. Escrow holders usually have a checklist, which they provide to the principals in a transaction that does not include real estate agents. A sample checklist should include the following:

■ Prepare a purchase contract (CAR form, if available, or standard forms available at office supply stores). Identify all contingencies of the contract, including dates on which they must be completed, waived, or removed.

- Suggest that the parties seek legal counsel or employ a real estate agent to prepare the contract.

- Determine the amount of deposit required of the buyer and place into escrow.

- Buyer must determine vesting, provide to escrow.

- Seller must provide escrow with vesting and information on all liens on property.

- Identify title insurance company. If escrow holder is owned by a title company, the escrow officer should still ask the parties which company they wish to use.

- Determine allocation of costs and fees between the parties.

- Identify any financing the buyer is to obtain, lender name and contact information, and terms and conditions of loan.

- Provide information on all third-party vendors and services: appraiser, home inspector, pest control inspector, home warranty company, and others.

- The seller should be advised that under the law, certain disclosures must be provided to the buyer.

The escrow officer must be prepared for considerably more work when the parties are not represented by either a real estate agent or an attorney. The escrow officer must also guard against offering legal advice or performing services that require a California real estate license. It is quite easy to accidentally and unintentionally perform such services when trying to answer the many questions the parties might ask.

■ OPENING INTERVIEW

Before the introduction of the CAR Purchase Agreement and Joint Escrow Instructions, escrow was opened by the escrow officer using a "take or order sheet" and completing it by guiding the real estate agent or principal through the process, asking the appropriate questions about the transaction. Typically, the escrow officer not only did not use the purchase contract but also did not want it. Some transactions may still require the escrow officer to use the take-or-order sheet, such as a refinance or a contract other than a CAR form.

Statement of Identity or Information (SI Form)

The escrow holder provides the buyer with a **statement of identity** or information form (Figure 8.2), which gives escrow important information in preparing the escrow instruction. It also provides the title company the necessary information regarding the buyer's identity to ascertain whether any public records about the buyer, such as tax liens, judgments, paroles, incompetency, attorneys in fact, guardianship proceedings, bankruptcies, probates, and any other matter that could affect title. The Statement of Identity or Information must be completed as thoroughly as possible by the buyer to avoid any confusion with a similarly named individual, especially if the other person has items of record that (if not verified as not belonging buyer) could prevent or delay escrow closing.

FIGURE 8.2

Statement of Information

STATEMENT OF INFORMATION

Fidelity Title & Escrow maintains procedural safeguards that comply with federal standards to protect the confidentiality and security of non-public personal information. This statement will serve to establish identity, eliminate matters affecting persons of similar name, protect you against forgeries, and speed the completion of your title and escrow services.

COMPLETION OF THIS FORM WILL EXPEDITE YOUR ORDER AND WILL HELP PROTECT YOU.

Confidential information to be used in conjunction with order no. _____

NAME

FIRST	MIDDLE	LAST
asdfadf		

BIRTHPLACE	YEAR OF BIRTH	SOCIAL SECURITY NUMBER	I HAVE LIVED IN CALIFORNIA SINCE

FIRST	MIDDLE	LAST

BIRTHPLACE	YEAR OF BIRTH	SOCIAL SECURITY NUMBER	I HAVE LIVED IN CALIFORNIA SINCE

WE WERE MARRIED ON ____/____/____ AT_____ WIFE'S MAIDEN NAME_____

MY DRIVER'S LICENSE NUMBER (STATE)   MY SPOUSE'S DRIVER'S LICENSE NUMBER (STATE)

RESIDENCE(S) FOR LAST 10 YEARS

NUMBER AND STREET	CITY	FROM	TO
NUMBER AND STREET	CITY	FROM	TO
NUMBER AND STREET	CITY	FROM	TO
NUMBER AND STREET	CITY	FROM	TO

OCCUPATION(S) FOR LAST 10 YEARS

HUSBAND

PRESENT OCCUPATION	FIRM NAME	ADDRESS	NO. YEARS
PRESENT OCCUPATION	FIRM NAME	ADDRESS	NO. YEARS

WIFE

PRESENT OCCUPATION	FIRM NAME	ADDRESS	NO. YEARS
PRESENT OCCUPATION	FIRM NAME	ADDRESS	NO. YEARS

FORMER MARRIAGES

IF NO FORMER MARRIAGES, WRITE "NONE" _____

NAME OF FORMER WIFE	DECEASED ( ) DIVORCED ( )	____/____/____ DATE FINAL	WHERE
NAME OF FORMER HUSBAND	DECEASED ( ) DIVORCED ( )	____/____/____ DATE FINAL	WHERE

THE STREET ADDRESS OF THE PROPERTY IN THIS TRANSACTION IS: _____

SIGNATURE _____ DATE ____/____/____

SIGNATURE _____ DATE ____/____/____

(____) _____   (____) _____
        HOME TELEPHONE   BUSINESS PHONE

PURPOSE OF THIS FORM

It is necessary to fill out this form completely, as the information contained herein will assist us to process your escrow more accurately and avoid timely delays. The growing population of California has greatly affected the processing of real estate transactions, in that there are many people with names that are the same or similar to your own. When the title company searches the title of the property in this escrow, they want to make sure that they there are no judgments, bankruptcies, income tax liens or any other situation that may effect you or the property. The information on this form allows them to reject all matters that do not effect you.

Source: Fidelity Title Insurance Co.

The Take Sheet

In order to ensure that all pertinent information regarding the transaction is clearly written in the escrow instructions, the **take sheet** form includes an orderly sequence of questions covering every important aspect of a transaction. It includes information regarding the property information, the buyer and the seller (marital status, address, vesting, and other personal information), the new loan of the buyer (amount, terms, rate, lender and other details), prorating property taxes based on the anticipated closing date, title company identification (policy number, officer, and any special consideration, coverage, or exclusions), and information regarding any existing loans of the seller that will be paid off.

Each element of the transaction must be evaluated properly in order to reduce all of them to a mutually satisfactory instruction. Today, the take sheet is a computer program that easily guides the escrow officer through the process of gathering the pre-escrow instruction information, managing and assembling it to become the formal instruction, and then transmitting the final product, the escrow instruction, or supplemental escrow instruction, to all parties involved, including the title company. At the same time, the escrow holder can transmit the instruction as a certified copy to the buyer's lender. Once the title company, whether independent of the escrow company or not, receives the escrow instruction information, it immediately has all the necessary data regarding the property, the buyer, and the seller to prepare the preliminary title report. This report, frequently called simply the "prelim" or "pre," will indicate those items or perils against which the title company will insure the buyer and the property and those it will not.

Primary Information Required for the Escrow Instruction

Information required for the escrow officer to adequately prepare a complete and accurate escrow instruction includes the sales price, loans, trust deeds in place that will remain (those being assumed by a buyer in a purchase transaction or those not being paid off in a refinance transaction), loans to be paid off, any new loans being obtained, whether the sales price includes any personal property, any real property not to be included, and other details of the transaction. Because considerable information is required and must be obtained from a variety of sources, escrow officers are aided in remembering the basic elements of the escrow by using a checklist. The following items provide the escrow officer with the basic information required to prepare a complete escrow instruction. Many of these items were discussed in detail earlier:

- *Legal description.* The exact and complete legal description of the property must be included, along with the street address, if any, of the property.

■ *Type of property.* The property type will be specified (i.e., single-family residence or apartment building).

■ *Names of lenders, present and proposed.* The escrow holder will provide the principals with a form to help them provide information regarding their lenders, whether the seller's existing lender or the buyer's proposed lender.

■ *Names of the parties.* All parties to the transaction must be named completely and accurately, to ensure that the names are indicated exactly as they appear or are to appear on title.

■ *Terms of the escrow.* Terms must be indicated, including the date escrow is to close and when possession of the property is to be given to the buyer. These are clearly spelled out in the CAR form, although if another contract is being used, the escrow holder must ascertain that all required terms have been addressed.

■ *Contingency removal.* The contingency removal procedure allows a principal a certain number of days to perform, such as obtain a loan approval or inspections. This time is certainly an important consideration, usually restricted to only 17 days as specified in the CAR purchase agreement unless otherwise agreed upon.

■ *Proration instructions.* Certain fees may be required to be prorated, some between the buyer and the seller and others applicable only to one of the parties. These include property taxes, homeowners association dues, maintenance fees, rents, and interest on loans. Prorations may be based on a 30-day month, regardless of the actual number of days in the month, or on the actual days. The principals may also agree not to prorate some items, or some items may not be subject to proration for the transaction, such as a new hazard insurance policy or supplemental taxes imposed after the transfer is affected.

■ *Title company.* The selected title company will be indicated by name. In Northern California, the title company is usually always the same as or affiliated with the escrow company. In Southern California, as discussed earlier, an independent escrow company is usually used. However, local custom does not mean the custom is universally followed.

■ *Hazard insurance.* As discussed earlier, homeowners or **hazard insurance** is a type of property insurance that covers private homes. It requires that at least one of the named insured occupies the home, unless otherwise indicated (such as a policy especially intended for rental properties). This type of insurance policy combines various personal insurance protections, which can include losses occurring to one's home, its contents, loss of its use, or loss of other personal possession of the homeowner, as well as liability insurance for accidents that may happen at the home. Property hazard insurance will be stated in the instruction both as to the lenders requirements and the parties. The escrow holder will require the contact information for the buyer's hazard insurance for buyer compliance with the lender's requirements. It is important for the escrow holder to arrange this as early as possible in the escrow process.

If there is any 11th-hour reason for a possible delay to the closing, it is that the insurance policy or information has not been provided to the escrow holder by the borrower's insurance agent. If the property is a condominium, the escrow holder will obtain the master insurance policy and insurance agent's contact information from the HOA. In addition to the standard hazard and fire insurance, the buyer, the lender, or both may desire or require additional protection, such as for earthquakes, flood, construction or any other extraordinary coverage. Some insurance companies also offer blanket or umbrella policies and may include additional liability coverage.

- *Pest control report.* Any requirement for a pest control inspection and the need for any work indicated by the report, and the agreement as to who will pay for any work, must be specified. Contingency removal dates should also be specified.

- *Home warranty company.* If the buyer is going to obtain a home warranty, that fact must be indicated, including the name of the home warranty company, the amount of the premium, and which party will pay for it. A home warranty is usually a one-year renewable service contract that covers the repairs or replacement of many of the most frequently occurring breakdowns of home system components, such as plumbing, heating, air conditioning, electrical, appliances, and swimming pool equipment.

- *Natural Hazard Disclosure (NHD) company.* Specify who will order the NHD, the name of the company selected, and the type of report.

- *Home inspection.* Indicate whether a home inspection is to be performed, the nature of the inspection (whole house, septic, well, roof, etc.), the name of the company, the amount of the fee, and the contingency removal date. Indicate also who will pay for the report.

- *Apportionment of charges.* The **apportionment of charges** are typically done in accordance with local custom, but the parties can agree on any division of costs and fees that do not conflict with any regulation or law, such as the tax service fee (for FHA financing, this cannot be paid by the buyer) or the typical lender's fees and costs in a VA loan (cannot be paid by the veteran borrower).

■ *Real estate agents' commission instructions.* The commission fee split, if any, between the listing agent and selling agent, must be specified. The **commission instructions** will be in addition to and separate from the instructions for and between the seller and the buyer in a purchase transaction.

■ *Contact information for the parties.* Full and complete names, Social Security numbers, phone numbers, and addresses for all parties must be indicated. This information will be provided to the escrow holder by the principals on a Statement of Information form delivered to them by the escrow officer. The escrow holder and the title company will use the information for a number of purposes, such as the seller's loan pay-off and to search public records for matters affecting the transaction and the title, such as judgments and liens.

■ *Special instructions.* Any other procedural or special consideration that may apply should be indicated, such as delivery of documents, certain requirements of the buyer or the seller, and other matters.

■ *Intent of the parties.* The escrow holder must insure that instructions drawn by the escrow officer accurately reflect the written contract and the intent of the parties.

Privacy

Understandably much of the information in the instructions is private and privileged, to be considered confidential, and not to be shared with any disinterested third party. It should be shared only with the parties to the transaction to the extent the information involves them or is necessary for them to perform their obligations and services. Any other disclosure requires the expressed written consent of the party whose information is to be disclosed.

Procedures and Customs

The actual time of preparing the escrow instructions at the beginning of a transaction or just prior to its closing may differ depending on local practice and customs. Whether the instructions are to be unilateral (typical with Northern California escrow), prepared in separate parts for the buyer and the seller, or bilateral (custom in Southern California), or prepared as one instruction for both buyer and seller (though signed separately), it is critical that the instruction be prepared exactly as the terms of the contract are specified and structured. As escrow progresses, it is not uncommon for changes or amendments to the original instructions to be required. Changes to a typical Northern California escrow are seldom required because it is prepared nearer the closing.

■ TRANSACTION OUTLINE

After obtaining all necessary information, the basic instruction will be prepared. Instruction formats may vary if the CAR Purchase Agreement is not being used as the basic instruction, but in all cases, a systematic method and approach will require that each item is included. It is absolutely imperative that all pertinent data be collected from the parties to fulfill the basic intent of the transaction.

Before actually beginning to prepare the instructions, the escrow officer will usually prepare a basic **transaction outline** after obtaining the initial information from the parties. When the preliminary title report is received, the escrow officer will update the information, correcting anything that differs from the information provided by the parties (after first confirming with them that the preliminary title report is correct). Outlining the details of the transaction in narrative form helps establish the objective of the principals.

Example: The Transaction

John and Mary Jones are buying a single-family residence from James and Martha Smith.

The property is located at 1223 Elmwood Street, Bakersfield CA 93312. They are paying $100,000 cash down and obtaining new financing in the amount of $400,000 from Bank of North America, a 30-year term loan with a fixed rate of 5%. James and Martha Seller have an existing loan to be paid off at closing, with an unpaid balance in the amount of $120,200 at Bank of the Far West, 1200 Willow Pass Road, Concord, CA 94500, loan number 120002, a rate of 6.25% and a monthly payment of $1,802.11.

The escrow holder will prepare an outline that will serve as a guide in preparing the narrative escrow instructions for this transaction as follows:

The Transaction Outline

Financial outline: Numerically, the financial details:
Down payment amount + financing = total consideration.

Example:

$ 100,000 cash down payment
+ 400,000 new loan
$ 500,000 total consideration)

Nature of transaction: Sale, escrow to close within 45 days

Legal description: Lot 12 of Tract 1445 in the city of Bakersfield, Kern County, as per map recorded in Book 1202, page 18 of Maps.

Property address: 1223 Elmwood Street, Bakersfield CA 93312

Sellers: James and Martha Smith

Sellers' address: 1223 Elmwood Street, Bakersfield CA 93312

Buyers: John and Mary Jones, taking title as husband and wife as joint tenants.

Buyers' address: 122 First Street, Apartment 3, Bakersfield CA 93308

New financing: First deed of trust from Bank of North America, $400,000, 30-year fixed-rate at 5%.

Payoffs: Bank of the Far West, 1200 Willow Pass Road, Concord, CA 94500; loan number 12002; balance $120,200; rate 6.25%; $1,802.11 monthly.

Adjustments: Taxes $1,955.10 annually; hazard insurance $642 annually

Buyer's deposit: $4,000

■ CHAPTER 8 QUIZ

1. If the escrow holder is using the CAR Purchase Agreement and Joint Escrow Instructions for the escrow's opening information,

   a. the escrow officer must still prepare a new and complete instruction.

   b. the escrow officer usually prepares only a supplemental instruction to begin with.

   c. the escrow officer is prohibited from using the CAR form as the instruction.

   d. the boilerplate language is contained in the CAR form so no additional instructions need to be prepared.

2. A For-Sale-By-Owner escrow in which the principals do not have a contract

   a. requires escrow to indicate that the escrow instruction is the contract.

   b. requires escrow to inform the parties to have a contract prepared.

   c. requires the escrow officer to prepare a contract for the parties.

   d. both b and c.

3. The Statement of Information or Statement of Identity

   a. is a statement of the buyers' personal information for the lender.

   b. is a statement provided to the buyer from escrow regarding fees.

   c. is a statement in which the buyer provides information necessary for the title company to adequately search public records in order to issue a policy.

   d. none of these.

4. The Statement of Identity is used to obtain which of the following information?

   a. Liens or judgments against the buyer

   b. The credit score of the buyer

   c. Bankruptcies or probates which may affect title

   d. Both a and c

5. The take sheet

    a. outlines the escrow process and is provided to the buyer.

    b. is an orderly sequence of questions the escrow holder asks the parties.

    c. is neither a nor b.

    d. is both a and b.

6. Information required for the escrow officer to adequately prepare a complete and accurate escrow instruction include, among other things,

    a. the sales price.

    b. new loans to be obtained and loans which will remain.

    c. loans to be paid off.

    d. all of these.

7. Unless indicated otherwise, the contingency removal period indicated in the CAR Purchase Agreement and Joint Escrow Instructions is

    a. 10 days.

    b. 14 days.

    c. 17 days.

    d. not specified, except as indicated by the parties in a separate agreement.

8. Prorations may be based on

    a. either a 30-day month or the actual days.

    b. only a 30-day month.

    c. only the actual days.

    d. 30.42 days per month (364 divided by 12).

9. The buyers' hazard insurance standard coverage will include

    a. earthquake insurance.

    b. flood insurance.

    c. both a and b.

    d. neither a nor b.

10.   Bilateral escrow instructions are prepared at the opening of escrow

    a.   as is the custom for Northern California escrow transactions.

    b.   as is the custom for Southern California escrow transactions.

    c.   are seldom prepared.

    d.   are illegal.

CHAPTER NINE

THE ESCROW
INSTRUCTIONS

■ KEY TERMS

allocation of costs
bar treaty
bill of sale
California Homestead
   Act

California tax
   withholding
closing statement
essential elements of a
   deed
financing statement

FIRPTA
grant deeds
HOA certificate
HUD-1
PCOR
supplemental tax bill

■ LEARNING OBJECTIVES

Upon completing this chapter, you will be able to

■ utilize the technological applications for the escrow process;

■ perform the procedures involved in the preparation of instructions and the escrow process, including closing statements;

■ understand the customary allocation of buyers' and seller' costs;

■ understand the FIRPTA and California tax withholding requirements;

■ understand the process involved in signing and processing loan documents;

■ understand the Preliminary Change of Ownership Report (PCOR); and

■ understand the supplemental tax bill.

■ ACCURACY THROUGH TECHNOLOGY

The probability of committing errors is fortunately reduced or eliminated through the implementation of systems and programs designed to safeguard against common errors.

Computer systems and software allow the escrow holder to prepare instructions that should be error free, however GIGO (garbage in, garbage out) applies to escrow programs just as it does to any computer software program. The resulting data and information is only as valid as the data and information entered. Therefore, the escrow holder who enters inaccurate information (garbage in) can only expect to receive inaccurate results (garbage out).

Attention to detail is always important; errors must be corrected, causing delays. Real estate and escrow professionals recognize that in every transaction "time is always of the essence."

■ PREPARATION OF THE INSTRUCTIONS

All basic data must be available to the escrow officer who is charged with completing the escrow instruction and with complying with the terms and conditions of the transaction, such as instruments of title and transfer, new liens created by the transfer, and any liens removed by it.

Using the data provided by the principals, an escrow instruction is drawn (prepared). Keep in mind that if the CAR Standard Purchase Agreement and Joint Escrow Instructions form is used, much of the foregoing process is eliminated, requiring instead only the preparation of the supplemental escrow instruction.

Basic Data

The escrow instructions begin by addressing the basic details of the escrow, legal descriptions of the property, its street address, vesting, and conditions of title.

Cash Summary

For the benefit of all parties, a summary list of the elements comprising the consideration is included at the head of the escrow instruction form. The memo box is included in the bilateral but not unilateral instruction because the unilateral is produced near closing and is therefore more complete.

- *Cash.* Note the amount of cash obtained from any source, whether a cash deposit or funds from new financing. This amount, plus or minus any fees and costs, adjustments, or prorations, represents the total actual cash that flows through the transaction. The escrow officer must account for this money in the financial **allocation of costs** in the settlement statement.

- *Non-cash consideration.* Account for any non-cash consideration, such as the equivalent value of personal property and encumbrances of record.

- *Exchange property transactions.* In an exchange transaction, the memo box would include the equities being transferred to or from the parties, and the total consideration would establish equity position (discussed later).

- *Prorations.* The escrow instructions include any prorations of property taxes, city and county transfer tax stamps, rents, interest on loans of record, hazard insurance, homeowners' association dues and assessments, and any other sales related items.

- *General instructions.* At one time, these provisions used to be printed on the back of the general escrow instructions and were obliquely referred to on the front with language such as "these instructions contain the general provisions included on the reverse side." With the advent of the CAR Purchase Agreement and Joint Escrow Instructions being the primary instrument used as the basic escrow instruction in most transactions, as well as an increasingly litigious society, general provisions are signed by all parties to the escrow instruction as a separate part of the instruction but considered a part of the entire instruction.

- *Buyer's and seller's costs.* Customary division and allocation of costs between the buyer and the seller are represented in Figure 9.1, though allocation of some costs may vary, depending on whether escrow is in Southern or Northern California.

FIGURE 9.1

Allocation of Costs in California

	Seller	Buyer
Drawing deed	X	
Documentary transfer tax	X	
Documentary local transfer tax	50%	50%
Recording deed		X
Drawing note		X
Drawing deed of trust		X
Recording trust deed		X
Notarizing grant deed	X	
Notarizing trust deed	X	
Title policy, owner's (buyer pays in Northern California)	X	
Title policy, lender's for buyer's loan		X
Beneficiary demand	X	
Reconveyance fee	X	
Recording reconveyance	X	
Sale escrow fee	50%	50%
Loan escrow fee		X

■ *Signatures and demand.* These recitals are followed by the buyer's and the seller's signatures. The paragraph preceding the seller's signature includes the seller's demand in the form of money for the deed less demands and costs allocated to the seller's portion of the transaction.

■ *Special provisions.* For each additional page required to complete the escrow instructions, a reference to each would be made in the first page of the instructions and a signature line for the buyer and the seller would be inserted.

■ *Foreign Investment of Real Property Tax Act (FIRPTA).* **FIRPTA** is a federal law intended to ensure that the U.S. Treasury receives income taxes that may be due and payable from a seller of real property who resides outside the United States. If the seller is a "foreign person," under FIRPTA every buyer must, unless an exemption applies, deduct and withhold 10% of the gross sales price from seller's proceeds (funds which would otherwise be paid to sellers) and send it to the Internal Revenue Service. While the law specifies that the buyer is to perform the withholding, in practice, it is the escrow holder who performs the service on behalf of the buyer from escrow funds provided by the buyer for the purchase price. Details of withholding requirements are discussed later in "Tax Reporting."

■ *California withholding.* Similar to FIRPTA, the state of California requires withholding for certain property sales. Originally implemented in 1988, **California tax withholding** was amended in 2002 with provisions that became effective for real property transfers that occurred on or after January 1, 2003. California withholding requires real estate transferees (buyers) to withhold a certain portion of the sales price paid for specified California real property from funds that would otherwise be paid to sellers. The amount withheld must be held in trust for the State of California, according to the law. Specific withholding requirements are found in "Tax Reporting."

■ *Other special considerations*. The escrow instructions will include any special requirements of the transaction or transfer of title, such as city or county retrofit, smoke detectors, residential property reports, or other ordinances and local city or county requirements.

Limited Authority of Escrow Holder to Draw Documentation

The preparation or "drawing" of certain documents by the escrow holder could be considered an unauthorized practice of law. Therefore, the escrow officer may not always be able to prepare some of the documentation necessary to effect the transfer of the property's title. If the preparation of such a document goes beyond "filling in the blanks" and requires legal judgment, an attorney must prepare it. Examples of this include unusual or complex terms, leases other than standard forms, and other detailed written agreements relative to property rights.

Printed Forms and Practice of Law

Escrow professionals are careful to not prepare any document in a manner that might be considered an illegal practice of law. In 1967, an agreement with the California State Bar described the documents that escrow holders were allowed to prepare. The Federal Trade Commission (FTC) ruled in 1979 that the **bar treaty,** or escrow treaty as it was called, was in violation of federal law. In general practice, the forms an escrow holder may prepare are recommended to be those in general use and of established form and be generally printed and commonly used in real or personal property transactions, including business opportunity transactions, generally still following the original provisions of the bar treaty.

Industry and legal professionals consider that a rigid and strict interpretation of this provision is not what the authors intended; rather it is meant to be a guide for the escrow holder to follow in a reasonable and practical application. Otherwise, even the mere preparation of escrow instructions itself might possibly be considered "practicing law."

■ *Variations*. The boilerplate and general instructions printed in the escrow instructions may vary and continue to change somewhat among escrow companies. Variations may occur due to new legislation and advanced technology, data processing systems, and programs.

■ *Liability*. The courts increasingly recognize the escrow holder as a person or entity more knowledgeable than the general public, making it somewhat difficult for the escrow holder to be protected by its "hold harmless" language. Much depends on the subject of the matter from which the escrow holder is claiming the ability to be held harmless.

Standard and Usual Escrow-Prepared Documents

Documents which may typically be prepared by the escrow holder include, but may not be limited to, the following:

■ *Escrow instructions*. Standard, joint, or supplemental instructions all fall within the list of documents acceptable under the law for the escrow holder to prepare.

■ *Transfer deeds*. These include grant deeds and quitclaim deeds.

■ *Declaration of homestead*. If the buyers will occupy the property as their primary residence, they may want to prepare and record a declaration of homestead (see "Homestead" in this chapter).

■ *Notes*. The escrow holder may legally draw notes secured by real or personal property. The note (technically called a promissory note, which is the promise to pay) is the evidence of the debt. It is signed but neither notarized nor recorded.

■ *Deeds of trust*. This document accompanies the note for seller carry-back financing. This would also include an all-inclusive deed of trust (or wraparound).

■ *Bills of sale*. The **bill of sale** is used for personal property transactions (e.g., the sale of a business).

■ *Security agreement*. In a transaction in which personal property is the collateral, this is the instrument that creates a lien against the property, usually in business opportunity transactions. The security agreement in a real property transaction is the deed of trust. Remember that the note, not the security agreement, is the evidence of the debt.

■ *Financing statement*. The **financing statement**, which is filed with the secretary of state of California but is not recorded, serves as public notice that a debt or security agreement exists with the specified personal property used and secured as collateral. The distinction between the financing statement and a deed of trust used for personal property is that a deed of trust is recorded by the county recorder in which the property (the collateral for a real estate loan) is located. The financing statement, however, does not create a lien against the personal property, as does the deed of trust. A typical transaction in which the escrow holder may process a financing statement using the California UCC form would be for a manufactured home, which would be personal instead of real property. However, other transactions utilize it as well, such as the sale of a business.

■ *Truth-in-lending documentation.* Usually prepared by the lender, the escrow holder is qualified to prepare some truth-in-lending documents, perhaps for a noninstitutional lender originating a loan to be secured by a one-to-four-unit property. In most cases, however, the escrow holder is not typically asked to perform this duty.

■ *Closing statement.* The escrow holder has the responsibility for preparing the **closing statement**, which accounts for all funds received and disbursed in accordance with the Real Estate Settlement Procedures Act (RESPA). As escrow closing approaches, the escrow officer will prepare an estimated settlement statement and **HUD-1** (Department of Housing and Urban Development closing statement form).

■ *Other forms.* Any other form or document required for the specific transaction may be prepared by the escrow holder if it essentially requires that the escrow officer only "fill in the blanks." If such a document would require narrative statements, an attorney must be employed to draw it.

■ *HOA certificate (Homeowners' Association Certification).* The **HOA certificate** form, although not prepared by the escrow holder, is one the escrow professional be familiar with because it becomes part of the escrow documentation. The buyer and the buyer's lender will require a Homeowner's Association Certification form (informally called the HOA cert) to be completed by the HOA and delivered to escrow with the HOA's information (bylaws, articles of incorporation, and insurance policy). The HOA cert provides a summary of the fundamental information regarding the HOA.

■ SPECIAL ESCROW DISCLOSURES

Escrow holders may be required to include disclosures of a protective nature in instructions intended to advise the buyer and/or the seller of certain legal requirements, actions, or limitations to which they may be subject. These protective clauses are described in the following paragraphs.

Local Code and Assessor's Requirements

Local (city and county) agencies and their respective regulations that may impose fees, penalties, requirements, or limitations on the principals must be disclosed by the escrow holder. These may include the following:

- *Supplemental tax bill.* Following the close of escrow, the county will prepare and issue a **supplemental tax bill**, which may either increase or decrease the tax level imposed on the property being transferred. The amount of the increase will be unknown to the buyer at escrow closing, and as such, the escrow holder is unable to indicate to the buyer any increase or decrease except to inform the buyer that it will occur.

- *Preliminary Change of Ownership Report (PCOR).* Required before closing, the **PCOR** form (Figure 9.2) is prepared by the buyers of a sale transaction or completes the memorandum of a lease. The form provides essential information regarding the terms of the sale. Each county in California has its own form. Escrow delivers the completed copy at closing to the county.

- *Retrofit ordinances.* State law under the Health and Safety Code Section 13113.8 requires smoke detectors to be placed and installed in all residential properties sold; a disclosure statement must be provided to the buyer. Also, some cities may require the installation of tempered safety glass in all sliding glass doors or that other safety issues be addressed.

FIGURE 9.2
Sample Preliminary Change of Ownership Report

BOE-502-A (P1) REV. 11 (07-10)

PRELIMINARY CHANGE OF OWNERSHIP REPORT

To be completed by the transferee (buyer) prior to a transfer of subject property, in accordance with section 480.3 of the Revenue and Taxation Code. A *Preliminary Change of Ownership Report* must be filed with each conveyance in the County Recorder's office for the county where the property is located. Please answer all questions in each section, and sign and complete the certification before filing. This form may be used in all 58 California counties. If a document evidencing a change in ownership is presented to the Recorder for recordation without the concurrent filing of a *Preliminary Change of Ownership Report*, the Recorder may charge an additional recording fee of twenty dollars ($20).

NOTICE: The property which you acquired may be subject to a supplemental assessment in an amount to be determined by the County Assessor. Supplemental assessments are not paid by the title or escrow company at close of escrow, and are not included in lender impound accounts. **You may be responsible for the current or upcoming property taxes even if you do not receive the tax bill.**

SELLER/TRANSFEROR	ASSESSOR'S PARCEL NUMBER

BUYER/TRANSFEREE	BUYER'S DAYTIME TELEPHONE NUMBER ( )

STREET ADDRESS OR PHYSICAL LOCATION OF REAL PROPERTY

MAIL PROPERTY TAX INFORMATION TO (NAME)

ADDRESS	CITY	STATE	ZIP CODE

☐ YES ☐ NO This property is intended as my principal residence. If YES, please indicate the date of occupancy or intended occupancy. | MO | DAY | YEAR

PART 1. TRANSFER INFORMATION   *Please complete all statements.*

YES NO

☐ ☐ A. This transfer is solely between spouses *(addition or removal of a spouse, death of a spouse, divorce settlement, etc.)*.

☐ ☐ B. This transfer is solely between domestic partners currently registered with the California Secretary of State *(addition or removal of a partner, death of a partner, termination settlement, etc.)*.

☐ ☐ *C. This is a transfer between: ☐ parent(s) and child(ren)   ☐ grandparent(s) and grandchild(ren).

☐ ☐ *D. This transaction is to replace a principal residence by a person 55 years of age or older. Within the same county? ☐ YES ☐ NO

☐ ☐ *E. This transaction is to replace a principal residence by a person who is severely disabled as defined by Revenue and Taxation Code section 69.5. Within the same county? ☐ YES ☐ NO

☐ ☐ F. This transaction is only a correction of the name(s) of the person(s) holding title to the property *(e.g., a name change upon marriage)*. If YES, please explain: _____

☐ ☐ G. The recorded document creates, terminates, or reconveys a lender's interest in the property.

☐ ☐ H. This transaction is recorded only as a requirement for financing purposes or to create, terminate, or reconvey a security interest *(e.g., cosigner)*. If YES, please explain: _____

☐ ☐ I. The recorded document substitutes a trustee of a trust, mortgage, or other similar document.

J. This is a transfer of property:

☐ ☐ 1. to/from a revocable trust that may be revoked by the transferor and is for the benefit of ☐ the transferor, and/or ☐ the transferor's spouse ☐ registered domestic partner.

☐ ☐ 2. to/from a trust that may be revoked by the creator/grantor/trustor who is also a joint tenant, and which names the other joint tenant(s) as beneficiaries when the creator/grantor/trustor dies.

☐ ☐ 3. to/from an irrevocable trust for the benefit of the ☐ creator/grantor/trustor and/or ☐ grantor's/trustor's spouse ☐ grantor's/trustor's registered domestic partner.

☐ ☐ 4. to/from an irrevocable trust from which the property reverts to the creator/grantor/trustor within 12 years.

☐ ☐ K. This property is subject to a lease with a remaining lease term of 35 years or more including written options.

☐ ☐ L. This is a transfer between parties in which proportional interests of the transferor(s) and transferee(s) in each and every parcel being transferred remain exactly the same after the transfer.

☐ ☐ M. This is a transfer subject to subsidized low-income housing requirements with governmentally imposed restrictions.

☐ ☐ *N. This transfer is to the first purchaser of a new building containing an active solar energy system.

* If you checked YES to statements C, D, or E, you may qualify for a property tax reassessment exclusion, which may allow you to maintain your previous tax base. If you checked YES to statement N, you may qualify for a property tax new construction exclusion. A claim form must be filed and all requirements met in order to obtain any of these exclusions. Contact the Assessor for claim forms.

Please provide any other information that will help the Assessor understand the nature of the transfer.

THIS DOCUMENT IS NOT SUBJECT TO PUBLIC INSPECTION

FIGURE 9.2

Sample Preliminary Change of Ownership Report (continued)

BOE-502-A (P2) REV. 11 (07-10)

PART 2. OTHER TRANSFER INFORMATION   *Check and complete as applicable.*

A. Date of transfer, if other than recording date: _____

B. Type of transfer:

  ☐ Purchase   ☐ Foreclosure   ☐ Gift   ☐ Trade or exchange   ☐ Merger, stock, or partnership acquisition (Form BOE-100-B)

  ☐ Contract of sale. Date of contract: _____   ☐ Inheritance. Date of death: _____

  ☐ Sale/leaseback   ☐ Creation of a lease   ☐ Assignment of a lease   ☐ Termination of a lease. Date lease began: _____

         Original term in years *(including written options)*: _____   Remaining term in years *(including written options)*: _____

  ☐ Other. Please explain: _____

C. Only a partial interest in the property was transferred. ☐ YES ☐ NO   If YES, indicate the percentage transferred: _____ %

PART 3. PURCHASE PRICE AND TERMS OF SALE   *Check and complete as applicable.*

A. Total purchase or acquisition price. Do not include closing costs or mortgage insurance. $_____

   Down payment: $_____   Interest rate: _____ %   Seller-paid points or closing costs: $_____

                                           Balloon payment: $_____

  ☐ Loan carried by seller   ☐ Assumption of Contractual Assessment* with a remaining balance of: $_____

             * An assessment used to finance property-specific improvements that constitutes a lien against the real property.

B. The property was purchased: ☐ Through real estate broker. Broker name: _____   Phone number: (____) _____

  ☐ Direct from seller   ☐ From a family member

  ☐ Other. Please explain: _____

C. Please explain any special terms, seller concessions, financing, and any other information (e.g., buyer assumed the existing loan balance) that would assist the Assessor in the valuation of your property.

_____

_____

PART 4. PROPERTY INFORMATION   *Check and complete as applicable.*

A. Type of property transferred

  ☐ Single-family residence   ☐ Co-op/Own-your-own   ☐ Manufactured home

  ☐ Multiple-family residence. Number of units: _____   ☐ Condominium   ☐ Unimproved lot

  ☐ Other. Description: (i.e., timber, mineral, water rights, etc.)   ☐ Timeshare   ☐ Commercial/Industrial

B. ☐ YES ☐ NO Personal/business property, or incentives, are included in the purchase price. Examples are furniture, farm equipment, machinery, club memberships, etc. Attach list if available.

   If YES, enter the value of the personal/business property: $_____

C. ☐ YES ☐ NO A manufactured home is included in the purchase price.

   If YES, enter the value attributed to the manufactured home: $_____

  ☐ YES ☐ NO The manufactured home is subject to local property tax. If NO, enter decal number: _____

D. ☐ YES ☐ NO The property produces rental or other income.

   If YES, the income is from: ☐ Lease/rent   ☐ Contract   ☐ Mineral rights   ☐ Other: _____

E. The condition of the property at the time of sale was: ☐ Good   ☐ Average   ☐ Fair   ☐ Poor

CERTIFICATION

I certify (or declare) under penalty of perjury under the laws of the State of California that the foregoing and all information hereon, including any accompanying statements or documents, is true and correct to the best of my knowledge and belief. **This declaration is binding on each and every buyer/transferee.**

SIGNATURE OF BUYER/TRANSFEREE OR CORPORATE OFFICER | DATE

►

NAME OF BUYER/TRANSFEREE/LEGAL REPRESENTATIVE/CORPORATE OFFICER (PLEASE PRINT) | TITLE

E-MAIL ADDRESS

The Assessor's office may contact you for additional information regarding this transaction.

Funds Deposited in Escrow

A purchaser of real property is required in most sales transactions to make a deposit against the sales price and to have the deposit monies placed into and held by escrow until closing. In California, a customary deposit is 3% of the sales price based on the state provisions for liquidated damages. If the buyer's deposit is substantial or if the escrow is for an extended term, the purchaser may request to have interest paid on funds held by escrow. In such a situation, an interest-bearing account must be established. The escrow holder will prepare a specific and separate instruction for the buyer to sign, which will require the inclusion of the buyer's Social Security number or, if a business, the tax ID number. Escrow will pass any fee charged by the bank for the maintenance of the account on to the buyer.

Release of Funds to Seller

Experienced escrow officers realize that most real estate professionals representing buyers are reluctant to allow a buyer to agree to releasing funds to a seller prior to closing. Occasionally, however, the purchase agreement and joint escrow instructions will specify that the buyer's cash deposit, or a portion of it, is to be released to the seller. The terms of the release will vary depending on the agreement between the parties. For example, it may provide that following the buyer's inspection and contingency removal period, usually 17 days unless stated otherwise in the agreement, the buyer's deposit is to be released to the seller. It may also provide that funds are nonrefundable to the buyer or will specify the conditions on which the funds are to be refunded. Release of funds out of escrow is usually not advisable and can offer serious consequences in the event problems closing are encountered. If and when funds are to be released, the escrow holder will prepare a separate instruction indicating the terms of the release exactly as the parties specified and which all will sign.

Tax Reporting

Withholding tax for the tax liability of a seller may be required of the buyer. Under both federal and state tax law and under certain conditions, the escrow holder may be required to have the buyer withhold an amount of funds otherwise due and payable to a seller at closing and instead have the escrow holder forward such funds to the Internal Revenue Service and the California Franchise Tax Board. In addition to tax withholding, other tax considerations may apply as well.

Foreign Investment in Real Property Tax Act (FIRPTA) Procedures

As discussed briefly earlier, Internal Revenue Service provisions state that the disposition (sale or transfer) of a U.S. real property interest by a foreign person (the transferor) is subject to Foreign Investment in Real Property Tax Act of 1980 (FIRPTA) income tax withholding. *Disposition* means for any purpose of the Internal Revenue Code, including but not limited to a sale or exchange, liquidation, redemption, gift, transfers, and other like transfers. A U.S. real property interest includes sales of interests in parcels of real property, as well as sales of shares, in certain U.S. corporations that are considered U.S. real property holding corporations.

Persons purchasing U.S. real property interests (transferees) from foreign persons, certain purchasers' agents, and settlement officers are required to withhold 10% of the sales price. Withholding is intended to ensure that the United States and its taxpayers are compensated for gains realized on disposition of such interests.

The transferee/buyer is considered to be the withholding agent. The transferee/buyer has the responsibility to determine if the transferor is a foreign person. If the transferor is a foreign person, the transferee who fails to withhold may be held personally liable for the tax. Withheld funds are sent to the IRS, along with form 8288.

If a U.S. business entity such as a corporation or partnership disposes of a U.S. real property interest, the business entity itself is the withholding agent. While the responsibilities for withholding, or providing proof that withholding is not required, rests with the buyer, it is the escrow holder who processes it.

Withholding Guidelines   The amount that must be withheld from the disposition of a U.S. real property interest can be adjusted pursuant to a withholding certificate. The following provisions apply:

- A disposition includes the sale of any U.S. real property interests in the United States or U.S. Virgin Islands.

- Generally speaking, in reference to the disposition of a U.S. real property interest, the foreign person disposing of the U.S. real property interest is called the transferor.

- The purchaser of the U.S. real property interest is called the transferee.

- The amount realized is the purchase/sales price of the U.S. real property interest but can also include any property received by the transferor and any liability relieved by the transferor.

■ The buyer/transferee must determine whether the seller is a foreign person. If so, the buyer/transferee is responsible for the withholding taxes.

■ The buyer/transferee may be held liable for the tax that should have been withheld on the purchase.

■ The amount withheld must be reported and paid to the IRS by the escrow holder within 20 days of closing.

Exemptions to Withholding   No such funds need be withheld under the following exemptions:

■ One of the most common exceptions to FIRPTA withholding is that the buyer/transferee is not required to withhold tax in a situation in which the buyer/transferee purchases real estate for use as the buyer's personal residence and the purchase price does not exceed a certain amount, as further explained in following paragraphs.

■ The seller's affidavit confirms that the seller is not a "foreign person."

■ The IRS has issued a "qualifying statement" that no withholding is necessary.

■ The buyer is purchasing the property for use as a personal residence, and the purchase price does not exceed $300,000.

■ The transferee/buyer is acquiring the property for use as a home, and the amount realized (generally sales price) is not more than $300,000. The buyer or a member of the buyer's family has definite plans to reside at the property for at least 50% of the number of days the property is used by any person during each of the first two years following the date of transfer. When counting the number of days the property is used, the days the property will be vacant are not included.

■ The property disposed of (other than certain dispositions of non-publicly traded interests) is an interest in a domestic corporation if any class of stock of the corporation is regularly traded on an established securities market. However, if the class of stock had been held by a foreign person who beneficially owned more than 5% of the fair market value of that class at any time during the previous 5-year period, then that interest is a U.S. real property interest if the corporation qualifies as a U.S. real property holding corporation (USRPHC), and withholding is required on any disposition.

■ The disposition is of an interest in a domestic corporation and that corporation furnishes the buyer with a certification stating, under penalty of perjury, that the interest is not a U.S. real property interest.

■ Generally, the corporation can make this certification only if the corporation was not a USRPHC during the previous five years (or, if shorter, the period the interest was held by its present owner), or as of the date of disposition, the interest in the corporation is not a U.S. real property interest by reason of section 897(c)(1)(B) of the Internal Revenue Code. The certification must be dated not more than 30 days before the date of transfer.

■ The transferor gives the buyer a certification stating, under penalty of perjury, that the transferor is not a foreign person and containing the transferor's name, U.S. taxpayer identification number, and home address (or office address, in the case of an entity).

■ The buyer receives a withholding certificate from the Internal Revenue Service that excuses withholding. A withholding certificate may be issued due to a determination by the IRS that reduced withholding is appropriate because either the amount that must be withheld would be more than the transferor's maximum tax liability, or withholding of the reduced amount would not jeopardize collection of the tax, the exemption from U.S. tax of all gain realized by the transferor, or an agreement for the payment of tax providing security for the tax liability, entered into by the transferee or transferor.

■ The transferor gives the buyer written notice that no recognition of any gain or loss on the transfer is required because of a nonrecognition provision in the Internal Revenue Code or a provision in a U.S. tax treaty. In this case, the buyer must file a copy of the notice by the 20th day after the date of transfer with the Internal Revenue Service.

California Tax Withholding

In 1988, the State of California implemented withholding under the basic guidelines of the federal FIRPTA, amending them in 2002, with the amendments becoming effective January 1, 2003. California withholding differs from federal FIRPTA. Under the law $3\frac{1}{3}\%$ of the sales price is to be withheld, or a percentage of the seller's gain as indicated in the paragraphs that follow, unless exemptions apply. The basic provisions relate to three classes of transferors, as follows:

■ Individuals

■ Persons (but not certain partnerships, or an individual or a corporation) where the funds are to be distributed to a transferor outside the state or to the financial intermediary of the transferor

■ The seller is a corporation with no permanent place of business in California immediately after the sale

Withholding Rates   The amount to be withheld is as follows: Either 3⅓% (0.0333) of the total sale price or alternatively the buyer may elect to withhold on the gain on sale at the following rates:

- 12.3% for individuals and non-California partnerships

- 8.84% for corporations

- 10.84% for banks and financial corporations

- 13.8% for S corporations

- 15.8% for financial S corporations

Withholding Rules   If withholding is required, the escrow agent would provide written notification of the withholding requirements to the parties, provide certification forms for the exemptions contained in the bill, provide instructions to be signed by the parties authorizing the withholding, and remit the amount to the Franchise Tax Board, along with any charge imposed for withholding and remitting, not to exceed $45. No withholding is required in the following circumstances or transactions:

- The sales price is less than $100,000.

- The property is the principal residence of an individual transferor, based on a written certification signed under penalty of perjury.

- The property is transferred to a corporate beneficiary by a foreclosure or a deed in lieu.

- The property transferred by an individual and will be replaced in a like-kind exchange, based on a written certification by the transferor or signed under penalty of perjury.

- The property is transferred by an individual as an involuntary conversion, and the transferor certifies intent to acquire replacement property eligible for deferral under Section 1033 of the Internal Revenue Code.

- The transferor is an individual who certifies under penalty of perjury that the transaction will result in a loss for California income tax purposes.

- The transferor is a corporation unless immediately after the transfer, the corporation has no permanent place of business in California.

Tax Reform Act of 1986

Amended in 1998 under the Taxpayer Relief Act of 1997, the Tax Reform Act of 1986 provides that the escrow holder as the final party responsible for closing a sales transaction and therefore the person responsible for reporting real estate sales transactions need not file an informational report for sales or exchanges of primary residences with a sales price at or less than $250,000 for an individual or $500,000 if the sellers are married.

The reporting person must obtain a certification from each seller in a form acceptable to the secretary of the Treasury. The sales are reported to the IRS on form 1099-S. If the transaction does not involve an escrow holder, the responsible reporting party. who would be the mortgage lender, the buyer's broker, or the seller's broker, must forward copies of the IRS form 1099-S to the buyer, seller, and IRS.

California Homestead Act

Owner-occupants of residential one-to-four-unit properties that are their primary residences are protected under the **California Homestead Act**. Unlike the Homestead Act of 1862, which provided lands for settlers, the California Homestead Act provides protection from the homeowner's property being seized by creditors and resold for the repayment of a debt. While the protection is not absolute, it guarantees the homeowner that any equity up to the amount of the homestead equity exemption is protected and at the same time reduces the property taxes on the homestead amount. The escrow holder usually assists in filing the Declaration of Homestead (Figure 9.3) at escrow closing. A fee may be charged. The equity protected is established by statute, essentially $75,000 for a single person; $100,000 if the debtor is married or the head of the family; or $175,000 if the debtor is at least 65 years old, is mentally or physically disabled, or is over 55 years old with an income of less than $15,000 per year ($20,000 annually if married). Any judgment lien will not attach to a declared homestead; that is, the homestead was recorded prior to the judgment lien was recorded and the homestead declaration names the judgment debtor as a declared homestead owner.

If a declared homestead is voluntarily sold and the proceeds from the sale are reinvested in a new residence within six months after closing (or after insurance proceeds are received if the property was damaged and destroyed), the new home may be selected as a declared homestead by recording the Declaration of Homestead within the six-month period. The prior homestead must first be removed. To remove a homestead from record when changing primary residences (only one homestead is allowed), the homeowner files a Declaration of Abandonment of Homestead (Figure 9.4) with the county recorder's office in which the property is located.

FIGURE 9.3
Declaration of
Homestead

RECORDING REQUESTED BY

AND WHEN RECORDED MAIL TO

HOMESTEAD DECLARATION

I, _____, hereby certify and declare:
(a) I hereby claim as a declared homestead the premises described as follows:

(b) I am the declared homestead owner of the above-declared homestead.
(c) I own the following interest in the above-declared homestead: _____.
(d) The above-declared homestead is _____ (my principal dwelling or the principal dwelling of my spouse), and _____ is currently residing in that declared homestead.
(e) My further act of causing this declaration to be recorded shall constitute a representation that _____ reside(s) in the above-declared homestead on the date this declaration is recorded.
(f) The facts stated in this Declaration are true as of my personal knowledge.
Dated: _____

_____

CERTIFICATE OF ACKNOWLEDGEMENT OF NOTARY PUBLIC

STATE OF CALIFORNIA,   )
COUNTY OF _____)

    On _____ before me, _____, (here insert name and title of the officer), personally appeared _____, who proved to me on the basis of satisfactory evidence to be the person(s) whose name(s) is/are subscribed to the within instrument and acknowledged to me that he/she/they executed the same in his/her/their authorized capacity(ies), and that by his/her/their signature(s) on the instrument the person(s), or the entity upon behalf of which the person(s) acted, executed the instrument.

I certify under PENALTY OF PERJURY under the laws of the State of California that the foregoing paragraph is true and correct.

WITNESS my hand and official seal.

Signature _____ (Seal)

FIGURE 9.4

Declaration of Abandonment of Declared Homestead

Recording Requested By:

When recorded mail document to:

NAME

ADDRESS

CITY/STATE/ZIP

APN: _____   Above Space for Recorder's Use Only

DECLARATION OF ABANDONMENT
OF DECLARED HOMESTEAD

The undersigned declare(s) that _____ hereby abandon(s) the homestead previously
(HE, SHE, THEY)

declared in the Homestead executed by _____

(FULL NAME OF DECLARANTS(S))

_____

on _____, 19_____, and recorded on _____,

19_____, in Book _____, Page _____, as Instrument No. _____, in

the Official Records of the County Recorder of _____County,

California.

Dated:_____, 19_____

_____   _____
(SIGNATURE OF DEcLARANT)   (SIGNATURE OF DECLARANT)

_____   _____
(PRINT FULL NAME)   (PRINT FULL NAME)

STATE OF CALIFORNIA   }
COUNTY OF_____ }

ON_____before me,_____,a Notary Public,
personally appeared _____
_____,
who proved to me on the basis of satisfactory evidence to be the person(s) whose
name(s) is/are subscribed to the within instrument and acknowledged to me that
he/she/they executed the same in his/their/her authorized capacity (ies), and that by
his/her/their signatures(s) on the instrument the person(s), or the entity upon behalf of
which the person(s) acted, executed the instrument.

I certify under PENALTY OF PERJURY under the laws of the
State of California that the foregoing paragraph is true and correct.

WITNESS my hand and official seal.   (SEAL)

Signature _____

Pro-Tip: Importance of Understanding the California Homestead Act

The homeowner's exemption provides significant benefits to the homeowner in protecting at least a portion of the equity in the property from creditors. However, the homestead may also create potential problems for the homeowner. If the homeowner refinances the property and reduces equity in the process, the increased debt is not subtracted from the equity subject to execution by creditors. For example, a homestead exemption of $75,000:

Property value	$250,000
First loan	80,000
Second loan from refinance	40,000

The equity available to a creditor would be $95,000, not $55,000 ($250,000 less the $80,000 first loan combined with the $75,000 homestead exemption).

■ CONVEYING TITLE: PREPARING THE TRANSFER DEEDS

There are two aspects to most escrow instructions: title and consideration. Title deals with preparation of the necessary documents to effect transfer of title while consideration involves allocation and accounting of the funds.

Three basic documents are involved in the processing of sale and loan escrows: the grant deed, the note, and the deed of trust (in some states, instead of a deed of trust, a mortgage is used with no trustee). Other documents may also be involved, such as security agreements, financing statements, bills of sale, and others, especially in specialty transactions such as bulk sales and transfer of liquor licenses. Chapter 1 introduced the basic elements of title and transfer. The following section discusses the practical application of them in the escrow process and what is needed to achieve a valid and insurable transfer of title.

Grant Deeds Conveying Title

As we learned in Chapter 1, the primary document of transfer of title in a real estate transaction is the deed, usually a **grant deed**. Escrow instructions usually contain language stating that the seller will provide "any instrument (document)" necessary to consummate the transaction. This statement is the authority for the escrow holder to prepare deeds of transfer to accomplish and complete the transaction. Usually the transfer deed used is a grant deed.

The grant deed may convey all the ownership or only a partial interest in a property.

The grant deed may contain special provisions, such as a clause that gives all the property to the grantee (the person receiving title, such as a buyer) with the exception of portions of the complete title—for example, an easement to be created for the grantor to use for egress and ingress to an adjoining parcel of land. An easement of this type would actually have been inherent in the future transfer of the property through the doctrine of what is known as "quasi-servient tenements" and "quasi-dominant tenements," discussed more fully in Chapter 17, "Advanced Title Insurance Underwriting." Such an exception is called a reservation.

Example: Seller (Grantor) Reservation in Title

For example, Henry Smith owns two parcels of land that are contiguous to each other. Each parcel has a commercial building on it, both of which are used by Henry in his business. One parcel has no access (ingress or egress) to a public street, therefore is landlocked. Henry has a driveway connecting the two properties and to the public street Henry and his employees use the driveway to travel from the landlocked parcel across the other parcel and to the public street. He has therefore established a quasi-servient tenement on the parcel which is NOT landlocked and which serves the benefit of the landlocked parcel which is the dominant tenement. Henry is selling the landlocked parcel to Frank Smith. The deed Henry, the grantor, gives to Frank, the grantee, will include, and specifically mention, an easement placed on the land Henry retains for the benefit of the land sold to Frank, and specifically for Frank's ingress and egress across Henry's land and to the public street. Henry's land relative to the easement is the servient estate and Frank's is the dominant estate.

The deed may contain other restrictions or reservations. It may prohibit certain activities or uses, such as any illegal activity enforcement executed through a clause indicating that if such use is conducted by the grantee, the property reverts back to the grantor (reversion).

Essential Elements of a Deed   Those items that must be present in a valid deed are called the **essential elements of a deed**, as follows:

- *In writing.* The deed must be written as required by the statute of frauds, the law that specifies that certain documents, including deeds, must be written. The escrow officer will prepare the deed, comparing the names and vesting with the instructions for accuracy.

- *Competent grantor.* The party must have the capacity to convey title without the need for a court-appointed representative. The title company's checks for records that would reveal any matter on the part of the seller that would prevent a transfer of title, such as competency.

- *Operative words of conveyance.* The instrument must have "operative language." The laws describe this language as creating a moving or operative force in the grant deed. The escrow officer checks for spelling errors and omissions.

- *Identified grantee.* Just as the grantor must have legal capacity to convey title, the grantee must have the capacity to receive title. Some exceptions, however, apply as discussed earlier. Although minors, except one who is emancipated, cannot convey title, they can acquire title.

- *Property to be conveyed.* The deed must contain a complete and adequate description of the property to be transferred. The full legal description may also include a street address.

- *Due execution by the grantor.* The party conveying the interest must sign the deed exactly as title is held. Attention must be given to names that may have changed after title was acquired. A common example would be a married woman who acquired title under a maiden or prior surname, in which case the granting clause would state, "Mary Smith who acquired title as Mary Jones." If the grantor is a corporation or partnership, the escrow officer will require documentation from the entity identifying and authorizing the person who has the capacity to sign the deed on behalf of the entity conveying title. The escrow officer guides the grantor through the process, indicating exactly how the document should be signed.

- *Delivery and acceptance.* In order for the deed to become effective, the deed must be "delivered" to and "accepted" by the grantee to move title from the grantor to the grantee. The escrow officer forwards the deed to the title company for recording to "deliver" the deed constructively.

  — Physical possession of the deed by the grantee presumes delivery has been executed.

  — The deed in the possession of the grantor, meaning the grantee has yet to receive it, presumes nondelivery and title has not transferred.

Recording   Recordation, while essential to protect the rights of the parties, does not guarantee that delivery has been executed. Acknowledgment is required by all executing parties for the document to be recorded. Although recordation of the deed is a presumption of delivery to the grantee, if the recorded deed is still in the possession of the grantor, it could be held that delivery has not been executed. Recordation also presumes acceptance by the grantee. If the grantee is a government agency, such as a city, county, state or any other, there must have been an actual and acknowledged act of acceptance by the agency for acceptance to have been accomplished.

■ CHAPTER 9 QUIZ

1. Escrow instructions begin with the basic information of the escrow, including

   a. legal description of the property.

   b. street address of the property.

   c. vesting and title.

   d. all of these.

2. Allocation of costs between the buyer and the seller customarily include the

   a. buyer paying for the documentary transfer tax.

   b. buyer paying for notarizing the grant deed.

   c. seller in Southern California paying for the owner's title insurance policy.

   d. buyer paying for the seller's reconveyance fee.

3. If the seller is a foreign person, unless exempt, the buyer must

   a. withhold and send 10% of the sale price from the seller's proceeds to the IRS.

   b. send 10% of the sale price to the IRS toward the buyer's income taxes.

   c. notify the seller of possible liability for taxes.

   d. authorize escrow to hold the seller's net proceeds until the IRS determines the tax liability, if any.

4. The forms escrow holders prepare or "draw," and which must be in "general use and of established form" in order to prevent them from the unauthorized practice of law, are essentially governed by the

   a. rule of "bar treaty."

   b. Treaty of Guadalupe Hidalgo.

   c. American Escrow Association.

   d. California Bar Association.

5. If the property being acquired has a homeowners association (HOA), the buyer and the buyer's lender will require a homeowner's

   a. confirmation report to be provided by the HOA.

   b. certification report to be provided by the HOA.

   c. certification report to be provided by the title company.

   d. certification report to be provided to the city.

6. Releasing buyer's deposit funds to the seller during the escrow is

   a. common.

   b. illegal.

   c. can offer serious consequences if problems are encountered during escrow.

   d. usually advisable.

7. California withholding, if the conditions apply, require the buyer to withhold

   a. 10% of the sellers' proceeds and send to the FTB.

   b. 3⅓% of the sale price and send to the FTB.

   c. 3⅓% of the seller's proceeds and send to the FTB.

   d. 3⅓% of the seller's proceeds and send to the IRS.

8. If a declared homestead is voluntarily sold and the proceeds from the sale are reinvested in a new residence, the new home may be selected as a declared homestead if it is

   a. selected within six months of closing.

   b. selected upon escrow closing.

   c. selected within 180 days of closing.

   d. both a and c.

9. FIRPTA stands for

    a. Foreign Investor Real Property Tax Act.

    b. Foreign Income Real Property Tax Act.

    c. Foreign Investment of Real Property Tax Act.

    d. Federal Investment Real Property Tax Act.

10. Documents that the escrow officer may prepare do NOT include

    a. those not of an established form.

    b. deeds of trust.

    c. notes.

    d. bills of sale.

CHAPTER TEN

10

NORTHERN AND SOUTHERN CALIFORNIA REGIONAL VARIATIONS AND PRACTICES

■ KEY TERMS

alienation clause
beneficiary statement
bilateral instructions

California good funds
  law
demand statement
easements

encumbrances
judgments
preliminary title report
vesting

■ LEARNING OBJECTIVES

Upon completing this chapter, you will be able to

■ understand the customary escrow process for that region of the state in which the escrow holder operates,

■ explain the preliminary title report,

■ explain the basic vesting requirements,

- identify and understand the significance of easements in the title report,

- understand the significance of encumbrances in the title report,

- process lenders' demands and beneficiary statements,

- explain California good funds law, and

- understand the California Recording Act and identify those documents that are required to be recorded.

■ NORTHERN CALIFORNIA ESCROW PROCEDURES

Northern California Versus Southern California

In Northern California, escrow procedure is closely related to the title insurance process. In fact, some title insurance companies have lenders' units that handle both title and escrow functions, with the officer in charge designated as a title-escrow officer. Clearly a benefit in expediting services for the borrower and the lender, the title-escrow officer handles not only the title activities, including facilitating the title search, reviewing the results, underwriting and issuing the preliminary title report, but also performs the functions and responsibilities of the escrow officer.

Real estate broker involvement in the closing process is greater in the north than in the south of the state, with the signing of escrow instructions occurring as one of the last items in the escrow process. Over the past several years, there has been a trend toward blending the differences between Northern and Southern California escrow procedures, with **bilateral instructions** and an up-front opening becoming a frequent practice in Northern California, as it is done in the South, and the increasing use of title company escrow services and procedures in Southern California, as has been the traditional practice in Northern California. Escrow and title procedures in Central California have used both approaches.

Northern California—Focus on the Title Report

After an acceptance has been obtained, the real estate broker begins processing the sales transaction by ordering the preliminary title report directly from the title company, usually through the escrow department. Typically, no escrow instructions are drawn at this time; if they are, they remain unsigned until the date of closing is near.

Preliminary Title Report

The title company's escrow department forwards the opening title order to its title plant after all information has been compiled to accomplish the search. Upon receipt of the search results from the title plant, the title officer will review it and write and issue the **preliminary title report**. The preliminary title report reveals the extent of coverage protection and any exclusion to it. It is essentially a report of the conditions discovered that affect title to the property and upon which the title company is willing to issue a title policy. Often, there are items noted that require resolution or elimination before the title policy will be issued. Necessary information may include the following:

- *Complete legal description.* Title records are usually retrieved by legal description. The assessor's parcel number is also helpful in making sure the property to be searched is correctly identified.

- *Current parties on title.* The title search includes determining who the correct parties on title are. Complete information regarding the identities of the parties is necessary for the title searcher to accomplish the task. Part of the searcher's job is to eliminate all parties who are named as a result of the search but who are not the actual party to the transaction. The reason is twofold: first, to insure that the party to the transaction does not have the satisfaction and release of lien of another party made a condition of the escrow and, second, to identify any lien, judgment, or some other matter that could affect title so the escrow holder can either facilitate its removal, if possible, or notify the responsible party of required action.

- *Prospective parties on title.* Names of the parties to acquire title must be provided accurately in order to prepare documentation correctly, as well as for the title search. Matters recorded against the buyer can prevent escrow from closing and must be resolved.

- *Type and amount of title insurance required.* The type of title insurance protection, depending on the nature of the transaction, must be indicated (see Chapter 3, "Common Title Policies and Endorsements").

- *Name and address of new lender.* As soon as the name, address, and contact information of the new lender is known, a copy of the title report will be forwarded to them.

- *Miscellaneous.* Any special requirements regarding the request for copies of covenants, conditions, and restrictions (CC&Rs) or special title endorsements or inspections should be included in the search request.

Receipt of Preliminary Title Report

After receiving the preliminary title report, the real estate broker will review it with the principals to ascertain what, if anything, is required to deliver title as indicated in the purchase agreement. Each aspect of the preliminary title report should be carefully reviewed. Additionally, some coverage protection may require a special endorsement (as covered in Chapter 3), which usually carries an additional fee. Some matters may not be insurable, so a report may indicate an exclusion, which will remain in the actual title policy. Remember that the title policy provides protection for the buyer and the buyer's lender against losses due to a defect in title. The title officer, in preparing the preliminary title report, reviews those conditions of and on the title, referring to matters affecting the ability to transfer or encumber the property as described on the title records, and which could result in a possible claim against the company. The title officer will take affirmative steps to minimize or mitigate its risk by excluding them.

- *Estate and interest.* The preliminary title report will indicate the type of estate and the interests in it. For example, the report might reveal that the property has a fee estate coupled with an easement appurtenant to the fee title interest. The title search will reveal both dominant tenements, which benefit the subject property, and servient tenements, which benefit another's property and which may affect the use of a portion of the subject property. Other interests might be life estates, leasehold estates, estates in reversion, or estates in remainder (see Chapter 1).

- *Vesting.* **Vesting** refers to the names and manner of the parties taking title, such as "John James and Mary James, Husband and Wife as Joint Tenants." The exact spelling should be compared with the names as indicated on the purchase agreement. If the names do not agree, a number of reasons might exist, such as the following:

  — An incorrect legal description is shown, and the property searched belongs to another party.

  — The parties are equitable owners under an unrecorded land contract (also called an installment contract or contract of sale).

  — Misrepresentation exists.

Legal Description as Indicated in the Report

The legal description as indicated in the preliminary title report should be compared with the information originally provided. The plat map should be reviewed and the lot's dimensions compared with those indicated on the original listing agreement or as represented by the seller or the listing agent.

Easements should be reviewed for ingress and egress, both dominant and servient, to determine whether the parties are aware of their existence and, if not, to have the agents resolve any issues that might prevent an escrow from proceeding.

Exceptions or Encumbrances

Among matters to title that may affect the buyer's ability to acquire title, to occupy, or to use and enjoy the property to the extent the buyer had been promised or had imagined are the following exceptions or **encumbrances**:

- *Taxes.* Delinquent or unpaid taxes or assessments must be dealt with. The responsible party for payment must be identified. If any amounts are to be prorated between the parties, the proration formula must be determined.

- *Easements.* **Easements** refer to the right to use the land of another for a particular use, such as utilities, ingress, and egress. The parties to a sales transaction, especially the buyer, must understand the type and significance of any existing easements.

- *CC&Rs.* Covenants, conditions, and restrictions (see Chapter 17) indicated in the preliminary report may require further review and examination by both the lender and the buyer, especially if new construction or a change of use is planned. For example, the buyer of a vacant lot or of property on which an existing dwelling is to be torn down to allow new construction should obtain copies of the CC&Rs.

Pro-Tip: Importance of Obtaining CC&Rs: Costly Mistake for Buyer

A buyer of a lot wishes to build a two-story, six-unit apartment building. After the purchase, the buyer obtains construction financing, without having read or closely reviewed the CC&Rs, and later discovers restrictions prohibiting two-story construction. The buyer may also be unable to build a single-story apartment building that would accommodate enough units to generate the income necessary to meet the investment objectives or even support the loan payment. Even worse, the buyer's construction lender also overlooks the CC&Rs, funds the loan, and construction begins. During construction, the restrictions are discovered. The remedy could be costly, both in legal fees if challenged by neighbors and in demolition and reconstruction costs.

- *Judgments.* These are court actions by and in favor of creditors against defaulting debtors. If **judgments** exist, before clear title can be delivered to the buyer, or if the judgment belongs to the buyer before the buyer's lender would allow escrow to close, a demand must be ordered from the creditor. If the debtor claims the judgment does not belong to him, the matter must be resolved through escrow and processing the statement of identity or statement of information.

■ *Loans of record.* If the property's seller has an existing loan, it must be dealt with by requesting a demand for payoff, which is processed by the escrow holder. If the seller allows the buyer to assume his loan, the escrow holder will order a **beneficiary statement** (a buyer's choice to either attempt to formally assume or to "take title subject to" the existing loan may affect the successful closing of an escrow). If the buyer is "taking title subject to" the existing loan, often the seller will provide the escrow holder with an "offset statement," indicating the seller's representation of the status of the loan, including the loan amount, interest rate, and periodic payment (typically monthly; however, if the property is other than residential, may be quarterly, semi-annually, or annually). The escrow holder will usually provide the seller with a lien information sheet for each loan recorded against the property. The form asks for information regarding the loan, such as the following:

— Lender's name, address, and phone number

— Loan number

— Current unpaid balance and interest rate

The seller will complete and return the form to escrow with the other documents delivered from escrow. The escrow officer is cautioned to not rely on the information provided by the seller as being completely accurate. It provides the basic information for the escrow officer to prepare the initial instructions and accounting that may need to be changed once the actual status and details of the loan is sent to the escrow holder from the seller's lender.

■ *Hold on funds.* Before escrow can close and funds disbursed, any funds deposited into escrow must be "good" and clear the depositor's banking institution. See "Buyer's Cash Requirements" in this chapter.

Statement of Information

Title and escrow companies provide the principals with a statement of information or statement of identity to verify that the escrow or title companies are working on behalf of the valid and true parties to the transaction. The information requested on the form will be used to ascertain the liability or not of any judgments, tax liens, incompetency, paroles, attorney-in-fact, guardianship proceedings, bankruptcies, probates, and other legal matters affecting the capacity or financial responsibility of the principals. The parties are asked to sign the form under penalty of perjury.

Demands

If existing liens are to be paid off, a demand is requested of the lienholder to provide actual payoff amounts and any documentation necessary to obtain the release of the lien.

When received from the lienholder, the funds required to pay off the seller's loan in order to comply with the demand should be reviewed with the seller to determine its accuracy. Compare the **demand statement** with the seller's statement and records. Also, if the demand calls for a payment of a penalty for earlier payoff (prepay penalty), advise the borrower to review the original note to confirm the terms of any prepay penalty.

Beneficiary Statement

If an existing mortgage lien is to be assumed and remain with the buyer, or in the case of a refinance, if the lienholders are asked to subordinate their liens to the new loan, a beneficiary statement will be requested from the lienholder. The statement will show the current unpaid balance of the note, the terms of payment, the insurance information, and the requirements for a buyer to assume the note and any changes to the note as a condition for its assumption.

- *Alienation clause.* An **alienation clause** is one that is detrimental to the objectives of the borrowers who seek to acquire title to the seller's property and simply take over making the loan payments but not assume legal responsibility for the loan. Most lenders include an alienation (acceleration) clause in the note in the event of a transfer of title to the property, requiring that the loan be paid in full. If a buyer and a seller have agreed to allow the buyer to "take title subject to" the seller's existing loan and a due-on-sale clause does not exist, the escrow holder will usually require a beneficiary statement to be ordered.

Pro-Tip: Taking Title Subject To

Taking title subject to is a technical term indicating that the buyer is not formally assuming the seller's loan and, in fact, that neither the buyer nor the seller will notify the lender that title to the property is being transferred because it may cause the lender to require the loan to be paid off in accordance with the alienation clause.

However, an escrow holder may proceed without the beneficiary statement by the seller's providing escrow with the seller's "offset" statement and representation of the status of the underlying loan. Even if the escrow holder consents to this action, the buyer would be well advised to seek legal counsel before proceeding, both for relying on the offset statement and to learn any risk inherent in "taking title subject to" the existing note and terms.

- *Buyer's acceptance of assumption terms.* If the buyer is formally assuming the seller's loan, with the seller being released of the liability (substitution of liability in the buyer), upon receipt of the assumption agreement, the buyer's broker should closely review it with the buyer. When considering a seller's request to allow a buyer to assume the legal responsibility of the existing loan, many, if not most, lenders change the original terms of the loan.

Example: Market Rates

For example, the seller's existing rate may be 5.5% and market rate is 6%. Instead of allowing the buyer to assume the note at 5.5%, the lender may raise the interest rate to 5.75%, better than the market rate that the buyer would otherwise have to accept on a new loan but higher than the seller's existing rate.

- *New financing.* If obtaining new financing, the buyer completes a loan application and the information required by the lender for processing and approving the loan. An appraisal would be ordered by the buyer's real estate broker. The buyer will usually be asked to pay for the appraisal in advance of escrow closing, but that's not always the case. The escrow holder must be informed if the appraisal has been "paid outside closing" (POC), meaning the buyer has already paid for it.

- *Vendor payables.* The escrow holder often assumes the responsibility for paying miscellaneous bills during the closing process on behalf of both the buyer and the seller. Typical vendors who submit invoices for work or services performed in conjunction with the escrow transaction include termite companies, roofers, home and appliance inspection companies, home warranty companies, insurance companies, appraisers, and contractors. The escrow holder will ask the party responsible for paying the bill to approve the invoice before arbitrarily paying it, unless it was submitted to escrow by the responsible party.

■ *Loan processing.* The Northern California escrow holder will receive and process loan documentation for signing, as discussed in "Basic Principles of the Escrow Process." The trust deed will be forwarded to the title department for eventual recording and the balance of the documents returned to the lender for funding when approved.

■ *Escrow instructions drawn.* In Northern California, the drawing of escrow instructions takes place near the end of the process. The escrow officer will prepare instructions in parts, one for the seller and one for the buyer, and to be signed separately, but both parts will reflect the same "meeting of the minds." The language used in the instructions is directed toward the respective party. For example, in a seller's instruction that says "a deed is being delivered in return for money received," the buyer's instruction may say "money is being delivered for a deed."

Few changes usually occur in the escrow process at this point. Unlike a typical escrow in Southern California, which is opened at the beginning of the process and which may allow for changes along the way that require amendments to the original instruction, few amendments take place in a Northern California escrow.

■ *Received signed instructions.* The buyer's and the seller's instructions are executed and returned to the escrow holder, along with the buyer's deposit monies. In the typical Northern California escrow process, all documents are prepared, signed and delivered to escrow with necessary buyer's deposit funds near the end of the process and the closing date. Among the final steps is the receipt of the buyer's loan funds.

■ *Final review.* The escrow officer reviews the file, accounting for all documentation and monies that were to be delivered. If anything is missing, the escrow officer will communicate to the appropriate party what is needed. If nothing remains, the escrow officer will prepare for closing, sending to the title department the items to be recorded, such as the grant deed conveying title and the buyer's trust deed, if not forwarded previously.

■ *Loan funds.* One of the remaining items prior to closing is receipt of the buyer's loan funds. The escrow officer will call for funds when instructed by the lender and the following requirements have been satisfied: both buyer and seller have complied with the instructions; the escrow holder has received all items necessary to close, transfer title, payoff and reconvey the seller's liens; and the buyer's funds have been received and considered "good."

- *Auditing the file*. Before ordering that the title department record the closing documents, the escrow officer audits the file, ensuring that all conditions and instructions have been completed. The officer will make a financial accounting to determine whether the escrow is in "balance" and that no additional funds are required from either party. All documents requiring signatures will be reviewed. After ensuring the file is complete, the escrow officer will call for the recording.

- *Final accounting and disbursement*. Once the recording has been confirmed, the escrow is officially closed. The final closing statements—Settlement Statement (HUD-1)—is prepared for delivery to all parties. The final accounting is performed, and checks are ordered to be "cut" for delivery with closing documents. When all this is accomplished, the final closing documents and funds due the parties are delivered. Usually in a sales transaction, the respective parties' agents prefer to pick up (or have delivered to them) the closing documents and checks to personally deliver to their principals.

■ SOUTHERN CALIFORNIA ESCROW PROCEDURES

Southern California escrow procedures focus on the financing aspect of the transaction. It is lender-oriented, except of course for an all-cash sale. Communications with the buyer's and the seller's lenders occur early in the escrow process, as do the preparation and signing of escrow instructions. While most of the steps followed in the Northern California escrow process are followed in the South's process, they occur in a different order and earlier in the process. The typical escrow process in Southern California is described in the following paragraphs. (Note: This discussion assumes principals are represented by real estate agents.)

Selecting the Escrow Holder

Upon the acceptance by the seller of a buyer's purchase offer, escrow is opened by one of the real estate agents. No actual custom exists as to whether it is the buyer's agent or the seller's agent who does this. As a practical matter, the responsibility usually falls to the agent who selects the escrow holder. The principal, not the agent, chooses the escrow holder. Most buyers and sellers, however, have no relationship with a particular escrow company or no preference as to which one is selected.

Preparation of Escrow Instructions

The real estate agent will fax or deliver a copy of the California Association of REALTORS® purchase agreement contract. For example, if the property being transferred is residential and will be owner-occupied, the contract used will be the Purchase Agreement Joint Escrow Instructions (CAR form RPA-CA). The purchase agreement serves as the initial escrow instructions and eliminates the need for the escrow holder to duplicate the information regarding the elements of the contract. The escrow holder instead prepares supplemental escrow instructions consisting of boilerplate information, which includes general disclosures, disclaimers, and other statements informing the parties of the obligations and limits of responsibility of the escrow holder. It also declares that the supplemental escrow instructions, including original escrow instructions, if prepared by the escrow holder (for transactions in which the CAR purchase agreement is not used), are not intended to supersede the original contract.

- *Bilateral escrow instructions.* Southern California escrow practice involves the preparation of bilateral instructions consisting of one set for both the buyer and the seller. The instructions may be signed in parts, with the buyer signing one set of instructions and the seller signing another, but they are identical. The instructions are more elaborate and all-inclusive partly because they contain the instructions for both parties, as well as considerable exculpatory language.

- *Signing instructions.* Escrow is not considered open until the instructions have been signed by both parties. It is imperative that the agents representing the parties facilitate the signing of the instructions by their respective principals. Failing to do so could jeopardize the entire transaction. While the purchase agreement may have been signed by both buyer and seller, indicating the acceptance of the terms contained in it, their failure to sign the escrow instructions in a timely manner (a condition of the purchase agreement) may cause termination of the agreement. The escrow holder will continue to process the escrow because it is not considered cancelled until or unless one of the parties orders it cancelled. If financing is involved, two separate activities commence, one regarding the sale transaction and the other for the loan. The lender's instructions are forwarded to them, along with the preliminary title report, when it is received (see "Preliminary Title Report") for their processing.

- *Escrow orders the title report.* The escrow officer will order the title report, usually concurrently with preparing escrow instructions. In most cases, the real estate agent who has selected the escrow company has also selected the title company as well. In Southern California it is not unusual for escrow and title companies not to be the same. If the escrow company chosen is owned by a title company or is the escrow department of a title company typically both escrow and title services will be provided by that company.

■ *Preliminary title report.* Upon receipt of the preliminary title report the escrow holder will deliver a copy to all parties named in the escrow instructions, such as the buyer and the seller, the real estate agents, and the buyer's lender (if the buyer is obtaining financing). Delivery is usually performed electronically.

■ *Review title report.* The real estate agents, the principals, and the lender will review the title report to determine whether the condition of title allows for transfer of clear title in the manner the buyer wishes and the lender requires. Any items that differ or may prevent transfer of clear title must be resolved and removed prior to delivery of a deed to the buyer. A simple example would be a seller's existing loan, which is a lien on the property that must be paid off and released or assumed by the buyer if the purchase contract calls for such an assumption. The parties would review the report for all other liens, which may or may not be required to be released, including property taxes. The tax status must be reviewed and determined whether it meets the agreement of the parties and satisfies the requirements of the buyer's lender.

■ *Demands.* The escrow holder receives the payoff demands from the seller's lender and places them into the escrow file. Because this occurs early in the Southern California escrow process, the escrow holder may be required to update the demand just before closing. Care should be taken to review the amounts indicated on the demands and compare them with the understanding of the parties. Attention should be given to any prepay penalties to determine whether they should exist at all and whether the amount conforms to the seller's note. Approval should be obtained by the seller before paying them at closing.

Buyer's Financing

Concurrently with the escrow instruction process, if the buyer is obtaining financing, the processing of such financing involves the escrow holder's interaction with the buyer's lender. The escrow officer transmits a copy of the escrow instructions and preliminary title report to the lender for action. Loan processing may take 30 days or longer; therefore, the anticipated closing date for escrow must be realistic and adequate to accommodate the time required to obtain approval and funding.

■ *Buyer's loan documents.* As previously discussed, upon approval of the buyer's loan, the lender will forward loan documents when ready to the escrow holder, usually electronically. If the loan documents are to be signed outside the escrow holder's place of business, arrangements must be made and coordinated with the notary public who will assist the buyer in signing the loan documents. The documents cannot be sent directly to the notary unless the lender sends lender's instructions separately to the escrow holder. The lender's instructions guide the escrow holder in the requirements the lender has for closing, such as hazard insurance, impound accounts for taxes and insurance, fees, and other conditions for closing. (See "The Loan Escrow" for more information.)

■ *Title company review for recording.* After the buyers have signed them, the loan documents are returned to the escrow holder for action. The escrow officer will forward certain documents, including the trust deed, to the title company to be reviewed and to insure they meet the conditions required to be recorded. Even if the escrow company is part of the title company, delivery to another physical location may be required, especially for escrow company branch operations. Loan documents, except those required to be recorded such as the trust deed, are returned to the lender for review and funding when ready.

■ *Request buyer's loan funds.* After all conditions have been met and escrow is in condition to close, including the buyer's cash funds that have been deposited into escrow, the escrow officer will "call" for the funding from the buyer's lender. Funding occurs with a wire transfer to the title company.

Buyer's Cash Requirements

As the closing date nears, the escrow officer calls the buyer (or buyer's agent) to make arrangement for the buyer to deliver to escrow the necessary funds required for closing—essentially the cash down payment, closing costs, and prepaid items as required by the lender or the terms of the contract, such as proration of property taxes.

California Good Funds Law   The so-called **California good funds law** specifies when funds deposited into escrow may be disbursed, as follows:

■ *Wire transfer.* Funds are considered to be good upon the receipt of the wire transfer and may be disbursed the same day.

■ *Cashier's check or certified check.* Funds are considered to be good the following business day, at which time they may be disbursed.

■ *Personal check.* Funds are considered to be good after three business days if the bank from which the funds are being delivered is local and may be disbursed at that time. If the funds are being delivered from a nonlocal bank, the funds are considered to be good after five business days and may be disbursed at that time.

Other Closing Requirements

Before escrow may close, other matters may require attention. Last-minute title issues requiring resolution may appear, such as a lien or judgment recorded against one of the parties that occurs after the initial title search was performed. Seldom does a seller need to bring monies into escrow to close; however, occasionally it does happen. For example, if the seller's loan payoff is greater than the net proceeds to the seller, the seller will be required to deliver funds to escrow to effect the closing. The seller's funds must be delivered in the same manner as the buyer's funds to be considered "good."

Recording the Documents

When the escrow is ready to close, the escrow officer will notify the title company to record the documents. Each document presented for recording must include or comply with the county's general requirements. Documents may be presented for recording in person, by mail, or by a courier service, or even electronically in some counties. The following county recording guidelines apply to real estate and loan documents to be recorded in Los Angeles County.

Before sending documents to the recorder's office, the California Recording Act requires the following:

- The property must be located within the county.

- The document must be authorized or required by law to be recorded.

- Signatures must be original unless the document is a certified copy issued by the appropriate custodian of the public record.

- The legibility of a document is important to the quality of the permanent record.

- Include the name of the party requesting the recording and a name and address where the document can be returned.

- The document must be properly acknowledged, unless exempt. California requires an all-purpose acknowledgment.

- The assessor's parcel number is required on deeds, trust deeds, and mortgages by local ordinance.

- The notary seal must be legible for a microfilm reproduction.

- When recording documents affecting a change in the ownership of real property, include a completed Preliminary Change of Ownership Report.

These forms can be obtained from the county assessor's office, as well as the county clerk-recorder's office.

■ Documents must be clearly legible in order to produce a readable photographic record. This pertains to the document text, notary seals, certificates, and other attachments, such as legal descriptions.

■ Payment for recording fees can be made by cash, personal check, cashier's check, or money order.

Final Accounting and Disbursements

The escrow officer will perform the final accounting, prepare the closing or settlement statement, and make the final disbursements to the parties. The closing statements and funds disbursed may either be mailed or made ready for pickup at the escrow holder's office, depending on the preferences of the parties. A typical if not common practice is for the buyers' and the sellers' respective agents to pick up the statements and checks to deliver to the principals.

■ CHAPTER 10 QUIZ

1. The preliminary title report

   a. reveals the extent of coverage protection and any exclusion to it.

   b. is essentially a report of conditions discovered that affect title.

   c. may often contain items that require resolution or elimination before the title policy will be issued.

   d. all of these.

2. Information that may be necessary for the title officer to issue a preliminary title report might include

   a. a complete legal description of the property.

   b. current parties on title.

   c. prospective parties on title.

   d. all of these.

3. The title report will show easements, including

   a. dominant tenements.

   b. dormant tenements.

   c. servient tenements.

   d. both a and c.

4. Covenants, conditions, and restrictions (CC&Rs) can apply to

   a. only condominiums.

   b. condominiums and planned unit developments.

   c. all real property.

   d. only new construction.

5. If the buyer is going to assume the seller's existing loan, the escrow officer will order

    a. a demand statement from the lender.

    b. a beneficiary statement from the lender.

    c. an offset statement from the lender.

    d. a beneficiary statement from the seller.

6. A clause in the lender's note that allows the lender to call the loan due and payable in the event of a transfer of title is alienation or

    a. acceleration.

    b. accommodation.

    c. amortization.

    d. assumption.

7. Southern California escrow practices usually focus on

    a. the loan aspect of the transaction except for an all-cash transaction.

    b. the title aspect of the transaction.

    c. the inspections aspect of the transaction.

    d. none of these.

8. Southern California purchase escrow instructions are

    a. unilateral.

    b. bilateral.

    c. individual.

    d. both b and c.

9. If only one party has signed the bilateral escrow instructions, escrow

    a. is not considered open.

    b. is considered open.

    c. must be cancelled.

    d. is considered cancelled.

10. California's good funds law provides that

    a.   wire transfer funds are good the same day received.

    b.   cashier's check funds are good the next business day.

    c.   both a and b.

    d.   neither a nor b.

CHAPTER ELEVEN

11

PRECLOSING

■ KEY TERMS

all-inclusive deed of trust   judgment liens   ratification
amendments   lender's demand   reconveyance
due-on-sale clause   mechanics' liens   third-party instructions
financing documents   MERS
installment note   PCOR process

■ LEARNING OBJECTIVES

Upon completing this chapter, you will be able to

■ understand and process the lender's demand statement;

■ understand the Mortgage Electronic Registration System (MERS);

■ understand and calculate property tax prorations and impounds;

■ understand the significance of liens;

■ understand the Preliminary Change of Ownership Report process;

263

- understand the basic escrow documents involved in financing and transfer of title including third-party instructions; and

- understand the significance of the due-on-sale-clause, as well as the limitations regarding the unlicensed practice of law.

■ SELLER'S MATTERS

During the escrow process, the escrow officer should review the file periodically to determine which, if any, conditions and contingencies remain to be satisfied for all parties. In both sale and refinance, close attention must be given to outstanding demands for the seller's loans, which are to be paid and the liens released. In a refinancing, it is possible that an existing loan will remain. The escrow officer will compare the demand for payoff from the lender against the loan information sheet provided by the seller at escrow opening. Other issues that usually require attention include property taxes and the possibility of other liens.

Lender's Demand

The escrow officer will request a beneficiary or **lender's demand** statement from the seller's lender to obtain the necessary information for determining the amount to deduct from the seller's proceeds for paying off the loan. It usually differs from the information provided by the seller to the escrow officer. The escrow officer should forward a copy of the demand directly to the seller or through the seller's agent for the seller to review, sign, and return.

Seller's Review of Demand   The seller will be instructed to review the demand statement for accuracy. If believed to be incorrect, it is the seller's responsibility to communicate with the lender to resolve any disputes. The escrow holder will not allow escrow to close until disputes are resolved and the seller has signed and returned the final corrected demand statement. It isn't unusual for the demand to reflect an amount that may be higher than what the seller believed it would be. Any payments made by the seller after the date of the demand will not be reflected in the demand. The escrow holder will contact the lender to determine whether the payment has been credited and, if so, have an updated demand sent to escrow. If the payment has not been processed and is not reflected on the lender's books, the demand will stand as it is. The seller will eventually receive a refund from the lender; however, the seller will have to understand that the proceeds will be less the amount of the outstanding payment.

Delays in Processing the Demand   Time is always of the essence in an escrow. Occasionally a lender's demand processing takes longer than expected for a number of possible reasons, such as the reasons noted in the next three paragraphs.

Servicer Does Not Own the Loan   The lender to which the borrower makes the payment may be the loan servicer rather than the actual owner of the note. The entity that receives the payment is called the loan servicer. The servicer may or may not own the note. Commonly, the loan is owned by an investor such as Fannie Mae, Freddie Mac, or some other investment firm or larger lender. Once the servicer receives the demand, it may have to be sent to the investor for processing.

Out of Area and Unfamiliar Lender   The lender may be out of state and unfamiliar to the escrow holder, and the lender's information may not be in the escrow database of lenders. (Most escrow companies have a database of mortgage lenders and banks, including the address for processing the demand.) The address to which the seller sends the payment may not be the location that processes demands for payoff. If the escrow officer is unfamiliar with the seller's lender, it may be wise for the escrow officer to call before sending the request for demand or to research the lender's information in the *Lane Guide*, a reference subscription service that provides information on virtually every bank and mortgage lender in the United States. The guide includes information regarding all services and departments of the bank, including payoff demands, assumptions, collections, REO services, and other useful information. (The *Lane Guide* is an excellent tool for the real estate agent as well, especially for learning contact information for REO property disposition and for the mortgage broker for discovering new lending relationships.) "Difficult to locate" servicers or lenders are seldom a problem today because many originating lenders use the services of **Mortgage Electronic Registration System, Inc. (MERS)**, created by the mortgage banking industry to streamline the mortgage process by using electronic commerce to eliminate paper. If you've ever tried to locate an owner of a mortgage or trust deed for any reason, tried to figure out who your lender was, or tried to find out who's servicing a particular loan and got nowhere, this service offers the consumer, escrow holder, and title company the help they need. MERS holds title technically as nominee for the true mortgagees and beneficiaries in its system, and as transfers occur, they are recorded in MERS's computer book-entry system similar to a stock-transfer system.

Reconveyance   This is the process of removing a lender's lien from the title. The title company will facilitate **reconveyance** by sending the Request for Full Reconveyance (Figure 11.1) to the trustee and, upon receipt, will record the Full Reconveyance.

Seller's Current Monthly Payment   To pay or not to pay? Questions may arise regarding the sellers' loan payment for the current month if closing is going to occur just before or after the payment is due. Sellers may wonder whether or not they should make the payment. For example, an escrow is scheduled to close on November 29 and the next payment is due on December 1; in this case, the sellers should not make the payment because escrow will have closed before the sellers' check has even cleared. Additionally, the payoff demand amount from the servicer will include the amount of that payment; so if the seller sends the payment to the lender, it will have been paid twice. The seller would eventually receive a refund from the lender for overpayment, though it may take some time for it to be processed. Even if the scheduled closing is not within a few days of the end or the beginning of the month, it would still be wise for the seller to deliver the monthly payment to escrow for handling. Providing that escrow will close before the 15th day of the month (after which a late charge will usually occur), the escrow holder will have the title company ensure that the payment is reflected through escrow closing and that the payoff amount is adjusted accordingly.

FIGURE 11.1
Request for Full Reconveyance

A Full Reconveyance will be issued only when the original Note or Notes, together with the Deed of Trust securing payment thereof, are surrendered to the Trustee for cancellation, accompanied by this Request signed by all owners of the Note or Notes, together with the required fees.

REQUEST FOR FULL RECONVEYANCE

TO ______________________________, TRUSTEE

The undersigned is the legal owner and holder of the Note or Notes for the original sum of $________________ , and of all other indebtedness secured by Deed of Trust dated _____________ made by ____, Trustor, to ______________________________ Trustee, and recorded on ________, as instrument number _____________ in Book ______ , Page ________, of Official Records, in the office of the County Recorder of ______________________, California.

Said Note or Notes, together will all other indebtedness secured by said Deed of Trust, have been fully paid and satisfied; and you are hereby requested and directed, upon delivery to you of said Deed of Trust and said Note or Notes and upon payment to you of any sums owing to you under the terms of said Deed of Trust, to cancel said Note or Notes above mentioned, and all other evidences of indebtedness secured by said Deed of Trust, together with the said Deed of Trust, and to reconvey, without warranty, to the parties legally entitled thereto, all the estate now held by you under the Deed of Trust.

Dated: ___________________________

____

Mail Reconveyance to ____

Source: Chicago Title Insurance Company

Property Taxes

Just as with a monthly loan payment coming due near escrow closing, the payment of property taxes may also be an issue. If the seller has not paid a property tax installment that is due but not yet delinquent, and if escrow will close before either December 10 for the property tax first-half payment or April 10 for the second-half payment, the seller should have the escrow holder pay the taxes from the seller's proceeds at closing. If escrow is not scheduled to close before the delinquent date and the seller has not paid an installment that is due, the seller should deliver the amount of taxes due to the escrow holder with "good funds" so the escrow holder can pay them to the county tax collector on the seller's behalf before the due date. In the rare event that the seller will not receive sufficient funds at closing to pay the property taxes, the seller should deliver "good funds" to the escrow holder for payment of the taxes. In either case, if the seller pays the property tax directly to the county tax collector, the escrow officer may be required to withhold an amount equal to the property taxes paid, plus penalties, until the county confirms receipt of the payment.

Delinquent Property Taxes   The escrow holder will have determined early in the escrow process whether the seller has any outstanding delinquent property taxes. Any delinquent property taxes must be paid through closing, along with any current amounts due.

Prepaid Property Taxes   Part of the property taxes paid by the seller may be the buyer's responsibility. The escrow holder will credit the seller with the prorated amount of the buyer's responsibility and charge (debit) the buyer accordingly. The following provisions of California property taxes are important for the new escrow professional to learn:

- Property taxes are based on a fiscal year beginning July 1 of each year and ending June 30 the following year.

- The first installment of the tax bill, although due November 1 and delinquent if not paid by 5:00 pm December 10, actually pays for taxes due from July 1 through December 31.

- The second-half payment due February 1, and delinquent if not paid by 5:00 pm April 10, pays taxes due for the period January 1 through June 30.

Example: Escrow and Taxes

If escrow closes September 1, the seller would not have paid property taxes but still owes for the period from July 1 to September 1. The buyer will owe the balance of the taxes due to the end of the tax year (June 30). The escrow officer will charge (debit) the seller with the taxes that will come due and payable November 1 for the period from July 1 to September 1 and issue the buyer a credit at closing for the same amount. Therefore, when the tax bill arrives, the buyer is responsible for paying the entire amount of the first half, including the amount due from July 1 to September 1 because the buyer was essentially reimbursed in advance for that amount at escrow closing.

The following prorations for property taxes are based on a banker's year of 360 days.

Assume escrow closes September 1; first half taxes are $2,000.

$2,000 ÷ 180 = $11.11 per day.

July 1 to September 1 = 60 days

$11.11 × 60 = $666.67 seller's responsibility, credit to buyer

Mechanics' Liens

An individual, vendor, contractor, or provider of materials who has performed work or delivered material to the seller and who was not paid might have filed a mechanic's lien. Such a lien is a recourse available to them under the law to help ensure that they will be paid. These claimants are categorized by law into four groups: contractors, subcontractors, laborers, and materialmen. The original contractor is the person hired and directed by the homeowner to perform the work. The contractor may also hire others, called subcontractors, to do much or most of the work. If the homeowner is directing all the work and personally hiring individuals to do the work, such as plumbing, concrete, electrical, etc., then each of those individuals is considered an original contractor. A materialman is anyone who provides goods, materials, or equipment to the jobsite.

Claiming the Lien   Subcontractors and materialmen may record the lien after they have finished their part of the work on or delivery of material to the project. The original contractor must wait until the project is completed before recording a claim. If recorded later than 90 days after the work was completed, the lien rights are considered expired. The property owner can record a notice of cessation if work has stopped. He can record a notice of completion if work has been finished and the project is completed. After such recordation, the subcontractor, materialman, or laborer must file a claim of lien within 30 days, not 90. The contractor has 60 days in which to file.

Paying the Lien   After paying the claim, the property owner must obtain a release of lien to be protected by record. If the property owner does not pay, the contractor must file suit in the county's superior court within 90 days after recording the claim of lien, otherwise the lien has no effect.

Judgment Liens

After obtaining a judgment against a debtor through the court, the claimant must obtain an abstract of judgment to have the judgment enforced through the court. Once recorded, the abstract of judgment becomes a lien against all real property of the debtor in that county. A judgment is valid for 10 years, though it can be renewed for another 10 years by the creditor. The **judgment lien** must be paid and released in order for escrow to close.

Homestead Exemption   One exception to the abstract of judgment is a homeowner's declaration of homestead exemption. In such a case, the judgment lien only attaches if the value of the homestead property is greater than the amount of all liens plus the amount of the homestead. The amount of the property's value that is greater than the homestead is called surplus equity, with the judgment creditor only entitled to that portion up to the amount of the judgment. If there is no surplus equity, the judgment cannot attach to the property.

Loans Paid but Still of Record

Occasionally, a homeowner has paid off a loan but the lien remains, having not been reconveyed (the process by which a loan, which has been recorded against a property and becomes a lien against it, is removed and released). It doesn't happen automatically.

Compare Loan Information Sheet with Preliminary Title Report   As soon as the preliminary title report is obtained and reviewed by the escrow officer, if loans are recorded against the title (other than those the seller has indicated on the loan information form), the escrow officer must alert the seller to determine whether they are valid. If they are not, the escrow officer must contact the beneficiary and have the trustee reconvey the lien, sometimes a difficult and time-consuming process.

Listing Real Estate Agent's Research   It is always a good idea for a listing agent to obtain a preliminary title report when first listing a property to review the status of the title, including liens of record. In the event an unreconveyed lien that has been paid off is discovered, the seller has more time to accomplish its release.

Income Tax Liens

A review of the preliminary title report will occasionally reveal a lien for delinquent income taxes. The escrow officer will alert the homeowner of the lien when delivering the report and note that the lien must be resolved and released before escrow can close. The escrow officer typically will process and send a demand, or help the seller send an inquiry if disputing the lien to the Internal Revenue Service (IRS) and/or the California Franchise Tax Board (FTB). The demand or inquiry might possibly be sent to the California Employment Development Department (EDD) if the seller is an employer with delinquent employment taxes.

Taxes Paid and Released but Not Recorded It is not uncommon for a tax lien that has been paid to appear on a preliminary title report. It is possible that the State of California or the IRS has not reported the payoff to the country recorder. It may be necessary for the seller to provide evidence of the lien's release to the county recorder to have it recorded.

Taxes Paid but Not Yet Released Liens are typically released by the IRS within 30 days of being paid; if the seller paid delinquent federal taxes less than 30 days before the preliminary title report was prepared, it is possible that the lien is still of record on the report.

Partial Releases It is possible that the seller owes delinquent taxes but does not have the ability to pay them in full. The seller must therefore negotiate with the taxing entity, whether it's the IRS, FTB, EDD, or other taxing agency. Occasionally, the seller's escrow or title officer can assist in the process by negotiating with the taxing agency to accept less than the full amount due. If the negotiation is successful, the lien against the property is released and escrow may close. It should be noted that the taxing agency does not relieve the taxpayer of the taxes due; only the lien against the property is removed. If the seller is buying another property, occasionally the taxing agency, especially the IRS, will allow the purchase to proceed but will attach a lien against the new property.

■ BUYER'S MATTERS

A buyer may have special considerations to resolve before escrow can close. Some of the buyer's issues may be the same as the seller's (e.g., taxes, judgments, and other liens that must be resolved and released). Much as with the seller, the escrow officer must advise the buyer that the outstanding issues must be resolved and certain **financing documents** must be provided to allow escrow to close. Other issues also may impact the ability of the buyer to perform under the contract and escrow provisions.

Buyer's Financing Documents

Notwithstanding the new financing contingency removal provision of the contract, which requires the buyer to remove the contingency to secure financing within a specified time frame (usually 17 days under the CAR Purchase Agreement and Joint Escrow Instructions), other issues and matters relative to the new loan may delay escrow from closing on the agreed-upon date.

Truth-in-Lending Requirements   Under federal law, new guidelines for the Truth-in-Lending (TIL) Disclosure Statement (Chapter 14) and annual percentage rate (APR) disclosures may delay loan processing and escrow closing if the buyers' interest rate is not locked in or expires before the closing date. Any 0.125% or greater increase over the originally disclosed interest rate requires a new TIL and an additional three-day waiting period. Escrow also may not close until at least seven days following the buyer's receipt of the new truth-in-lending statement.

Appraisals   Under today's more rigid loan guidelines, lender's look closely at values represented by the appraiser. Most lenders have their own appraisal department review the results of the appraiser, performing at least a computer validation of value to determine whether their search supports the appraiser's opinion of value. Occasionally, it does not agree. A disagreement might cause a delay and even prevent escrow from closing and the sale being cancelled. The typical review procedure first involves a computer search of comparable sales, called a desk review, to determine whether the appraiser's opinion of value can be supported. If the desk review cannot support the value found in the appraisal, a lender may allow a field review in which the lender's appraiser visits the subject property and all comparable sales. If the field review then supports the value, the loan will proceed through the approval process. If the field review cannot support the appraiser's value, three things are possible: the buyer must pay more cash down if the lender allows, the sales price must be renegotiated, or the sale must be cancelled.

REO (Real Estate Owned) Tenant-Occupied Properties

A bank-owned foreclosed property, called an REO (real estate owned), might be occupied by a tenant with a lease. Under the federal Protecting Tenants at Foreclosure Act of 2009, the tenant must be allowed to stay in the property until the end of the lease under certain conditions. Effective January 1, 2013, the California Civil Code was changed to comply with federal law. Escrow closing can be affected when a buyer is unaware, and later learns, of the law and its tenant protections. If a contingency covered by the circumstance is not removed, the buyer may possibly cancel the escrow. Or if the contingency removal date has passed, a buyer may still prefer to cancel and seek compensation for agent nondisclosure.

Buyer Not Intending to Occupy the Property An investor-buyer who will not occupy the property and intends to rent it to another party must allow a current tenant with an existing lease to stay until the lease's termination date. The existing terms and conditions of the lease will remain. An existing tenant with a month-to-month rental agreement must be given 90 days notice under both the federal and California laws.

Buyer Who Will Be an Owner-Occupant. Buyers who intend to occupy the property are not subject to the survival of lease regulation; however, they must still comply with the 90-day notice provision.

Arm's-Length Transactions. Any transaction in which the buyer is related to the seller is not covered by this act or by California law.

■ PRECLOSING DOCUMENTATION REVIEW

As escrow closing approaches, the escrow officer should use the original take sheet, outline, and instructions (CAR Purchase Agreement and Joint Escrow Instructions) as a guide to audit the escrow file to ensure compliance with all conditions, terms, agreements, and understanding of the parties.

The Audit Process

Because events taking place during the escrow may have changed some of the terms and conditions, it is necessary to review all documents prepared and received, comparing the amendments with the original instructions, to determine compliance. In a Southern California escrow, which requires amendments to escrow, such an audit is especially critical.

Documents to Review All documents, items, and information should be reviewed to determine their correctness and the status of action items. If any condition remains outstanding, the escrow officer should contact the appropriate party for action. Communication is critical during the escrow—and especially as the closing date approaches. The following list includes typical documents to review or actions required during auditing:

- Legal description of the property and current ownership data
- Exact names of the buyers and the method of taking title (vesting)
- Special considerations of the transfer, such as a contingency sale of the buyer's property

■ Status of buyer's loan approval

— Outstanding conditions of lender (either new loan or formal assumption)

— Hazard insurance requirements (agent and policy information received)

— Commission instructions

— Pest control report, including completion of work report

— Prorations

— Invoices to be paid for services (pest control, appraisal, inspections, etc.)

— Trust deeds to be created by escrow (seller carryback). Note: Trust deeds to be assumed by the buyer must be reviewed to determine whether an impound account is required for the future payment of property taxes and/or hazard insurance, and if the loan is current.

— Is a formal assumption required? This is important if the buyer and the seller are entering into a transaction in which the property is being "taken subject to." If so, the lender's instructions to the escrow holder will include requiring the buyer to prepare and submit a loan application and certain documentation verifying the buyer's financial qualifications. Upon approval and closing of escrow, the buyer will have formally assumed the seller's loan and, in the process, assumed all responsibility and liabilities for repaying it. The seller is relieved of all such responsibility and responsibility. This process is technically referred to as substitution of liability.

Special Considerations of Unilateral Instructions

While fewer changes and amendments occur in an escrow involving unilateral instructions (these are common in Northern California), the escrow officer must review and compare the instructions for the buyer with the instructions for the seller to be certain there is a "meeting of the minds." A unilateral instruction may be prepared closer to the end of the escrow or perhaps prepared earlier but not presented to or signed by the parties until near closing. The instruction is a recap of the entire transaction, including any changes made during its process, requiring no amendments. It describes the final agreement between the parties, establishing responsibilities for compliance and for allocation of closing costs. At this point in the escrow, all that is usually required is for the parties to review and sign the instructions and for any funds required to close to be placed into escrow by the responsible party or parties.

Content of the Documents   The primary difference between the buyer's and the seller's unilateral instructions is that the seller's instruction provides the necessary documents to transfer the title in exchange for delivery to the seller of consideration, usually money. The buyer's instruction provides that the consideration is to be given to the escrow holder when title is in a condition to allow it to be transferred.

Meeting of the Minds   The inherent problem when using unilateral instructions is that a meeting of minds may not be present. A problem may arise if the nature or amount of the consideration changes or is different between the two instructions. At some point during the escrow, for example, the buyer and the seller may have agreed for the buyer to increase the amount of cash to be placed into escrow, which would then reduce the amount of the buyer's loan (either a new origination or a loan carried by the seller). The seller's escrow may reflect the change but not the buyer's. Before escrow can close, a change must be made to one of the instructions to make them the same, which then reflects a meeting of the minds.

Ratification   In Northern California, unilateral escrow instructions are typically a ratification of what the escrow holder has been doing in the form of instructions to escrow from the principals, but they do not necessarily create the subsequent contract between the parties. The **ratification** process is based on the completion of items promised to be performed or provided, such as receipt of payoff demands, delivery of title reports, ascertainment of pest control work, and approval of new loans. The principal part of the unilateral instruction process is the estimated closing statement that, because closing is near, should be the same as the statement to be delivered on the anticipated closing date.

Preclosing and Bilateral Instructions

Because bilateral instructions include the mutual promises of the parties in a single instruction at the beginning of the escrow process, it is possible that some information is incomplete or to be provided. The instruction consists initially of the terms of the buyer's purchase offer, which is likely to be relatively complete, but it may only indicate the seller's acceptance, with much of the seller's information still to be provided.

General Instructions   General instructions vary among escrow companies, especially regarding the protective or exculpatory clauses they insert in the instructions. These typically include a provision that in the event escrow is not in a position to close on the proposed closing date, the escrow will continue unless objected to by either party. General instructions must be retained by the escrow holder for five years from the date of closing under California law.

Amendments   Because the general instructions are prepared at the beginning of the escrow (when using bilateral instructions), changes commonly occur as escrow progresses. Instead of preparing entirely new instructions, an additional or amended instruction is prepared to reflect the change. Any **amendment** must be signed by both principals. Some typical reasons for amendments are as follows:

- *Newly discovered or disclosed facts, such as the title company's discovery of a recently recorded lien against the property, which must be resolved.* An agreement must be made and executed by the parties as to the resolution and the allocation of cost, if any, between the parties.

- *Continuing negotiations that may cause a change in the meeting of the minds.* Once a change is agreed upon, it must be reflected in an amendment signed by both parties. For example, the results of an inspection for the buyer may indicate a defect that previously wasn't discovered or disclosed, or there may arise a greater cost to perform repairs or to correct a condition subject to inspection.

- *The results of other third-party reports or requirements, such as an appraisal that reflects a value less than the agreed-upon sales price.* The buyer's lender may not approve a loan in an amount for which the buyer previously had applied, or the buyer may not be prepared to pay a price that exceeds the appraised value. In order for the escrow to proceed, the buyer and the seller must reach a mutual agreement that is also acceptable to the buyer's lender.

Third-Party Instructions Sometimes parties other than the principals become involved in the transaction, requiring amendments or additional instructions to accommodate the requirements of these third parties. Occasionally, a party other than the principal who has a financial interest in the transaction may execute a **third-party instruction** to the escrow holder. A typical third-party instruction is when the broker entitled to a commission, as identified in the agreement, orders a separate instruction to the escrow holder to pay the third party at the closing. Other examples of third-party instructions include the following:

- Instructions for an interspousal transfer grant deed from one spouse to the other without the payment of consideration (no money)

- Lender's instruction relating to the payoff or assumption of the existing loan and trust deed

- Other special instructions relating to the release of mechanics' liens, judgments, tax liens, and other such matters

Transfer and Financing Documents

At this point in the escrow, the grant deed, plus the note and trust deed if financing is part of the transaction, will have been prepared for signing by the parties.

Preparing the Grant Deed The grant deed is a notarized document containing language that transfers title from the seller to the buyer (grantor to grantee). It will have been prepared based on the instructions from the parties; therefore, the escrow officer should review to ensure that it complies with their instructions. Special attention should be given to the following:

- *Transfer tax.* The state/county transfer tax is $0.55 per $500 of value of cash and new loans in the transaction. Additionally, some cities in California also have a transfer tax. The escrow officer should check the grant deed to determine whether the total transfer tax is correct.

- *Assessor's parcel number (APN).* The escrow officer should be certain the APN is correct. If it is incorrect, the grant deed cannot be recorded.

- *Form and content.* If these are incorrect, the recorder will reject the grant deed for recording. Common errors include an inadequate notary seal, an expire notary commission, missing or questionable signatures of the parties, property location in another county, among other items.

Installment Note A promissory note, commonly called an **installment note,** is prepared by a borrower's lender and will show the exact terms of the loan. The note is the evidence of the debt, signed and dated but not notarized. If the note has been prepared by escrow, such as in a seller carryback loan, using the Seller Financing Addendum as a guide (this form is required by law to be completed by the agent with the seller if seller financing will be a part of the transaction), both buyer and seller must agree that it is correct as to the term, amount, interest rate, and any other conditions, such as a late charge, prepay penalty, or due-on-sale provision.

Due-on-Sale clause The **due-on-sale clause** is a provision in the note that gives the lender the ability to call the loan due and payable if the borrower transfers title, or any part of it (such as quitclaiming a partial interest to another person), and the loan is not paid off and the lender has not given its expressed approval.

Deed of Trust The deed of trust is the security or debt instrument for the loan and the collateral securing the loan (the real estate). It is used almost exclusively by lenders in California, instead of a mortgage (Figure 6 in Chapter 2). It is signed, notarized, and recorded. The trust deed creates a lien on the property with recordation giving constructive notice. A major provision of the deed of trust is the Transfer of Rights in the Property clause. In this clause, the borrower grants and conveys to the trustee on behalf of the beneficiary, with the power of sale, legal title (technically "bare legal title") to the property. The borrower, by signing the deed of trust, agrees that the beneficiary has the right to foreclose and sell the property (and this may be executed without court action) as allowed and through the process described under "Nonuniform Covenants" and "acceleration." The deed of trust form used by lenders is called the fictitious deed of trust.

Fictitious Deed of Trust   A *fictitious deed of trust* is a legal term that refers to a deed of trust that is recordable in any county in California as authorized by California Civil Code Section 2952. It contains the standard provisions normally used in actual transactions. This prerecorded fictitious deed is inherently included by its reference in the "short form" deed of trust. The recording information of the fictitious deed of trust is referred to on the front page of the short form with the boilerplate language reprinted on the back page. Because the front page of the short form deed of trust refers to the recording information of the fictitious deed of trust, it is not necessary to record the back page, which may include an instruction such as "Do Not Record."

Short Form Deed of Trust   Trust deeds are usually referred to as "short form deeds of trust," eliminating much of the language that otherwise would have been included. Using the short form deed of trust not only eliminates much of the paperwork but also reduces the cost of recording because recorder's offices charge a specified amount for each page recorded. The short form is allowed to be used because it makes reference to the previously recorded master deed of trust (the fictitious deed of trust). The deed of trust is used to convey the "dormant title" to land to another person or company as a "trustee," in order to secure debts or other obligations evidenced by an installment (promissory) note. The trustee is given the "bare legal title," accompanied by the power of sale of the land encumbered in the event of a default by the borrower. The primary reason for the use of the short form deed of trust is to reduce the recording fees payable to the county by eliminating the pages that contain the complete language of the deed of trust.

All-Inclusive Deed of Trust   The **all-inclusive deed of trust** (AITD; also informally called a wraparound deed of trust) is the security instrument used when a seller is carrying back financing in which an underlying senior lien is included in a new note along with the seller's equity position being carried. In an AITD transaction, the buyer (borrower) "takes title subject to" the seller's existing note and trust deed. Typically, neither the seller nor the buyer informs the underlying note holder of the transaction, unless no due-on-sale clause exists, which is unlikely. The recourse of the lender holding the note, and the impact and liability to both the buyer and the seller, is the same as described earlier in the traditional method of taking title subject to. The new note, drawn by the escrow holder, although including the senior underlying note, is still junior to it. A grant deed transferring title to the buyer is executed and escrow closes.

Risks   "Taking title subject to" the existing note and deed of trust carries with it some potential risk to both the buyer and the seller. In the usual transaction the seller's lender is not contacted to approve the transaction as it would if the buyer was "formally" assuming the loan. The major risk to the parties is the lender eventually discovering title has transferred and the possibility it will enforce the note's due on sale clause. The escrow holder prepares the note and the title company usually serves as the trustee. The agent must prepare the CAR Seller Financing Addendum.

What Happens if the Lender Calls the Loan Due and Payable   If the lender calls the note due and payable, it sends a letter to the trustor of record (the former seller) demanding payment in full within 30 days. The seller naturally would inform the homeowner (the former buyer) of the lender's demand, expecting the homeowner to make arrangements to pay off the loan. The possibility exists that the homeowner will be unable to obtain pay-off funds in a timely manner. Typically, the homeowner in this situation will attempt to refinance the property to accommodate the payoff. The homeowner's refinancing lender and the escrow holder need to be made aware of the urgency of the transaction. Providing copies of the loan escrow instructions to the lender with a request for a payoff demand may get the lender's cooperation, even if the refinance will take longer than the 30 days. The real difficulty arises when the homeowner is unable to obtain refinancing and has no other access to funds. Unless the trustor (the technical term for a borrower in a deed of trust), which in this case is the former seller, is able to help, the lender will file foreclosure, an action impacting both the current homeowner and the trustor. The homeowner loses the property, and all the monies invested, and is forced to vacate; the trustor gets a foreclosure on his credit report.

Request for Full Reconveyance   Upon satisfaction of the debt, meaning the debt has been paid in full, the beneficiary (lender) will request that the lien be removed from the property by completing a Request for Full Reconveyance (Figure 11.1) and submitting it to the trustee, along with the original note and deed of trust. The trustee will then execute and either record or deliver the reconveyance deed directly to the trustor (borrower), who should have it recorded to give constructive notice of the removal of the lien.

Documents and Action Required for Closing

The balance of the documents required to close would include those related to the title, such as any document required to release the seller's trust deed of record and a statement of the amount necessary to pay it off in full. The escrow officer will audit the balance of the escrow documents and requirements.

Preliminary Title Report   The escrow officer will review the title report to be certain that nothing has been omitted or overlooked, comparing it to the escrow instructions as to action or disclosure requirements.

Demands   The escrow officer will order the payoff demands from the seller's lenders of record that are being paid off.

Change of Ownership Report   The buyer will also be required to complete the county's Preliminary Change of Ownership Report (PCOR) (Figure 9.1). The escrow holder will conduct the **PCOR process**. California Revenue and Taxation Code Section 480 requires that whenever there is a change in ownership of real property, the property owner must actually file a Change in Ownership Statement (COS), which is different from the PCOR. However, there is no penalty for failing to file the statement unless the assessor prompts the property owner to file the statement by making a written request. If requested, then the taxpayer has 45 days to file the COS or incur penalties, as specified. Generally, the penalty for failing to timely file a COS after a written request is 10% of the taxes applicable to the new base year value reflecting the change in ownership. The amount may not exceed $2,500, provided the failure to file the statement is not willful. Thus, at the basic 1% tax rate, the maximum penalty threshold of $2,500 applies to any property with a new base year value in excess of $2.5 million.

Preliminary Change of Ownership Report (PCOR)   In actual practice, many persons file a PCOR rather than a COS. The two forms are nearly identical. If a PCOR is filed at the time a deed is recorded, an extra fee of $20 is avoided. The COS and/or PCOR provide the assessor with information necessary to value the property for tax purposes, such as details about the purchase price and the terms of the sale. It also assists in determining whether the transfer of property might be eligible for one of the many change in ownership exclusions that would avoid the need to reassess the property. Both the COS and the PCOR are confidential documents pursuant to Section 481 (Revenue & Taxation Code). The primary purpose of the law is to insure that all government entities (state, city, and county, as well as other agencies) receive appropriate revenues for which they are entitled under the law. California's system of property taxation under Article XIII A of the California Constitution (Proposition 13) values property at its 1975 fair market value, with annual increases limited to the inflation rate, as measured by the California Consumer Price Index or 2%, whichever is less, until the property changes ownership or is newly constructed. At the time of the ownership change or new construction, the value of the property for property tax purposes is redetermined based on current market value. The value initially established, or redetermined where appropriate, is called the base year value. Thereafter, the base year value is subject to annual increases for inflation. This value is called the factored base year value.

■ TRANSMITTAL OF DOCUMENTS

Approaching the date of closing, the following documents will be forwarded to the title company for review, issuance of the title insurance policy, and recording of the necessary documents to transfer title and secure the loan (deed of trust).

Title Officer's Review

The title officer will review the grant deed to determine whether it has been properly completed and acknowledged, all the names are correct, the property description is correct and valid, and vesting is in accordance with the instructions. A similar review of the deed of trust will be conducted. The Statements of Information of the parties will also be reviewed not only to ensure that the parties have been correctly identified for recording but also to ascertain that no exceptions to the title policy are required other than those previously determined. The PCOR, which should have been prepared by this time in the escrow, will be reviewed for completeness and accuracy and submitted with the other documents that must be recorded (if the PCOR is recorded separately, a penalty is assessed by the county).

■ FINAL AUDIT BY ESCROW

With recording ready, a final audit of the escrow file helps avoid last-minute errors, which could be costly or delay or prevent closing. Most escrow officers use a checklist to avoid missing any item. The escrow officer will also perform another accounting of all funds, debits, and credits of the parties and "balance" the file and will use this to complete the Settlement Statement (HUD-1). The items on the escrow officer's checklist should include the items listed in the paragraphs that follow.

Signed Escrow Instructions

All parties having a vested interest in the matter must sign the instructions, including all amendments and additional or third-party instructions to which they are a party.

Authorized Disbursements

Does the escrow holder have the signed commission authorization, payoff approval with updated demand information, approvals for loan escrow, title fees, termite work, withholding of any funds for work to be performed, bills and invoices to be paid including buyer's hazard insurance, and other such items?

Legal Description Confirmed

One last check of the legal description, both by the escrow officer and the title company, can avoid a last-minute problem in recording.

Review Escrow Instructions

Events may occur late in the escrow, including just before recording is to take place, that result in the preparation of a final amendment. If so, is it correct and has it been signed by all parties?

Lender's Requirements

Have all the outstanding conditions of the lender before funding the loan been accomplished or received, such as pest control, insurance, and impound accounting? If the loan documents have yet to be signed, review the lender's instructions to insure compliance. Last-minute issues usually involve hazard insurance documents not received, or incorrect coverage, as well as missing documents the buyer was to return to the lender with signed loan documents (i.e., signed tax returns).

Buyer's Hazard Insurance

The importance of verifying that the hazard insurance policy has been received, is correct, and meets the lender's requirements, including accurate loss payee information, cannot be stressed enough. It is not necessary to wait until loan documents have arrived to obtain the loss payee information and forward it to the insurance agent long before closing. Escrow is, at times, delayed because the buyer's insurance agent hasn't been available or fails to respond in a timely manner. Upon receipt of the loan documents, double-check to be certain that insurance requirements and loss payee Information have not changed.

Correct Names on All Documents

Does the seller's name agree with ownership as indicated on the preliminary title report, and have the buyers' names, status, and vesting been correctly indicated on all appropriate documents?

Sufficient and Good Funds

There must be sufficient and "good" funds from the buyer, and from the seller, if required. Funds delivered to escrow for closing must be "good" as defined by the State of California. Funds wired to escrow are good upon receipt and may be disbursed the same day. Funds delivered to escrow in the form of a cashier's check or certified check are good the next business day, at which time they may be disbursed. Funds delivered to escrow in the form of a personal check drawn on a local bank must be held by escrow for three business days before disbursement is. Funds must be held for five business days before disbursement if the bank on which they are drawn is out of state.

Tax Reporting

Have funds been withheld, if necessary, in compliance with FIRPTA and California withholding, or has an exemption been filed, if necessary (see "Tax Reporting")?

Pest Control Completion and Compliance

Has any remedial work as indicated and required by the pest control inspection report been completed? Has the final inspection been performed and is it in the file? Is payment authorization in the file, along with the invoice? If work has not been completed, has an authorization to withhold sufficient funds been received?

Documents for the Title Company

Are all documents to be recorded at the title company? Have any documents previously sent to the title company and returned to escrow as being incorrect or incomplete been corrected or replaced and delivered back to the title company?

Presettlement Accounting

Has the file been "figured" once again to prevent any shortages at closing? Closing short is not an acceptable escrow practice.

■ CLOSING AND RECORDATION

After documents have been recorded, the final accounting performed, closing statements drawn, and funds disbursed, escrow is said to be closed. The final closing process is described in the following paragraphs.

Deposit of Buyer's Funds

Some of the buyer's deposit may have been forwarded to the title company, if necessary, to pay any buyer's liens of record and to pay for a sub-escrow if the escrow company is not part of the title company. (If the title company and escrow company are related, no sub-escrow fee is charged.)

Final Audit

Escrow holder verifies again that all instructions are fulfilled and that there are adequate funds for closing.

Recording

The escrow holder arranges for the title company to record the deed and trust deed and any other documents, such as those for releasing seller's liens of record.

■ CHAPTER 11 QUIZ

1. The entity that receives the borrower's payments is called the

   a. loan servicer.

   b. loan processor.

   c. Freddie Mac.

   d. investment servicer.

2. Many originating lenders today use the services of MERS, which stands for

   a. Mortgage Escrow Registration System.

   b. Mortgage Escrow Recording System.

   c. Mortgage Electronic Registration System.

   d. Mortgage Electronic Recording System.

3. The primary benefit of MERS to the escrow holder is that

   a. it allows for more rapid loan payoff.

   b. it eliminates closing delays.

   c. it eliminates the question as to who owns or services the loan.

   d. all of these.

4. Property taxes in California are based on a fiscal year beginning

   a. July 1.

   b. June 30.

   c. March 1.

   d. January 1.

5. The first half of California property taxes is due

   a. December 1 and delinquent if not paid by February 1.

   b. November 1 and delinquent if not paid by December 10.

   c. July 1 and delinquent if not paid by September 1.

   d. November 10 and delinquent if not paid by December 1.

6.   Claimants under a mechanic's lien are divided into which four groups under the law?

   a.   Contractors, subcontractors, laborers, and materialmen

   b.   Contractors, homeowners, lenders, and materialmen

   c.   Contractors, homeowners, laborers, and materialmen

   d.   Subcontractors, vendors, laborers, and materialmen

7.   Under the federal truth-in-lending (TIL) disclosure laws, if a borrower's interest rate increases by 0.125% or greater than first disclosed before the close of escrow,

   a.   a new TIL is sent to the borrower and escrow may not close for seven days.

   b.   escrow may not close until the borrower receives a new TIL.

   c.   escrow may close regardless.

   d.   escrow may not close for three days after receipt of the new TIL.

8.   The escrow holder must retain general escrow instructions under the law for

   a.   one year.

   b.   three years.

   c.   five years.

   d.   seven years.

9.   The Preliminary Change of Ownership Report

   a.   provides the assessor with information necessary to value the property for tax purposes.

   b.   assists in determining whether the transfer of property might be eligible for one of the many change in ownership exclusions that would avoid the need to reassess the property.

   c.   both a and b.

   d.   neither a nor b.

10.   The value initially established by the PCOR is called the

    a.   base year value.

    b.   baseline value.

    c.   basic year value.

    d.   factored base year value.

12

ESCROW ACCOUNTING

■ KEY TERMS

California property tax chart	estimated closing statement	per diem
credits	HOA dues	prorations
debits	impound accounts	Settlement Statement
documentary transfer tax	ledger sheet	(HUD-1)
	lien date	supplemental tax bills

■ LEARNING OBJECTIVES

Upon completing this chapter, you will be able to

- ■ prepare, balance and explain the escrow ledger sheet,

- ■ prepare and explain the estimated closing statement,

- ■ understand and explain basic accounting principles of debits and credits,

- ■ calculate and explain prorations including property taxes and HOA,

- ■ calculate and explain lenders' impound account requirements,

- ■ calculate and explain documentary transfer taxes, and

- ■ explain the California property tax chart and lien dates.

■ THE CLOSING STATEMENT

The obligations and responsibilities for the payment of services, fees, and costs of the parties involved in the escrow transaction may vary depending upon the item, custom, and laws or regulations. The escrow holder must reflect these obligations properly in the form of a closing statement, called the settlement statement, for each party. This statement provides the flow of all consideration through escrow, as well as listing the adjustments and authorized disbursements for payment of the obligations.

Escrow Holder's Ledger Sheet

The escrow holder accounts for all funds, payments, and credits on the **ledger sheet**, which is then transferred to the Settlement Statement (HUD-1). Except for an all-cash sale, although the entire consideration and adjustments will still be subject to an accounting, the actual total dollar amounts will not flow through the transaction if the escrow is a Southern California transaction. For example, in Southern California, if the title company is one other than that of the escrow holder, loan proceeds and the payment of demands will flow through a sub-escrow by the title company (which charges a fee for this service), with only the net amount disbursed to the escrow holder. In Northern California, all funds flow through the escrow.

Escrow Closing Statements

The **estimated closing statement** usually reflects debit and credit columns, as in standard bookkeeping practice, with columns headed "Seller," "Borrower," "Buyer," and "Lender," and is transferred to the HUD-1 Settlement Statement, the form and format required by the U.S. Department of Housing and Urban Development. In Northern California, this is used as a worksheet and is included in the escrow instructions as the estimated closing statement. The escrow holder will indicate the appropriate party (seller, borrower, buyer, or lender) to which the statement is being provided.

Seller's Closing Statement

The following represent typical entries, in the form of credits or debits, on the seller's closing statement:

> **Pro-Tip: Credits or Debits? Remembering Which Is Which**
>
> Credit = Money received or a credit against monies owed by the party
>
> Debit = Money owed by the party

- **Credits** reflected on the closing statement for the seller would include the following:

  — The buyer's consideration (total sales price) is shown as a debit on the buyer's statement.

  — Taxes prepaid by the seller and for which the buyer is responsible would be shown as a credit, as would any homeowners association dues; both are shown as debits on the buyer's statement.

  — Monies to be returned by the seller's lender for an impound account are shown as a credit (this would not be shown as a debit on the buyer's statement).

- **Debits** are items to be paid by the seller; the following would be shown as debits on the closing statement (and would not be shown as credits on the buyer's statement):

  — Unpaid loan balance of the seller to be paid off at closing

  — Owner's title policy, if seller is to pay (customary)

  — Commission payable to real estate agents

  — Any other vendor service or fee that the seller agreed to pay.

Buyer's Closing Statement

Credits and debits reflected on the buyer's closing statement may include the items listed here. Some, as already noted, would also be shown on the seller's statement, while others would not. Those would not show on the seller's statement include fees and costs the buyer is paying to others, such as an appraisal fee.

- *Credits.* Items prepaid by the buyer or to be advanced by the lender (such as the buyer's loan) would be shown as a credit on the buyer's statement:

  — Buyer's deposit toward the purchase price

  — Buyer's new loan

  — Balance of buyer's remaining funds to be placed into escrow

- *Debits.* Debits would reflect those fees for expenses and vendors for which the buyer is responsible for paying, including but not limited to the following:

  — Loan processing fees

  — Interest to be paid on buyers loan at closing (represents interest due from the date the loan funds to end of the calendar month)

  — Escrow and title fees

  — Hazard insurance

  — Appraisal

  — Recording

  — Total consideration (sales price)

Funds Held After Escrow Closes (Holding Escrow)

Occasionally, the escrow holder will be asked by one of the parties to hold funds following the close of escrow because of special circumstances. It may be a requirement of the buyer's lender for work that the lender allows to be performed after the close of escrow. The lender will usually require an amount equal to one-and-one-half times to estimated cost of the work to be held. Upon completion of the work, the escrow holder will usually pay the contractors from funds held, releasing the balance to the appropriate party, usually the buyer.

■ ESCROW MATHEMATICS

Among the tasks the escrow officer performs are those that require an understanding of basic mathematical concepts, especially in prorating fees, charges, and other costs to be paid by the buyer and the seller. Determining and correctly calculating these various **prorations** requires careful and diligent attention to the process.

Some fees (e.g., the interest on a loan) may not be shared by both the buyer and the seller and are the responsibility of only one party. Others fees and charges that are commonly prorated between both the buyer and the seller include property taxes, transfer taxes, rents, and homeowners association dues.

Proration Concepts

Financial calculations for prorating items at closing (i.e., fees, taxes, and expenses between or among the buyer, seller, or third parties charges such as the interest payable by the buyer or the seller for their respective loans) are easily performed using the escrow holder's software. However, the escrow officer should have a thorough understanding of the mathematical and financial principles behind the calculations, as well as be able to manually perform some of the simple calculations.

- *Time period.* The first step is to establish the appropriate time period governing the prorations. Financial calculations are based on either an amount per day or as a percentage of the total for the period. For example, property taxes may be prorated on a basis of either 180 days or six months.

- *Insurance.* Insurance policies are prorated based on a 12-month, or one-year, term. For example, if the buyer's monthly loan payment will include hazard insurance, the escrow company's prorations will reflect 14 months, representing a one-year policy prepaid plus a prorated amount equaling 2-months' insurance premium payments.

- *Rents.* Prorations are based on 30 days or one month.

Property Taxes

California property taxes are ad valorem taxes levied on real property at a base rate of 1% of the assessed value of the property. An ad valorem tax is one based on the value of the item being taxed. Additional assessments may include taxes for other services, such as public schools and colleges, streetlights, parks, fire and other emergency services, sewers, and other community infrastructure. An actual total tax rate of nearly 2% is possible, depending on the public services performed or provided by a local government. Taxes on real property extend to both land and improvements that are permanently affixed to the land, such as homes and other buildings, and become a lien on the title. It is possible for the escrow officer to encounter a transaction in which, although rare, the improvements and land are owned by different persons. The owner of the land and the owner of the improvements most likely have a separate assessment and a separate tax bill on the property that each owns. Such a complex transaction requires careful attention to detail when it comes time to computing and calculating the buyers' and the sellers' closing costs and fees.

Priority of Property Tax Liens   Property tax liens have priority over all other liens attached to the property, including judgments, state, IRS, purchase money (loans to purchase property), and trust deeds, regardless of when any of the other liens were created and recorded.

Lien Date   The lien of the tax attaches to the property each year at noon on the January 1 preceding the fiscal year for which the taxes are levied; this is the **lien date**. The lien is placed on the property at this time; however, the amount of the taxes will not be known until later in the year. For example, January 1, 2013, property taxes become a lien for taxes due for the tax year of 2013–2014, which begins July 1, 2013, and terminates at midnight June 30, 2014.

Tax Collection   Most real property is assessed on the secured roll. On or before July 1, the county assessor completes and delivers the tax roll to the county auditor. The assessor sends a notice to each property owner of the assessed value that will appear on the tax bill. California law requires the assessor to fix tax rates and levy taxes on or before September 1. Taxes may be adjusted between that time and when the taxes are actually due and payable.

Due Date and Payment of Taxes   Property taxes in California may be paid in two installments. The first installment is due and payable November 1 and becomes delinquent if not paid by 5:00 pm on December 10. A 10% penalty is assessed if paid after December 10. The second half of the taxes is due February 1 of the following year and becomes delinquent if not paid by 5:00 pm on April 10, with a 10% penalty due as well.

Proration is based on the lien dates for the various taxes due. In general, every tax on real property is a lien on the property assessed. The lien of the tax is only removed when it's paid or legally cancelled or when the property is sold to a private party or the state for nonpayment. Property may be sold to the state for nonpayment only after five years of nonpayment has occurred.

The escrow professional is guided by a chart indicating when taxes are due and how many months of the installment term have been or are to be paid. The chart is used to determine the proration of taxes between a buyer and a seller. These amounts vary depending on the closing month of the year.

California Property Tax Chart   Figure 12.1 shows the **California property tax chart**, which shows when taxes are due by the respective parties according to the escrow closing date.

FIGURE 12.1

Property Tax Chart

Buyer		Seller	
Jan 1	6 months of 2nd Installment	Jan 1	6 months of 1st Installment
Feb 1	5 months of 2nd Installment	Feb 1	1 month of 2nd Installment
Mar 1	4 months of 2nd Installment	Mar 1	2 months of 2nd Installment
April 1	3 months of 2nd Installment	Apr 1	3 months of 2nd Installment
May 1	2 months of 2nd Installment	May 1	4 months of 2nd Installment
Jun 1	1 month of 2nd Installment	Jun 1	5 months of 2nd Installment
Jul 1	6 months of 1st Installment	Jul 1	6 months of 2nd Installment
Aug 1	5 months of 1st Installment	Aug 1	1 month of 1st Installment
Sep 1	4 months of 1st Installment	Sep 1	2 months of 1st Installment
Oct 1	3 months of 1st Installment	Oct 1	3 months of 1st Installment
Nov 1	2 months of 1st Installment	Nov 1	4 months of 1st Installment
Dec 1	1 month of 1st Installment	Dec 1	5 months of 1st Installment

Delinquent Taxes and Tax Defaults   On or before June 8, a list of tax delinquent properties is published and notes the date upon which delinquent property will be "sold to the state." As of June 30, these properties become tax defaulted. Pursuant to California State Revenue and Tax Code Section 3436, all properties appearing on the published list of delinquent taxes remaining unpaid are deemed to have been "sold to the state." This does not actually mean the properties have been sold or that there was an auction. It refers to the process by which the state records and accounts for such properties and taxes. The list also establishes a five-year period for residential properties and a three-year period for nonresidential properties during which the property owner has the right to own, use, and enjoy the property and may redeem it by paying all delinquent taxes, costs, and penalties along with interest.

Redemption   Redemption period terms provide that the owner retains legal title to the property. During the five- or three-year term, whichever applies, there is no additional sale to the state for subsequent tax delinquencies while the original sale to the state is in effect.

Supplemental Tax Bills Due to Value Change

A point of confusion for a buyer, especially a first-time homebuyer, is the fact that the State of California issues an additional tax bill, called a **supplemental tax bill**, sometime after the close of a purchase transaction escrow. Although escrow holders do not become involved with supplemental property taxes, they should have a fundamental understanding of them and be able to explain to buyers that the bill will be forwarded to them sometime after escrow closing. They should also advise buyers that any amounts due were not included in the escrow accounting. State law requires the assessor's office to reappraise real property upon change in ownership or completion of new construction. The assessor's office must issue a supplemental assessment, which reflects the difference between the prior assessed value and the new assessment. This value is prorated based on the number of months remaining in the fiscal year (July 1 through June 30).

Increase in Assessed Value   An increase in value will result in a supplemental tax bill reflecting the change in value for the balance of the tax year. In some cases, the market value is higher than the owner's assessed value in effect as of the January 1 lien date. If this situation occurs, a supplemental tax bill will be issued. Additionally, a supplemental assessment must be made to reflect the new assessed value for the remainder of the fiscal year in which the activity occurred. Due dates for supplemental tax bills depend on when the bill is mailed. The buyer must understand that these supplemental taxes are in addition to the regular property tax and must be paid in accordance with the tax bill.

Decrease in Assessed Value   A decrease in the assessed value, such as that of an REO or short sale property having a sales price less than the current assessed value, will result in a negative supplemental tax, meaning a credit toward taxes coming due in the future. Reassessment reducing taxes for a construction project prior to completion of construction typically will result in a negative supplemental assessment. All these negative assessments (refunds) will not cause a change in the current annual tax bill, which was based on the current assessed value and which must be paid as indicated to avoid penalties. The difference will be adjusted, and reflected on the next year's bill. The current taxes must be paid before the county will refund the difference.

In some cases, a property changes ownership before a secured or unsecured supplemental bill is issued for a prior change of ownership or completion of new construction. This will occur when the buyer sells the property within a short period of time. The buyer's supplemental tax bill will cover only those months when the buyer owned the property, and the new owner will receive a separate supplemental tax bill.

Two Supplemental Tax Bills May Be Issued   If a change in ownership occurs or the new construction is completed on or between January 1 and midnight May 31, there will be two supplemental assessments. One supplemental assessment will be issued; it will represent the difference between the new assessed value and the taxable value on the tax roll in existence for these dates. The second supplemental assessment will be the difference between the new assessed value and the taxable value on the next year's tax roll.

Additional Taxes   Additional property taxes may be assessed against a property after the close of a sale escrow or as a result of the construction of additional improvements to or on the property. The impact and responsibility for the supplemental taxes should be a matter of agreement between the parties, as reflected in the purchase agreement and escrow instructions. The escrow officer should not get involved in attempting to prorate or explain these taxes. The additional and new tax is customarily based on 1% of the market value, usually considered to be the sales price. The difference is issued as a prorated supplemental tax due and payable.

Due Date for Supplemental Taxes   The date on which supplemental tax bills become delinquent varies depending upon when they are mailed by the tax collector.

- If the bill is mailed between July 1 and October 30, the taxes may be paid in two installments, and they become delinquent for the first installment at 5:00 pm on December 10 and at 5:00 pm on April 10 for the second installment (the same delinquency schedule as for the annual tax bill mailed in November).

- If the bill is mailed between November 1 and June 30, the taxes may be paid in two installments and they become delinquent for the first installment if not paid by 5:00 pm on the last day of the month following the month in which the bill was mailed. The taxes become delinquent for the second installment if not paid by 5:00 pm on the last day of the fourth month following the month in which the bill was mailed.

California Property Tax Calendar

The escrow officer must have a basic knowledge of the primary dates during the year that affect property taxes as shown in Figure 12.2.

FIGURE 12.2

California Property Tax Calendar

Date	Event
January 1	Property taxes become a lien on real property as of 12:01 am
February 1	2nd half of property taxes become due and payable
February 15	Last day to file for homeowner's exemption ($7,000)
February 15	Last day to file for disabled veteran's exemption (5:00 pm)
April 10	Last day to pay 2nd half of property taxes without a penalty (5:00 pm)
June 30	End of the fiscal tax year
June 30	Delinquent taxes become tax defaulted
July	Assessor sends property tax roll to auditor-controller
July	Assessor mails property value notice to homeowners
July 2	First day to file property tax assessment appeal
September 15	Last day to file property tax assessment appeal
October 1-31	Tax collector mails annual tax bills
November 1	First half of property taxes becomes due and payable
December 10	Last day to pay 1st half of property taxes (5:00 pm)

Disabled Veteran's Property Tax Exemption

According to the U. S. Department of Veteran Affairs, there are presently over 243,000 disabled veterans in California. Many more also continue to return home daily. California offers a number of benefits to all veterans, and especially to those who have become disabled because of service-connected injuries or diseases. Among these many benefits is possible eligibility for an exemption to California property taxes if the veteran meets certain eligibility requirements. (Note that California also has an exemption for veterans who are not disabled; however, the value of the property owned by the veteran cannot exceed $5,000; therefore, most veterans will want to obtain the basic homeowner's exemption instead). The qualifying guidelines for the disabled veteran's exemption are as follows:

- *Qualifying disabilities.* The veteran should obtain qualifying information from the appropriate county assessor's office (the county in which the property is located). Basic qualifying guidelines include disability due to

  — loss of sight in both eyes, or

  — loss of the use of two or more limbs, or

  — result of a service-connected disability or disease.

  The unmarried surviving spouse of a veteran who met, or would have met, the qualifying guidelines may also qualify.

- *Amount of exemption.* The exemption is \$100,000 (\$150,000 for low-income veterans; other criteria also noted in this section). The exemption amount may increase annually based on a cost-of-living index.

  — The exemption for the tax year 2013 is \$122.128 (\$183,113 for low-income veterans).

- *Low-income eligibility.* Veterans may be eligible if household income does not exceed the 2001 base of \$40,000 annually increased each year on the cost-of-living index.

  — The maximum 2013 qualifying household income is \$54,842.

- Veterans may not use both the \$7,000 homeowner's exemption and the disabled veteran's exemption.

Buyer's Loan Impound Accounts for Property Taxes

The buyer's lender may require property taxes and, in some instances, hazard insurance to be paid with the monthly payment. An **impound** or escrow **account** (this does not refer to the escrow company) must be established with funds in a specific amount forwarded to the lender at closing. The lender, in turn, holds the fund in the borrowers' account and it is used to pay property taxes and hazard insurance when they are due each year. Many borrowers, even if the lender does not require such an account, may voluntarily wish to do it because it saves them from the responsibility of making one large payment each year. The escrow account replaces writing one or two large checks with 12 more easily manageable payments, paid each month as an addition to the monthly loan payment. Such a system also avoids the possibility of not making the payment on time and incurring a penalty of 10% of the tax due.

The hazard insurance impound, an amount equal to two months' insurance, is required to be impounded. Property taxes are more complex.

The following guidelines are for impounding or escrowing the property taxes in California.

California Property Tax Impound Account

Depending on the month escrow closes, the chart in Figure 12.3 shows the amount of property taxes required to be impounded at escrow closing. It also indicates the installments that are due and payable, or should have already been paid, at closing.

For example, if the first month's loan payment will be due January 1, four months of property taxes must be paid at closing. An annual property tax of $4,200 would require an initial account of $1,400, determined as follows:

$4,200 ÷ 12 = $350 amount of monthly taxes; $350 × 4 months = $1,400 to impound.

Refer to Figure 12.3 to determine the amount of tax impounds required. The chart also shows the status of installments due and payable at the time of closing. Refer to the tax computation chart to determine the responsible party, buyer or seller, for installments due.

FIGURE 12.3
Tax Computation Chart

Closing Month	1st Payment	Months' Impound	Installment Due	Closing Month	1st Payment	Months' Impound	Installment Due
Nov.	Jan.	5	1st	May	July	5	1st and 2nd
Dec.	Feb.	6	1st	June	Aug.	6	1st and 2nd
Jan.	Mar.	7	1st	July	Sep.	7	1st and 2nd
Feb.	April	2	1st and 2nd	Aug.	Oct.	8	1st and 2nd
Mar.	May	3	1st and 2nd	Sep.	Nov.	9	1st and 2nd
Apr.	June	4	1st and 2nd	Oct.	Dec.	4	1st

The newer escrow professional may become confused as to the difference between the taxes actually due and payable (Installment Due) and the amount required to be placed into the borrower's tax impound account to be held by the mortgage lender (Months' Impound).

The former refers to taxes now due and payable or should have already been paid. The latter refers to taxes due in the future.

Additionally 1/12 of annual property taxes are paid each month with the loan payment in addition to the amounts paid into the impound account at escrow closing. The taxes actually due would be those based on Figure 12.3, "Tax Computations." Those taxes due will be charged to the appropriate party, buyer or seller, as indicated in the chart and paid to the county tax collector at closing. The impound taxes due will be sent to the borrower's lender at closing to be used when taxes become due and payable at the next installment due date.

Documentary Transfer Tax

A "point of sale" tax or fee is a government's means of raising additional revenues by taxing the sale of a certain product or service. The **documentary transfer tax** (see Figure 12.4) is such a tax. It is an ad valorem tax, just as property taxes are. The documentary transfer tax was originally a federal stamp tax used to raise revenue for the federal government. The stamps were first required in December 1914 and were used with brief interruptions until December 31, 1967, when the federal law was repealed. The cost for stamps ranged from $0.50 for each $5,000 of value or $10.00 on a $100,000 transaction in 1914 to $1.10 per $1,000 of transaction value or $110.00 on a $100,000 transaction at the time of repeal. The U.S. document stamps were designed and printed by the government, appearing quite similar to postage stamps. At the close of escrow, the county recorder sold the stamps on behalf of the federal government and then physically attached them to the transfer documents, usually a grant deed.

The federal stamp act was eventually repealed, but the California Legislature implemented the procedure and process, authorizing counties and municipalities to continue as collection agents and sharing in the revenues.

FIGURE 12.4
Documentary Transfer Tax Disclosure

DOCUMENTARY TRANSFER TAX DISCLOSURE

Statement of tax due and request that said amount not be made part of permanent record in the office of the county recorder.

TO: _____   County Recorder

The amount of remittance below is in full payment of the Documentary Transfer Tax for the document attached and described below. When tax payment is verified and after the permanent record is made, attach this request to the document pursuant to Section 11932 R & T Code.

GRANTOR:

GRANTEE:

AMOUNT OF REMITTANCE: $_____

( ) Computed on full value of property conveyed, or

( ) Computed on full value less liens and encumbrances remaining thereon at time of sale.

Documentary Transfer Tax Basic Calculation

The tax is now collected at the time of recording, but stamps are no longer used. The documentary transfer tax is based on a simple formula of $0.55 per $500. To calculate the transfer tax, simply divide the sales price by $500 and multiply the result by $0.55 as shown below.

■ **EXAMPLE:** Sales price of $400,000 ÷ $500 = 800 × $0.55 = $440 tax stamps

■ It is easy to calculate the purchase price of a property if one knows the amount of transfer taxes collected. Using the sample numbers, divide the transfer tax paid ($440) by $ 0.55, then multiply that result (800) by $500; the result is the sales price ($400,000). The calculation becomes more complicated in certain transactions as described later in this section.

Special Considerations and Alternate Calculations
There are three situations where calculating the transfer tax as described does not work.

■ A *loan being assumed.* The transfer tax is based on taxing "new money" being paid to purchase the property, typically the entire value or price of the property. Sometimes, however, the tax is calculated on less than the full value of the transaction. Such is the case if a buyer is assuming a seller's existing mortgage loan. The tax then is calculated on the purchase price less the existing liens being assumed. For example, a house had a $100,000 sales price, and the buyer paid $10,000 down and assumed an existing loan of $90,000. If the buyer were obtaining an entirely new loan (new money), it would count toward the full value and the transfer tax would be $110.00. [$100,000 sales price (all new money) × $1.10 tax]. However, in the case of the example, the transfer tax would be only $1.10 ($0.55 × 2) times $10,000, or $11.00. It is almost impossible for the person searching public records to determine how much was paid for a property by looking only at the transfer tax paid if an existing loan was assumed. The researcher would need to know the amount of the assumed loan(s) to know the full purchase price.

■ **EXAMPLE:**

$100,000 − $90,000 existing loan (old money) = $10,000 new money
$10,000 new money (cash paid) × $1.10 = $11.00

■ *Multiple parcels being transferred through a single document.* In the second case, the tax will be paid on a single document that transfers several parcels of property. One would need to know the allocation of the purchase price among those parcels to determine the price of any one parcel.

■ *Confidential tax stamps.* Finally, a buyer may file a Declaration of Transfer Tax, which keeps the amount of tax paid confidential. In this case, unless someone has other access to the purchase transaction details, the only way to discover one opinion of the full market value of the property is to wait until the assessed value for property tax purposes appears on the next assessment roll.

Prorating Taxes

Property taxes are paid in arrears. California property taxes are paid in two installments, as described in "Tax Computations" above, with the first half due November 1 and the second half due February 1 (the following calendar year). To determine the amount of tax liability of a seller during their ownership term and the amount of taxes a buyer will assume for the remaining term of the tax year (July 1 through June 30 of the following year), the first step is to determine how many days the seller has owned the property during the tax year through the estimated closing date. Dividing the total annual property tax bill by 365 yields the daily, or **per diem**, tax rate. Next multiply the daily tax rate times the number of days for which the seller has owned the property (round down to three decimal points). The result will be the amount of tax responsibility of the seller and the buyer. The per diem calculation is performed as shown in the example below:

■ **EXAMPLE** Assuming escrow will close October 23, the seller has owned the property for 114 days during the current tax year. Because taxes are paid in arrears, neither the first half nor the second half have been paid. The tax liability of the seller remains unpaid at closing. The buyer receives a credit for the seller's tax liability at closing and then is responsible for paying the entire amount due for the tax period on November 1. The annual property tax is $1,960.

$$\$1,960.00 \div 365 = \$5.369$$
$$\tfrac{1}{2} \text{ tax year} = \$980$$
$$114 \times \$5.369 = \$612.06 \text{ amount of tax seller owes}$$

Escrow credits $612.06 to buyer at closing.

Prorating Homeowners Association (HOA) Dues

Just as with property taxes, the escrow holder may be required to prorate the **HOA dues** if the property has such an association, such as a condominium or planned unit development. The dues are those typically paid by the property owner on a monthly basis for the maintenance of the property's common area.

Determining Credit or Debit for Buyer and Seller Proration of any amount due by the buyer for which the seller has already prepaid (providing for a credit to the seller at closing) would be treated in the same manner as that discussed for property taxes.

■ **EXAMPLE**   Assuming a homeowners' association dues of $300 per month with 10 days remaining in the month after the close of escrow, and assuming the seller paid the dues and there are no dues in arrears, the proration would be as follows:

$$\$300 \div 30 \text{ (days)} = \$10 \text{ per diem HOA dues}$$
$$\$10 \times 10 \text{ days} = \$100 \text{ HOA dues to be paid by buyer (credited to seller)}$$

Prorating Rents

An escrow for an investment property requires that rents paid during the closing month be prorated between the buyer and the seller. The rent information obtained from the seller is critical for accurately determining the amount credited or debited to the appropriate party. Making the process more difficult and time consuming is the fact that often a tenant will have either paid a prior month's delinquent amount during the closing month or will have prepaid rent for a future month during the closing month. Rental proration usually is based on a 30-day month, whether the month actually has 31, 30, or 28 days. Rents differ from loan interest in that they are paid and collected in advance.

■ **EXAMPLE**   Assume a single-family rental house, with a tenant who will remain.

The monthly rent is $2,500, which the tenant has paid for the current month. There will be 10 days remaining in the month following the close of escrow.

$$\$2500 \div 30 \text{ (days)} = \$83.33 \text{ daily rent}$$
$$\$83.33 \times 10 \text{ days} = \$833.33 \text{ rent paid to the buyer and debited to seller.}$$

■ SETTLEMENT STATEMENT (HUD-1)

The Department of Housing and Urban Development (HUD) has prepared the following information to guide the escrow holder in completing the **Settlement Statement (HUD-1)** (see Figure 12.5). The HUD-1 was revised in 2009 to allow the parties to more easily understand the closing statement and to make it compatible with the good-faith estimate of settlement charges (GFE) (see Figure 14.1).

FIGURE 12.5
Settlement Statement (HUD-1)

 A. **Settlement Statement (HUD-1)**

B. Type of Loan

1. ☐ FHA 2. ☐ RHS 3. ☐ Conv. Unins.	6. File Number:	7. Loan Number:	8. Mortgage Insurance Case Number:
4. ☐ VA 5. ☐ Conv. Ins.			

C. Note: This form is furnished to give you a statement of actual settlement costs. Amounts paid to and by the settlement agent are shown. Items marked "(p.o.c.)" were paid outside the closing; they are shown here for informational purposes and are not included in the totals.

D. Name & Address of Borrower:	E. Name & Address of Seller:	F. Name & Address of Lender:

G. Property Location:	H. Settlement Agent:	I. Settlement Date:
	Place of Settlement:	

J. Summary of Borrower's Transaction

100. Gross Amount Due from Borrower	
101. Contract sales price	
102. Personal property	
103. Settlement charges to borrower (line 1400)	
104.	
105.	
Adjustment for items paid by seller in advance	
106. City/town taxes to	
107. County taxes to	
108. Assessments to	
109.	
110.	
111.	
112.	
120. Gross Amount Due from Borrower	
200. Amount Paid by or in Behalf of Borrower	
201. Deposit or earnest money	
202. Principal amount of new loan(s)	
203. Existing loan(s) taken subject to	
204.	
205.	
206.	
207.	
208.	
209.	
Adjustments for items unpaid by seller	
210. City/town taxes to	
211. County taxes to	
212. Assessments to	
213.	
214.	
215.	
216.	
217.	
218.	
219.	
220. Total Paid by/for Borrower	
300. Cash at Settlement from/to Borrower	
301. Gross amount due from borrower (line 120)	
302. Less amounts paid by/for borrower (line 220)	( )
303. Cash ☐ From ☐ To Borrower	

K. Summary of Seller's Transaction

400. Gross Amount Due to Seller	
401. Contract sales price	
402. Personal property	
403.	
404.	
405.	
Adjustment for items paid by seller in advance	
406. City/town taxes to	
407. County taxes to	
408. Assessments to	
409.	
410.	
411.	
412.	
420. Gross Amount Due to Seller	
500. Reductions In Amount Due to seller	
501. Excess deposit (see instructions)	
502. Settlement charges to seller (line 1400)	
503. Existing loan(s) taken subject to	
504. Payoff of first mortgage loan	
505. Payoff of second mortgage loan	
506.	
507.	
508.	
509.	
Adjustments for items unpaid by seller	
510. City/town taxes to	
511. County taxes to	
512. Assessments to	
513.	
514.	
515.	
516.	
517.	
518.	
519.	
520. Total Reduction Amount Due Seller	
600. Cash at Settlement to/from Seller	
601. Gross amount due to seller (line 420)	
602. Less reductions in amounts due seller (line 520)	( )
603. Cash ☐ To ☐ From Seller	

FIGURE 12.5
**Settlement Statement
(HUD-1) (continued)**

L. Settlement Charges			Paid From Borrower's Funds at Settlement	Paid From Seller's Funds at Settlement
700. Total Real Estate Broker Fees				
Division of commission (line 700) as follows :				
701. $	to			
702. $	to			
703. Commission paid at settlement				
704.				
800. Items Payable in Connection with Loan				
801. Our origination charge		$	(from GFE #1)	
802. Your credit or charge (points) for the specific interest rate chosen		$	(from GFE #2)	
803. Your adjusted origination charges			(from GFE #A)	
804. Appraisal fee to			(from GFE #3)	
805. Credit report to			(from GFE #3)	
806. Tax service to			(from GFE #3)	
807. Flood certification to			(from GFE #3)	
808.				
809.				
810.				
811.				
900. Items Required by Lender to be Paid in Advance				
901. Daily interest charges from to @ $ /day			(from GFE #10)	
902. Mortgage insurance premium for months to			(from GFE #3)	
903. Homeowner's insurance for years to			(from GFE #11)	
904.				
1000. Reserves Deposited with Lender				
1001. Initial deposit for your escrow account			(from GFE #9)	
1002. Homeowner's insurance months @ $ per month $				
1003. Mortgage insurance months @ $ per month $				
1004. Property Taxes months @ $ per month $				
1005. months @ $ per month $				
1006. months @ $ per month $				
1007. Aggregate Adjustment -$				
1100. Title Charges				
1101. Title services and lender's title insurance			(from GFE #4)	
1102. Settlement or closing fee		$		
1103. Owner's title insurance			(from GFE #5)	
1104. Lender's title insurance		$		
1105. Lender's title policy limit $				
1106. Owner's title policy limit $				
1107. Agent's portion of the total title insurance premium to		$		
1108. Underwriter's portion of the total title insurance premium to		$		
1109.				
1110.				
1111.				
1200. Government Recording and Transfer Charges				
1201. Government recording charges			(from GFE #7)	
1202. Deed $ Mortgage $ Release $				
1203. Transfer taxes			(from GFE #8)	
1204. City/County tax/stamps Deed $ Mortgage $				
1205. State tax/stamps Deed $ Mortgage $				
1206.				
1300. Additional Settlement Charges				
1301. Required services that you can shop for			(from GFE #6)	
1302.		$		
1303.		$		
1304.				
1305.				
1400. Total Settlement Charges (enter on lines 103, Section J and 502, Section K)				

FIGURE 12.5

Settlement Statement (HUD-1) (continued)

Comparison of Good Faith Estimate (GFE) and HUD-1 Charrges		Good Faith Estimate	HUD-1
Charges That Cannot Increase	**HUD-1 Line Number**		
Our origination charge	# 801		
Your credit or charge (points) for the specific interest rate chosen	# 802		
Your adjusted origination charges	# 803		
Transfer taxes	# 1203		

Charges That In Total Cannot Increase More Than 10%		Good Faith Estimate	HUD-1
Government recording charges	# 1201		
	#		
	#		
	#		
	#		
	#		
	#		
	#		
Total			
Increase between GFE and HUD-1 Charges		$ or %	

Charges That Can Change		Good Faith Estimate	HUD-1
Initial deposit for your escrow account	# 1001		
Daily interest charges $ /day	# 901		
Homeowner's insurance	# 903		
	#		
	#		
	#		

Loan Terms

Your initial loan amount is	$
Your loan term is	years
Your initial interest rate is	%
Your initial monthly amount owed for principal, interest, and any mortgage insurance is	$ includes ☐ Principal ☐ Interest ☐ Mortgage Insurance
Can your interest rate rise?	☐ No ☐ Yes, it can rise to a maximum of %. The first change will be on and can change again every after . Every change date, your interest rate can increase or decrease by %. Over the life of the loan, your interest rate is guaranteed to never be **lower** than % or **higher** than %.
Even if you make payments on time, can your loan balance rise?	☐ No ☐ Yes, it can rise to a maximum of $
Even if you make payments on time, can your monthly amount owed for principal, interest, and mortgage insurance rise?	☐ No ☐ Yes, the first increase can be on and the monthly amount owed can rise to $. The maximum it can ever rise to is $
Does your loan have a prepayment penalty?	☐ No ☐ Yes, your maximum prepayment penalty is $
Does your loan have a balloon payment?	☐ No ☐ Yes, you have a balloon payment of $ due in years on
Total monthly amount owed including escrow account payments	☐ You do not have a monthly escrow payment for items, such as property taxes and homeowner's insurance. You must pay these items directly yourself. ☐ You have an additional monthly escrow payment of $ that results in a total initial monthly amount owed of $. This includes principal, interest, any mortgage insurance and any items checked below: ☐ Property taxes ☐ Homeowner's insurance ☐ Flood insurance ☐ ☐

Note: If you have any questions about the Settlement Charges and Loan Terms listed on this form, please contact your lender.

Appendix A to Part 3500—Instructions for Completing HUD-1

The following are instructions provided by the FDIC for completing the HUD-1 settlement statement, as required under Section 4 of RESPA and 24 CFR part 3500 (Regulation X) of the HUD regulations. This form is to be used as a statement of actual charges and adjustments paid by the borrower and the seller, to be given to the parties in connection with the settlement. The instructions for completion of the HUD-1 are primarily for the benefit of the settlement agents who prepare the statements and need not be transmitted to the parties as an integral part of the HUD-1. There is no objection to the use of the HUD-1 in transactions in which its use is not legally required. Refer to the definitions section of HUD's regulations (24 CFR 3500.2) for specific definitions of many of the terms used in these instructions.

General Instructions for completing the HUD-1:

Information and amounts may be filled in by typewriter, hand printing, computer printing, or any other method producing clear and legible results. Refer to HUD's regulations (Regulation X) regarding rules applicable to reproduction of the HUD-1 for the purpose of including customary recitals and information used locally in settlements; for example, a breakdown of payoff figures, a breakdown of the Borrower's total monthly mortgage payments, check disbursements, a statement indicating receipt of funds, applicable special stipulations between Borrower and Seller, and the date funds are transferred.

The settlement agent shall complete the HUD-1 to itemize all charges imposed upon the Borrower and the Seller by the loan originator and all sales commissions, whether to be paid at settlement or outside of settlement, and any other charges which either the Borrower or the Seller will pay at settlement. Charges for loan origination and title services should not be itemized except as provided in these instructions. For each separately identified settlement service in connection with the transaction, the name of the person ultimately receiving the payment must be shown together with the total amount paid to such person. Items paid to and retained by a loan originator are disclosed as required in the instructions for lines in the 800-series of the HUD-1 (and for per diem interest, in the 900-series of the HUD-1).

As a general rule, charges that are paid for by the seller must be shown in the seller's column on page 2 of the HUD-1 (unless paid outside closing), and charges that are paid for by the borrower must be shown in the borrower's column (unless paid outside closing). However, in order to promote comparability between the charges on the GFE and the charges on the HUD-1, if a seller pays for a charge that was included on the GFE, the charge should be listed in the borrower's column on page 2 of the HUD-1. That charge should also be offset by listing a credit in that amount to the borrower on lines 204-209 on page 1 of the HUD-1, and by a charge to the seller in lines 506-509 on page 1 of the HUD-1. If a loan originator (other than for no-cost loans), real estate agent, other settlement service provider, or other person pays for a charge that was included on the GFE, the charge should be listed in the borrower's column on page 2 of the HUD-1, with an offsetting credit reported on page 1 of the HUD-1, identifying the party paying the charge.

Charges paid outside of settlement by the borrower, seller, loan originator, real estate agent, or any other person, must be included on the HUD-1 but marked "P.O.C." for "Paid Outside of Closing" (settlement) and must not be included in computing totals.

However, indirect payments from a lender to a mortgage broker may not be disclosed as P.O.C., and must be included as a credit on Line 802. P.O.C. items must not be placed in the Borrower or Seller columns, but rather on the appropriate line outside the columns.

The settlement agent must indicate whether P.O.C. items are paid for by the Borrower, Seller, or some other party by marking the items paid for by whoever made the payment as "P.O.C." with the party making the payment identified in parentheses, such as "P.O.C. (borrower)" or "P.O.C. (seller)."

In the case of "no cost" loans where "no cost" encompasses third party fees as well as the upfront payment to the loan originator, the third party services covered by the "no cost" provisions must be itemized and listed in the borrower's column on the HUD-1/1A with the charge for the third party service. These itemized charges must be offset with a negative adjusted origination charge on Line 803 and recorded in the columns.

Blank lines are provided in section L for any additional settlement charges. Blank lines are also provided for additional insertions in sections J and K. The names of the recipients of the settlement charges in section L and the names of the recipients of adjustments described in section J or K should be included on the blank lines.

Lines and columns in section J which relate to the Borrower's transaction may be left blank on the copy of the HUD-1 which will be furnished to the Seller. Lines and columns in section K which relate to the Seller's transaction may be left blank on the copy of the HUD-1 which will be furnished to the Borrower.

Line Item Instructions

Section A: This section requires no entry of information.

Section B: Check appropriate loan type and complete the remaining items as applicable.

Section C: This section provides a notice regarding settlement costs and requires no additional entry of information.

Section D and E: Fill in the names and current mailing addresses and zip codes of the Borrower and the Seller. Where there is more than one Borrower or Seller, the name and address of each one is required. Use a supplementary page if needed to list multiple Borrowers or Sellers.

Section F: Fill in the name, current mailing address and zip code of the Lender.

Section G: The street address of the property being sold should be listed. If there is no street address, a brief legal description or other location of the property should be inserted. In all cases give the zip code of the property.

Section H: Fill in name, address, zip code and telephone number of settlement agent, and address and zip code of "place of settlement."

Section I: Fill in date of settlement.

Section J: Summary of Borrower's Transaction.

Line 101 is for the contract sales price of the property being sold, excluding the price of any items of tangible personal property if Borrower and Seller have agreed to a separate price for such items.

Line 102 is for the sales price of any items of tangible personal property excluded from Line 101. Personal property could include such items as carpets, drapes, stoves, refrigerators, etc. What constitutes personal property varies from state to state. Manufactured homes are not considered personal property for this purpose.

Line 103 is used to record the total charges to Borrower contained in Section L and totaled on Line 1400.

Line 104 and 105 are for additional amounts owed by the Borrower, such as charges that were not listed on the GFE or items paid by the seller prior to settlement but reimbursed by the Borrower at settlement. For example, the balance in the Seller's reserve account held in connection with an existing loan, if assigned to the Borrower in a loan assumption case, will be entered here. These lines will also be used when a tenant in the property being sold has not yet paid the rent, which the Borrowers will collect, for a period of time prior to the settlement. The lines will also be used to indicate the treatment for any tenant security deposit. The Seller will be credited on Lines 404-405.

Lines 106 through 112 are for items which the Seller had paid in advance, and for which the Borrower must therefore reimburse the Seller. Examples of items for which adjustments will be made may include taxes and assessments paid in advance for an entire year or other period, when settlement occurs prior to the expiration of the year or other period for which they were paid. Additional examples include flood and hazard insurance premiums, if the Borrower is being substituted as an insured under the same policy; mortgage insurance in loan assumption case; planned unit development or condominium association assessments paid in advance; fuel or other supplies on hand, purchased by the Seller, which the Borrower will use when Borrower takes possession of the property; and ground rent paid in advance.

Line 120 is for the total of Lines 101 through 112.

Line 201 is for any amount paid against the sales price prior to settlement.

Line 202 is for the amount of new loan made by the Lender when a loan to finance construction of a new structure constructed for sale is used as or converted to a loan to finance purchase. Line 202 should also be used for the amount of the first user loan, when a loan to purchase a manufactured home for resale is converted to a loan to finance purchase by the first user. For other loans covered by 24 CFR part 3500 (Regulation Z) which finance construction of a new structure or purchase of a manufactured home, list the sale price of the land on Line 104, the construction cost or purchase price of manufactured home on Line 105 (Line 101 would be left blank in this instance) and amount of the loan on Line 202. The remainder of the form should be completed taking into account adjustments and charges related to the temporary financing and permanent financing and which are known at the date of settlement.

Line 203 is used for cases in which the Borrower is assuming or taking title subject to an existing loan or lien on the property.

Lines 204-209 are used for other items paid by or on behalf of the Borrower. Lines 204-209 should be used to indicate any financing arrangements or other new loan not listed in Line 202. For example, if the Borrower is using a second mortgage or note to finance part of the purchase price, whether from the same lender, another lender or the Seller, insert the principal amount of the loan with a brief explanation on Lines 204-209. Lines 204-209 should also be used where the Borrower receives a credit from the Seller for closing costs, including seller-paid GFE charges. They may also be used in cases in which a Seller (typically a builder) is making an "allowance" to the Borrower for items that the Borrower is to purchase separately.

Lines 210 through 219 are for items which have not yet been paid, and which the Borrower is expected to pay, but which are attributable in part to a period of time prior to the settlement. In jurisdictions in which taxes are paid in the tax year, most cases will show the proration of taxes in these lines. Other examples include utilities used but not paid for by the Seller, rent collected in advance by the Seller from a tenant for a period extending beyond the settlement date, and interest on loan assumptions.

Line 220 is for the total of Lines 201-219.

Lines 301 and 302 are summary lines for the Borrower. Enter total in Line 120 on Line 301. Enter total in Line 220 on Line 302.

Lines 303 must indicate either the case required from the Borrower at settlement (the usual case in a purchase transaction), or cash payable to the Borrower at settlement (if, for example, the Borrower's earnest money exceeds the Borrower's case obligations in the transaction or there is a cash-out refinance). Subtract Line 302 from Line 301 and enter the amount of cash due to or from the Borrower at settlement on Line 303. The appropriate box should be checked. If the Borrower's earnest money is applied toward the charge for settlement service, the amount so applied should not be included on Line 303 but instead should be shown on the appropriate line for the settlement services, marked "P.O.C. (Borrower)", and must not be included in computing totals.

Section K: Summary of Seller's Transaction.

Instructions for the use of Lines 101 and 102 and 104-112 above, apply also to Lines 401-412. Line 420 is for the total of Lines 401 through 412.

Line 501 is used if the Seller's real estate broker or other party who is not the settlement agent has received and holds a deposit against the sale price (earnest money) which exceeds the fee or commission owed to that party. If that party will render the excess deposit directly to the Seller, rather than through the settlement agent, the amount of excess deposit should be entered on Line 501 and the amount of the total deposit (including commissions) should be entered on Line 201.

Line 502 is used to record the total charges to the Seller detailed in section L and totaled on Line 1400.

Line 503 is used if the Borrower is assuming or taking title subject to existing liens which are to be deducted from sales price.

Lines 504-505 are used for the amounts (including any accrued interest) of any first and/or second loans which will be paid as part of the settlement.

Line 506 is used for deposits paid by the Borrower to the Seller or other party who is not the settlement agent. Enter the amount of the deposit in Line 201 on Line 506 unless Line 501 is used or the party who is not the settlement agent transfers all or part of the deposit to the settlement agent, in which case the settlement agent will note in parentheses on Line 507 the amount of the deposit that is being disbursed as proceeds and enter in the column for line 506 the amount retained by the above-described party for settlement services. If the settlement agent holds the deposit, insert a note in Line 507 which indicates that the deposit is being disbursed as proceeds.

Lines 506 through 509 may be used to list additional liens which must be paid off through the settlement to clear title to the property. Other Seller obligations should be shown on Lines 506-509, including charges that were disclosed on the GFE but that are actually being paid for by the Seller. These Lines may also be used to indicate funds to be held by the settlement agent for the payment of either repairs, or water, fuel, or other utility bills that cannot be prorated between parties at settlement because the amounts used by the Seller prior to settlement are not yet know. Subsequent disclosure of the actual amount of these post-settlement items to be paid from settlement funds is optional. Any amounts entered on Lines 204-209 including Seller financing arrangements should also be entered on Lines 506-509.

Instructions for the use of Lines 510 through 519 are the same as those for Lines 210 to 219 above.

Line 520 is for the total of Lines 501 through 519.

Lines 601 and 602 are summary lines for the Seller. Enter the total in Line 420 on Line 610. Enter the total in Line 520 on Line 602.

Line 603 must indicate either the cash required to be paid to the Seller at settlement (the usual cash in a purchase transaction), or the cash payable by the Seller at settlement. Subtract Line 602 from Line 601 and enter the amount of cash due to or from the Seller at settlement on Line 603. The appropriate box should be checked.

Section L: Settlement Charges

Line 700 is used to enter the sales commission charged by the sales agent or real estate broker.

Lines 701-702 are to be used to state the split of the commission where the settlement agent disburses portions of the commission to two or more sales agents or real estate brokers.

Line 703 is used to enter the amount of sales commission disbursed at settlement. If the sales agent or real estate broker is retaining a part of the deposit against the sale price (earnest money) to apply towards the sales agent's or real estate broker's commission, include in Line 703 only that part of the commission being disbursed at settlement and insert a note on Line 704 indicating the amount the sales agent or real estate broker is retaining as a "P.O.C." item.

Line 704 may be used for additional charges made by the sales agent or real estate broker, or for a sales commission charged to the Borrower, which will be disbursed by the settlement agent.

Line 801 is used to record "Our origination charge," which includes all charges received by the loan originator, except any charge for the specific interest rate chosen (points). This number must not be listed in either the buyer's or seller's column. The amount shown in Line 801 must include any amounts received for origination services, including administrative and processing services, performed by or on behalf of the loan originator.

Line 802 is used to record "Your credit or charge (points) for the specific interest rate chosen, " which states the charge or credit adjustment as applied to "Our origination charge", if applicable. This number must not be listed in either column or shown on page one of the HUD-1.

For a mortgage broker originating a loan in its own name, the amount shown on Line 802 will be the difference between the initial loan amount and the total payment to the mortgage broker from the lender. The total payment to the mortgage broker will be the sum of the price paid for the loan by the lender and any other payments to the mortgage broker from the lender, including any payments based on the loan amount or loan terms, and any flat rate payments. For a mortgage broker originating a loan in another entity's name, the amount shown on Line 802 will be the sum of all payments to the mortgage broker from the lender, including any payments based on the loan amount or loan terms, and any flat rate payments.

In either case, when the amount paid to the mortgage broker exceeds the initial loan amount, there is a credit to the borrower and it is entered as a negative amount. When the initial loan amount exceeds the amount paid to the mortgage broker, there is a charge to the borrower and it is entered as a positive amount. For a lender, the amount shown on Line 802 may include any credit or charge (points) to the Borrower.

Line 803 is used to record "Your adjusted origination charges," which states the net amount of the loan origination charges, the sum of the amounts shown in Lines 801 and 802. This amount must be listed in the columns as either a positive number (for example, where the origination charge shown in Line 801 exceeds any credit for the interest rate shown in Line 802 or where there is an origination charge in Line 801 and a charge for the interest rate (points) is shown on Line 802) or as a negative number (for example, where the credit for the interest rate shown in Line 802 exceeds the origination charges shown in Line 801).

In the case of "no cost" loans, where "no cost" refers only to the loan originator's fees, the amounts shown in Lines 801 and 802 should offset, so that the charge shown on Line 803 is zero. Where "no cost" includes third party settlement services, the credit shown in Line 802 will more than offset the amount shown in Line 801. The amount shown in Line 803 will be a negative number to offset the settlement charges paid indirectly through the loan originator.

Lines 804-808 may be used to record each of the "Required services that we select." Each settlement service provider must be identified by name and the amount paid recorded either inside the columns or as paid to the provider outside closing ("P.O.C."), as described in the General Instructions.

Line 804 is used to record the appraisal fee.

Line 805 is used to record the fee for all credit reports.

Line 806 is used to record the fee for any tax service.

Line 807 is used to record any flood certification fee.

Line 808 and additional sequentially numbered lines, as needed, are used to record other third party services required by the loan originator. These Lines may also be used to record other required disclosures from the loan originator. Any such disclosures must be listed outside the columns.

Line 901-904 This series is used to record the items which the Lender requires to be paid at the time of settlement, but which are not necessarily paid to the lender (e.g., FHA mortgage insurance premium), other than reserves collected by the Lender and recorded in the 1000-series.

Line 901 is used if interest is collected at settlement for a part of a month or other period between settlement and the date from which interest will be collected with the first regular monthly payment. Enter that amount here and include the per diem charges. If such interest is not collected until the first regular monthly payment, no entry should be made on Line 901.

Line 902 is used for mortgage insurance premiums due and payable at settlement, including any monthly amounts due at settlement and any upfront mortgage insurance premium, but not including any reserves collected by the Lender and recorded in the 1000-series. If a lump sum mortgage insurance premium paid at settlement is included on Line 902, a note should indicate that the premium is for the life of the loan.

Line 903 is used for homeowner's insurance premiums that the Lender requires to be paid at the time of settlement, except reserves collected by the Lender and recorded in the 1000-series.

Lines 904 and additional sequentially numbered lines are used to list additional items required by the Lender (except for reserves collected by the Lender and recorded in the 1000-series), including premiums for flood or other insurance. These lines are also used to list amounts paid at settlement for insurance not required by the Lender.

Lines 1000–1007. This series is used for amounts collected by the Lender from the Borrower and held in an account for the future payment of the obligations listed as they fall due. Include the time period (number of months) and the monthly assessment. In many jurisdictions this is referred to as an "escrow", "impound", or "trust" account. In addition to the property taxes and insurance listed, some Lenders may require reserves for flood insurance, condominium owners' association assessments, etc. The amount in line 1001 must be listed in the columns, and the itemizations in lines 1002 through 1007 must be listed outside the columns.

After itemizing individual deposits in the 1000 series, the servicer shall make an adjustment based on aggregate accounting. This adjustment equals the difference between the deposit required under aggregate accounting and the sum of the itemized deposits. The computation steps for aggregate account are set out in 24 CFR §3500.17(d). The adjustment will always be a negative number or zero (0), except for amounts due to rounding. The settlement agent shall enter the aggregate adjustment amount outside the columns on a final line of the 1000 series of the HUD-1 or HUD-1A statement.

Lines 1100–1108. This series covers title charges and charges by attorneys and closing or settlement agents. The title charges include a variety of services performed by title companies or others, and include fees directly related to the transfer of title (title examination, title search, and document preparation), fees for title insurance, and fees for conducting the closing. The legal charges include fees for attorneys representing the lender, seller, or borrower, and any attorney preparing title work. The series also includes any settlement, notary, and delivery fees related to the services covered in this series. Disbursements to third parties must be broken out in the appropriate lines or in blank lines in the series, and amounts paid to these third parties must be shown outside of the columns if included in Line 1101. Charges not included in Line 1101 must be listed in the columns.

Line 1101 is used to record the total for the category of "Title services and lender's title insurance." This amount must be listed in the columns.

Line 1102 is used to record the settlement or closing fee.

Line 1103 is used to record the charges for the owner's title insurance and related endorsements. This amount must be listed in the columns.

Line 1104 is used to record the lender's title insurance premium and related endorsements.

Line 1105 is used to record the amount of the lender's title policy limit. This amount is recorded outside of the columns. (Back)

Line 1106 is used to record the amount of the owner's title policy limit. This amount recorded outside of the columns. (Back)

Line 1107 is used to record the amount of the total title insurance premium, including endorsements, that is retained by the title agent. This amount is recorded outside of the columns. (Back)

Line 1108 is used to record the amount of the total title insurance premium, including endorsements, that is retained by the title underwriter. This amount is recorded outside of the columns.

Additional sequentially numbered lines in the 1100-series may be used to itemize title charges paid to other third parties, as identified by name and type of service provided.

Lines 1200–1206. This series covers government recording and transfer charges. Charges paid by the borrower must be listed in the columns as described for lines 1201 and 1203 with itemizations shown outside the columns. Any amounts that are charged to the seller and that were not included on the Good Faith Estimate must be listed in the columns.

Line 1201 is used to record the total "Government recording charges" and the amount must be listed in the columns.

Line 1202 is used to record, outside of the columns, the itemized recording charges.

Line 1203 is used to record the transfer taxes, and the amount must be listed in the columns.

Line 1204 is used to record, outside of the columns, the amounts for local transfer taxes and stamps.

Line 1205 is used to record, outside of the columns, the amounts for State transfer taxes and stamps.

Line 1206 and additional sequentially numbered lines may be used to record specific itemized third party charges for government recording and transfer services, but the amounts must be listed outside the columns.

Line 1301 and additional sequentially numbered lines must be used to record required services that the borrower can shop for, such as fees for survey, pest inspection, or other similar inspections. These lines may also be used to record additional itemized settlement charges that are not included in a specific category, such as fees for structural and environmental inspections; pre-sale inspections of heating, plumbing or electrical equipment; or insurance or warranty coverage. The amounts must be listed in either the borrower's or seller's column.

Line 1400 must state the total settlement charges as calculated by adding the amounts with each column.

Comparison of Good Faith Estimate (GFE) and HUD-1/1-A Charges

The comparison chart must be prepared using the exact information and amounts from the GFE and the actual settlement charges shown on the HUD1/1A Settlement statement. The comparison chart is comprised of three sections: "Charges that Cannot Increase", "Charges That Cannot Increase More Than 10%", and "Charges That Can Change."

"Charges That Cannot Increase" The amounts shown in Blocks 1 and 2, in the Line A, and in Block 8 on the borrower's GFE must be entered in the appropriate line in the Good Faith Estimate column. The amounts shown on Lines 801, 802, 803 and 1203 of the HUD-1/1A must be entered in the corresponding line in the HUD-1/1A column. The HUD-1/1A column must include any amounts shown on page 2 of the HUD-1 in the column as paid for by the borrower, plus any amounts that are shown as P.O.C. by or on behalf of the borrower. If there is a credit in Block 2 of the GFE or Line 802 of the HUD-1/1A, the credit should be entered as a negative number.

"Charges That Cannot Increase More Than 10%" A description of each charge included in Blocks 3 and 7 on the borrower's GFE must be entered on separate lines in this section, with the amount shown on the borrower's GFE for each charge entered in the corresponding line in the Good Faith Estimate column. For each charge included in Block 4, 5 and 6 on the borrower's GFE for which the loan originator selected the provider or for which the borrower selected a provider identified by the loan originator, a description must be entered on a separate line in this section, with the amount shown on the borrower's GFE for each change entered in the corresponding line in the Good Faith Estimate column. The loan originator must identify any third party settlement services for which the borrower selected a provider other than one identified by the loan originator so that the settlement agent can include those charges in the appropriate category. Additional lines may be added if necessary. The amounts shown on the HUD-1/1A for each line must be entered in the HUD-1/1A column next to the corresponding charge from the GFE, along with the appropriate HUD-1/1A line number. The HUD-1/1A column must include any amounts shown on page 2 of the HUD-1 in the column as paid for by the borrower, plus any amounts that are shown as P.O.C. by or on behalf of the borrower.

The amounts shown in the Good Faith Estimate and HUD-1/1A columns for this section must be separately totaled and entered in the designated line. If the total for the HUD-1/1A is greater than the total for the Good Faith Estimate column, then the amount of the increase must be entered both as a dollar amount and as a percentage increase in the appropriate line.

"Charges That Can Change" The amounts shown in Blocks 9, 10 and 11 on the borrower's GFE must be entered in the appropriate line in the Good Faith Estimate column. Any third party settlement services for which the borrower selected a provider other than one identified by the loan originator must also be included in this section. The amounts shown on the HUD-1/1A for each charge in this section must be entered in the corresponding line in the HUD-1/1A column, along with the appropriate HUD-1/1A line number. The HUD-1/1A column must include any amounts shown on page 2 of the HUD-1 in the column as paid for by the borrower, plus any amounts that are shown as P.O.C. by or on behalf of the borrower. Additional lines may be added if necessary.

Loan Terms

This section must be completed in accordance with the information and instructions provided by the lender. The lender must provide this information in a format that permits the settlement agent to simply enter the necessary information in the appropriate spaces, without the settlement agent having to refer to the loan documents themselves.

Source: 6500 – Consumer Protection, FDIC Law, Regulations, Related Acts, www.fdic.gov/regulations/laws/rules/6500-2525.html

■ CHAPTER 12 QUIZ

1. The closing statement usually includes columns headed "Seller," "Borrower," "Buyer," and "Lender" and in standard bookkeeping practice also includes

   a. credits and debits.

   b. debits and rebates.

   c. debts and rebates.

   d. rebates and credits.

2. The buyer's consideration is shown on the closing statement as a

   a. credit.

   b. debit.

   c. debt.

   d. none of these.

3. Items prepaid by the buyer or to be advanced to the buyer would be shown as a credit on the buyer's statement and may include

   a. buyer's deposit toward the purchase price.

   b. buyer's new loan.

   c. balance of buyer's remaining funds to be placed into escrow.

   d. all of these.

4. Debits would reflect the buyer's

   a. new loan.

   b. appraisal.

   c. escrow and title fees.

   d. both b and c.

5. If a buyer's loan payment will include a monthly reserve for hazard insurance, the escrow closing statement shows prepaid and impound insurance covering

   a. 12 months.

   b. 13 months.

   c. 14 months.

   d. 16 months.

6. Property taxes in California become a lien on the property

   a. at 12:00 pm on January 1.

   b. at 12:00 pm on March 1.

   c. at 12:00 pm on June 30.

   d. at 12:00 pm on July 1.

7. The second half of property taxes becomes due on

   a. April 10.

   b. February 1.

   c. February 10.

   d. June 30.

8. Documentary transfer taxes are based on

   a. $1.55 per $1,000 of the purchase price.

   b. $1.10 per $500 of the purchase price.

   c. $0.55 per $500 of the cash paid and new loans obtained by the buyer.

   d. 1.25% of the sales price.

9. To find the sales price if the transfer tax is known, divide the transfer tax

   a. by $0.55, then multiply the result by $500.

   b. by $1.10, then multiply the result by $1,000.

   c. by $1.10, then multiply the result by $500.

   d. both a and b.

10.   Rental prorations are usually based on

  a.   a 30-day month, regardless of the actual number of days in the month.

  b.   only the actual number of days in the month.

  c.   365 days a year.

  d.   both a and c.

CHAPTER THIRTEEN

13

LENDING AND THE ESCROW PROCESS

■ KEY TERMS

CalHFA loan program
CalVet loan program
conventional loans
Fannie Mae
Federal Housing
   Administration
   (FHA)

Freddie Mac
Housing and Urban
   Development (HUD)
loan correspondent
mortgage bankers
mortgage brokers
mortgage insurance

portfolio loans
salable loans
secondary mortgage
   market
Veterans Affairs

■ LEARNING OBJECTIVES

Upon completing this chapter, you will be able to

■ understand the function of the secondary mortgage market;

■ understand the role of Fannie Mae and Freddie Mac in the mortgage marketplace;

■ understand the difference between portfolio and salable loans;

■ understand the role of and the difference between mortgage bankers, loan correspondents, and mortgage brokers;

- understand the function of mortgage insurance; and

- understand the role of HUD, as well as the basic governmental loan programs, including Cal HFA, CalVet, FHA, and VA and how they differ from conventional loan programs.

■ A HISTORY OF LENDING

Introduction to Lending

Escrow is the process of accepting, holding, accounting for, and delivering documents and funds, including those for the buyer's loan. Escrow officers are involved in a variety of loan transactions, including buyer financing and homeowner refinancing. An introduction to the various loan programs offered by lenders, including typical terms, guidelines, qualifying procedures, and limitations or restrictions may assist the escrow officer in understanding the lender's role and requirements during the escrow process. The escrow holder must know the basic government guidelines and regulations that apply to lending and borrowers' rights. Learning how lenders operate in the marketplace is also helpful, especially given the escrow officer's daily communications with real estate agents, loan officers, processors, and the principals. Knowing simply that lenders may retain a loan after it is originated for the borrower or may sell it to some other entity soon after escrow closes can be valuable information for the escrow officer. And, of course, the escrow holder must have an understanding of the fees, interest costs, and other matters of the loan that will require closing calculations.

Evolution of Lending in America

To fully appreciate the availability of long-term, low-down-payment loan plans buyers have access to today and their positive impact on the growth and services of escrow and title providers, it's necessary to look at how loan plans have evolved over the years, from the relatively risk-free loans of the early 19th century to the so-called "risk-based" loans of the 21st century. Financing to purchase or build a home was not readily available in early America, at least not to the average working person. Liquidity was a constant problem without a national banking system to provide a uniform source of monies and the ability to inject capital into the banking system, regardless of the state where the bank was located.

Politics and Opposition to a National Bank

Alexander Hamilton, our first secretary of the treasury, proposed a central banking system to first pay off the federal debt incurred during the Revolutionary War and also to offer a uniform and stable currency. Thomas Jefferson, the secretary of state, believed such a system was unconstitutional. He proposed that banking be the business of each state. Jefferson also believed that a central bank would favor industrialism and the wealthy, abandoning the nation's farms and working class.

Bank Act of 1791   With President George Washington's support, Hamilton succeeded in establishing a banking system with the first Bank Act of 1791 and the creation of the Bank of the United States. Short-lived, its charter expired in 1811 and Jefferson was able to prevent it from continuing until the Second Bank of the United States was established in 1816. It too lost to national banking foes, including President Andrew Johnson, and its charter expired in 1832.

A Nation of State Banking   After the Second Bank of the United States ceased to exist, banking was left to the business of state governments, each issuing its own currency supposedly backed by adequate reserves of gold and silver to pay the bearer of the bank notes on demand.

National Currency Act of 1863 and the Bank Act of 1864   Finally, with the passage of the National Currency Act of 1863 and the National Bank Act in 1864, signed into law by president Abraham Lincoln, a new national banking system was born under the supervision of a comptroller of the currency. Under this new system, national banks would buy U.S. government securities and place them on deposit with the Comptroller of the Currency in exchange for government issued national bank notes. Although the Bank Act brought more stability to the nation's banking system, especially in requiring each bank to maintain certain capital reserves, there was no actual central federal banking structure to adequately regulate the money supply in response to economic conditions. The nation was at the mercy of the aggregate total of each individual bank's capitalization. The act also prohibited banks from making loans secured by real estate, considered too risky a practice. The financial panics of 1893 and 1907 underscored the problem causing severe financial losses in all markets with no central federal bank available to pour money into the system.

The Federal Reserve Act of 1913

With the passage of the Federal Reserve Act in 1913, the banking system was provided with the central control it required and a regulatory body that could monitor and govern the nation's money supply as necessary. The act did away with the national bank system with its individual notes and established a central bank that would issue Federal Reserve bank notes. It provided a more stable source of liquidity for the financial markets and the ability to inject capital into the banking system, if needed, including lending. The Federal Reserve Act also granted banks the authority to lend on real estate; this was limited, however, to only farmland, and then up to only 50% loan to value and with a five-year term.

In spite of the significant improvements resulting from the Federal Reserve Act, and the extension of real estate lending in 1927 to homes (but again only up to 50% loan to value and with a five-year term), it would take the Great Depression to make real estate lending a major part of the business of commercial banks. It is easy to see, therefore, why today's major home lending institutions evolved from other sources.

18th and 19th Century Financial Institutions

It was not until well after the turn of the 19th century that commercial banks began to offer long-term lending for any purpose. Prior to that, most loans were short term, payable in 30 to 60 days, and usually were provided to merchants to pay costs of manufacturing or to purchase goods until they could sell them to their customers. Real estate lending was usually the business of insurance companies.

Terminating Building Societies   The real evolution of today's real estate lending began around the early- to mid-19th century. Borrowing the concept from the English who had been financing homes through Terminating Building Societies (TBS) since 1775 (and, in fact, continued to do so until 1980), Americans began forming village-based lending associations composed of a town's citizens, who would pool their money for the purpose of financing the purchase or construction of homes. Today we would consider the TBS to be a "portfolio" lender because no secondary mortgage market existed in which a lender could sell its loans to replenish funds for lending. Most contributors were working class people who generally would not have access to the banking system or insurance lenders to finance a home. The terminating society would be created and begin accepting members who would make small periodic, usually weekly, savings deposits into it, continuing until the desired amount of funds had been raised, usually 10 to 15 years. No interest was paid to depositors. The order in which each member had the opportunity to obtain a home loan from the society was determined by ballot or lottery. The winner would receive an interest-free loan from the association for about 50 to 60% of the home's purchase price. Repayment was made to the society and distributed to the membership usually in semi-annual installments. After the last member received his home loan, the society was terminated. Any remaining funds in the society's loan pool would be distributed among the members according to their deposit contributions.

Permanent Building Societies   Terminating Building Societies evolved into "permanent building societies," which remained open to new members after those wishing to obtain home loans had done so. Many depositors joining the permanent societies had no intention of buying or building a home, increasing the chances for others to obtain financing, and leading to the development of permanent savings institutions. Interest was paid to all depositors and charged on all home loans.

Building and Loan Associations   Permanent building societies led to the birth of building and loan associations, the forerunners of today's savings and loan industry. The first record of a savings institution in the United States was the Oxford Provident Building Association in Frankfort, Pennsylvania, established in 1831. The building and loans were community rather than neighborhood-based, but they still, for the most part, relied on depositors' savings accounts to make real estate loans. As with the permanent building societies, interest was earned on savings and financing was not interest free. However, earning the highest return on capital invested was not the most important principle of the building and loan but rather operating in the best interest of all members of the association. Its policy would be continued some years later with the creation of the savings and loan industry and its original public policy by which it was governed. Loan terms of both the building societies and building and loans were usually from 5 to 10 years, with semi-annual non-amortizing (interest only) payments and only adjustable rates. Later loan plans offered 10-year amortizing payments with the entire balance due in three to five years. All programs required 50% down payment. Liquidity issues would plague the building and loan industry. Because there was no such thing as a secondary mortgage market place in which a bank or a building and loan could sell its mortgage paper, they relied on depositors' savings accounts and investors' contributions to make real estate loans. Once deposits were depleted, they were out of the lending business.

Early Mortgage-Backed Securities   The securitization of mortgages (the practice of issuing bonds backed by the value and security of a group of loans, with the bonds paying interest to those who buy them) is generally considered a product of the 20th century. However, they were used briefly beginning around 1880. Western U.S. mortgage brokers would originate farm loans, package them into pools of about $100,000 each, and issue debentures (bonds) secured by the loans. They would then sell the bonds to investors and insurance companies in the East. This early experiment of a "secondary mortgage market" would be short-lived. There was considerable risk to the broker, who would remain liable to the investor in the event of default because of being required to repurchase loans if the borrowers couldn't bring them current. Default was a constant possibility with inconsistent underwriting practices of the time. Securitization lasted only about a decade. Beginning in 1890, several years of severe weather took their toll on farm income, resulting in numerous losses and foreclosures. Then the financial Panic of 1893 caused the entire market to collapse.

Easy Credit and Good Times   One could likely say the root cause of the recent so-called subprime explosion the country witnessed in the mid-1990s and the subsequent implosion in 2007 was easy credit, just as it was during the good times following World War I. The stock market had become to the average mom and pop investor what real estate has become today. Everyone wanted for themselves what the major investors and the wealthy were enjoying: a leveraged ride on a runaway stock market, with the end to attractive values and profits nowhere in sight. It was the Roaring Twenties and Americans—businesses and consumers alike—became hooked on easy credit, with a "dollar down and a dollar a week" allowing them to buy homes, automobiles, home furnishings, and stocks. Thousands of homeowners went to non-banking sources (the subprime lending community of the time) and pledged the family home in order to finance their purchase of stocks.

The Great Depression and a Changing Mortgage Industry

The Great Depression gave birth to innovative change in the lending industry, establishing for the first time universal lending standards and creating a real estate lending system that would allow banks to no longer rely solely on depositors' savings to stay in business. It also would shield the originating bank from losses due to default by borrowers. This evolutionary, perhaps more appropriately "revolutionary," process in lending is the result of forward and creative thinking by bright individuals who rose to the challenge and strayed far outside the box. They are responsible for the loan products offered today by both **Federal Housing Administration (FHA)** and conventional originators, which in spite of several troubled financial times made homeownership available to millions of Americans who would have otherwise remained disenfranchised. By the spring of 1933, when president Franklin D. Roosevelt was sworn into office, unemployment had risen from 1929's high of 8 million to over 15 million—nearly one-third of the work force. His predecessor, Herbert Hoover, believed local governments and charities should provide relief to the homeless and unemployed, not the federal government. By 1932, only one-quarter of unemployed families had received any kind of help. Hoover, however, can be credited with some measure of progress. In 1931, he had convened the President's Conference on Home Building and Home Ownership, attended by over 3,700 members of the building industry. By the end of the conference, they had recommended a number of recovery programs, which were finally implemented during Roosevelt's term.

Hoover's administration and the 1932 Congress also established the Federal Home Loan Bank (FHLB), which would become a critical part of the success of the National Housing Act introduced by FDR. Initially, however, the FHLB was a failure. With a job of providing funds to savings and loans for home loans, of the 41,000 loan applications submitted in its first two years, only three were approved. The FHLB created the savings and loan industry and provided a source of liquidity. As the legislation establishing it was driven by a public policy goal of encouraging home ownership, it set the stage for the introduction of FDR's National Housing Act. As foreclosures continued to rise at an alarming pace, Congress offered help to homeowners in distress. By 1933, half of all home loans in the United States were in default, with over 1,000 foreclosed upon each day. In 1933, the Home Owners' Loan Act was passed, creating the Home Owners' Loan Corporation

(HOLC). The HOLC was a government agency whose sole purpose was to provide financing assistance to borrowers in default and foreclosure. It would operate for three years, originating loans from 1933 to 1936, continuing thereafter only to service the loans they originated and collect payments.

It should be noted that over 80% of loans originated were paid back in full and in a timely manner. The HOLC would buy loans in default from the originating bank, paying for them with government bonds with a guaranteed yield of 4% to the bank. The HOLC would then provide new financing for the homeowner in default with a 15-year loan with a 5% fixed rate, fully amortized with no balloon payment, novel for the time.

The Federal Housing Administration (FHA)   Established by the National Housing Act in 1934, the FHA introduced the long-term mortgage, which continues today. The Federal Housing Administration goals were, first, to promote jobs in the housing construction trades and related industries, such as building products and suppliers and transportation of materials. Second, it was to provide affordable housing through government-insured loans, with long-term financing for both rehabilitation and purchases of owner-occupied homes.

And, finally, the National Housing Act established national mortgage associations, private corporations that would buy these new FHA loans from originating lenders to replenish their funds so they may continue lending. No longer would they be subject to relying on depositors' savings to stay in the real estate lending business. The National Housing Act had four major objectives:

- Provide insurance against loss on property improvements

- Establish mutual mortgage insurance, providing a guarantee of return on investment to investors purchasing newly originated FHA loans

- Establish national mortgage associations to buy the new FHA loans

- Establish insurance for savings accounts with the creation of the Federal Savings and Loan Insurance Corporation (FSLIC)

Creation of a Secondary Mortgage Market Place   By 1937, no commercial bank or investor had stepped up to become a national mortgage association. One of the primary requirements for eligibility was to retain $5 million in reserve to operate. Because the United States had just entered a recession, right in the middle of trying to recover from a depression, it is little wonder there were no takers. The Federal Home Loan Bank Board (FHLBB) provided temporary liquidity to the FHA loan program by purchasing loans from originating lenders. In 1938, FHA created its own national mortgage association to do the job. The Federal National Mortgage Association, Fannie Mae, (more fully explained later) was established to provide a **secondary mortgage market** by purchasing, as a government agency, FHA loans originated by banks and the new savings and loans created as a result of Hoover's Federal Home Loan Bank Act.

Federal Housing Administration Loan Program (FHA) The original FHA loan program allowed a minimum down payment of 20% of the sales price and a fully amortized term of 20 years with low monthly payments, based on the prediction that the new government programs would promote stable and long-term employment lasting about 20 years. When it came time to retire, the home mortgage would have been paid off. In 1938, FHA extended the loan term to 25 years and reduced the maximum down payment to 10%. In 1948, the loan term was extended to 30 years and reduced the minimum down payment to 5% with further modifications made in 1957 and 1958.

Housing and Urban Development (HUD) FHA operated under several "owners." In 1939, the Federal Loan Agency assumed control of FHA, along with the Fannie Mae, the Federal Home Loan Bank Board, and the HOLC. Three years later, FHA and the Federal Home Loan Bank became part of the new National Housing Agency (NHA). The following year, NHA was replaced by the Housing and Home Finance Agency (HHFA). In 1965, HHFA became part of the newly created cabinet-level department of **Housing and Urban Development (HUD)**. The stated mission of HUD today is "to promote adequate and affordable housing, economic opportunity, and a suitable living environment free from discrimination." HUD's role and responsibilities extend beyond the FHA program. The escrow officer will work with HUD regulated forms, regulations and procedures on a daily basis.

Conventional Non-FHA Lending Subject to the federal and state regulators' "safety and soundness" laws, which were waived for lenders originating FHA loans, banks originating non-FHA loans were restricted by federal and state laws to originating home homes having loan-to-value ratios no greater than 50%, with terms either fully amortized over five years or amortized over a longer term but still due in five years. It was not until 1955 that laws were changed to increase non-FHA loan terms up to 66.7% loan-to-value (LTV) ratios and allowed up to a 20-year term. In 1959, the loan-to-value ratio was increased to 75% but were still not competitive with FHA's 97% of 1960. Only in 1968, with the establishment of Fannie Mae as a private mortgage association and its new role of providing a secondary mortgage market for **conventional loans** (non-FHA and non-VA) did the loan-to-value ratio increase and down payment requirements drop. With a new lending industry standard program and qualifying guidelines established by Fannie Mae, and later Freddie Mac, the largest investors in the secondary mortgage market (see "The Secondary Mortgage Market Today"), conventional loan origination began to escalate, capable of competing in the marketplace with loan programs having maximum loan amounts and other terms not available through FHA loan plans.

■ THE SECONDARY MORTGAGE MARKET TODAY

Those who buy loans in the secondary mortgage marketplace are called investors. The largest and best known investor is **Fannie Mae**, the Federal National Mortgage Association (FNMA), which was originally established as a government agency in 1938 to buy FHA, and later VA, loans. Next to Fannie Mae in size is **Freddie Mac**, the Federal Home Loan Mortgage Corporation (FHLMC), established in 1970 as a government agency to initially buy "seasoned" loans (a *seasoned loan* is defined as an "aged" loan, with at least one year lapsed since its origination).

Fannie Mae

In 1968, the process to privatize Fannie Mae as a government-sponsored enterprise (GSE) and with a new role of establishing a secondary mortgage marketplace for loans began. The privatization was accomplished by dividing Fannie Mae into two parts. One part retained the name Fannie Mae and became a private shareholder-owned corporation. The other part was renamed the Government National Mortgage Agency (GNMA, or Ginnie Mae) and remained a government agency. By 1970, privatization was completed and Fannie Mae was authorized to purchase conventional loans. The secondary market for FHA loans was given to the Government National Mortgage Agency and placed under the regulation of the HUD.

Freddie Mac

Another government sponsored investor, Freddie Mac, the Federal Home Loan Mortgage Corporation, (FHLMC), was created in 1970 as a non-profit government agency under the supervision of the Federal Home Loan Bank as part of the government's economic recovery program following the recession of 1969. Its initial role was to provide a secondary mortgage market for Savings and Loans that were in dire need of capital. To that end it began buying seasoned loans held by these S&Ls, an industry that had been struggling for years with many institutions failing. S&Ls were restricted until 1981 to originating only fixed-rate home loans. They were also prohibited from making either adjustable-rate loans—which help avoid "interest rate risk" to the lender (interest rate risk is the possible liability to the lender of originating and holding a fixed-rate investment in an inflationary market)—or loans for commercial projects, which offered higher profits to the S&L. S&L depositors had been withdrawing their savings for several years to deposit in the higher-yielding money market accounts offered by nonregulated investment banks. As a result, lending funds were evaporating.

The S&Ls were unable to sell their portfolios of fixed-rate loans for two reasons. First, there was no institutional secondary mortgage market for conventional fixed-rate residential loans (only FHA and VA loans had such, through Fannie Mae). Second, the rates of these loans were too low at the time to attract many buyers. Congress stepped in with Freddie Mac to offer aid. Freddie Mac assistance helped somewhat, but by the time legislation was signed into law in 1989 to resolve the S&L crisis once and for all, 747 S&Ls had closed their doors and over 300 others were forced into "technical mergers" with healthy partners. Freddie Mac was then privatized that same year as a GSE, joining Fannie Mae as a primary investor in the secondary mortgage market with the authority to buy newly originated conventional loans.

Fannie Mae and Freddie Mac's Role in the Mortgage Market

Both Fannie Mae and Freddie Mac were subject to government regulation and supervision by the Office of Federal Housing Enterprise Oversight (OFHEO). On July 30, 2008, the OFHEO, along with the Federal Housing Finance Board and the mission office of the GSEs within HUD, were merged into a new regulatory agency under the Housing and Economic Recovery Act of 2008. This new agency, the Federal Housing Finance Agency (FHFA) is now responsible for supervising and regulating the activities of not only Fannie Mae and Freddie Mac but also the 12 Federal Home Loan Banks. On September 8, 2008, Fannie Mae and Freddie Mac were seized by the U.S. government as a result of an audit revealing major accounting discrepancies.

Placed Under U.S. Government Conservatorship   Following their seizure by the government, Fannie Mae and Freddie Mac were placed, and remain today, under U.S. government conservatorship. The federal government acquired a 79.9% ownership position in each; however, they continue to provide the same services as before, under greater governmental control and scrutiny. Fannie Mae and Freddie Mac, along with the FHA loan programs, provide an essential source of residential loan funds to originating lenders, especially for providing affordable housing through affordable lending.

Fannie Mae and Freddie Mac's Role in Today's Marketplace   Fannie Mae and Freddie Mac buy and hold loans for their own portfolio, plus they pool others and sell them as mortgage-backed securities. Because FNMA and FHLMC are the two largest U.S. suppliers of mortgage capital through their loan purchases, their lending guidelines are often accepted as the industry standard by most other investors who also buy loans in the secondary mortgage market. By supplying a constant flow of funds to the financial housing market, FNMA and FHLMC play a crucial role in the nation's housing finance system. Presently, Fannie Mae and Freddie Mac are able to purchase first mortgages on single-family residential properties, two-unit properties, three-unit properties, and four-unit properties. Maximum loan amounts depend on the number of units and are re-established at the beginning of each calendar year, based on national median home prices. There are limitations on the loans that Fannie Mae and Freddie Mac purchase. These include maximum LTVs and loan amounts. Presently the maximum LTV on an owner-occupied one-unit home is 97%; two-unit is 90%; and three- or four-unit is 80% for traditional plans.

General Underwriting Guidelines

For single-family detached housing, townhomes, and condos (generally with an owner occupancy ratio of 60–70%), Fannie Mae and Freddie Mac look for 28% (front ratio) for housing and 36% (back ratio) for total debt. Properties purchased for investment or rental properties generally require a 10 to 25% down payment.

Loan approval is usually provided through an automated underwriting system and program. Fannie Mae's Desktop Underwriting and Freddie Mac's Loan Prospector are the automated underwriting software developed by the agencies. These special software programs allow for almost instant loan approval and do not necessarily restrict the borrower to maximum debt ratios. Nearly every mortgage banker and broker today uses these programs, which have significantly changed the way conforming loan programs have been underwritten. Similar automated underwriting software now also exists for jumbo loans.

Private Mortgage Insurance (PMI)

Private mortgage insurance (PMI) is required for all loans sold to FNMA/FHLMC with loan-to-value ratios in excess of 80%. Combined LTVs above 80% do not require PMI as long as the first mortgage is at or below 80% LTV. The **mortgage insurance** must cover the amount of the loan above 75%. Mortgage insurance compensates the lender for all or part of any losses that incur in the event of the borrower's default and foreclosure. Without mortgage insurance, most lenders would not assume the risk of a borrower defaulting on a loan because the property it secured was so highly leveraged. They would require a greater down payment for a couple of reasons. First, the more of the buyer's hard-earned money that's invested, the less likely it is for the buyer to walk away from it. Second, if the lender needs to foreclose, the less likely it is for the lender to suffer a loss because there is some real equity in the home. However, the latter assumes that the real estate market hasn't devalued and the property doesn't require substantial repair. Thus, the borrower pays a monthly mortgage insurance premium for the lender's protection.

■ LOAN PROGRAMS AND LENDER'S REQUIREMENTS

Today's contemporary loan programs that involve escrow and that evolved from the FHA original program created in 1934 include both government programs—such as the FHA, VA, and Cal-Vet—and nongovernment programs such as conventional loans originated by lenders and sold to Fannie Mae and Freddie Mac in the secondary mortgage market. A variety of loan programs exist for residential properties.

Portfolio Loans

Depending on the originating lender or bank, loans may be retained by the lender. These are called **portfolio loans**; the lender receives monthly payments from the borrower and retains all the interest. A lender holding a loan in its portfolio, while not selling the loan itself, may sell the rights to *service it*, the term used to describe the activity of collecting the borrower's monthly payments.

Salable Loans

Instead of retaining a loan in its portfolio, the lender may instead sell the actual loan to investors such as Fannie Mae and Freddie Mac in the secondary mortgage marketplace. These loans are called **salable loans**.

Loan Servicing

A lender who sells some or all of its loans might retain the servicing rights and responsibility for collection of the monthly payments, retaining a portion of the interest for compensation and submitting the balance to the investor who has purchased the loan. The lender may instead sell both the loan and the servicing rights. In fact, once a loan is sold, it is the servicing rights that may be resold more than once. A borrower who says, "My home loan has been sold again," usually doesn't realize it's the servicing rights rather than the loan that has been sold.

An escrow officer who is asked by a buyer signing loan documents if the loan will be sold should refer the question to the buyer's loan officer. Many (though not all) loan officers are present during the signing for reasons such as this. When arranging for signing documents, the escrow officer is advised to ask whether the loan officer plans to be present.

Institutional Lenders

Institutional lenders are the common lenders with whom the escrow officer will work. These include commercial banks, S&Ls, credit unions, and mortgage bankers. The escrow officer will work frequently with loan brokers (mortgage brokers), as well as those who act as the intermediary with the foregoing institutional lenders in originating a loan for their buyers. Private lenders, including individuals and investment groups, are considered noninstitutional.

Mortgage Bankers and Loan Correspondents   A **mortgage banker** is an entity that takes the borrower's loan application, performs the processing and underwriting, issues the loan approval, and funds the loan. After funding, the banker will assign (sell) the loan to another entity, such as a commercial bank, mortgage company, or more substantial mortgage banker. Mortgage bankers act as **loan correspondents** on behalf of these other lenders, approved by them to perform the described services as their authorized representative.

Mortgage or Loan Brokerage   The mortgage or loan broker is a third-party agent, licensed by either the California Department of Real Estate, or less commonly, the California Department of Corporations. **Mortgage brokers** originate loans through the institutional sources listed previously, providing access to a variety of lenders for the borrower in an efficient and time-saving process. The escrow officer will be required to know those obligations and disclosures, especially at closing, required of the mortgage broker that differ from or do not apply to other lenders.

Yield Spread Premiums (YSP)   Until recently, borrowers who were signing loan documents commonly asked about the payment of a rebate to a mortgage broker, called a yield spread premium (YSP), from the lender. If applicable, the YSP amount is shown only in the "description" portion of the closing statement and not in the financial columns showing debits and credits. For example, a YSP in the amount of $4,500 being paid to a mortgage broker by the lender will be indicated on the settlement statements as "YSP of $4,500 to American Financial Corporation POC," meaning a yield spread premium in the amount of $4,500 is being paid outside closing (POC) to American Financial Corporation; therefore, the escrow holder will not receive nor will be required to account for those monies. The question and any controversy arise when the borrowers have no previous knowledge of the rebate or when the rebate is larger than previously disclosed. Either situation may violate truth-in-lending regulations. YSP disclosures and explanations are seldom a concern because new government regulations prohibit the payment of such fees to mortgage brokers in originating most loans secured by one-to-four-unit residential properties.

New YSP and POC Regulations   Effective January 1, 2010, new laws essentially prohibit the payment of yield spread premiums (YSPs) for loans subject to the Real Estate Settlement and Procedures Act (RESPA). These regulations apply to loans originated for the purchase or refinancing of one-to-four-unit residential properties. Under the new rules, a loan originator (mortgage broker) may only lender pays the compensation, it will not be indicated as a POC on the closing statement as other such fees are shown (i.e., such as an appraisal paid in advance of escrow closing) but rather as a credit to the borrower (shown as a negative amount on line 802 of the HUD-1).

Exemptions to the Regulations It is important to remember that loans for properties other than one-to-four-unit residential properties are not subject to RESPA.

Private Lenders (Noninstitutional)

Private-party lending is relatively common in certain transactions, especially for commercial, business brokerage, and apartment sales. Private-party financing typically carries higher interest rates and higher costs and fees. A private lender may actually be quasi-institutional in that it may be a corporation rather than an individual but offers similar loan plans. Loan plans offered include those directed to credit issues or certain special transactions.

Credit Issues Less creditworthy borrowers are the frequent customers of some lenders who may offer a loan plan, subject to government regulation, with considerably relaxed underwriting standards that meet the need of buyers with credit problems. Federal laws and regulations implemented through a number of new laws enacted between 2009 and 2013, however, placed more restrictions on these loans. While these restrictions may prevent some prospective buyers from obtaining financing, they also prevent a predatory lender from taking advantage of them.

Special Transactions Buyers and sellers in unusual transactions may require additional contingencies or disclosures. Such transactions might involve properties that, because of certain characteristics or conditions, do not qualify for conventional institutional or governmental loan plans, or they may involve mixed-use buildings consisting of both commercial and residential uses.

General Loan Plans and Guidelines

A representation of the most common and affordable loan programs offered to homebuyers and with which the escrow officer should become familiar are listed here.

Pro-Tip: Misled by Borrower

The escrow officer who knows or learns that the borrowers are intentionally misleading the lender regarding any requirement or provisions of the loan program should consult management or legal counsel before guiding the borrower in signing loan documents.

FHA 203(b), the Primary Mortgage Program   The FHA's Better Housing Program is known to us today as the FHA 203(b). It is probably the most popular of all loan programs in the United States. The program's general guidelines and provisions (which change from time to time) are as follows:

- The property must be owner occupied and the primary residence only.

- The property may consist of one to four units, including condominiums.

- Rental income of two-to-four-unit properties may be included in the borrower's income for qualifying. The current rents being charged, or rents validated by the appraiser, will be reduced by 25% as a reserve for vacancies and expenses. No rent credit will be given for the unit occupied by the borrower.

- The maximum LTV for a purchase loan or for a refinance in which the borrower does not receive cash-out (called a rate-and-term refinance) may not exceed 96.5% of the property's appraised value or sales price, whichever is less.

- The maximum LTV for a cash-out refinance may not exceed 85% of the appraised value if the borrower has less than a 12-month mortgage payment history with no late payments.

- Borrowers' documenting a 12-month or greater history of mortgage payments with no late payments may be eligible for a cash-out refinance loan of up to 95% of the appraised value.

- The borrower is required to make a minimum 3½% cash down payment.

- The maximum loan amounts, modified by the Housing and Economic Recovery Act of 2008, are set by FHA for each county (metropolitan statistical area or MSA) independently throughout the United States. Loan amounts are established during the fourth quarter of each year to become effective January 1 of the following year.

- Current FHA limits allow a maximum loan based on 115% of the average housing cost of each MSA, up to a maximum of 150% of the base conforming loan limit, which presently equals $625,500. In areas where 115% of the average housing cost is equal to or less than the base conforming loan amount, the maximum loan is 65% of the base conforming loan amount, or $271,050 (65% of $417,000). Remember, these loan amounts may change annually.

■ The borrower's maximum debt-to-income ratio (DTI) is 31% of the borrowers' gross monthly income for the housing payment, defined as principal, interest, taxes, insurance, mortgage insurance, and homeowners association dues, if any.

■ FHA does not require reserves for principal, interest, taxes, insurance (PITI), except for three-to-four-unit properties, where three months' reserves are required.

■ Impounds for the payment of renewing property taxes and homeowners insurance is required regardless of the loan to value. The escrow officer should review loan documents for any errors regarding impounds that could prevent timely funding. If, for example, the lender audits the documents after signing and discovers an error in the impounds, they must be corrected. Funding can be delayed, placing a closing in jeopardy.

■ Borrower eligibility, including coborrowers and cosigners:

— U.S. citizenship is not required.

— Non-U.S. citizens must be legal aliens, have a Social Security card, and be able to work legally in the United States.

— Nonpermanent resident aliens must occupy the property as their primary residence.

■ Military personnel are considered owner-occupants even if they reside elsewhere, providing the immediate family occupies the property.

■ Coborrowers are defined as follows:

— Their income is used to qualify for the mortgage.

— They will take title to the property.

— They will obligate themselves on the mortgage.

— Non-occupant co-borrowers must be family members.

■ A cosigner is defined as follows:

— Their income is used to qualify for the mortgage.

— They will obligate themselves on the mortgage.

— They will not take title to the property.

— Their income may not be used as the primary source of income.

— Their credit may not be used as the primary source of credit.

■ FHA MORTGAGE INSURANCE

When first introduced in 1934, the FHA loan program offered mortgage lenders three fundamental elements that made it a hit. One was the terms of the loan itself: long term, fully amortized, and low down payments. Another was the ability for the lender to sell the loan to another entity (eventually Fannie Mae was established to do that job in 1938) and to have the loan funds immediately replenished to make more loans. Third, because of the lingering effects of the Great Depression and the resultant losses to lenders from defaulting mortgagors, the FHA mortgage insurance program promised to reimburse lenders for such losses in the future. Prior to FHA's creation, no such insurance was available to protect mortgage lenders from mortgage default losses. Mortgage insurance is required on all FHA loans. Called the mortgage insurance premium (MIP), it consists of both an up-front premium paid at closing and an annual renewal premium included in and paid with the monthly loan payments. These amounts are set by Congress and may change from time to time.

Up-Front MIP   The up-front premium may be paid by borrower's funds or paid through a credit to the borrower by the seller. The up-front MIP may also be added to the borrower's loan, providing the sum total of the loan, including the MIP, does not exceed the maximum allowable loan for the property's MSA. The current up-front amounts are

■ 1.75% for purchase loan transactions and full documentation refinance, or

■ 0.01% for streamline refinance subject to specific conditions.

■ **EXAMPLE**

> $352,000 FHA loan amount
> × 1.75% MIP
> $ 6,160 MIP amount, paid as follows:

■ In cash by borrower and included in borrower's closing costs

■ Credited to borrower by seller to be paid in cash at closing in borrower's closing costs

■ Added to loan amount and reflected in borrower's loan documents

Annual Renewal MIP The current annual MIP is paid monthly and, as such, will be ¹⁄₁₂ of the annual amount. The current annual MIP, which became effective June 3, 2013, but is always subject to change, is shown in Figure 13.1.

FIGURE 13.1
Annual MIP Amounts

Loan terms greater than 15 years	Loan terms 15 years or less
Loans $625,500 and less and LTV 95% or less: 1.30%	Any loan amount with LTV 78% or less: 0.45%
Loans $625,500 and less and LTV greater than 95%: 1.35%	Loans $625,500 and less and LTV 78.01% to 90%: 0.45%
Loans over $625,000 and LTV 95% or less: 1.50%	Loans $625,500 and less and LTV greater than 90%: 0.70%
Loans over $625,500 and LTV greater than 95%: 1.55%	Loans over $625,500 and LTV 78.01% to 90%: 0.70%
	Loans over $625,500 and LTV greater than 90%: 0.95%

Pro-Tip: Escrow Holder Should Not Try to Explain MIP to Borrower

The MIP process and its calculations are somewhat complex. A borrower will often have a number of questions regarding MIP, such as, Will the monthly payment change during the term of the loan, and can it be removed? These and other questions may only be answered by the lender or loan officer and therefore should be referred to them.

Costs Borrower Cannot Pay at Closing FHA has established costs which the borrower is not allowed to pay, which is limited to only the tax service.

Seller's Assistance Toward Borrower's Costs In no case may the buyer receive from the seller any cash or credit that exceeds the actual costs. Allowable seller contributions may not exceed 6% of the sales price and may include the following:

- Discount points
- Prepaid taxes, insurance, escrows, and interest
- Interest rate buy-downs
- Closing costs (including the up-front MIP)

CalHFA Home Loan Program

The California Housing Finance Agency (**CalHFA**) provides low down payment fixed-rate financing at below-market interest rates. CalHFA receives annual allocations of tax-exempt mortgage revenue bond authority (MRBs). CalHFA loans are either conforming fixed or FHA fixed.

Eligibility CalHFA loans are available for first-time buyers who have not owned a home within past three years. Borrowers are subject to income and purchase price restrictions established by federal law, and they must be U.S. citizens. These restrictions change annually and are based on regional (county) average home prices and median household income. The first-time buyer restriction is currently waived if the buyer purchases a home in a "targeted area," which are neighborhoods specifically designated by the state.

Rates and Terms Standard CalHFA loans are available with as little as 3% down. CalHFA offers up to a 40-year fixed term.

CalHFA Loans Require Either FHA or Private Mortgage Insurance
Underwriting criteria generally follow those of either FHA or the private insurer. Interest rates vary with each bond issue, but generally are between 1% and 2% below current fixed rates. CalHFA maximum back-debt ratio is 55%.

Eligible properties CalHFA loans are available for new construction and existing homes, townhomes, and condos. Resale condos are only eligible in high-cost areas. Any property must be owner-occupied for the life of the loan.

CalHFA offers no-down and matched-down payment plans. There is no prepayment penalty on any CalHFA loan program.

Conventional Loan Plans

Conventional loans, meaning "nongovernment," are available through most originating lenders and are ideal for most homebuyers. Conventional lenders and loan plans vary in their guidelines and standards, offering a variety of options and qualifying criteria. The lenders who originate these nonstandard or nonconforming loans do not sell their loans to Fannie Mae and Freddie Mac, which have standard and consistent requirements of all loans they purchase.

Conventional Conforming Loans Standard conforming loans are called agency conforming loans, meaning that the originating lender plans to sell them to Fannie Mae or Freddie Mac. Conforming loans offer attractive rates, carry sensible and nonpredatory underwriting standards, and feature a few benefits not available through government loan plans, such as the following:

- Lower rates than FHA and VA, usually 0.25 to 0.50 less for loans up to $417,000; somewhat higher rates for jumbo conforming

- No up-front mortgage insurance as with FHA's 1.75% premium

- No mortgage insurance if the buyer pays 20% down or more

- Buyer's debt ratios not considered in approval process using automated underwriting

A universal national minimum loan amount exists for all properties located in the continental United States, presently $417,000. Unlike the FHA loan program, the minimum loan amount extends to all states and counties, regardless of the MSA average sales price. Maximum LTVs are as high as 95% of the sales price.

A high-cost maximum loan limit up to $625,500 exists for properties located in states having average sales prices that would result in a loan exceeding the base loan limit of $417,000.

Seller contributions toward the buyers' closing costs are limited to the following:

- 3% for LTV exceeding 90%

- 6% for LTV from 75 to 90%

- 9% for LTV less than 75%

VA Guaranteed Loans

The Department of **Veterans Affairs** (VA) provides guaranteed (meaning the lender originating the loan is protected against the borrower's default) loans to qualified veterans of the U.S. armed forces.

No-Down Payment Loans   The VA offers up to 100% financing and up to an amount based on four times the veteran's entitlement, presently $104,250. The VA automatically increases the veteran's eligibility to one-fourth the conforming loan amount when it is established each year. This means the maximum no-down VA loan is the same as the maximum conforming loan, currently $417,000 (as of 2013).

Loans Requiring Down Payment   Properties having sales prices exceeding the maximum no-down loan amount may be financed with the veteran paying the 25% difference between the no-down loan amount and the sales price. VA has no maximum loan limit; however, lenders generally will not originate a loan greater than $1,000,000.

■   **EXAMPLE**

$ 695,000	Sales price of home
× 75%	Down payment factor (100% – 25%)
$ 521,250	
+ 104,250	Entitlement
$ 625,500	Maximum loan

$ 695,000	Sales price
– 625,500	Loan
$ 69,500	Required down payment = 10% of total sales price making an overall 90% LTV and no PMI.

Veterans using the program for the first time pay a 2.15% funding fee (indemnity fee) when no down payment is made, 1.5% for a 5% down payment, and 1.25% for a 10% down payment. The fee may be added to the loan, providing the total does not exceed the maximum allowed.

The Reserve or National Guard funding fee is 2.4%.

A disabled veteran pays no funding fee.

Veterans with no down payment using the program a subsequent time pay a 3.3% funding fee.

For all VA loans originated on or after March 1, 1988, assumptors must undergo a full credit check and reunderwriting. VA loans prior to March 1, 1988, are fully assumable (i.e., can be assumed "subject to").

Veterans can use the VA program again only if they have repaid the original VA loan and sold the home, or if they have a partial entitlement remaining.

VA loan discount points are negotiable and may be paid by the veteran. Discount points may not be financed in VA loan amounts, except for refinancing and then not to exceed two points, with any remainder being paid in cash.

The VA imposes some restrictions on certain fees and closing that may or may not be paid by the veteran. The following fees are allowed to be paid by the veteran:

■   VA appraisal

■   Credit report

■   Loan origination fee (usually 1% of the loan)

- Discount points

- Title search and title insurance

- Recording fees

- State and/or local transfer taxes,

- Survey, if applicable

The veteran cannot pay the following fees. These fees must be paid by the lender (out of the 1% origination fee, if the lender chooses), the seller, or other third party:

- Lender's appraisals

- Lender's inspections (except in construction loan cases)

- Loan closing or settlement fees

- Document preparation fees

- Underwriting fees

- Pest inspection fees

- Well and septic inspection fees

- Preparation of title company papers or conveyance fees

- Attorney's services, other than for title work

- Photographs

- Stationary, telephone calls, postage, and other mailing charges

- Amortization schedules

- Escrow fees or charges

- Notary fees

- Commitment fees

- Trustee fees

- Loan application or processing fee

- Fees for preparation of the truth in lending statement

- Fees to loan brokers, finders, or other third parties

- Tax service

Income qualifying is a two-tiered process, using both a maximum 41% back-debt ratio and a minimum required residual income based on family size, with the debt ratio not considered if actual residual income is 20% or greater than the minimum.

Seller's Contributions   All of the buyer's closing costs, including prepaids, may be paid by the seller, plus up to 4% in sales concessions. Sales concessions may even include paying off some of the veteran buyer's debts for qualifying. In no case, however, may the actual seller's contribution exceed these amounts.

CalVet Loan Program

The California Department of Veterans Affairs, referred to as CalVet, provides real estate loans for qualified veterans. It was established by the Veterans Farm and Home Purchase Act of 1974. **CalVet loan program** funds come from a combination of tax-exempt general obligation (GO) bond issues approved by state voters, as well as tax-exempt mortgage revenue bonds. Application for a CalVet loan must be made before completing the purchase or acquisition of an interest in the property. This does not apply if the veteran has an interest of record in the building site, the dwelling has not been completed, or a certificate of occupancy has not been issued. CalVet loan applications can be acquired from a participating lender or from any of CalVet's 13 regional offices. Proof of eligibility must be submitted with the completed application, along with a $50 application fee. Although ample money is generally available for new CalVet loans, there are times when bond proceeds for new loans become scarce. When funds are scarce, CalVet has established the following priorities for funding loans:

1. Top priority is given to disabled vets (whose income must be at least 10% from a government source) or veterans who have been wounded (e.g., received a Purple Heart). These veterans are not affected by the time limit of 30 years from date of discharge for application.

2. Former POWs, unremarried spouses of veterans killed in the line of duty, and un-remarried spouses of veterans designated as missing in action (MIA) are granted second priority.

3. Veterans who served during the Vietnam period (August 5, 1964, through May 7, 1975) and Native American veterans applying for loans on reservation or trust land have third priority.

4. All other qualified California veterans have the lowest priority.

Applicants must be a California resident at time of application. (The former requirement that veteran must have been from California or residing in California at time of entrance into service has been eliminated.)

The veteran applicant must have served at least 90 days consecutively, not including training, on active duty, except if the applicant was

- discharged sooner because of a service connected disability,

- called to active duty from the Reserves or National Guard because of a presidential executive order, or

- received a U.S. campaign or expeditionary force medal.

The applicant must have been honorably discharged.

CalVet must approve any secondary financing in advance, and the total amount financed cannot exceed 90% of appraised value.

A maximum loan origination fee of 1% of the loan amount is charged on CalVet loans (which includes the nonrefundable $50 application fee).

Interest rates on CalVet loans may be adjusted from time to time during the loan term. Rates on both new and existing CalVet loans are periodically adjusted. Interest rates on CalVet loans reflect the blended average cost of all outstanding bonds sold and the administrative costs of running the program.

CalVet offers a no-down CalVet/VA loan program. The standard CalVet 97 program, which provides for a 3% down payment, allows secondary financing up to 100% combined LTV with the approval of CalVet.

A loan may be paid in full at any time. However, if a loan is prepaid in whole or in part within the first five years, a service charge must be paid, equal to 6 months' advance interest on the amount prepaid that exceeds 20% of the original loan amount.

Rather than a housing debt-to-income ratio or a total debt-to-income ratio, at least 40% of a borrower's net income must remain after subtracting the monthly mortgage payment (including principal, interest, taxes, insurance, and other long-term debt) to qualify for a CalVet mortgage.

Seller's may pay all of a buyer's closing costs, including prepaids, but cannot exceed the actual costs.

■ THE LOAN REFINANCE ESCROW

The escrow holder prepares the complete escrow instructions (not simply supplemental instructions, as with a purchase escrow). Using a special take sheet designed for refinance transactions, the escrow officer will guide the borrower or the loan officer through the opening process. The escrow holder's processing of the escrow is similar to a purchase transaction in many respects, but it obviously includes procedures not involved in the purchase transaction.

Opening Process

The basic opening steps for the escrow holder are described in the paragraphs that follow.

Borrower Information   The escrow officer will obtain the borrowers' names, Social Security numbers, vesting, and mailing addresses, if different from the subject property. A statement of identity will be delivered to the borrowers for all other necessary information for the title company's search.

Property Information   This includes the address of the property and property description (single family, condominium, duplex, commercial, apartment building, etc.).

Owner-Occupant or Investment Property   This is important in that if the property is owner-occupied, California's right of rescission law prohibits the borrowers' new loan from funding and closing for at least three business days following the date the borrowers' sign loan documents. Sundays and holidays are not included in the waiting term.

Amount of New Loan   The amount of the new loan and lender's name are included.

New Loan Interest Rate and Term   If the rate and term are known, the loan officer will provide it; otherwise it will be provided near escrow closing. If the rate has been locked (a rate lock is a guarantee by the lender to the borrower that the interest rate quoted will be valid until a specified date), and for whatever reason escrow is not in a position to close at the time the rate lock expires, the lender will be required to either obtain a rate lock extension or may possibly be required to offer the borrower a different rate. The new rate and term information must be provided to the escrow holder.

Homeowners Insurance   The escrow holder will ask the borrower to provide the name and contact information for the borrower's insurance agent.

Loans to Be Paid Off   Any existing loans to paid off and the name of the servicing lenders will be identified. The escrow holder usually has the address and contact information for most major lenders; however, it is always a good practice for the escrow officer to also obtain the information from the borrower or the loan officer.

Loans Requiring Subordination   If the borrower has an existing loan that will remain, requiring the lender to subordinate to the new loan, the escrow holder will assist in the process. Subordination processing varies among lenders; however, the existing lender usually requires a copy of the borrower's new loan application and approval or commitment letter, along with a fee. The borrower, with the assistance of the refinancing lender and the escrow holder, will submit a request for subordination to the lender. The approved subordination agreement will be delivered by the existing lender to the escrow holder for the borrower to sign at escrow closing to return with loan documents.

Preparation of Escrow Instructions

The next step in the process is the preparation of the escrow instructions, which are drawn and delivered (mailed) to the borrower; concurrently, the escrow officer orders the preliminary title report. In some cases, the title company may require the statement of information form before providing it.

Request for Demand for Pay-Off

The escrow holder will deliver a request to the existing lender for pay-off information (a demand for pay-off). Upon receipt of the demand, the escrow officer should compare the actual pay-off amount with what the borrower or loan officer originally provided. Any significant differences should be communicated to the parties for acknowledgment or for them to contact the lender to resolve any disputes.

Review Preliminary Title Report

The escrow officer will deliver the preliminary title report to the lender and the borrower. The officer should also review it to ascertain any unresolved issues, such as old liens of record that reportedly should have been reconveyed, delinquent property taxes, state or IRS tax liens, or other matters. All such matters may need to be resolved before the lender approves or funds the loan. Income tax liens may be subordinated to the new loan with the approval of the taxing authority, although property tax liens, which supersede all liens, usually must be paid. The escrow officer will also verify that the parties on the title are those obtaining the loan.

Loan Fees and Closing Statement

The escrow officer will obtain the lender's fees and costs, preparing and delivering to the lender and the borrower an estimated closing statement (Figure 13.2). The escrow officer's estimates usually are inflated or "padded" with a surplus amount to ensure that the borrower isn't required to bring in monies (or more monies) at closing if the final pay-off or other fees, costs, or prepaid items (property taxes and homeowners insurance) exceed the original estimate.

FIGURE 13.2
Estimated Refinance Closing Statement

General Escrow Services, Inc.

Date: February 8, 2011   Time: 16:04:38
Escrow No. 4196-9C   Closing Date: March 10, 2011

Estimated Closing Statement

Lender: Atlas Capital Corp.

Borrower: John T. Borrower and Jane S. Borrower

Property: 1234 Elm Street, Anytown, USA

	$ Debit	$ Credit
Financial		
New 1st trust deed to Atlas Capital		385,000.00
Title charges		
ALTA loan policy for $385,000	360.00	
Endorsement fee(s)	50.00	
Recording trust deed(s)	100.00	
Wire fee	50.00	
2nd-half taxes	1,708.77	
Escrow Charges		
Escrow fee	450.00	
Courier fee	30.00	
Wire fee	25.00	
Payoffs—Washing National Bank		
Total Payoff $229,198,77		
Principal balance	227,500.00	
Interest to 02/19/11	1,659.77	
Forwarding/Demand fee	39.00	
Payoffs—General Bank		
Total Payoff $100,475.51		
Principal balance	99,506.84	
Interest to 02/19/11	968.67	
Miscellaneous Charges		
Insurance	900.00	
Balance to Borrow		$ 51,651.95
Total	$ 385,000.00	$ 385,000.00

Borrower's Hazard (Homeowners) Insurance

The escrow holder should have received the borrowers' homeowners insurance information by this time. If not, the officer should enlist the borrowers' or the loan officer's assistance. If any one thing delays escrow closing for a refinance loan it is usually not obtaining the hazard insurance policy from the borrower's insurance agent. The experienced escrow officer knows all too well the many reasons for such delays and counsels the borrower regarding the importance of contacting the insurance agent or company as soon as escrow has been opened. Oftentimes, it may be necessary for the homeowner to renew the policy. Because that's the time when most homeowners explore different insurance companies and plans, it is understandable that more time is necessary. Also, most lenders require a renewal for insurance if the policy will renew in three months or sooner. Occasionally, the local insurance agent may personally handle renewals. If the agent is not readily available and both the termination date for interest rate protection ("lock") and escrow closing are approaching, it may be necessary to prepare the loan paperwork all over again. Even worse, if the rate lock has expired, the borrower may have to accept a higher rate. Losing the desired interest rate is one of the most common reasons that refinance escrows fail to close.

Loan Processing, Underwriting, and Approval

The time required to underwrite and approve the borrowers' loan depends on the type of financing, the type of property, and the amount of processing work required to obtain information regarding the borrowers' employment, income, and assets. There may also be unresolved credit issues. If the loan application is approved, the underwriter issues a conditional approval. It indicates any remaining conditions that must be satisfied before the loan may actually fund. The underwriter will usually indicate those conditions that must be resolved before loan documents can be prepared and delivered to escrow for signing, appropriately called "prior to docs" (PTD) conditions. There may also be certain conditions remaining to be completed after the loan documents are signed but before the loan may fund, referred to as "prior to funding" (PTF) conditions. Some of these are procedural and apply to practically every loan, such as requiring evidence of hazard insurance.

The Lender's Loan Approval Process The fundamental steps of the lender in the loan process are as follows:

1. The application is prepared by the loan officer and the borrowers.

2. The loan officer submits application and supporting documents from borrower to lender for "processing."

3. The loan officer, or the lender's administration, orders the appraisal. The appraisal may have to be ordered through an appraisal management company in accordance with the regulations of Fannie Mae and Freddie Mac, which prohibit a mortgage broker from directly ordering the appraisal.

4. Processing is performed, including entering application information into lenders' loan origination software for underwriting (the next step). The processor sends requests to the borrowers' employers for verification of employment (VOE form) and may send requests to the borrowers' banks for verification of deposits (VOD) to verify and confirm the amount of funds that the borrowers say they have.

5. When all the information and verifications have been received, the processor submits the file to the underwriter for approval.

6. The underwriter reviews the application package and renders a decision.

Loan Documents and Signing

Upon loan approval, the lender will deliver the loan documents to the escrow holder electronically. The escrow officer should request to receive the documents at least one day prior to the borrowers' signing for time to review the documents and to "figure" the file, determining how much cash the borrowers will either receive at closing or be required to deliver to escrow in order to close. Not uncommonly, the borrowers request to sign documents at a location other than the escrow company, such as at their home or places of employment. The escrow officer or the lender contracts with a "mobile" notary public to perform the signing. Logistics can be somewhat complex if the escrow holder has certain requirements of the lender that are contained in the lender's instructions. Usually the escrow holder will have the lender forward the lender's instructions to it and the loan documents directly to the notary public. However, many escrow officers prefer that the entire loan document package be delivered to them for review first, along with the loan officer, if possible. Errors can be and have been committed in the preparation of loan documents. Having to do them all over again can be costly. Following signing of the documents, a mobile notary who performed the signing will return the documents to the escrow holder. In either case, with or without the services of a mobile notary, after the documents have been signed, the escrow officer will review them for errors or omissions and return them to the lender. Among the forms included with the loan documents will be final disclosures to the borrower and will include a Mortgage Loan Disclosure Statement.

Lender's Audit and Funding

Upon receipt from escrow of the loan documents, the lender will review the documents to determine whether they have been completed and signed satisfactorily. If the property is owner-occupied, funding may not take place for at least three business days after the borrowers signed the documents. In a purchase transaction, the escrow officer usually calls the lender to initiate funding. In the refinance transaction, the funding date is usually prearranged and will take place on that date unless there remains any condition that needs to be removed. The lender and the escrow officer communicate closely at this point to facilitate a successful closing.

Final Accounting and Delivery of Proceeds

After escrow closes, the escrow officer prepares the final closing statement, just as with a purchase transaction, and if the borrower is receiving a cash-out, meaning an amount of cash given to them at escrow closing, the escrow officer will prepare either a check to deliver to them or, if prearranged, wire funds to the borrowers' designated bank account.

■ CHAPTER 13 QUIZ

1. The Federal Housing Administration was established by

    a.   the National Housing Act of 1934.

    b.   the HOLC.

    c.   the FHLB.

    d.   Herbert Hoover.

2. The government agency responsible today for promoting adequate and affordable housing, economic opportunity, and a suitable living environment free from discrimination is

    a.   NHA.

    b.   HHFA.

    c.   HUD.

    d.   HOLC.

3. The largest and *BEST* known investor in the secondary mortgage market is

    a.   FHA.

    b.   HUD.

    c.   Fannie Mae.

    d.   the VA.

4. Mortgage insurance is required for all loans sold to Fannie Mae and Freddie Mac

    a.   without exception.

    b.   having LTVs greater than 80%.

    c.   having LTVs less than 80%.

    d.   having LTVs greater than 75% but less than 80%.

5. All mortgage brokers in California must be licensed by the

   a. Department of Real Estate only.

   b. Department of Real Estate or Department of Corporations.

   c. Department of Housing and Urban Development.

   d. Department of Finance.

6. FHA loans require that impound accounts be established for taxes

   a. and insurance regardless of loan-to-value.

   b. and insurance only if LTV exceeds 90%.

   c. only regardless of LTV.

   d. only if LTV exceeds 90%.

7. The borrower obtaining an FHA loan cannot pay

   a. the lender's closing costs, such as processing and underwriting.

   b. the escrow and title insurance.

   c. discount points to obtain a lower interest rate.

   d. the tax service.

8. The practice of adding to the estimated closing statement a surplus to the amount of funds necessary for the buyer to close escrow is

   a. called padding.

   b. called packing.

   c. unethical.

   d. illegal.

9. The loan underwriter's approval letter may require additional conditions that must be satisfied before the loan may close and that include

   a. PTD items, meaning "prior to documents" being drawn by the lender.

   b. PTF items, meaning "prior to funding" the loan.

   c. Both a and b.

   d. Neither a nor b.

10. When all the lender's conditions have been satisfied and funding is approved by the lender, the person who initiates the request for funding is the

    a. loan officer.

    b. lender's processor.

    c. escrow officer.

    d. title officer.

CHAPTER FOURTEEN

PROTECTING THE CONSUMER

■ KEY TERMS

Consumer Financial
   Protection Bureau
Equal Credit
   Opportunity Act
   (ECOA)
Fair Housing Act
Fair Housing
   Amendments Act

Good Faith Estimate
Holden Credit Denial
   Disclosure Act
predatory lending
Real Estate Settlement
   Procedures Act
   (RESPA)
release clauses

right of rescission
Subdivided Lands Act
Subdivision Map Act
Truth in Lending Act
   (TILA)
Unruh Civil Rights Act

■ LEARNING OBJECTIVES

Upon completing this chapter, you will be able to

■ understand the significance and consequences of predatory lending,

■ understand the provisions of the Federal Truth in Lending Act (Regulation
Z) and the Real Estate Settlement Procedures Act (RESPA),

■ understand and explain the good-faith estimate of settlement costs,

■ understand and explain the Mortgage Loan Disclosure Statement,

■ understand the provisions of the federal and state discriminatory practices laws and acts, and

■ understand the essential elements of the Subdivided Lands Act and the Subdivision Map Act.

■ CONSUMER FINANCIAL PROTECTION BUREAU

In June 2009, the Obama administration proposed enhancing consumer protection in our financial markets by establishing a new financial agency to focus directly on consumers—rather than on bank soundness or monetary policy. This new agency would consolidate responsibilities that were previously those of a number of agencies scattered across government. The new agency would also have responsibility for supervision and enforcement with respect to the laws over providers of consumer financial products and services, and in particular the residential mortgage lending industry. This agency would provide regulations to protect families from unfair, deceptive, and abusive financial and lending practices.

In July 2010, Congress passed and President Barack Obama signed the Dodd-Frank Wall Street Reform and Consumer Protection Act. The act created the **Consumer Financial Protection Bureau (CFPB)**, which consolidates most federal consumer financial protection authority in one place. The consumer bureau is focused on one goal: watching out for American consumers in the market for consumer financial products and services.

■ LENDER'S DISCLOSURES AND RESTRICTIONS

During the escrow, a number of required disclosures are intended to protect buyers and borrowers from certain predatory, unethical, or abusive practices. Restrictions are placed on lenders, brokers, and others regarding their business practices which the government considers not to be in the best interest of their principals. Many of the required disclosures relate to financing, especially predatory lending practices. A variety of disclosures are required of a borrower's lender.

The U.S. Department of Housing and Urban Development (HUD) warns homebuyers and refinancing borrowers to be wary of practices such as real estate agents selling a home for much more than it is worth using false appraisals or loan officers who encourage borrowers to lie about their income, expenses, or cash available for down payments in order to get a loan.

Predatory Lending Practices

The U.S. government has established certain guidelines that lenders must follow regarding **predatory lending** practices and loans having interest rates higher than the average market rates. Additionally, HUD provides the prospective home-buyer with a list of high-pressure tactics that are designed to coerce the buyer into obtaining financing for which they are clearly unqualified or which has onerous term and conditions. HUD also cautions consumers to be aware of these predatory and illegal practices of lenders:

- Knowingly lend more money than a borrower can afford to repay

- Charge high interest rates to borrowers based on their race or national origin and not on their credit history

- Charge fees for unnecessary or nonexistent products and services

- Pressure borrowers to accept higher-risk loans. such as balloon loans, interest-only payments, and steep prepayment penalties

- Target vulnerable borrowers to cash out refinancing offers when they know the borrowers are in need of cash because of medical, unemployment, or debt problems

- "Strip" homeowners' equity from their homes by convincing them to refinance again and again when there is no benefit to the borrower

- Use high-pressure sales tactics to sell home improvements and then finance them at high interest rates

Good Faith Estimate of Costs

The federal Truth in Lending Act (TILA) requires a mortgage lender to provide the borrower with certain information before the borrower becomes obligated to receive loan funds. The truth-in-lending disclosure form, called the **Good Faith Estimate**, must include the following settlement cost information: the identity of the creditor, the amount financed, the finance charge (including interest and fees), the annual percentage rate (APR), and the payment schedule. Disclosure must be made before consummation of the credit transaction or within three business days after receiving the consumer's written application, whichever is earlier. These disclosures are provided to the buyer, or borrower, by delivery of the Good Faith Estimate (see Figure 14.1) and a Truth-in-Lending Disclosure Statement (see Figure 14.2). The Mortgage Loan Disclosure Statement, a California-required disclosure—not part of the requirements of the Truth in Lending Act—providing a borrower with details regarding the loan and the lender's compensation, will also be delivered to the borrower.

> **Pro-Tip: Right of Rescission: Three-Day Waiting Period Until Funding**
>
> For refinance loans on primary residences, the borrower must be given the right to rescind (cancel) the loan within three days before loan funding and closing. The borrower cannot waive this right.
>
> The right of rescission does not apply to investment properties.
>
> The right of rescission does not apply to purchase loans.

The lender must provide the consumer with a notice of **right of rescission**. The borrowers have the right to rescind until three business days following the last of these events: consummation of transaction and delivery of truth-in-lending disclosures or delivery of notice of right to rescind. In December 2007, the Federal Reserve Board proposed amendments to Regulation Z, Truth in Lending Act, under the Home Ownership and Equity Protection Act (HOEPA), which were finalized and approved in July 2008 and became effective October 1, 2009. Not restricted to only adjustable-rate mortgages, these amendments address and strengthen consumer protection in certain mortgages, identifying prohibited abusive practices.

FIGURE 14.1
Good Faith Estimate

OMB Approval No. 2502-0265

Good Faith Estimate (GFE)

Name of Originator		Borrower	
Originator Address		Property Address	
Originator Phone Number			
Originator Email		Date of GFE	

Purpose

This GFE gives you an estimate of your settlement charges and loan terms if you are approved for this loan. For more information, see HUD's *Special Information Booklet* on settlement charges, your *Truth-in-Lending Disclosures*, and other consumer information at www.hud.gov/respa. If you decide you would like to proceed with this loan, contact us.

Shopping for your loan

Only you can shop for the best loan for you. Compare this GFE with other loan offers, so you can find the best loan. Use the shopping chart on page 3 to compare all the offers you receive.

Important dates

1. The interest rate for this GFE is available through [   ]. After this time, the interest rate, some of your loan Origination Charges, and the monthly payment shown below can change until you lock your interest rate.
2. This estimate for all other settlement charges is available through [   ].
3. After you lock your interest rate, you must go to settlement within [ ] days (your rate lock period) to receive the locked interest rate.
4. You must lock the interest rate at least [ ] days before settlement.

Summary of your loan

Your initial loan amount is	$
Your loan term is	years
Your initial interest rate is	%
Your initial monthly amount owed for principal, interest, and any mortgage insurance is	$ per month
Can your interest rate rise?	☐ No ☐ Yes, it can rise to a maximum of %. The first change will be in .
Even if you make payments on time, can your loan balance rise?	☐ No ☐ Yes, it can rise to a maximum of $
Even if you make payments on time, can your monthly amount owed for principal, interest, and any mortgage insurance rise?	☐ No ☐ Yes, the first increase can be in and the monthly amount owed can rise to $. The maximum it can ever rise to is $.
Does your loan have a prepayment penalty?	☐ No ☐ Yes, your maximum prepayment penalty is $.
Does your loan have a balloon payment?	☐ No ☐ Yes, you have a balloon payment of $ due in years.

Escrow account information

Some lenders require an escrow account to hold funds for paying property taxes or other property-related charges in addition to your monthly amount owed of $[   ].
Do we require you to have an escrow account for your loan?
☐ No, you do not have an escrow account. You must pay these charges directly when due.
☐ Yes, you have an escrow account. It may or may not cover all of these charges. Ask us.

Summary of your settlement charges

A	Your Adjusted Origination Charges *(See page 2.)*	$
B	Your Charges for All Other Settlement Services *(See page 2.)*	$
A + B	Total Estimated Settlement Charges	$

FIGURE 14.1

Good Faith Estimate (continued)

Understanding your estimated settlement charges

Your Adjusted Origination Charges	
1. Our origination charge This charge is for getting this loan for you.	
2. Your credit or charge (points) for the specific interest rate chosen ☐ The credit or charge for the interest rate of [＿＿] % is included in "Our origination charge." (See item 1 above.) ☐ You receive a credit of $[＿＿＿＿] for this interest rate of [＿＿] %. This credit **reduces** your settlement charges. ☐ You pay a charge of $[＿＿＿＿] for this interest rate of [＿＿] %. This charge (points) **increases** your total settlement charges. The tradeoff table on page 3 shows that you can change your total settlement charges by choosing a different interest rate for this loan.	
A Your Adjusted Origination Charges	$

Some of these charges can change at settlement. See the top of page 3 for more information.

Your Charges for All Other Settlement Services	
3. Required services that we select These charges are for services we require to complete your settlement. We will choose the providers of these services. *Service* *Charge*	
4. Title services and lender's title insurance This charge includes the services of a title or settlement agent, for example, and title insurance to protect the lender, if required.	
5. Owner's title insurance You may purchase an owner's title insurance policy to protect your interest in the property.	
6. Required services that you can shop for These charges are for other services that are required to complete your settlement. We can identify providers of these services or you can shop for them yourself. Our estimates for providing these services are below. *Service* *Charge*	
7. Government recording charges These charges are for state and local fees to record your loan and title documents.	
8. Transfer taxes These charges are for state and local fees on mortgages and home sales.	
9. Initial deposit for your escrow account This charge is held in an escrow account to pay future recurring charges on your property and includes ☐ all property taxes, ☐ all insurance, and ☐ other [＿＿＿＿＿].	
10. Daily interest charges This charge is for the daily interest on your loan from the day of your settlement until the first day of the next month or the first day of your normal mortgage payment cycle. This amount is $[＿＿＿]per day for [＿＿] days (if your settlement is [＿＿＿]).	
11. Homeowner's insurance This charge is for the insurance you must buy for the property to protect from a loss, such as fire. *Policy* *Charge*	
B Your Charges for All Other Settlement Services	$
A + B Total Estimated Settlement Charges	$

 Good Faith Estimate (HUD-GFE) 2

FIGURE 14.1

Good Faith Estimate
(continued)

Instructions

Understanding which charges can change at settlement

This GFE estimates your settlement charges. At your settlement, you will receive a HUD-1, a form that lists your actual costs. Compare the charges on the HUD-1 with the charges on this GFE. Charges can change if you select your own provider and do not use the companies we identify. (See below for details.)

These charges **cannot increase** at settlement:	The total of these charges **can increase up to 10%** at settlement:	These charges **can change** at settlement:
■ Our origination charge ■ Your credit or charge (points) for the specific interest rate chosen *(after you lock in your interest rate)* ■ Your adjusted origination charges *(after you lock in your interest rate)* ■ Transfer taxes	■ Required services that we select ■ Title services and lender's title insurance *(if we select them or you use companies we identify)* ■ Owner's title insurance *(if you use companies we identify)* ■ Required services that you can shop for *(if you use companies we identify)* ■ Government recording charges	■ Required services that you can shop for *(if you do not use companies we identify)* ■ Title services and lender's title insurance *(if you do not use companies we identify)* ■ Owner's title insurance *(if you do not use companies we identify)* ■ Initial deposit for your escrow account ■ Daily interest charges ■ Homeowner's insurance

Using the tradeoff table

In this GFE, we offered you this loan with a particular interest rate and estimated settlement charges. However:

■ If you want to choose this same loan with **lower settlement charges**, then you will have a **higher interest rate**.
■ If you want to choose this same loan with a **lower interest rate**, then you will have **higher settlement charges**.

If you would like to choose an available option, you must ask us for a new GFE.

Loan originators have the option to complete this table. Please ask for additional information if the table is not completed.

	The loan in this GFE	The same loan with lower settlement charges	The same loan with a lower interest rate
Your initial loan amount	$	$	$
Your initial interest rate[1]	%	%	%
Your initial monthly amount owed	$	$	$
Change in the monthly amount owed from this GFE	No change	You will pay $ **more** every month	You will pay $ **less** every month
Change in the amount you will pay at settlement with this interest rate	No change	Your settlement charges will be **reduced** by $	Your settlement charges will **increase** by $
How much your total estimated settlement charges will be	$	$	$

[1] For an adjustable rate loan, the comparisons above are for the initial interest rate before adjustments are made.

Using the shopping chart

Use this chart to compare GFEs from different loan originators. Fill in the information by using a different column for each GFE you receive. By comparing loan offers, you can shop for the best loan.

	This loan	Loan 2	Loan 3	Loan 4
Loan originator name				
Initial loan amount				
Loan term				
Initial interest rate				
Initial monthly amount owed				
Rate lock period				
Can interest rate rise?				
Can loan balance rise?				
Can monthly amount owed rise?				
Prepayment penalty?				
Balloon payment?				
Total Estimated Settlement Charges				

If your loan is sold in the future

Some lenders may sell your loan after settlement. Any fees lenders receive in the future cannot change the loan you receive or the charges you paid at settlement.

 Good Faith Estimate (HUD-GFE) 3

FIGURE 14.2
Truth-in-Lending
Disclosure Statement

TRUTH-IN-LENDING DISCLOSURE STATEMENT

LOAN #: 601480
LOAN AMT: $385,000.00

BORROWER(S):

PROPERTY ADDRESS: 1312 CHESTNUT STREET

ANNUAL PERCENTAGE RATE The cost of your credit as a yearly rate.	FINANCE CHARGE The dollar amount the credit will cost you.	Amount Financed The amount of credit provided to you or on your behalf.	Total of Payments The amount you will have paid after you have made all payments as scheduled.	
7.056 %	$ 584,676.10	$ 379,803.50	$ 964,479.60	

Your payment schedule will be:

No. of Payment(s)	Amount of Payment(s)	Due Monthly Beginning	No. of Payment(s)	Amount of Payment(s)	Due Monthly Beginning	No. of Payment(s)	Amount of Payment(s)	Due Monthly Beginning
60	$2,005.21	4/01/2006						
300	$2,813.89	4/01/2011						

Your loan contains a variable rate feature. Disclosures about the variable rate feature have been provided to you earlier.

INSURANCE: THE FOLLOWING INSURANCE IS REQUIRED TO OBTAIN CREDIT: PROPERTY INSURANCE. YOU MAY OBTAIN THIS INSURANCE FROM ANYONE YOU WANT THAT IS REASONABLY ACCEPTABLE TO THE CREDITOR. CREDIT LIFE AND CREDIT DISABILITY INSURANCE ARE NOT REQUIRED TO OBTAIN CREDIT.

SECURITY: YOU ARE GIVING A SECURITY INTEREST IN THE PROPERTY LOCATED
        AT: 1312 CHESTNUT .

FILING/RECORDING FEE: $0.00

LATE CHARGE: IF A PAYMENT IS MORE THAN 15 DAYS LATE, YOU WILL BE CHARGED 5.000% OF THE PAYMENT.

PREPAYMENT: IF YOU PAY OFF EARLY, YOU WILL NOT HAVE TO PAY A PENALTY AND YOU WILL NOT BE ENTITLED TO A REFUND OF PART OF THE FINANCE CHARGE.

ASSUMPTION: SOMEONE BUYING YOUR PROPERTY MAY, SUBJECT TO CONDITIONS, BE ALLOWED TO ASSUME THE REMAINDER OF THE MORTGAGE ON THE ORIGINAL TERMS.

High-Cost Loan Restrictions Under Regulation Z

The Federal Reserve Board's amendments include the formal inclusion of a new category of "higher-priced mortgages," those mortgages whose APR exceeds the average prime offer rate (average market rate) as follows:

- A loan with a rate of 1.5% or greater than conventional market rate for first trust deed loans

- A loan with a rate of 3.5% or greater for subordinate loans

The amendments for these higher-priced loans, which include not only subprime loans but some of the "alt-A mortgages" as well, include the following:

- Prohibit a lender from engaging in a pattern or practice of lending without considering the borrowers' ability to repay the loan from sources other than the home's value.

- Prohibit a lender from making a loan by relying on income or assets that it does not verify.

- Prohibits prepayment penalties on loans having payments that adjust within the first four years. On all other loans a prepay penalty may not last longer than two years.

- Require the lender to establish an escrow account for the payment of property taxes and homeowners insurance for the first year of the loan, at which time the borrower can opt out of the escrow account (this provision became effective April 1, 2010).

Amendments for All Mortgages Under Regulation Z

Amendments for all mortgages, including higher-priced loans, are as follows:

- Prohibit certain lending practices, such as failing to credit a payment to a consumer's account when the servicer receives it, failing to provide a payoff statement within a reasonable period, and "pyramiding" late fees (the practice of charging late fees to a borrower who has not paid a prior late fee).

- Prohibit a creditor or a broker from coercing or encouraging an appraiser to misrepresent the value of a home.

- Prohibits advertising "fixed" rates or payments without adequately disclosing that the rate or payment amounts are fixed only for a limited period of time, rather than for the full term of the loan.

- Comparing an actual or hypothetical consumer's current rate or payment obligations and the rates or payments that would apply if the consumer obtains the advertised product, unless the advertisement states the (actual) rates or payments that will apply over the full term of the loan.

- Advertisements that characterize the products offered as "government loan programs," "government-supported loans," or otherwise endorsed or sponsored by a federal or state government entity, unless the loans are government supported or sponsored loans such as FHA or VA loans.

- Advertisements that prominently display the name of the consumer's current mortgage lender, unless the advertisement also discloses the fact that the advertisement is from a mortgage lender not affiliated with the consumer's current lender.

- Advertising claims of debt elimination if the product advertised would merely replace one debt obligation with another.

- Advertisements that falsely create the impression that the mortgage broker or lender has a fiduciary relationship with the consumer.

- Foreign-language advertisements in which certain information, such as a low introductory "teaser" rate is provided in a foreign language, while required disclosures are provided only in English.

- Require truth-in-lending disclosures to borrowers early enough for them to use while shopping for a mortgage. Lenders could not change fees until after the consumer receives the disclosure, except for a fee to obtain a credit report.

The new regulations also extend early disclosure of good-faith estimate disclosures to both purchase money and non-purchase-money (refinance) closed-end transactions (previous regulations provided only for the disclosure on purchase money loans).

The Federal Reserve Bank has said that the goal of these changes and of the Federal Reserve Bank is to ensure they are likely to protect consumers from unfair practices "without shutting off access to responsible credit." Fed Chairman Ben Bernanke said the board responded to deceptive lending problems with rules that were carefully crafted with an eye toward deterring improper lending and advertising practices without unduly restricting mortgage credit availability.

Real Estate Settlement Procedures Act (RESPA)

Under the **Real Estate Settlement Procedures Act (RESPA)**, lenders are required to distribute information booklets authorized by HUD and provide a good-faith estimate of closing costs to borrowers before the close of escrow. Among other things, the booklet describes the settlement process and the nature of the charges, which are generally incurred by the principals in the transaction. The booklet sets forth information as to rights and remedies available under RESPA; it describes unfair or illegal settlement practices and provides an item-by-item explanation of closing costs and services. The act requires the escrow holder to provide a full and complete accounting of all costs paid and monies received by or on behalf of the parties.

Rights of the Borrower Under RESPA   As mentioned earlier, the principal has the right to select third-party service providers, such as the escrow company and the title company. RESPA guaranteed this right to the principals. The act also prohibits offering unequal rates, costs, or fees; the amount one person pays in a transaction is the amount all others must be charged in their transactions relative to level or flat fees and those based on a percentage of value or some other factor. The caveat for the escrow holder is the penalty for anyone who violates a provision of RESPA: a fine of $10,000 or imprisonment for not more than one year, or both, for each violation.

Applicability to Lenders   RESPA provisions apply to lenders making more than $100,000 per year in real estate loans or any lender regulated by a government agency, such as the Federal Reserve Bank, the Comptroller of the Currency, the Federal Deposit Insurance Corporation, Veterans Affairs, or HUD agencies.

Restrictions on Borrowers' Escrow (Impound) Accounts   RESPA regulates the maximum amount a lender can require a borrower to deposit in escrow impound accounts (trust or impound accounts for payment of future taxes and insurance).

Kickbacks Prohibited Under RESPA   RESPA prohibits giving or accepting any compensation or "thing of value" for the referral of any settlement service business (i.e., no "kickbacks" or "naked" referral fees).

Loans Covered by RESPA   RESPA applies to first and second mortgages, including home equity loans for residential one-to-four-unit properties.

The Equal Credit Opportunity Act (ECOA)

The **Equal Opportunity Act (ECOA)** prohibits discrimination in the extension of credit. The Federal Reserve Board's Regulation B dictates what information may be solicited in an application for credit, how a lender may proceed in evaluating an applicant's credit worthiness and in making a decision whether to extend credit or not, and what a lender may or must do after a decision is made.

The Holden Credit Denial Disclosure Act of 1976

The **Holden Credit Denial Disclosure Act** of 1976 is a state law imposing substantially the same requirements as the Equal Credit Opportunity Act and Regulation B with respect to providing notice to an applicant of a lender's decision to extend credit or not.

The Unruh Civil Rights Act

The **Unruh Civil Rights Act** is a state law expressing a policy of nondiscrimination in very broad terms. This law applies to all business establishments of any kind and prohibits certain discrimination in the rendering of "services" without further specification.

The Fair Housing Act

The **Fair Housing Act** is a federal law prohibiting discrimination against any applicant for financial assistance for purchasing any housing accommodation.

The Housing Financial Discrimination Act of 1977

The Housing Financial Discrimination Act is a state law prohibiting "redlining," the practice of blocking off entire areas of a city or a county and refusing to lend on the security or property within those areas, solely because of the location of the property relative to other properties occupied or owned by certain groups or kinds of people.

Fair Housing Amendments Act of 1988

The federal **Fair Housing Amendments Act** broadened the protected classes to explicitly include families with children and people with physical or mental disabilities. In addition, the revisions substantially increased the fines that can be levied for fair housing violations and provided HUD the power to represent discrimination victims in court in individual cases, not just in so-called "pattern and practice" cases. Finally, the Fair Housing Initiatives Program provides federal funding to private fair housing groups to fund local testing efforts to discover fair housing abuses.

■ PROPERTY USE RESTRICTIONS DISCLOSURES

In the transfer of either real or personal property, restrictions or limitations placed on the use of the property can make the property unsuitable for the buyer's intended use or lessen its value to the buyer.

Disclosures of private restrictions or public laws, ordinances, and regulations help the buyer make an informed decision relative to the purchase offer, the amount to offer, and any issues and procedures needed to make the property conform to the buyer's needs.

These disclosures are described in this section.

Zoning Reports

Some cities or counties require a seller to obtain a zoning statement from the appropriate agency and deliver it to the buyer in escrow.

Zoning Is Example of Police Power   Zoning is an example of police power: the right of the government to control or restrict the use of real property. Zoning helps assure a buyer that the property conforms to the zoning required for its intended use.

Excluded From Most Title Insurance Coverage   Zoning is one of the exclusions from insurance coverage; however, a title policy zoning endorsement may provide limited coverage.

Subdivision Map Act

If the sale involves new construction in a subdivision, it is regulated under the **Subdivision Map Act**. Before 1929, there was no real control over the development of subdivisions. Not uncommon was the developer who sold unfinished lots (no streets, curbs, or gutters yet constructed) indicating that street access existed, but it did not. In other cases, municipal street lighting was funded with improvement bonds, but the bonded indebtedness exceeded the value of the lot. The Map Filing Act of 1929, which later evolved into the Subdivision Map Act, served to protect the interests of the unsuspecting public. The act is the authority granting cities and counties the right to implement subdivision ordinances. It applies to all subdivisions of land into two or more parcels and is designed to coordinate lot design, street patterns, and easements for public utilities, and it assures that dedicated public areas (streets and alleys) are improved properly. While it is the title company that serves as the focal point for map processing and recording, escrow holders who handle subdivision escrows must be aware of the state and local requirements for processing the subdivision maps.

Release Clauses   Any lien of record on a subdivision must contain a partial **release clause** allowing the individual lots to be released subsequent to map filing.

Parties of Interest   All parties in interest (property owners) are required to sign the map and indicate their interest in the project.

Approval Process   The approval process for the subdivision begins with the developer conducting feasibility studies, progressing through applicable state, local, title company, and lender requirements.

Environmental Impact Reports (EIR)   These reports might include the following steps:

- Coastal commission approval, if subject to its authority

- Preparation of a tentative map for local planning approval

- Preparation of the final map with required signatures

- Submission of the final map to local government for approval

- Recording of the approved map.

  — If Subdivided Lands Act applies (see "Subdivided Lands Act" in this chapter), a copy of the recorded map is delivered to the California Department of Real Estate by the developer for issuance of a public report.

  — The escrow holder must be aware of the time involved for processing the map. Filing a parcel map can take from 6 to 9 months, while a formal tract map takes from 12 to 18 months.

Subdivided Lands Act

The **Subdivided Lands Act** directly affects the activities of escrow holders. The act was intended to protect the consumer from fraudulent marketing practices in the sale of subdivided parcels including condominium projects.

California Department of Real Estate (DRE) Approval Required   The Subdivided Lands Act requires DRE approval prior to the sale of certain types of real estate interests. To get the approval, the prospective seller submits a lengthy application describing the project in detail.

Pink Paper   The preliminary approval is called the pink report or pink paper. It is the instrument used to inform the prospective purchaser of the details of the project in the public report.

White Paper   Once all required work is performed by the developer to obtain a final approval, a request is made to the DRE for a Final Subdivision Public Report (also sometimes referred to as a white report or white paper). The final report must be distributed to all buyers before they commit to purchasing.

Undivided Interests   Originally, the Subdivided Lands Act required public reports only in situations where a parcel of real estate was legally subdivided into five or more smaller parcels, such as entirely independent lots or condominiums. To avoid the cost and delay of getting a public report, some developers chose not to divide the lots they wished to sell, opting instead to sell percentage interests. At the request of the DRE, the California legislature responded by amending the Subdivided Lands Act so that it also required a public report for the sale of undivided interests. The portion of the Subdivided Lands Act that applies to sales of undivided percentage interests does not require a public report for the sale of four or fewer shares. When 5 to 10 shares are to be sold, the act requires a public report but also provides for an exemption from this requirement.

Interim Public Report   An interim report may also be used by the developer; however, it may only be used to take reservations from prospective buyers before the issuance of an amended or renewed subdivision public report, unlike the preliminary subdivision report. The interim subdivision report process requires reservation funds to be impounded in a neutral escrow depository. As is the case with preliminary subdivision public reports, Department of Real Estate forms RE 612 and RE 612A do not constitute binding contracts. The forms have been modified for use with either a preliminary or an interim subdivision public report.

The Escrow Holder's Responsibility   The escrow officer with experience in working with developers and subdivisions should be capable of complying with the legal requirements regarding the Subdivided Lands Act. However, it is often difficult for the escrow officer to know whether the seller of a condominium owns five or more units in the project, which would fall under the requirements of the Subdivided Lands Act, until the title search is completed. The escrow holder can only rely on the information from the seller or the title company report. Most escrow holders include exculpatory language in the general provisions of their escrow instructions to avoid any liability.

Home Warranty Protection

The home warranty protection policy being provided to a buyer, while not a required disclosure, should have its terms and exclusions from coverage clearly discussed with the buyer. A variety of home warranty protection policies exist with varying amounts of protection, including those for preexisting defective conditions. The home warranty policy may be delivered through escrow; however, the escrow officer should not interpret the coverage protection for the buyer but rather refer the buyer to the home warranty company representative. The seller may obtain coverage as well during the escrow. The escrow holder will be provided an invoice for payment through escrow.

■ CHAPTER 14 QUIZ

1. The federal Truth in Lending Act requires a mortgage lender, before the borrower becomes obligated to receive loan funds, to provide the borrower with

    a. creditor's identity, amount financed, finance charge (including interest and fees), annual percentage rate, and payment schedule.

    b. only the amount financed, annual percentage rate, and payment schedule.

    c. only the identity of the creditor, amount financed, interest rate, and payment.

    d. only the amount financed, finance charge, annual percentage rate, and payment schedule.

2. Federal truth-in-lending disclosures are provided to the borrower by

    a. a good-faith estimate of settlement costs.

    b. a Truth-in-Lending Disclosure Statement.

    c. the title officer.

    d. both a and b.

3. The borrower must be given a three-day right of rescission, with the lender prohibited from funding and the escrow holder prohibited from closing, for

    a. a refinance loan of the borrower's primary residence.

    b. all loans.

    c. all refinance loans.

    d. a refinance loan of rental properties only.

4. Under RESPA, the lender is required to provide the borrower with

    a. information booklets authored by HUD and a good-faith estimate of closing costs to borrowers before the close of escrow.

    b. only a good-faith estimate of closing costs at closing.

    c. only information booklets authorized by HUD.

    d. none of these.

5. The penalty for anyone who violates any provision of RESPA is a

   a. $5,000 fine for each violation.

   b. $10,000 fine or not more than one year in prison for each violation.

   c. $10,000 fine and/or not more than one year in prison for each violation.

   d. cease and desist order to discontinue the practice.

6. RESPA provisions apply to lenders

   a. making more than $100,000 per year in real estate loans.

   b. regulated by the Federal Reserve Bank.

   c. regulated by the VA or HUD agencies.

   d. all these.

7. The Unruh Civil Rights Act is a state law prohibiting discrimination by

   a. all businesses.

   b. only lenders.

   c. only lenders and real estate agents.

   d. only lenders, real estate agents, escrow holders, and title companies.

8. Zoning is an example of

   a. eminent domain.

   b. police power.

   c. liens.

   d. easements.

9. The Subdivision Map Act applies to the subdivision of land into

   a. two or more parcels.

   b. no fewer than five parcels.

   c. no fewer than four parcels.

   d. housing tracts of 10 parcels or more.

10. The Subdivided Lands Act applies to subdivisions of five lots or more and provides for both a preliminary approval and a final approval, referred to as

    a. pink paper and white paper, respectively.

    b. yellow paper and white paper, respectively.

    c. pink paper and yellow paper, respectively.

    d. white paper and pink paper, respectively.

CHAPTER FIFTEEN

APARTMENT BUILDINGS, COMMERCIAL PROPERTIES, AND EXCHANGES

■ KEY TERMS

accommodator
apartment buildings
commercial properties
debt service coverage
estoppel certificates
exchanges

franchise agreements
IRS Code Section 1031
like-kind
operating expenses
Phase I environmental
   site assessment (ESA)

Phase II inspection
Phase III work
prepay penalties
rent roll

■ LEARNING OBJECTIVES

Upon completing this chapter, you will be able to

■ understand the essential requirements of apartment and commercial property building transactions and lenders' requirements for each;

■ understand the environmental inspection process in Phase I and Phase II;

■ understand the significance and consequences of Phase III mitigation work;

■ understand the advantages and disadvantages of franchises relating to lenders' requirements;

■ understand, perform, and explain the escrow process involving IRS Section 1031 tax-deferred exchanges, including "reverse exchanges"; and

■ identify and explain "like-kind" properties.

■ SPECIAL REQUIREMENTS

Processing the escrow for the sale or refinancing of apartment buildings and commercial real estate includes a number of additional disclosures, reports, and special provisions that involve the escrow officer. In order to provide the level of service required in these special transactions, the escrow officer must possess the knowledge and skills essential not only to orchestrate a successful escrow closing but also to meet the fiduciary obligation to the principals in the process. A number of special requirements are involved in escrows involving each of these property types, and an escrow officer must be intimately familiar with them to be able to property handle their escrows. More often than not, the apartment or commercial property transaction involves a Section 1031 exchange. Escrow officers experienced in exchange transactions acquire considerable training and education relative to the IRS and the Franchise Tax Board regulations to be qualified and capable of handling these complex escrows.

■ APARTMENT BUILDINGS

Apartment Buildings, called multifamily properties, and especially those with five housing units or more, require additional inspections, reports, and contingencies that are not required for typical owner-occupied single-family homes. They may be subject to rent control or other governmental restrictions with which the escrow officer must be familiar. The escrow officer will be involved with, or must be cognizant of, additional responsibilities in an apartment building escrow. These are described in the paragraphs that follow. If the buyer is obtaining financing, the lender will require compliance with most of these conditions.

Rental Income   A **rent roll** (a list indicating the names of all tenants, along with the amount of their individual rents and security deposits) and rental or lease agreements will be requested by the buyer from the seller or listing agent. The seller usually delivers these to the escrow holder, who forwards them to the buyer or the buyer's agent. The buyer's lender will require this same information:

- Name of each tenant

- Tenant's move-in date (when the tenant first rented the apartment)

- If under a lease, the expiration date of the lease

- Current rent amount

- Security deposit

- Date of the last rent increase

- Date the last rental payment was made

- Amount of any delinquency

- Any other special terms of the rental agreement or lease

Rent Control   If the property is located in a community subject to rent control affecting the subject property, this fact must be conveyed to the buyer in the escrow instruction.

Estoppel Certificates   Estoppel certificates for verifying rents will be delivered to the escrow holder who will, in turn, deliver it to the buyer. Estoppel certificates are prepared by the buyer's lender (or by escrow for the buyer paying all cash), requesting that each tenant confirm the amount of the periodic rent payment, the security deposit paid, and any other special terms of the lease or rental agreement, such as parking or concessions.

Operating Expenses   In obtaining and reviewing additional rental information regarding the property, the buyer (and the lender if the buyer is obtaining financing) will ask the seller to provide a list of itemized **operating expenses**. It is not always easy to get the expense information, and often, unless the buyer is obtaining financing, the buyer may decide to not make delivery of operating expenses a condition of the escrow.

Financing   Buyer's loan requirements are far more complex than those of the buyer obtaining a loan for a single-family home. The lender considering originating a loan on an apartment building will rely on the ability of the property to generate adequate income to "service" the monthly loan payment—meaning it will have adequate cash flow to make the monthly payment when due. The lender will ask either the escrow holder or the seller's agent to provide a record of income and itemized operating expenses for the past two complete calendar years plus the current year to date.

Debt Coverage Ratio   The lender utilizes a process called a **debt service coverage** ratio (DSCR) calculation to determine this. *Debt service* is the term lender's use to refer to the loan payment. The term *coverage ratio* means the net operating income required to "cover" (pay) the loan payment plus yield the cash flow amount. Simply put, the lender's DSCR represents the amount of cash flow the lender will require the property to generate after the monthly loan payment.

■ **EXAMPLE**   An apartment building is listed for $1,250,000. The lender allows up to 75% LTV, which would be a loan of $937,500. However, the actual maximum loan will be the lesser of 75% of the sales price or the loan amount based on the debt service coverage ratio calculation. The property generates $150,000 in annual gross scheduled income. The area has a 10% vacancy rate, and the property's expenses total $52,500 yearly. The net operating income (NOI), therefore, is $82,500. The lender requires a minimum debt service coverage ratio (DSCR) of 1.2. The borrower is applying for a loan offering a 30-year amortization and an 8% interest rate. The following calculation will determine the actual maximum loan amount:

$82,500 annual NOI ÷ 12 = $6,875 monthly NOI payment

$5,729.17 P&I payment, 30-year amortization, 8% rate = $780,791 maximum loan, and an adjusted LTV down to 62.46%.

The DSCR limitation, more than anything else, causes escrow fallout in apartment transactions. There could be one or more of several reasons the income is too low for the loan amount as specified in the escrow instructions. The rents may simply be too low and under market or the property may have high vacancies. A common cause for both is that the property requires renovation or rehabilitation. Some lenders offer a solution referred to as an earn-out. The lender will fund the loan based on current rental income to close escrow, allowing the buyer usually up to one year to improve the property to the extent it will justify the higher loan based on the higher rental income. At that time, the lender will release the balance of the loan proceeds back to the buyer. The funds typically are not retained in escrow.

Other Causes That Reduce the LTV   The LTV may be further reduced by other factors such as the property age, condition, or construction (brick, not earthquake retrofitted), low capitalization (cap) rate (lower than area averages), unit mix (too many singles or one-bedroom units), and expenses understated by the seller.

The seller will be asked to submit to the escrow holder for delivery to the buyer, and to the buyer's lender, certain items (i.e., representation of the income and itemized expenses for the property for the past two complete calendar years plus the current year-to-date). If the transaction is a refinance, the borrower's lender will require an actual IRS 1040 Schedule E for the past two years, as well as an operating statement (profit and loss statement) for the current year through the most recent quarter's ending. Also, the lender will want a list of capital improvements made during the current year or during the last tax return year. This is important to the buyer in that the seller's operating expenses will influence the amount of the buyer's loan. Capital improvements are typically of such a large amount that if treated as a repair expense rather than a capital improvement, they might negatively impact the amount of the loan available to the buyer, reducing the loan amount available to the buyer and jeopardizing the closing of the escrow.

Personal property included in the transaction, such as appliances, including a bill of sale or indicating "to which no value is attached," must also be included. Compliance with state and local health and safety requirement will be required, such as smoke detector information and fire extinguisher requirements, if any. A list of vendors (e.g., gardener; pool-service company; trash and cable service; water, gas and electrical service providers; and other similar services) will be necessary, and tenant concessions (as indicated in the estoppel certificates) regarding parking, free rent or discounts, and other items are also a part of the required documentation.

■ COMMERCIAL (NONRESIDENTIAL) PROPERTIES

Most of the foregoing provisions and requirements, including the loan analysis and debt-service-coverage-ratio calculation process, are also applicable to commercial nonresidential properties. Additional requirements, however, also apply.

The Commercial Property Transaction

A **commercial property** transaction involves the transfer or refinance of a business, and as such the business is subject to local and state regulations. The escrow holder may be required to assist in the preparation or delivery of additional documentation or reports necessary for accomplishing the closing of escrow. A greater number of inspections, government reports, studies, and evaluations are done in a commercial property sale—more so than in the typical apartment transaction. If the property is going to be used by the buyers in their business or trade, inquiries regarding any restrictions or limitations on its use are made with the appropriate governmental agencies.

Maximum LTV for Commercial Properties
Commercial properties are generally defined as any type of property that is not intended for residential dwelling use. These properties usually have lower maximum loan-to-value (LTV) ratios

than residential properties, including apartment buildings. The maximum LTV is commonly 75% and often considerably less than that. Some commercial lenders will not loan more than 60% to 65% LTV for commercial real estate. It is helpful for the escrow holder to have an understanding of the typical LTV, especially if the buyer is unrepresented by a commercial real estate agent. It's possible that the buyer has not discussed financing with a lender, and both the buyer and the seller may be unaware of commercial lending guidelines. In such a case, the escrow officer may be instrumental in encouraging the buyer to visit a lender before becoming obligated in the transaction.

Property Types Commercial properties may be divided into the following property types, some of which require additional inspections, reports, and disclosures by government agencies or the lender who might originate the buyer's loan. General commercial property types are as follows:

- Office buildings, including medical
- Free-standing retail buildings
- Mixed use (usually retail and residential combined)
- Retail strip centers, unanchored (no major tenant)
- Retail strip centers, anchored
- Retail shopping centers or malls
- Industrial buildings
- Industrial condominiums or planned unit developments
- Medical office buildings and hospitals
- Restaurants
- Recreational facilities (health clubs, amusement parks)
- Golf courses
- Automotive repair facilities
- Automobile car-wash facilities, full service
- Automobile "coin-op" car-wash facilities
- Mobile home parks
- Hospitality (i.e., hotels and motels)
- Hospitality, non-flag (independent)

■ Agriculture properties (crop lands, vineyards, and orchards)

■ Other properties (usually owner-user), liquor stores, dry cleaners, coin-op Laundromats, theaters

Contingencies and Conditions of the Commercial Property Transaction

A buyer, either an investor or one intending to occupy and use a commercial property, will have a number of concerns requiring an extensive investigation of factors which may impact the use of the property. The buyer's research may include physical inspections of the property and surrounding properties, as well as the area's infrastructure. The investigation may also involve visiting or contacting various government agencies. Some of the factors are described in the paragraphs that follow.

Government Agencies   The buyer's use of the property may require compliance with certain city, county, state or federal laws, regulations, and ordinances:

■ Walls or fences to be constructed

■ Landscaping requirements or restrictions

■ Water conservation

■ Sign restrictions and ordinances

■ Noise abatement

■ Trash containers and disposal

■ Zoning (variances and conditional-use permits)

■ Underground tanks

■ Registration, if necessary, with state board of equalization

Appraisals   An appraisal for the commercial or multifamily property is more detailed, and considerably more expensive, than one for a one-to-four-unit property. The lender may require the appraiser to have the MAI or SRPA professional appraisal designations, which is seldom required in one-to-four-unit appraisals. Commercial and apartment appraisals take considerably longer to complete than smaller residential properties because of the additional work and time required. The agent and the escrow holder, therefore, should suggest that the principals consider at least 60–90 days for escrow closing. The appraisal process considers the following:

- *Cap rates.* The appraiser considers the market cap rate (capitalization rate), which essentially reveals the yield or return on investment that the typical investor is requiring. Rents will be validated, comparing the subject property's rents to the market. Additionally, the appraiser will be asked to provide **estoppel certificates**, as previously described, to the tenants confirming the amount of rent they are paying and the terms and conditions of leases.

- *Appraisals.* Apartment appraisals typically cost $150 to $200 per unit or more. Some lenders, especially those using staff appraisers, charge a flat rate, regardless of units. Fees for commercial appraisals depend on the size and character of property and range from $1,500 to $3,500 or more.

Environmental Inspection

An environmental inspection, either a limited or full Phase I environmental assessment report, is required for many commercial properties. They are typically not required for most apartment loans unless the property appraisal called attention to a condition of the property or the property is adjacent to or near commercial properties whose current or prior occupants used toxic or other contaminating materials or processes or the property is or was the site of

- automotive and manufacturing chemical spills,

- hazardous waste,

- PCBs,

- abandoned industrial operations, or

- underground storage tanks.

Adjacent property history can have a significant impact on the liability found by a buyer, seller, or lending institution.

A lender may require an environmental questionnaire to be completed by the seller before arbitrarily ordering a Phase I environmental inspection and report. The results of the questionnaire and the lender's physical inspection of the property will determine whether a Phase I inspection is to be performed. A growing number of lenders, however, are requiring a Phase I inspection for all larger properties and higher loan amounts.

The **Phase I environmental site assessment (ESA)** is the standard nonintrusive environmental investigation, limited to visual inspections and historical data research, to assess various potential environmental concerns or to ensure the environmental soundness of a property and its surroundings. When a property is to be sold, transferred, refinanced, or foreclosed, the report provided by a thorough investigation into current and past practices at the property will identify potential toxic materials or contaminants and other environmental hazards that will influence both the buyer's purchase decision and the lender's loan decision. It should be noted by the principals and the escrow officer that federal law prohibits the transfer of any real property to a new owner if known (identified) environmental hazards or hazardous materials are present.

A typical Phase I ESA includes the following tasks:

- Site reconnaissance with a review of neighboring property use

- Review of multiple historical sources, including aerial photographs, historical maps, and city directories

- Review of regulatory agency records; interview local fire, health, building, and water quality agencies

- Interviews with property representatives, including owners, occupants, past owners and tenants, neighbors, etc.

- Review surrounding area regulatory agency database reports

- Review of physical setting information, including site topography, geology, and hydrology

- Visual survey of asbestos, lead, and PCB-containing building materials and equipment

Thorough and Concise Conclusions and Recommendations   If the results of the Phase I inspection indicate that contamination may be present, a Phase II inspection is ordered (the engineer considers both the possibility of contamination and the probability of contamination). Because the Phase II inspection may require the engineer to drill into the property's surface or perform other potentially expensive actions, which will have to be repaired after the inspection, all parties should discuss the impact on the others before proceeding, including who may be responsible for incurring costs for each step of the process.

> **Pro-Tip: Phase II Environmental Inspection: Intrusive and Expensive**
>
> The Phase II engineer may need to drill into the surface of the property, possibly even in the interior. Depending upon the property characteristics, drilling may be two to four feet deep. The Cost of a Phase II can be as high as $5,000 or more.

The **Phase II inspection** obtains findings relating to the possible contamination of surface soils, subsurface soils, and groundwater. The buyer and the seller must be made aware of the intrusive nature of the Phase II inspection, which may involve drilling into the property's exterior and/or interior. The following are the various methods employed by the engineer:

- Hand auger borings and sampling (for shallow-depth sampling)
- Direct push borings and sampling (for medium-depth sampling)
- Drill rig borings and sampling (for deeper sampling)
- Limited-access drill rig
- Groundwater sampling
- Soil gas survey
- Geophysical survey

Phase III Mitigation Work   If remedial or removal work is indicated by the Phase II report, depending on the site-specific goals, regulatory requirements, and the costs required to accomplish them (which can run from $10,000 to over $100,000), corrective actions may be required.

The buyer and the seller should be aware that some lenders may not approve a loan, subject to **Phase III work**. The work involved may include the following processes:

- Vapor extraction
- Soil excavation
- Underground storage tank and pump removal
- Groundwater purging
- Groundwater monitoring

- Air strippers installation and maintenance

- Hazardous waste disposal

Lender's Insurance Requirements

Hazard insurance for apartment and commercial properties is considerably more expensive than that for one-to-four-unit residential properties. In addition to the typical coverage offered by homeowners insurance policies, the following coverages may be requested by the buyer or required by the buyer's lender:

- Loss of rents due to property damage

- Loss of rents due to reduction in percentage lease income from damage

- Loss of business income

- Glass coverage (retail stores)

- Environmental hazard insurance

- General business liability

Special form or special extended coverage may offer coverage for items usually excluded from basic policies, such as water damage

Special Concerns for Unique Properties

Certain commercial properties may require the escrow officer to have knowledge of special requirements that are unique and specific to the property type. Some are discussed in Chapter 16, "Specialty Escrow Transactions." These special commercial properties include hospitality (primarily hotels and motels), gas stations, restaurants, and dry cleaners.

Hospitality Properties   Hotels and motels are either owned and operated independently or franchised. Franchise hotels and motels are referred to as "flag" operated and considered by lenders to be a safer and more secure lending risk than non-flag properties.

Franchise Agreement   The contract involves the owner of a business "name," along with its products and services, referred to as the franchisor. The buyer, licensee or dealer, is referred to as the franchisee. The escrow officer involved in a flag transaction will often be involved in communicating, corresponding, providing, and receiving documentation to and from the franchisor, including obtaining copies of the franchise agreement for the buyer's approval (and the buyer's lender). Major considerations of the lender are the terms, conditions, restrictions, and obligations indicated under the franchise agreement. A **franchise agreement** may be so restrictive that the lender may not approve the loan. For example, franchise agreements for some franchises exist with conditions and terms that make the franchisee a de facto employee of the franchisor, even though she is the owner-operator. Such a franchise business is ineligible for a loan guaranteed by the U.S. Small Business Administration (SBA). Learning this early in the escrow, preferably even before escrow is opened, can help avoid escrow fallout, giving the buyer time to explore other lending sources or alternatives to financing.

Construction or Rehabilitation   Often a hotel or motel requires work, sometimes substantial. The work required may include construction and renovation of the real estate, as well as acquisition or replacement of personal property, including furniture and equipment. If any of the work is to be performed during the escrow, the escrow officer may be providing documentation to and from vendors, contractors, and lenders, as well as government agencies. Typically, in cases where the lender will allow escrow to close, the escrow officer will be instructed by the parties to continue the escrow for "hold-back" funds. This can also be true for other commercial properties and apartment buildings.

Gas Stations   Gas stations present even greater challenges to the parties. Just as with hospitality properties, gas stations are either independent or franchise and are subject to the same challenges in obtaining financing, especially relative to restrictive franchise agreements. Often environmental issues present time-consuming and costly inspections and possible renovation both to the aboveground improvements and the underground tanks. The time necessary to close escrow may be six months or longer.

Dry Cleaners   A major concern to both the buyer and the buyer's lender is local governmental restrictions on dry cleaners having a "plant on the premises." Zoning and environmental issues are of major importance. The escrow will include a number of additional inspections and investigation processes on the part of the buyer and the buyer's lender. Some commercial lenders will not originate loans secured by real estate with a dry cleaning plant on the premises.

Restaurants   Additional considerations in the restaurant transaction include the application process with the local health and fire departments and perhaps zoning and parking issues. While the loan process isn't complex or necessarily lengthy, the lender's underwriter rigidly follows the guidelines when ascertaining the credit risk to the bank. Restaurants have the highest failure rate of all businesses, and accordingly financial statements—especially pro formas—are evaluated closely. Escrows can easily fall out if the buyer isn't prepared in advance to resolve qualifying issues.

Prepay Penalties Levied on Seller's Loan at Payoff

Nearly all loans for commercial and apartment buildings with five or more units carry **prepay penalties**, some severe. In fact, some of the penalty programs do not allow the loan to be paid off at all for a period of time. Other penalties require the borrower to compensate the lender for the interest income revenue lost from the payoff if the current market interest rate is less than the borrower's. Another onerous program requires the borrower to substitute the yield lost to the lender with a similar yield from other vehicles. If the seller of the property has a prepay penalty it may significantly reduce the net proceeds to the seller at closing or impact the equity available for an exchange.

Common Prepay Penalty Programs   The common prepay programs include a 3-to-10-year level or declining prepay penalty, a "capped fee" with no prepay penalty after the specified term.

Level prepay   If the loan has a three-year prepay penalty and is paid off within three years and carries a 2% penalty, the borrower will be charged 2% of the unpaid loan balance. After the third year, no penalty is charged.

Declining prepay   The declining percentage varies among lenders. For example, a four-year prepay could feature a 4% penalty charged if the loan is paid off during the first year, 3% penalty the second year, 2% penalty the third year, and 1% penalty the fourth year. No penalty is charged after that.

Yield Maintenance   A lump sum payment to the lender is required to cover any loss to the lender from reinvesting the prepaid amount if the reinvestment rate (based on a U.S. Treasury note with a term equal to the remaining term of the yield maintenance) is less than the interest the lender would have received. Usually there is a minimum 1 percent penalty regardless of yield difference. The yield difference is calculated on unpaid loan balance times the difference in the yield times the number of years remaining.

The next example reflects the typical calculation used in determining the amount of penalty, if any, that would exceed the minimum required yield maintenance of a lender.

■   **EXAMPLE**   A $5,000,000 note with a 6.5% note rate and a 25-year term is being paid off after five years, having a yield maintenance for the life of the loan with a minimum penalty of 1% of the unpaid loan balance. The current U.S. treasury 20 year bond (the reinvestment rate) is 6.0%.

$5,000,000	Original loan amount
6.5%	Original note rate
25	Year term
6.0%	Current corresponding Treasury yield at payoff

$4,496,604	Unpaid balance at time of loan pay-off
.5%	Yield difference
$ 22,483	Yield maintenance per year
× 20	Years remaining
$ 449,660	Yield maintenance
44,497	Minimum penalty (unpaid balance times 1%)
$ 449,660	Total penalty ($449,660 is greater than minimum)

Upon receipt of the lender's demand, the escrow holder will identify the prepayment penalty and its amount on the closing statement.

Defeasance The borrower must provide a mix of different Treasury instruments to the lender in an amount that will yield the cash flow that the lender would have received from loan interest. Defeasance requires complex and costly structuring for which the borrower usually hires a company who specializes in the process. The note remains in effect with the real estate as original collateral replaced with Treasury notes. Often, defeasance is less costly than yield maintenance and, in fact, can be accomplished at par or even at a discount if the Treasury yields exceed the note rate.

Lockout The loan can't be paid off at all for a specified term without the borrower being required to pay the entire interest due and payable during the term of the lockout. Lockouts usually are for a limited number of years, followed by a standard "capped fee" prepay penalty for a number of years.

■ EXCHANGES

The Exchange Professionals

Exchanges, when used in a discussion about real estate, refers to **IRS Code Section 1031,** which allows for the tax-deferred disposition and acquisition of investment real estate in which any tax otherwise due on gain (profit) may be deferred to a later date. An experienced escrow officer knowledgeable in real estate exchanges is a valuable asset to real estate professionals and principals. As a key member of the exchange team, typically consisting of the principal's tax advisors or accountants, their attorneys, and the exchange **accommodator**, (a third party used to execute the exchange of property under the guidelines of Section 1031), the exchange escrow officer understands the importance of properly drawn escrow instructions with appropriate language for meeting IRS and California Franchise Tax Board guidelines for deferring taxes that may otherwise be due and payable in a real estate sale transaction. The escrow officer will work more closely with the accommodator than any other third parties, except perhaps the real estate agents. The accommodator actually accepts title to the properties, accepts monies, and disburses the monies to escrow. The primary purpose of the accommodator is to prevent title and monies being received by the principals before the escrows are able to close. The escrow holder's role in facilitating the procedures necessary and the steps essential to accomplishing the parties' objectives is paramount.

Property Types

Property is either "real" or "personal." The primary concept in exchanging investment property (property used in a trade or business; a personal residence is ineligible for a tax exchange) is that the properties must be like-kind or "like for like."

Like-Kind

To meet the tax-deferred test, personal property must be exchanged for personal property and real property must be exchanged for real property. The IRS does not actually identify specific eligible properties; however, it does offer the following as a guide: Properties are of **like-kind** if they are of the same nature or character, even if they differ in grade or quality.

Personal Property

Personal properties of a like class are like-kind properties. However, livestock of different sexes are not like-kind properties. Also, personal property used predominantly in the United States and personal property used predominantly outside the United States are not like-kind properties, meaning one cannot effect a tax-deferred exchange between personal property in the United States with personal property outside the United States.

- ■ *Ineligible properties.* Six types of property are not eligible for an exchange:

  — Stock in trade or property held primarily for sale, such as a retailer's merchandise

  — Stocks, bonds, or notes

— Evidences of indebtedness or interest

— Partnership interests

— Certificates of trust or beneficial interests

— Chose in action (a legal term meaning the title to or right to something).

Real Property

Real properties generally are of like-kind, regardless of whether the properties are improved. However, real property in the United States and real property outside the United States are not like-kind properties.

■ *Typical real property types (eligible).* The IRS does not specifically identify qualified properties, except as previously stated, that properties are considered like-kind if they are of the same nature or character, even if they differ in grade or quality. Because it has been the practice of the IRS to accept exchanges of any kind of real estate used in a trade or business (investment and rental real estate is considered among acceptable businesses), it makes no difference whether an office building, for example, is exchanged for an apartment building. They are both considered like-kind. Eligible real property many include the following:

— Apartment buildings

— Commercial properties (office, retail, industrial, etc.)

— Farms, lands, orchards, and vineyards, including unharvested crops

— Other unimproved land

Deferring Taxes

The Section 1031 exchange allows an owner of an investment property or property used in a trade or business to sell that property and reinvest the proceeds in a property of equal or greater value, without having to pay capital gains tax.

■ *Deferred, not exempt, taxes.* The seller is not exempted from paying the capital gains tax but is deferring payment until it is actually sold. Nothing prevents the property owner from exchanging any number of times subsequent to the first exchange.

■ An *eventual "sale" triggers all taxes due.* Once an actual sale occurs, the property owner will pay the combined capital gains tax due from any profit realized on both properties. Not only does the seller avoid paying capital gains tax in the year of sale, but he is able to use the equity otherwise used to pay taxes to purchase a larger property and potentially achieve a greater future gain.

Exchange Accommodator

In order to accomplish a Section 1031 exchange, an owner of investment property should use the services of a 1031 exchange accommodator. An exchange accommodator will prepare all the necessary paper work, hold the exchange funds, and guide the exchangor through the process. The exchange accommodator should be bonded, insured, and knowledgeable in the process and preferably be a corporation that is in the full-time business of offering qualified intermediary services. It is obviously helpful to the parties if the exchange accommodator is professionally qualified to give tax advice. An exchange accommodator who is a certified public accountant (CPA) or an attorney will be able to guide the principal through especially complex transactions.

The Exchange Transaction

An ideal exchange transaction would be one in which the exchanger (otherwise a seller) locates the desired property to acquire and trades "equities" with the other property owner, paying any difference. Such a transaction seldom happens, if at all. At best, an exchangor finds the property to be acquired but determines its seller isn't interested in the exchangor's property. The exchangor's property is then listed for sale by the agent, subject to a buyer's agreeing to cooperate with the exchangor processing.

Delayed Exchange: 45–180 Day Rule

Exchangors have only 45 calendar days from the close of the sale of their property (called the relinquished property) to identify the replacement property and then only 180 calendar days from the close of the sale (not an additional 180 days, but including the 45-day identification term) to acquire a replacement property. It may be difficult to find a suitable property within 45 days. Section 1031 exchanges must be completed within these strict time limits with absolutely no extensions, except for federally declared disasters. Identification of a property may be revoked in writing anytime during the 45-day term.

Reverse Exchange

If the exchangor purchases a replacement property before selling the relinquished property, a reverse Section 1031 exchange is used. The accommodator must take title to either the property being sold before the replacement property is acquired, or the accommodator must take title to the replacement property.

Identifying the Replacement Property

An exchangor may have several options in identifying the replacement property, depending on certain conditions being present.

Three-Property Rule Up to three replacement properties may be identified within the 45-day maximum identification period.

200% Fair Market Value Rule Any number of properties may be identified, as long as their aggregate fair market value does not exceed 200% of the aggregate fair market value of the property relinquished.

95% Fair Market Value Rule The exchangor acquires at least 95% of the aggregate fair market value of all the identified replacement property before the end of the 180-calendar-day period.

> ### Pro-Tip: Role of the Escrow Holder and Exchange Accommodator
> Keep funds and title away from the exchangor!
>
> The escrow holder and the accommodator work together to prevent proceeds from a sale being delivered to the exchangor.
>
> The exchangor cannot take delivery of any funds or title to any new properties until the final escrow is ready to close.
>
> All proceeds and all titles are delivered to the accommodator until ready for the final closing.
>
> Funds received by the exchangor and not reinvested at escrow closing may be subject to income taxes.

The Accommodator's Process and the Escrow Holder

Once a replacement property has been identified as the final choice, the escrow process begins. Although more than one escrow company may be involved, a smoother and more efficient escrow occurs if one escrow company handles the escrow for all properties, keeping in mind that there may be several properties and several property owners involved.

■ *Accommodator forwards deposit to escrow.* The accommodator will usually send the exchangor's funds to the escrow holder of the replacement property (the property being acquired by the exchangor) when escrow opens. In turn, the escrow company handling the escrow for the replacement property sends the escrow instructions to the accommodator, along with the preliminary title report.

■ *Exchange escrow instruction sent to escrow by accommodator.* Using the escrow instructions and preliminary title report information, the accommodator prepares an Amendment to Escrow Instructions—Exchange of Replacement Property form. These documents are returned to escrow to obtain the signatures of the exchangor and the seller (the owner of the replacement property). Escrow on the replacement property must close no later than 180 calendar days after the close of escrow of the relinquished property. If a tax return is due during the 180-calendar-day period, an extension of time to file the return must be obtained.

■ *Considerations regarding deferring taxes.* Generally speaking, to completely defer all capital gain taxes, the following apply:

— All of the net proceeds from the relinquished property must be applied to the purchase of the replacement property.

— A mortgage must be obtained on the replacement property equal to, or greater than, the mortgage on the relinquished property.

— The amount of mortgage obtained on the replacement property may be reduced by putting the equivalent amount of additional cash into the exchange.

— The escrow holder must prevent delivery of the actual or "constructive receipt" of the funds during the 1031 exchange process to the exchangor. No funds from the transaction should be received by the taxpayer until all replacement property has been acquired.

■ CHAPTER 15 QUIZ

1. The buyer of a multifamily property may request, and if obtaining a loan, the lender will require

   a. a rent roll reflecting current monthly rents and security deposits.

   b. copies of lease and rental agreements.

   c. amount of any rental delinquency.

   d. all of these.

2. The buyer's lender will require tenants to verify their current monthly rent and security deposit. This is provided on a form called

   a. Stoppel Certificate.

   b. Estoppel Certificate.

   c. Certificate of Rent.

   d. Verification of Rent (VOR).

3. The apartment lender determines the maximum loan amount based on its cash flow requirement using a factor called

   a. debt ratio (DR).

   b. debt-to-income ratio (DTIR).

   c. debt service coverage ratio (DSCR).

   d. debt servicing ration (DSR).

4. An apartment LTV may be reduced by

   a. property age, condition, or construction.

   b. capitalization rate lower than the average.

   c. unit mix.

   d. all of these.

5. In a refinance transaction for an apartment building, the lender will require the borrower to provide the IRS income tax form that indicates rental income received during the year and lists the itemized operating expense. That form is the

    a. Schedule C.

    b. Schedule E.

    c. Schedule L.

    d. Form 2106.

6. If the escrow property involves rehabilitation or renovation, the lender may allow the work to take place after escrow closing, providing the escrow holder

    a. keeps an escrow account open for hold-back funds.

    b. keeps an escrow account open for kickback funds.

    c. forwards funds to the lender in the amount of the work to be returned to the borrower after the work is completed.

    d. draws a note and trust deed for the amount of the work required.

7. Prepay penalties are common for commercial real estate loans and include

    a. declining prepay penalty.

    b. yield Maintenance.

    c. defeasance.

    d. all of these.

8. In Section 1031 exchange, the term "like for like," or "like-kind," is defined as

    a. properties of the same nature or character, even if they differ in quality.

    b. improved for improved only and unimproved for unimproved only.

    c. real properties, both within and outside the United States.

    d. if the property is real estate, any real estate whether investment or personal residence.

9. In a delayed Section 1031 exchange, the exchanger, in order to defer any capital gains tax, must comply with the "45-180" rule, which means the exchangor has 45 days from

   a. closing escrow on his property to identify the new property has and then another 180 days to close that escrow.

   b. closing escrow on his property to identify the new property and then has, including the initial 45 days, a total of 180 days to close that escrow.

   c. opening escrow on his property to identify the new property and then another 180 days to close that escrow.

   d. opening escrow on his property to identify the new property and then has, including the initial 45 days, a total of 180 days to close that escrow.

10. If the exchangor buys a replacement property before selling the property to be relinquished, the exchange is called a

    a. reverse exchange.

    b. 200% rule exchange.

    c. 95% rule exchange.

    d. relinquished exchange.

16

SPECIALTY ESCROW TRANSACTIONS

■ KEY TERMS

Alcoholic Beverage
   Control
Board of Equalization
bulk sales law
construction draw
covenant not to
   complete

Health and Safety Code
Housing and
   Community
   Development
manufactured housing
manufacturer's certificate
   of origin

mobile homes
new home sellout
off-sale license
on-sale license
sales tax clearance
UCC-1

■ LEARNING OBJECTIVES

Upon completing this chapter, you will be able to

■ understand and perform escrow functions as they relate to the bulk sales law;

■ understand and explain the sales tax clearance process, the UCC-1;

■ understand the process and escrow responsibilities under the law regarding the transfer of liquor licenses;

- understand and explain the processing involved in the transfer of title of manufactured homes, both on permanent foundations and in a "park";

- understand, perform, and explain the subdivision escrow process; and

- understand the lenders' construction loan procedures, including construction draws.

■ ESCROW SPECIALISTS

It is common to find a particular escrow officer capable of handling more than one of these special transactions, though it is not uncommon for that escrow officer to specialize in only one or two. For example, an escrow officer may have a specialty in mobile home escrows. Mobile homes may be located on fee land owned by the owner of the mobile home or located in a "park," with the mobile home owner paying rent for a "space" on which to locate it. Both have some similar yet different requirements and escrow procedures.

Other specialty transactions involve bulk sale transfers (business opportunities), the transfer of liquor licenses, and other personal property transactions, including notes and commodities. The escrow officer representing buyers and sellers in the sale of a business (which is personal property, not real property) requires an in-depth knowledge of the mechanics and laws regarding the transfer of the business assets. The sale of a business is referred to as a bulk sale transfer, which is governed by state law.

■ BULK SALE TRANSACTIONS

Bulk Sales Laws and Requirements

Bulk sales laws are designed to prevent sellers from defrauding creditors by either selling the business for less than the market price and not paying creditors in full, or not paying the creditors at all in the event an escrow is not used (bulk sale transfers in California do not require an escrow except for the transfer of a liquor license). Any sale outside the ordinary course of the seller's business of more than one-half of the seller's inventory and equipment, as measured by the fair market value on the date of the bulk sales agreement, is defined as a bulk sale subject to the requirements of state law.

The procedures involved in the bulk sale transfer include, but are not limited to, the following list. Because additional guidelines and penalties apply for non-compliance, buyers and sellers are advised to investigate fully with the State of California.

Filing and Publishing the Notice of Sale California law requires a buyer to record and publish advance notice of the sale for the protection of the seller's creditors. If the sale is "all cash" and does not exceed $2 million, the buyer or the escrow agent is authorized to impound and control the distribution of the proceeds and must apply the sale proceeds to the seller's debts before paying the seller. Notification to the Franchise Tax Board is also required.

Sales Tax Clearance Under the sales and use tax law, the state **Board of Equalization** must be notified before the sale of all or part of a business or the stock of goods of an enterprise engaged in selling tangible business personal property. The purpose of the notification is to obtain a certificate of **sales tax clearance** and a seller's permit. Any unpaid sales tax could become the liability of the buyer, whose identity must be made known to the state Board of Equalization. An escrow holder will generally not close a bulk sale escrow without notice to, and clearance from, the state Board of Equalization.

Transactions Exempt From Bulk Sales Law Several exemptions may apply, though the most common exemption relates to a sale of a business having a net worth less than $10,000 or valued value of over $5 million on the date of the bulk sale agreement.

Sales Subject to Bulk Sales Law To be subject to the law, first the seller's principal business must be the sale of inventory from stock, including a manufacturer who sells its own merchandise, or the seller is a restaurant owner, and second the business must be located in California.

Failure to Comply With Bulk Sales Law A buyer who fails to comply with the bulk sale notice requirements is liable for damages in the amount of any claims against the seller, less any amount that the claimant would not have realized if the buyer had complied with the notice requirements, subject to each validating their respective arguments. An exception applies where the buyer made a good-faith effort to comply with the requirements of the bulk sales law and therefore is not liable.

Time Limit for Claims The bulk sales law requires a claim to be valid against a buyer (or an auctioneer or liquidator) who fails to comply with notice requirements. Generally, it must be filed within one year after the date of the bulk sale.

Recording, Publishing, and Delivering the Notice of Sale   The buyer must take the following action **no less than** 12 business days before the date of the bulk sale:

- The buyer must record the notice in the office of the county recorder of the county in which the tangible assets are located or, if located in another county, the county in which the seller is located.

- The buyer must publish the bulk sale notice in a newspaper of general circulation published in the judicial district where the assets are located or, if not located in that district, in the district in which the seller is located.

- The buyer must deliver the notice or send the notice by registered or certified mail to the county tax collector in the California county in which the tangible assets are located.

Paying Creditor Claims   When the consideration for the bulk sale is $2 million or less and is either substantially all cash, an obligation of the buyer to pay cash in the future to the seller, or a combination of the two, the bulk sales law additionally requires the following:

- *Obligations of buyer.* The buyer (or an escrow agent if the transaction is handled through an escrow) has a duty to apply the consideration in accordance with the law, and this includes paying those debts of the seller for which claims are due and payable on or before the date of the bulk sale.

- *Submission of claims to sellers.* The buyer or the escrow agent should submit all creditor claims to the seller for approval. If the seller disputes whether a claim is due and payable on the noticed sale date, or disputes the amount of any claim, the buyer or the escrow agent must withhold an amount specified by statute.

- *Payment of undisputed claims.* Unless disputed by the seller, within 45 days after the close of escrow, the buyer or the escrow agent must either pay the creditors' claims to the extent of the cash consideration or institute an interpleader action with the courts.

Pro-Tip: Financing Statement for Business Assets (Personal Property)

In financing business opportunities, the UCC-1 financing statement is the instrument recorded and used with the buyer's "security agreement" to secure the business assets, which are personal, not real, property as collateral for the lender. Its use is similar to the trust deed for real property.

Financing the Business   If the purchase of the business involves financing, the lender will require the loan to be secured by collateral. In a real estate transaction, the collateral is the real property. The security instrument to "secure" the collateral in the State of California is a deed of trust. In the sale of personal property, such as the tangible assets of a business a deed of trust, cannot be used as it applies to only real property. The instrument used to secure the business assets is a security agreement coupled with a financing statement.

- The financing statement for California transfers of business property is the **UCC-1**. It may be used as the security agreement, though typically a separate security agreement is prepared. The following must exist for a security agreement to be valid and enforceable:

  — The debtor (buyer) must have rights in the collateral.

  — The secured party (seller) must give something of value (extension of credit).

  — The collateral must either be in the secured party's possession or the security agreement must be in writing.

- The UCC-1 financing statement is publicly filed with the California secretary of state and recorded with the clerk of the county in which the business is located. A financing statement must include the following:

  — The names and addresses of the debtor (buyer)

  — The debtor's signature (not necessary if the filing is authorized in the Security Agreement)

  — The name and address of the secured party (seller), from which further information about the security interest can be obtained

  — A description of the collateral

Escrow Holder Responsibilities   The escrow holder performs many of the same duties as required in a real estate transaction, such as handling and holding documents and monies and facilitating the delivery of the buyer's casualty insurance per the lender's instructions. Note: Business property is covered by casualty insurance, whereas real property is covered by hazard insurance. The escrow holder may also be asked to prepare additional documents or instructions, such as preparing a note in favor of the seller if the seller is going to carry the financing.

Covenant Not to Compete   An additional escrow instruction may be an agreement between the buyer and the seller that the seller will not compete against the buyer by reopening his business at another location within a specified distance, or by opening a new but similar business if the buyer's purchase of the property included buying the business' "name." This agreement is called a **covenant not to compete**. The buyer and the seller should have the actual agreement drawn by an attorney or obtain a standard form from an office supply store for the parties to complete. The escrow officer should not prepare the agreement.

Inventory   If the business sale will include the buyer's purchase of the seller's inventory of merchandise, the escrow officer will be asked to prepare an instruction spelling out its terms as agreed to between the buyer and seller and reflected in the purchase agreement. The terms may include the following:

- The maximum dollar amount of inventory to be paid by the buyer at the time of closing.

- Specific inventory items to be excluded from the sale.

- The date on which the inventory is to be performed (no earlier than the day before the buyer takes possession of the property).

- The disposition of "shop-worn" inventory.

- The basis for determining the cost to the buyer, such as the seller's actual wholesale cost as evidenced by invoice, the wholesaler's catalog (paper or electronic), or by some arbitrary yet reasonably established discount from the retail price as indicated on or for each stock keeping unit. (All businesses have an average "gross markup" or "gross mark-on" for all products or for the type of business, which could be the basis for arriving at the wholesale cost to the buyer.)

- Method of performing inventory, such as personally performed by both the buyer and the seller or by a professional inventory company that provides such services. If such a third party will be used, the fee for its services must be negotiated between the buyer and seller.

■ LIQUOR LICENSE TRANSFER

State Regulatory Agencies

The transfer of a liquor license requires an escrow and is regulated by the California Department of **Alcoholic Beverage Control** (ABC). The escrow officer must not only be well versed in the state's requirements relative to the buyer and seller's obligations but, except for title-insurer-owned escrow holders, also must be licensed and incorporated by the Department of Corporations as an escrow holder. Liquor license laws in California, including their issuance, are rigidly enforced. There are essentially two categories of licenses: new and previously issued.

Liquor Licenses: On-Sale and Off-Sale   Licenses are divided into two groups: **on-sale licenses**, where the alcohol will be consumed on the premises (such as a bar and grill, night club, or similar establishment) and **off-sale licenses**, in which the alcohol will be purchased but not consumed on the premises (such as a liquor store). Technically, there are a number of different licenses, though only 11 are commonly issued. There are only two off-sale licenses (beer and wine and a general license that includes beer, wine, and spirits). New licenses are difficult to obtain under California's guidelines.

- *New liquor licenses.* A new liquor license may be issued by the State of California only under certain conditions. New licenses are not always available.

- *Existing licenses.* Typically an existing license accompanying the sale of the liquor store or other retailer is the type involved in the escrow transaction.

Escrow Holder Responsibilities

If there is any purchase price or consideration in connection with the transfer of a business operated under a retail license, an escrow must be established with an escrow holder that is not a party to the transfer and before filing the transfer with the ABC. The full amount of the purchase price or consideration must be placed in escrow. Escrow agreements must provide for payment only after the transfer of the license is approved by the ABC. The applicant, within 30 days of application, must furnish the ABC a statement, under penalty of perjury, that the purchase price or consideration has been deposited with the escrow holder. The applicant must also submit a copy to the seller and a copy to the escrow holder.

A misrepresentation may be grounds for denial of the license or subsequent revocation of the license, if issued. Consideration includes cash, checks, promissory notes, or other items of value that have been agreed to be paid to the transferor for the license, inventory, fixtures, leasehold interest, realty, goodwill, covenant not to compete, or other property connected with the licensed business. Among the issues and responsibilities with which the escrow holder will be involved are the following:

- *Release of funds.* The escrow officer may not release any funds to the seller until the ABC has approved the transfer.

- *Monies and taxes owed to the State of California by the buyer.* If the buyer owes monies to the state for sales taxes (the State Board of Equalization is the tax agency responsible for the collection of sales taxes), employment taxes (the Employment Development Department is responsible for collecting and enforcing employment taxes to be paid by the employer), and personal income taxes (the Franchise Tax Board is the responsible agency), the ABC may not approve the sale until they are paid. The escrow officer must obtain a written release from the State Board of Equalization prior to allowing escrow to close.

■ *Processing time*. ABC is required to mail a copy of each application to certain local officials. Additionally a 30-day posting period is required before the transfer may occur. According to the Department of Alcoholic Beverage Control, "most investigations take 45 to 50 days. The license (approval) can average about 75 days for a Person-to-Person transfer and 90 days for an Original. Circumstances often result in a longer waiting period; therefore, before final approval and issuance of a license, caution should be used regarding extensive financial commitments, plans for grand openings, etc."

■ MANUFACTURED HOUSING AND MOBILE HOMES

Manufactured housing or **mobile homes** that have been registered with the Department of Motor Vehicles for at least one year and are greater than 8 feet wide and 40 feet long may be sold by real estate agents licensed by the California Department of Real Estate. Any manufactured or mobile home that does not meet the requirements may only be sold by a manufactured housing or mobile home dealer. The mobile home may be placed in a mobile home park that rents a space to the homeowner, or it may be located on fee land owned by the homeowner. If located in a park, the mobile home offers a safe and secure environment. Certain areas in the state are a natural for a mobile home, such as the beaches, mountains, and deserts, both for homeowners wanting a reasonably priced home on their own lot and for people who enjoy the "community" and security afforded by the mobile home park.

Escrow considerations are unique for mobile homes, and not all escrow officers are familiar with the process. Those officers with the knowledge and skills required to successfully handle a mobile home escrow usually have a sizable "following" in their market. An escrow officer who has acquired the California Escrow Association professional designation of Mobile Home Specialist (MHS) is well qualified to represent buyers and sellers of mobile homes. It should be noted that technically the term *mobile home* has been replaced by *manufactured housing*, but the term is still frequently used in the industry and the market.

California Law Regarding Escrow for Mobile Homes

The Mobile Homes-Manufactured Housing Act of 1980, **Health and Safety Code** (HSC) Sections 18000 et seq. is the authority and law governing the sale and transfer of mobile homes in California and is enforced by the California Department of **Housing and Community Development** (HCD).

Basic Escrow Requirement Under the Law   Section 18035(a) of the HSC requires that most mobile home transfer transactions be handled through an escrow:

> For every transaction by or through a dealer ... of a new or used manufactured home or mobile home subject to registration under this part, the dealer shall execute in writing and obtain the buyer's signature on a purchase order, conditional sale contract, or other document evidencing the purchase ..., shall establish an escrow account with an escrow agent, and shall cause to be deposited into that escrow account any cash or cash equivalent received at any time prior to the close of escrow. . . . The parties shall provide for escrow instructions that identify the fixed amounts of the deposit, down payment, and balance due prior to closing consistent with the amounts set forth in the purchase documents and receipt for deposit. . . . If an item of cash equivalent is, due to its size, incapable of physical delivery to the escrow holder the property may be held by the deliver and if available its certificate of title shall be delivered to the escrow holder.

According to Information Bulletin 2001-06 (MH, OL, MP, RT) from the Department of Housing and Community Development, dated July 16, 2001, the following are critical elements of the law's escrow provisions.

Escrow Opening Requirement and Placement of Funds – HSC § 18035(a) requires that an escrow account be opened for dealer sales and leases of new or used manufactured homes subject to registration by HCD. Additionally, HSC § 18035 requires that payments received from the buyer shall be deposited into the escrow account within five (5) working days (meaning all days except Saturdays, Sundays, and state and federal holidays) of receipt, one of which shall be the date of receipt. Checks, money orders, or any other similar type of payment must be made payable to the escrow company. Under no circumstances may such funds be retained outside of escrow, even if they are deposited in a commercial bank account or other secured account. These requirements apply to manufactured homes installed pursuant to HSC § 18613 and § 18551(b), which are subject to HCD registration. Manufactured homes installed on a foundation system pursuant to HSC § 18551(a) as an improvement to real property are subject to the escrow requirements of HSC § 18035.2.

Placement of the Manufacturer's Certificate of Origin (MCO) into Escrow – HSC § 18035(b) requires that the escrow instructions provide for the placement of the original MCO into escrow on or before the close of escrow on all new manufactured home sales that are subject to registration with HCD. HSC

§ 18035.2(b)(1) requires the same on all new manufactured homes that will become a fixture of the underlying real estate.

Current Registration Card(s) and All Copies of the Registration Cards into Escrow – HSC § 18035(c)(1) requires that the escrow instructions provide that the certificate of title and the current registration card and all copies be placed into escrow on all sales of used manufactured homes.

Replacement Label/Insignia Requirement – Although there is no escrow provision requiring that a federal label or a California insignia be affixed on the manufactured home at the close of escrow, HSC § 18026 requires that all new and used manufactured homes and mobile homes that were manufactured on or after September 1, 1958, bear either a federal label or a California insignia when offered for sale, rent, or lease in California.

When needed, replacement insignia can be obtained from HCD prior to offering the manufactured home for sale, rent, or lease. This includes replacement insignia for manufactured homes constructed on and after June 15, 1976, in which the Department issued the original federal label in our capacity as the primary inspection agency.

Withdrawal of Escrow Funds – HSC §18035(e)(1) requires that the escrow instructions shall provide that funds shall be disbursed from a manufactured home escrow account only upon delivery and, in some circumstances installation, of the home. There are exceptions for early payment of governmental fees and permits required as a precondition for an installation acceptance or a Certificate of Occupancy. Pursuant to § 5062(d) of the regulations, funds withheld for accessories may only be withdrawn on or after the close of escrow upon receipt of written notice from the dealer that the accessory actually has been installed or received by the purchaser in the event that installation is not required under the terms of the purchase document.

Failure To Disclose Resale Commission – HSC § 18035(c)(2)(A)(i) requires that the escrow instructions provide for the placement into escrow of a written statement from the registered owner acknowledging the amount of the commission to be received by the dealer in the resale of the manufactured home, pursuant to a listing agreement. Violations of the escrow provisions by escrow companies may subject them to discipline by the California Department of Corporations. Violations of the manufactured housing law and regulations may subject an HCD licensee to discipline such as citation with monetary fine or suspension or revocation of the HCD license. In addition, HCD may request that the local District Attorney or the State Attorney General pursue a violation as a misdemeanor conviction pursuant to HSC §18020.5. Law enforcement agencies may also prosecute felony violations such as embezzlement or fraud, or unfair business practices under the California Business and Professions Code.

Mobile Homes Not on a Permanent Foundation   Mobile or manufactured homes are often located in a mobile home park. These facilities may offer the homeowner a safe and secure environment with many of the same amenities found in condominium or apartment complexes, such as swimming pools and other recreational facilities. The buyer of the mobile home will rent the space on which the home is placed. The State of California has laws and regulations required of the park owner regarding rental policies, including the approval process of a new rental applicant who is in the process of buying a home in the park.

- A mobile home not placed on a permanent foundation is considered personal property. The transfer of its title does not include recording with the county recorder office. A bill of sale may be used to transfer interest, with the certificate of title and registration card along with a security agreement and UCC-1 if financing is involved (as in a bulk sale escrow) and filed with the secretary of state of California.

- Escrow closing takes place when all the buyer's monies are deposited into escrow, any financing for the buyer has funded and forwarded to escrow (there is no title policy; therefore, escrow receives the funds instead of a title company), and all documents have been signed by the parties.

- If financing is involved, because the home is considered personal property, at closing there is no deed of trust to record but rather the security agreement, UCC-1, and promissory note executed and delivered to the beneficiary by registered mail. A copy is not required to be delivered to HCD.

Manufactured Homes on a Permanent Foundation   The escrow process for a manufactured home that rests on a permanent foundation and that together are being sold is handled the same as a conventionally constructed home ("stick" construction), with escrow and title processed as usual. Once placed permanently on a foundation, the manufactured home becomes real property.

- Transfer of title will be recorded with the county recorder's office, and the buyer will obtain a title policy from the title insurer.

- If the mobile home is being placed on a permanent foundation for the first time as a result of the sale, the county generates an HCD form 433 for the permits after the unit, if new, has been inspected. The county (not escrow) records the form. Escrow receives a copy after recordation and forwards it to HCD at closing, which completes the conversion from personal to real property.

■ Escrow closes after the buyer's funds have been deposited into escrow; the buyer's loan, if any, has funded and been delivered to the title company; all documents, as appropriate, have been signed by the parties; and those to be recorded have been recorded with the county recorder's office. For more information, visit the Department of Housing and Community Development website at www.hcd.ca.gov.

■ SUBDIVISION ESCROW

Subdivision escrow is a unique specialty for the escrow professional. It is not uncommon for an escrow officer who handles subdivisions to do nothing else. A developer of a new housing tract establishes a relationship with the escrow holder in the very beginning of construction, even before touching the land, with interaction involving plans, permits and government agencies. The escrow officer develops an intimate understanding of the project early in the process and, when it's time to begin the "sellout," is well prepared to do the job. The builder-developer goes through the process (described in Chapter 14), complying with the provisions of the Subdivided Map Act or Subdivided Lands Act, usually with a public report submitted to the commissioner of the Department of Real Estate. A number of considerations and requirements unique to land development and subdivision must be addressed.

Developer's Financing

The developer may obtain financing for both the acquisition of the land and for the construction. The lender provides **construction draws**. This begins with an initial draw (the advance of monies to the developer), usually through the title and escrow companies, to fund the purchase of the property. Then the lender provides additional draws as each phase of the construction is completed and inspected. This process can be time-consuming, especially for larger projects, and it depends on the availability of inspectors from the city or county building departments to inspect and "sign off" on the completed portion.

Title Insurance Company Inspection

The title company inspects the land before construction begins to ascertain that no work has commenced for which it might be liable for paying a possible mechanic's lien that predated the issuance of the title policy.

Title Company Ancillary Services   The title policy and ancillary services provided by the title company may include the following:

- Land acquisition title processing

- Mapping with qualified assistance

- Full engineering department expertise

- Development and construction loan title services

- Expert DRE processing

- Sale-out title processing

- Full local escrow services

Escrow Holder's Services During Construction

The escrow holder may be used for taking reservations on a subdivision project. Properties may not be sold until the final report (White Paper) has been issued, so the developer will offer the properties to be reserved by interested buyers. When the project is developed to the extent that homes may be sold, escrow may proceed as normal.

Post-Construction Escrow Process

When the infrastructure has been completed (streets, curbs, gutters, street lighting, sewers, and utilities provided to each lot), lots graded, and home construction commenced, the lender requires a payment of a portion of the principal before reconveying the lien against the individual lots being sold. Otherwise, a homebuyer would be unable to secure financing for the new home. The escrow holder becomes involved in this process. At the end of construction and prior to the title company issuing a title policy, a notice of completion is required.

New Home Sellout

As the builder begins to sell the new homes, called the **new home sellout**, the escrow holder provides two services for the builder. First, the escrow holder will provide the necessary documentation to the construction lender as each home is sold to facilitate the reconveyance of the lien against the lot being purchased, called a partial reconveyance, which would be accomplished either in advance of or concurrently with the closing of the homebuyer's property. Additionally, the escrow holder may also handle the escrow for the homebuyer. Although state law prohibits the developer from requiring the prospective buyer from using a specific escrow company, most homebuyers have no objections and recognize the efficiency of doing so. Additionally, due to economies of scale, the escrow holder may be able to offer a preferred escrow fee for the buyer.

■ CHAPTER 16 QUIZ

1. Bulk sales laws are designed to prevent

    a. sellers from defrauding their buyers.

    b. sellers from defrauding the State of California.

    c. sellers from defrauding their creditors.

    d. creditors from defrauding their debtors.

2. Bulk sales laws require that an escrow be opened

    a. for all sales involving personal property.

    b. for all sales involving a business in which real estate is not a part.

    c. for all sales involving a liquor license.

    d. only voluntarily.

3. The purpose of notifying the state Board of Equalization of the bulk sale is to

    a. obtain a certificate of sales tax clearance and a seller's permit.

    b. impound and control the distribution of proceeds.

    c. both a and b.

    d. neither a nor b.

4. If a buyer fails to comply with the bulk sale notice requirements, the buyer is

    a. liable for damages in the amount of any claims against the seller.

    b. liable for double damages in the amount of any claims against the seller.

    c. not liable for damages against the seller.

    d. not liable if a good-faith effort was made to comply.

5. The bulk sales law requires that for any claim to be valid, it must be filed within

    a. one year of the date of the sale.

    b. two years of the date of the sale.

    c. 180 days of the date of the sale.

    d. 45 days of the date of the sale.

6. The document to be recorded as constructive notice for the security instrument for personal property involved in a bulk sales transaction is the

    a. deed of trust.

    b. financial statement.

    c. California UCC-1.

    d. security statement.

7. An agreement that the seller of a business will not compete against the buyer by reopening his business at another location within a specified distance, or by opening a new but similar business if the buyer's purchase of the property included buying the business's "name," is called the

    a. condition not to compete.

    b. restriction not to compete.

    c. covenant not to compete.

    d. declaration not to compete.

8. The two basic categories of liquor licenses are

    a. off-sale and on-sale.

    b. new and previously issued.

    c. "beer and wine" and "general."

    d. all of these.

9. The two basic groups of liquor licenses are

    a. on-sale and off-sale.

    b. new and previously issued.

    c. "beer and wine" and "general."

    d. all of these.

10. If the buyer of a liquor license is liable for taxes to the Franchise Tax Board, the Board of Equalization, or the Employment Development Department, the escrow holder must

    a. obtain a written release from the department to whom the taxes are due prior to allowing escrow to close.

    b. hold back the amount of the taxes due at the close of escrow.

    c. withhold the monies due from the buyer's funds and forward to the appropriate agency.

    d. obtain a written release from the Department of Alcoholic Beverage Control before allowing escrow to close.

ADVANCED TITLE INSURANCE UNDERWRITING

■ KEY TERMS

appurtenant	latitude	principal meridian
base line	license	profit á prendre
CC&Rs	longitude	range
condemnation	metes and bounds	rectangular survey
dominant estate	natural rights	system
easements in gross	negative easements	servient estate
implied easements	point of beginning	true easements
judicial survey		

■ LEARNING OBJECTIVES

Upon completing this chapter, you will be able to

- understand the different types of easements, the methods by which they may be established, and the difference between true easements, implied easements, and other rights that only appear to be easements;

■ understand the necessity of not only searching public records but also inspecting the property and making inquiries of the occupants;

■ understand basic land survey methods and coordinates;

■ understand the concept of principal meridians and base lines; and

■ understand and demonstrate the ability to write a land description using townships and sections, and metes and bounds.

■ EASEMENTS

The presence of easements in the title search and policy considerations may require the services of a title officer with a greater degree of technical knowledge and experience necessary to determine the effect of insurability of title. Many title and other real estate industry professionals do not have a comprehensive understanding of the concepts of easements, especially those that are complex. Some easements may be insurable, while others may not. To clearly understand and describe easements requires the title professional to be familiar with a number of terms that will be discussed in this chapter.

True Easements

Many easements as described are actually not easements at all because they do not possess all the necessary characteristics required of **true easements**. The fundamental characteristic of a true easement is that it benefits another particular piece of land, called the **dominant estate**. The land that is encumbered by the easement, that which gives up a right for the benefit of the dominant estate, is called the **servient estate**.

> ### Pro-Tip: Explaining Easements
> Servient estate "SERVES" the interest of the dominant estate, which "DOMINATES" the servient estate's use of the easement.

The most common true easements may be easily recognizable and include roadways or other conduits allowing for ingress and egress to a property. However other interests in land exist that are also considered true easements, some of which may not be so easily identifiable. These include sewers, water and drain pipes, and utility lines, both for overhead and underground transmission. An easement may be granted to accommodate the flow of water from or across the servient estate, such a river or stream. It may be given to allow livestock to graze on the servient estate. It may also include rights that may seem inherent in basic ownership rights but must actually be explicitly granted, such as unrestricted light and air from it. Additionally, such easements may include the right to use and enjoy both real and personal property that is attached to or located on the servient property of another. An example of this is the right to use a parking structure or space within it belonging to the owner of the servient estate. It is important to remember that a true easement does not include the arbitrary right of the owner of the servient estate to allow or disallow the use of the easement by the dominant estate. Any true easement always includes a "servitude" upon the servient estate for the use and benefit of the dominant estate. The two go hand in hand in that both servient and dominant estates must exist. Also, it is not necessary for the two estates to be connected to each other, meaning they do not need to be contiguous (adjoining). Such an estate is called an easement **appurtenant**.

Pro-Tip: What Appurtenant Means

Appurtenant means simply something that belongs to something else or someone else, accompanies it, is attached to it, or is annexed to it.

Easements in themselves do not constitute an estate in the land or title to it. They are, however, an "interest" in the land and can be transferred to or inherited by another. Even though a grant deed may make no mention of these easements, they are usually automatically transferred along with fee title. As with most interests in land, they are subject to being lost through adverse possession by another or prescription. The owner of the servient estate cannot sell them separately, and they are assumed by any purchaser of the dominant estate.

The title officer must be aware of the fact that these easements, as long as they are true easements, along with title to the dominant estate are typically insurable.

Pro-Tip: Interest in Land

"Interest" in land or estate does not necessarily mean "Title to" it.

The title officer during the examination process of a transaction involving the servient estate must also search and examine the dominant estate to determine that the easement is actually a true easement.

True easements must be in writing, meaning they are not created by an oral agreement. The true easement is customarily, but not always, created by a deed or a grant. It is little wonder that they are created by the owner of the servient estate.

It is that owner who will be "served" by the easement, enjoying and benefiting from it. In addition to being established by deed, it is possible for an easement to be created by other means as well. Described more fully later, these other means include the following:

- *Implied.* Due to the characteristics of a parcel of land and the use by the owner of it, an easement by implication could be established upon the division of the land and reselling one of the divided parcels.

- *Necessity.* As easement may be established due to the obvious necessity of it, such as a land-locked parcel requiring ingress and egress (however such an easement may not always be automatically granted from and by a particular parcel).

- *Prescription.* The open and notorious use of the servient estate by the owner of a dominant estate may also establish an easement, called an easement by prescription.

- *Estoppel.* Easements may be established by estoppel, explicitly granted by an act or statement of the owner of the servient estate.

- *Condemnation.* A public agency may exercise its right of **condemnation** to acquire an easement just as it may use condemnation to acquire fee title to land. An easement created through condemnation differs in that courts have held that they are true easements and enjoy the same characteristics as **easements in gross** (easements that are not appurtenant and convey the right to use the land of another for some particular use and not necessarily for an adjoining land)

These easements, except for condemnation, are usually considered true easements in that there is a presumption that the owner of the servient land granted the easement in the first place because of the nature of the dominant estate's use of that which constitutes an easement and, therefore, such a grant should be made officially evident. In fact, the actual dimensions of the easement need not be specified to allow the owner of the dominant estate to enjoy and use what would be considered a reasonable amount of land necessary for the purpose of the easement.

Implied Easements

A future or potential easement is called a quasi-easement. This easement is the part that is benefited and that would otherwise be the dominant estate if it were located on another parcel of land and is called the quasi-dominant tenement. The part of the owner's land that serves the quasi-dominant tenement is called, quite understandably, the quasi-servient tenement.

■ **EXAMPLE**   A retail shopping center consists of two separate buildings, each with 10 stores. The buildings are located on one parcel of land, which has a parking lot accessed by a single entrance-exit driveway from the roadway. Vehicle traffic travels across the land on which one building rests to reach the other building's parking area, and returns to exit. The two buildings would be considered to be located on portions of the property that would constitute the quasi-servient and quasi-dominant tenements, respectively.

If and when the owner of the shopping center were to divide the land into two parcels, each with one of the two buildings, the quasi-dominant easement would then become a true easement benefiting and transforming the quasi-dominant easement into a dominant estate.

Remember that the quasi-servient and quasi-dominant tenements are merely the terms that refer to the possible or potential easement that could be established in the future. They, as true easements, do not really exist unless and until the land is divided. Upon such division and sale to another person of the portion that has been inherently the quasi-dominant tenement, a dominant estate in the acquired parcel now exists. Therefore, a true easement has been established by the implication of such an easement that has previously existed due to the nature, characteristics, and use of the property by the original owner. The legal concept is that all rights under the control of the original owner that are obviously necessary to use and enjoy the land are also necessary for the use and enjoyment of the buyer and therefore are conveyed upon its sale. The title officer must interpret the facts of such transactions to determine the validity of these types of easements. An underlying rule is that the use of the easement must be continuous and not require any act of man to perpetuate its use. Most important, if the grantor is required to perform any act in order for the grantee to enjoy the same benefit of the easement as enjoyed with the quasi-dominant tenement, an **implied easement** does not exist and cannot be established as such.

Easements by Prescription

The open and notorious use of another's land with the knowledge of the servient estate landowner, and the landowner's passive failure to stop such use, may establish an easement by prescription. Such use must also be adverse, exclusive, uninterrupted, and continuous for the period of time necessary to establish the right by prescription (five years under California Civil Code Section 1008). Easements by prescription are based on the presumption that a grant of an easement exists on land where the exclusive right to its use has been essentially given up by the owner of the servient estate; it is also presumed that the owner must not have been under any duress or disability for the prescriptive right of the dominant estate to develop completely. Any acknowledgment by the dominant estate's owner of the fee title and rights of the servient estate's owner's prevents the use from being adverse and therefore does not establish an easement by prescription. Also, mere possession or use alone is not adequate to constitute adverse possession. In addition to the use for a minimum of five years, it must be for the exclusive benefit of the dominant estate alone and not in common with any other. Because these easements may not appear on public record, they must be confirmed by the title officer by visually inspecting the land or by some verifiable proof from the owner of the dominant estate as the claimant of the easement. If the inspection reveals that such an easement has most probably been acquired, a release from the owner of the dominant estate should be obtained by the title officer or it should be "excepted" in the policy (meaning not covered in the event of any challenge or claim by another).

Easements by Way of Necessity

The law of "way of necessity" is based on the basic law of easements. The title officer's primary objective is to recognize its existence, locate it, and provide for an exception to coverage in any title policy issued on the servient estate, or through which the easement passes. Essentially, where a parcel of land is granted by its owner to another and it is surrounded by other lands sill belonging to that property owner as the grantor, the grantee as the owner of the dominant estate has a right of way by necessity across the grantor's land for ingress and egress. Because the easement is not specified in writing and, therefore, does not indicate its dimensions, the right of way is allowed to be of an appropriate and adequate size to accommodate passing across the servient estate by the owner of the dominant estate. It does not include this owner's right to use and enjoy any other portion of the servient estate. Conversely, the owner of the servient estate who retains land surrounding the easement conveyed to the dominant estate has an implied right of way to use the easement, otherwise that owner's land would be landlocked. The title officer must recognize circumstances that would prevent such crossing and include a resolution in the policy.

In issuing title policies for the sale of raw lands, the title officer may come across a transaction involving lands located on or near interstate highways. Federal highway programs, as well as some state, county, and city programs, provide for limited-access highways, such as the interstate highway system. In existence since 1894, the Bureau of Public Roads was transferred in 1966 from the Department of Commerce to the Department of Transportation and its role and functions assigned to the Federal Highway Administration. In its administration of the Federal Aid Highway Act of 1956, Congress gave the Federal Highway Administration the authority, and equally important, the funding to proceed in developing the National Interstate and Defense Highway program. It also provided additional funding for the construction of secondary connecting roads. The original National

Interstate Highway Program involved the acquisition of approximately 800,000 separate parcels of land.

The rights of owners of both servient and dominant estates involved in transactions concerning land near interstate highways should be spelled out in the deed conveying interest, with the title policy clearly specifying such terms. Therefore, when issuing policies for land located near an interstate, the title officer should examine and investigate the possibility of the insured property being subject to rights-of-way based on the doctrine of easement by necessity from other properties that have had access for ingress and egress restricted or eliminated.

Easements by Condemnation

One element missing in an easement by condemnation is the lack of a dominant estate. Created under the power of eminent domain in favor of public agencies or common carriers such as rail service, these easements, while recognized and insurable, do not conform to the definition of the typical true easement because it is established for the benefit of a particular and specific use and not for any particular dominant estate. Confusing? Perhaps, especially because there is, in fact, generally no dominant estate. These are actually considered to be a form of an easement in gross, discussed next, but are somewhat of an exception to a traditional easement in gross.

Easements in Gross

The fundamental difference between an easement appurtenant and an easement in gross is that the easement appurtenant is attached to a dominant estate, whereas the easement in gross is not attached to anything specific based on ownership in a piece of land that would otherwise constitute a dominant estate. It is instead the personal right of an individual or entity to use the servient estate land of another for some particular and specified use. It is not assignable, transferable, or inheritable and expires upon the death of the holder. It is not, therefore, an interest or right capable of being insured. Even valid easements for a road right-of-way for ingress and egress over a specified parcel of land are not always an insurable easement.

■ **EXAMPLE**   A homeowner whose property is located in a remote location requires traveling along several roadways, avoiding certain properties over which travel is prohibited by the landowner to reach his daily place of employment. In his path and blocking continued travel to the closest public road is a cattle ranch. The homeowner contracts with the cattle rancher to allow him to travel across the ranch to the public road and then to his property, creating a written agreement for an easement for ingress and egress and executing the contract with paid consideration. Sometime later, the homeowner decides to sell an interest in this easement to a neighbor with a similar problem. In attempting to obtain title insurance coverage for easement, he discovers it cannot be insured. The problem rests with the fact that it is not appurtenant to the estate, being only a personal right, and under the law is not saleable, assignable, transferable, or inheritable. There was no interest in the land that was insurable. Additionally, the easement provided a benefit only to him and was not for the public good. However, had there been a public good attached to the easement, it could have conveyed and insured.

Easements in gross are not limited to roadways and may cover a vast range of rights relating to the servient land. (An exception to this rule is the easement in gross created by the power of condemnation through the doctrine of eminent domain). To makes rules about easements a bit more complex and difficult for the title officer to immediately determine insurability, some easements—such as those for water, oil, and gas pipelines, electric transmission lines, telephone lines and towers, and railroad rights-of-way—although all are easements in gross, are transferable even though no dominant estate exists. The fundamental principle is that the holders of these easements should have the right to sell, assign or otherwise transfer them for the benefit of public good for the services they provide. As such, they do present an exception and may be insured. The difference between these examples and that of the landlocked property is that of public good. In that case, the easement benefited only the person who had the easement and was not for the good of the public.

■ OTHER RIGHTS AND PRIVILEGES

There may exist other agreements, both expressed in writing and implied, which deserve consideration as to insurability. Not all such rights, as discussed, are insurable. Uninsurable rights are discussed in this section.

Profit á Prendre

A true easement prohibits a right to the profits or proceeds from the servient estate land, called **profit á prendre**, which is the right of a person to remove part of the earth on land belonging to another, or something growing in or on it. However, it may explicitly include the right to harvest and keep crops on the land, but such an agreement is typically covered by an agreement called a **license**.

License

A license is written permission for a personal and revocable right. However, it does not convey any legal interest in the estate. It grants only a right to enter someone's land when it would be otherwise unlawful to do so. A license, unlike an easement, is a personal, revocable, unassignable, and uninheritable permission that expires with the death of the holder. A license can even be created by an oral agreement between the parties. Recognizing the elements of a true easement and comparing those with the rights under a license, the title officer understands that a license cannot be insured.

Natural Rights

Natural rights are inherent in and incidental to the right of ownership. They include the right to benefit from the path of a natural water course, the right to discharge surface water onto another's land that lies unobstructed in its path, and to have one's land supported by adjacent land. It also includes the right to have the air in the immediate vicinity of one's land reasonably free from annoying odors, noises, and contaminants. These rights are a matter of law and are defined as natural rights. A property owner may be concerned with these issues, but they are not a concern of the title officer, nor do they affect the title insurance examination process or title policy coverage.

Negative Easements

A **negative easement** is one that prohibits or prevents the owner of land subject to the easement from doing that which, if no easement existed, he would otherwise be entitled to do. For example, the restrictive conditions placed on the height of dwellings in a housing subdivision are meant to prevent blocking the view of neighboring properties. Such easements are also called reciprocal negative easements, as each dwelling in the subdivision receives the same benefit as all the others.

Covenants, Conditions, and Restrictions (CC&Rs)

CC&Rs are private rights established by prior owners of the land that impose limitations on the use and occupancy of it, including any improvements on it. CC&Rs are always important to the buyer of a common interest development property (CID), as well as the builder or developer of vacant land.

Title Officer's Conclusion

Although the title officer may mentally question whether rights or privileges granted to a purchaser constitute easements in gross, licenses, profits á prendre, or any other type of easements, they are all rights or privileges, interests, or estates that must be searched from public records. If record searches are insufficient to provide the necessary information for the title officer to arrive at a conclusion, an inspection of the property may be necessary, a survey of the premises may be warranted, or both. The title officer will provide the appropriate exceptions in the policy based on the findings of all research.

Of course, the title officer must keep in mind that easements are not confined to the surface. Other matters below, above, and surrounding the property may include easements that must be researched. The subsurface (minerals, water, gas, and other elements), light to the property, the view from the property or impacted by the property, the air above and surrounding the property (aircraft and airport flight paths, smoke to and from the property), and structures on the property all may require research and a conclusion as to the existence of easements regarding the impact they may have on insurability.

■ COMPLEX LAND DESCRIPTIONS

The title professional's career may include working closely with engineers and surveyors in those transactions that require identifying complex legal descriptions of land. It is helpful for the title officer to have acquired a fundamental knowledge of the characteristics of the earth and the means and methods by which parcels of land may be accurately measured and described.

Every parcel of land sold, leased, or financed must be properly identified or described. According to the California Department of Real Estate, a good description is said to be one describing no other piece of property but the one involved in the transaction. The senior title officer, therefore, must have the knowledge and skills necessary to research, identify, and satisfactorily describe more complex land and legal descriptions beyond the typical lot, tract, and map descriptions. Such complex and detailed descriptions include identifying the property using township and section and metes and bounds.

An elementary understanding of the characteristics of the earth includes a thorough working knowledge of latitude and longitude and the coordinates they establish. In that regard, it is important to understand the essential elements of the U.S. rectangular survey system, which guides every survey in some way. Understanding the role of principal meridians, base lines, and range lines in creating and identifying townships is critical in the daily performance of the title professional's duties. Title professionals will be able to apply in practice much of what they learn in the classroom regarding townships and sections, especially because the actual size of townships and sections may differ from the theoretical dimensions.

The Earth

Learning the fundamentals of surveying begins with learning the fundamentals about the earth itself. The most common way to locate points on the surface of the earth is by standard reference points in the form of geographic coordinates. The escrow or title professional who has served in the military, or was a Boy Scout, understands the concept and use of coordinates. The earth is divided into uniform measurements extending both horizontally and vertically; these are called **latitude** (horizontal) and **longitude** (vertical). They serve as the basis for establishing land descriptions. The units of measure are called degrees (shown as °). Calculated from the center of the earth, degrees are then divided into minutes and finally into seconds. It is appropriate that the terminology is the same as keeping track of time. As we learned in kindergarten, the earth revolves around the sun once each 24 hours, with each hour consisting of 60 minutes and each minute consisting of 60 seconds. In identifying the coordinates of the earth, there are 60 minutes (shown as ') in each degree, and 60 seconds (shown as ") in each minute.

Written Coordinates

A coordinate may be written as 65° 32' 15"—verbalized as 65 degrees, 32 minutes, and 15 seconds. It may also be written as decimals: 65.5375—verbalized as 65 "point" 5375 degrees. It could be written as a combination of both degrees and decimal minutes: 65° 32.25'—verbalized as 65 degrees and 32 "point" 25 minutes. Or it may be written as a combination of them all (degrees, minutes, and decimal seconds): 65° 32' 15.275"—verbalized as 65 degrees, 32 minutes, and 15 "point" 275 seconds. Any one of these enable the surveyor to locate places on the earth to within inches.

Pro-Tip: Latitude Versus Longitude

An easy memory trick for recalling that latitude lines are horizontal is this: Latitude lines extend north and south to and from the equator; when stacked on top of one another, one might say they indicate the "altitude," inverting the "l" and the "a" of *latitude*.

Latitude Lines

Latitude lines are horizontal and parallel to the equator; they are sometimes referred to as parallels. Basic math tells us that there are 360 degrees in a circle, or in a "pear" as is the shape of the earth. There are 180 degrees from the top of one side of the earth to the bottom of it, or from the North Pole to the South Pole. Parallels are equally spaced, having a total of 90 degrees of latitude extending from the equator to the North Pole. We describe the location of the North Pole in degrees as 90 degrees N. Conversely, there are 90 degrees from the equator to the South Pole, described as located at 90 degrees S. Oftentimes, in a written description, the north or south directional designators are omitted, in which case latitudes from the equator to the North Pole are given positive values and latitudes from the equator to the South Pole are given negative values.

Longitude Lines

Lines of longitude, called meridians, run vertically and are perpendicular to lines of latitude. Longitude lines extend from pole to pole. Each longitude line represents an equal portion of the 360 degrees that encompass the earth. This 360-degree circle is divided by prime meridian. There are 180 degrees of longitude to the east of the prime meridian, written as a positive value if the east directional designator is not used. Completing the circle, the 180 degrees of longitude to the west of the prime meridian are written as a negative value if the west directional designator is not used.

Measurement of Latitude and Longitude Lines

A degree of latitude is approximately 69 miles, per minute, approximately 1.15 miles per second, and approximately 0.02 miles, or slightly over 100 feet. A degree of longitude varies in size as it extends from the equator north and south to the poles. At the equator, it is approximately 69 miles, the same size as a degree of latitude. However unlike the latitudes, which are all the same size, the size of each longitude diminishes the farther north and south it is located. Visualize the spherical shape of the earth and you will see that because all lines of longitude meet at the poles, the point at which they meet must be zero. As the title professional becomes involved in writing legal descriptions that may involve latitudes and longitudes, it will be important to remember that because a degree of longitude varies in size, minutes and seconds of longitude also vary. As previously noted, the degrees of longitude decrease in size as they near the poles. This importance, and the difference in sizes, manifest themselves in range lines and townships. Although the uniform surveying method developed through the rectangular survey system provided uniformity in the creation of townships (each in theory being six miles square consisting of 36 one-mile square sections), they actually may differ in size and acreage.

Legal Descriptions using Townships and Sections

According to the U.S. Bureau of Land Management (BLM), over the past two centuries, almost 1.5 billion acres of land have been surveyed into townships and sections and monumented. The BLM historical account of surveying practices in the United States claims that this

> represents the greatest land surveying project ever undertaken; there are about 2.6 million section corners throughout the United States, each one located about a mile apart. Placing these corners required a vast expenditure of human energy in carrying heavy surveying equipment, dragging chains, cutting trails, climbing mountains, placing monuments, digging pits, and blazing "witness" trees.

Rectangular Survey System   According to the Bureau of Land Management, the **rectangular survey system** was first proposed by Thomas Jefferson, once a surveyor (as were George Washington and Abraham Lincoln), and enacted into law by the Land Ordinance of 1785, which forms the backbone of the nation's land surveys. The task began with surveying over 1.8 billion acres of public domain lands acquired through the Louisiana Purchase, the Alaska Purchase, and other acquisitions. Today's survey methods and instruments are a far cry from the early techniques discussed in Chapter 1. The U.S. rectangular survey system, and the public land survey system (PLSS) it established, is the basis for the creation of townships and sections and established 42 initial beginning points. The north-south line that runs through the initial point of the survey is a true meridian and is called the **principal meridian**. There are 37 principal meridians. Each is named and used to distinguish the various surveys in the PLSS.

Base Line   The east-west line that runs through the initial point is called a **base line**. This line is perpendicular to the principal meridian. Each township is identified with a township and range designation. Township designations based on township lines, which run east and west, indicate the location north or south of the base line, and range designations based on **range lines** which run north and south indicate the location east or west of the principal meridian. As covered in Chapter 1, California has three sets of base lines:

- Humboldt base line and meridian located in the northwestern part of the state

- Mt. Diablo base line and meridian located in the central part of the state

- San Bernardino base line and meridian in the southern part of the state

A land description, for example, indicating "township 4 north, range 3 east, Humboldt Base Line and Meridian" locates the township, which is four townships north from the Humboldt Base Line and three townships east from the Humboldt Meridian. A township, as we know from Chapter 1, is six-miles square (six miles on each side) and consists of 36 sections, each one-mile square (one mile on each side). One mile is 5,280 feet. One square mile is 27,878,400 square feet. An acre is 43,560 square feet. Each section is 640 acres. A half-section is 320 acres, one-quarter section is 160 acres, and one-quarter of one-quarter section, the smallest parcel in the township plat, is 40 acres. A legal description using the township and section as shown in Figure 17.1 may read like this one from the *California Department of Real Estate Reference Manual*, Chapter 4:

Beginning at the NW. corner, of the SE 1/4 of Sec. 17, thence southeasterly to the NW. corner of the SE. ¼ of Sec. 21, thence southwesterly to the NW. corner of the SE. ¼ of Sec. 29, thence northwesterly to the NW. corner of the SE. ¼ of Sec. 19, thence northeasterly to the point of beginning.

FIGURE 17.1

A Sample Township

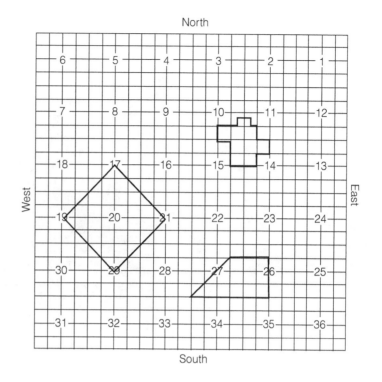

Source: *California Department of Real Estate Reference Manual*

Legal Descriptions Using Metes and Bounds

Occasionally, a property may be covered by a properly recorded map, but its shape makes it impractical to describe using simply a section and township. Using a description that employs **metes and bounds** can be complex, lengthy, and possibly difficult for anyone but a civil engineer or surveyor to understand. Title companies may employ such professionals, or a senior title officer may possess the skills to understand and complete such a description. The metes-and-bound description starts at a fixed **point of beginning** (POB) and continues outlining the boundaries of the land being described, measuring distances from one point to another and then back to the POB. (See Figure 17.2.)

FIGURE 17.2

A Sample Plat Map

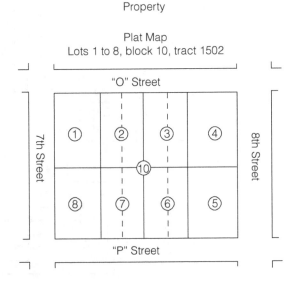

Source: *California Department of Real Estate Reference Manual*, Chapter 4

Point of Beginning Probably the most important aspect of the land description is the POB. Without such a permanent, fixed, and clearly identifiable starting point, the land being described cannot be located. The concept is quite easy to understand when comparing it with the mapping devices and programs used by today's global positioning systems (GPS). One cannot get the automobile's GPS to identify a desired destination and its route without first establishing the beginning point. An error in the point of beginning makes the entire description useless—and a possible case for damages against the title company insuring the title.

There are two different types of points of beginning. The first type is the one first used by early surveyors: natural and unique objects (e.g., boulder, creek or stream crossing, tree, or other similar and easily identifiable object). Lacking such unique natural objects, surveyors then uses certain man-made objects, such as a corner of a building or fence. Over time, however, some of these objects deteriorated or vanished. The other type of POB is more permanent. Those used today are the coordinates based on an intersection of a specific latitude and longitude. These are identified by a permanent steel object driven into the ground by the surveyor; these monument markers identify the location.

Metes Metes are measures of length, such as feet and yards.

Bounds The boundaries of a land description are referred to as bounds. These can be both natural and man-made, and they include monuments. Many, if not most, of natural or less than permanent man-made monuments have been replaced by newer permanent ones such as steel spikes.

■   **EXAMPLE**   A typical description using metes and bounds is as follows:

Beginning at a point on the southerly line of "O" Street, 150 feet westerly of the SW corner of the intersection of "O" and 8th Streets; running thence due south 300 feet to the northerly line of "P" Street; thence westerly along the northerly line of "P" Street, 100 feet; thence northerly and parallel to the first course, 300 feet, to the southerly line of "O" Street; thence easterly along the southerly line of "O" Street, 100 feet, to the point or place of beginning.

Record of Survey

After completing a survey, the land surveyor (or the civil engineer) must file a record of the survey in the county where the survey was made. The record of survey map discloses the following:

- Any change in an earlier survey not previously recorded in the office of that county recorder

- Any discrepancy with previously recorded information

- Any findings that conflict with previously recorded points

- The establishment of new lines not previously recorded and which are not identifiable on a map

Performing the Survey

Title companies often employ the services of professional land surveyors. A survey made for the purpose of supplying a title company and lender with survey and location data necessary for the issuing of title and/or mortgage insurance. A detailed map must be done to American Land Title Association (ALTA) specifications. The title company may require or be requested by principals to order a survey to be performed for these purposes, as indicated by ALTA: boundary, cadastral, construction, control, elevation, judicial, lot split, mortgage location, plat plan, subdivision, and topographic.

Boundary Survey   A boundary survey establishes the true property corners and property lines of a parcel of land. Boundary surveys are typically performed to obtain building permits, to resolve property disputes, and for establishing property boundaries through fences and walls. The surveyor may also be asked to locate or establish easement lines.

Cadastral Survey   The original survey or a resurvey of public lands within the public land survey system in order to locate or reestablish property lines is accomplished through a cadastral survey.

Construction Survey   A construction survey is performed prior to the construction of a building, or in some instances during the construction process, to provide for and conform with the design, location, and architectural requirements of the project, such as orientation, height, dimensions, and placement of fences, walls, and roads.

Control Survey   A control survey is performed to locate and determine boundaries and is often employed in mapping aerial photographs.

Elevation Survey   Elevation surveys are provided to do exactly as the name implies, to identify and determine the elevation of the building and the land on which it rests. Quite often an elevation survey, also referred to as a floodplain survey, is utilized to establish location within a floodplain.

Judicial Survey   Again, as the name implies, a judicial survey would be performed to provide professional evidence regarding the legal description, including boundaries of a property to be used in a court of law.

Lot Split Survey   A lot split survey would be employed in the process of dividing an existing parcel of land into multiple parcels.

Mortgage Location Survey   While not a true land survey, a mortgage location survey may be used by title companies and mortgage lenders to verify that the subject property does not encroach on another property or impairs a recorded easement.

Plat Plan Survey or Lot Survey   The plat plan (or lot) survey combines both boundary and topographic surveys to prepare for the construction of improvements and for obtaining building permits.

Subdivision Survey   A developer wishing to create a subdivision utilizes the subdivision survey in order to develop and create the individual lots. It shows the monuments used in the survey and provides the dimensions.

Topographic Survey   An escrow or title professional with prior experience, as in the military or the Scouts, will be familiar with the topography of a property and its survey. It includes and incorporates the elevations (height and depressions) of the land, both of natural and man-made elements.

Specifications of some of these types of surveys may include (but are not limited to) determining property lines, location of improvements, and identifying all easements, utilities, and other conditions affecting the property. ALTA surveys are very comprehensive, typically cost thousands of dollars, and take weeks to complete. Any ALTA land survey must meet the "Minimum Standard Detail Requirements for ALTA/ACSM Land Title Surveys" as adopted by ALTA, the American Congress on Surveying and Mapping, and the National Society of Professional Surveyors. The ALTA survey is most often performed on commercial properties.

A survey may be considered by the title company for a number of purposes. Cost, however, is a major factor in determining whether it may be required or not. The objective is to ensure as much as possible that a claim against the policy is unlikely to occur. If a survey may assist toward that end, the title company will first balance survey cost against possible loss.

■ CHAPTER 17 QUIZ

1. True easements may consist of rights that may not be obvious, such as easements for

   a. sewer lines.

   b. private utility lines that cross over or under the surface.

   c. the right to receive unrestricted light and air from an adjacent servient estate.

   d. all of these.

2. Characteristics of true easements include which of the following?

   a. They may be created by oral agreements.

   b. They must always be created by a deed or grant.

   c. They must be created by the owner of the servient estate.

   d. They must be created by the owner of the dominant estate.

3. The open and notorious use of another's land, or with the knowledge and acquiescence of that servient estate landowner,

   a. is a requirement to establish an easement by prescription.

   b. is a required to occur for three years to create an easement by prescription.

   c. is both a and b.

   d. is neither a nor b.

4. An easement by condemnation is

   a. considered an easement in gross.

   b. created under the power of eminent domain.

   c. has no dominant estate.

   d. all of these.

5. A true easement prohibits a right to the profits or proceeds from the servient estate land, which is called

    a. profit á prendre.

    b. prescription.

    c. appurtenant.

    d. incorporeal.

6. A license is distinguishable from an easement in that it

    a. conveys an interest in the land.

    b. expires with the death of the holder.

    c. is assignable to another.

    d. is unrevocable.

7. Geographic coordinates

    a. are not commonly used to locate points of the surface of the earth.

    b. consist of the intersection of a latitude and a longitude.

    c. are measured in feet and yards.

    d. are none of these.

8. The U.S. rectangular survey system, which has been conducted throughout the United States and through the public land survey system,

    a. is the basis for the creation of townships and sections.

    b. established 42 initial beginning points.

    c. is both a and b.

    d. is neither a nor b.

9. A township

    a. is one-mile square.

    b. is six-miles square.

    c. is six square miles.

    d. has 42 sections.

10. The metes-and-bounds description starts at a fixed POB, which refers to

    a. point of beginning.

    b. path of beginning.

    c. point of beacon.

    d. point of base line.

CHAPTER EIGHTEEN

DEFAULT, FORECLOSURE, AND THE TITLE INSURER

■ KEY TERMS

beneficiary	mortgagee	short sale
deed in lieu of	mortgagor	trustee
foreclosure	notice of default	trustee sale guarantee
foreclosure time line	notice of sale	trustee's sale
mortgage	regulated lender	trustor

■ LEARNING OBJECTIVES

Upon completing this chapter, you will be able to

- understand the preforeclosure options available to borrowers and the escrow holder's and title insurer's participation in the process;

- understand the short sale process and the additional procedures that may be required of the escrow holder;

■ understand the standard foreclosure process and time line, as well as the special provisions that may apply from time to time, such as the California foreclosure time line;

■ understand and explain the trustee sale guarantee (TSG) and how it differs from a standard title insurance policy; and

■ understand, prepare, and process the various documents involved in a short sale, foreclosure, and subsequent REO sale.

■ PREFORECLOSURE CONSIDERATIONS

Foreclosure

Foreclosure is one remedy available to a lender that has a security instrument filed against real property as collateral for a loan it provided to a borrower who is now in default. When a mortgage lender forecloses on a borrower's property and takes title to it at the foreclosure sale, the property, now owned by the lender, is real estate owned, or REO, for short. Lenders quite naturally want to sell REO properties as quickly as possible in order to eliminate the cost to maintain them, as well as to turn them into liquid and profitable assets. The time, therefore, between the acquisition date at the foreclosure sale and the resale of the property is relatively short. However, following the beginning of the Great Recession in the fall of 2007, REOs entered the market at a slower pace because of government moratoriums and foreclosure-avoidance programs, some now expired, that required mortgage lenders and banks to offer homeowners in default some alternatives to foreclosure.

Government Alternatives: Federal and State Foreclosure Moratoriums   The following paragraphs are an overview of the primary government foreclosure alternative programs and an insight into many mortgage lenders' proprietary loss-mitigation programs.

Helping Families Save Their Homes Act of 2009   On May 20, 2009, President Barack Obama signed the Helping Families Save Their Homes Act of 2009 into law. The law's Making Home Affordable Program continues to offer assistance to homeowners in default through an evolution of the previous moratoriums and assistance programs with the Home Affordable Refinance Program (HARP) and the Home Affordable Modification Program (HAMP).

Featuring a two-step process to determine a homeowner's eligibility for loan modification, HAMP requires all loan servicers of loans owned by Fannie Mae and Freddie Mac, before filing foreclosure, to offer the program to homeowners in default, in foreclosure, and to those current with their loan payment but at risk of imminent default. The borrower must first determine eligibility for refinancing under HARP and is guided easily through the online process. If the result reveals that the homeowner is ineligible for refinancing, the program automatically continues with the determination for loan modification eligibility under HAMP. Once the modification plan is identified and established, the servicer grants a 90-day "trial" loan modification period based on the verbal financial analysis.

During the trial period, the servicer gathers and reviews all the required documentation from the borrower and about the property, including valuation, usually utilizing the service's automated valuation model appraisal system but which may instead require a broker price opinion. If the analysis of the homeowners' documentation and the property analysis differ from the verbal information, the modification plan must be revised if the homeowner qualifies for another option. Otherwise, foreclosure proceedings will begin, unless the lender agrees to a short sale alternative and, in fact, may be required to consider the borrower's eligibility for such under the third element of Making Home Affordable, the Home Affordable Foreclosure Alternative.

A similar program was implemented for FHA loans. Homeowners wishing to determine their eligibility for either refinancing or modification may obtain details and perform self-determination of eligibility at www.makinghomeaffordable.gov. Although these programs are in effect only until January 1, 2014, many lenders have implemented their own foreclosure-alternative programs to become effective upon the expiration of Making Home Affordable and for loans not subject to the government guidelines. Not surprisingly, many of the features of their programs parallel those of the government. Most of the lender's own programs (referred to as "proprietary") do not terminate but are part of the permanent loss mitigation guidelines of the lender.

Fannie Mae and Freddie Mac replaced the government programs with their own, effective January 1, 2013. Understanding the government programs, although they will all eventually expire by year's end 2013 (unless extended by Congress), will aid the escrow and title professional in understanding those proprietary guidelines offered by many lenders.

Short Sales: an Alternative to Foreclosure

A **short sale** may offer a more attractive solution for both the homeowner and the lender. Among the possible benefits to the lender is that following the close of escrow of a short sale, the homeowner usually vacates. If the lender proceeds to foreclosure, the homeowner has a minimum of 111 days until required to vacate. The lender may begin foreclosure with the first late payment, though in reality usually waits a few months. Currently, the lender may not immediately commence foreclosure action against many delinquent borrowers. A borrower with an unpaid loan balance that exceeds the value of the property may be interested in exploring a short sale.

Typically, lenders will only consider a short sale if the borrower is in default or is likely to default, such as having a mortgage interest rate that will soon "reset" to a higher rate and payment and that the borrower cannot afford. Instead of foreclosing, the lender allows the property owner to seek a buyer. Once a sales price has been agreed upon and a contract executed, the lender may negotiate the short sale terms and conditions with the borrower. The government's Making Home Affordable Program offers some assistance to homeowners wishing to utilize the short sale process. In the event the homeowner is found to be either ineligible for HAMP or fails to successfully complete it, a third element in the Making Home Affordable Program offers the possibility of a short sale instead of foreclosure. The Home Affordable Foreclosure Alternative (HAFA) program was implemented to assist those homeowners who met certain qualifying standards to sell their homes through a structured government-sponsored program and avoid foreclosure. HAFA, along with the other Making Home Affordable programs, expires December 31, 2013.

Short Sale Defined   The short sale occurs at escrow closing when the lender agrees to accept less for the loan payoff than the total amount due. The terms of the short sale may include additional documents provided by the lender to be processed by the escrow holder. The borrower may be asked to sign a promissory note for the difference, and the borrower may incur tax consequences. A growing practice among some real estate agents has been the use of a third-party short sale "negotiator." Escrow holders are cautioned to seek legal advice for any procedure they are asked to perform, which is unusual or outside the normal or customary practice, such as participating in "side agreements" or assisting with disbursements of monies to any party after both the closing and the accounting of and for funds has been completed.

California Law and Short Sale Deficiencies   Among legal issues of importance regarding short sales is California Civil Code Section 580(e), which prohibits a mortgage lender from requiring the borrower to remain liable for the deficiency balance as a condition of the lender agreeing to the short sale. This law applies to all lenders, senior and junior, and applies to all one-to-four-unit residential properties, whether owner-occupied or investor-owned.

Short Sales and the Foreclosure Time Line   Real estate licensees recognize the reluctance of a prospective homebuyer to purchase a home subject to the homeowners' lender agreeing to a short sale, especially if negotiations haven't begun or are still in the process. Short sale negotiation should begin well before the lender starts foreclosure. Of course, many homeowners facing financial difficulties don't consider selling their home until they are several payments past due. By the time the licensee gets involved, the foreclosure clock has already begun. The California **foreclosure time line**, which refers to the length of time it takes for a lender to begin and complete the foreclosure process under the law, is a minimum of 111 days. Understanding the California foreclosure process and time line helps real estate licensees in determining the amount of time they have to help the homeowner negotiate a short sale, and it allows the escrow holder and the title insurer to determine the ability to request, obtain, or process everything necessary to effect a closing that meets the lender's time consideration. The foreclosure process is discussed later in this chapter.

Why a Short Sale May Be Best for the Lender   Lenders typically don't want to foreclose if there are other reasonable options. Most lenders recognize the benefit of considering a short sale instead of foreclosing. They avoid the costs of property maintenance, repairs, and utilities; they avoid the additional possible decreased value of the property due to vandalism; and their total sales costs are usually less than selling an REO property. Negotiating a short sale on behalf of the homeowner with the lender includes estimating the financial benefit to the lender of a short sale as in the example shown.

■ **EXAMPLE**

Costs to Foreclose and Sell as an REO

1.	$ 350,000	loan balance
2.	× 3%	estimated foreclosure costs
3.	$ 10,500	foreclosure cost
4.	$ 300,000	sales price if sold as REO
5.	− 350,000	loan balance
6.	$ 50,000	loss at REO sales price
7.	$ 300,000	sales price if sold as REO
8.	× 8%	sales costs as a % of sales price
9.	$ 24,000	sales costs
10.	$ 350,000	loan balance
11.	× 1%	estimated holding costs rate
12.	$ 3,500	monthly holding costs
13.	× 6	number of holding months before closing
14.	$ 21,000	total income lost from holding costs
15.	$ 105,500	loss from selling as REO

Regulated Lender

A lender may be a **regulated lender**, which is a financial institution that accepts and holds monetary deposits from customers and allows for the disbursement of their monies through a variety of instruments or means. They are by law regulated by federal and state governments. Lending institutions such as banks, thrifts, and credit unions are among these regulated lenders, and they must maintain specified capital reserves as a safeguard against the risk of failure from losses. Regulated institutions include the following:

- National banks (identified by "NA" or "National Association"), regulated by the U.S. Office of the Comptroller of the Currency

- California state-chartered banks, regulated by the California Department of Financial Institutions

- Federal savings banks and savings & loans, regulated by the U.S. Office of Thrift Supervision

- Federal credit unions, regulated by the National Credit Union Administration

Reserves are in the form of cash held untouched in the bank's vaults or in their regional banks and are maintained for a variety of categories. In addition to reserves that must be maintained in a specified percentage of depositors funds held by the banks, reserves are also required for lending activity as follows:

- Reserves are maintained in a specified percentage of the outstanding balance of performing loans (nondelinquent) and vary depending on the loan product.

- Reserves are required for a specified percentage of nonperforming (delinquent) loans. As a loan becomes nonperforming, the bank must add more capital to its reserves, which reduce funds available for lending.

- Reserves are also required to be set aside in a specified percentage of the bank-owned value of REO properties.

As a result, banks lose the opportunity for revenues from loan fees and interest they otherwise could earn if these reserves were not required. Accepting a short sale instead of going to foreclosure usually expedites the process and allows the bank to receive its proceeds much sooner than through a foreclosure.

Deed in Lieu of Foreclosure

One alternative to foreclosing is a process referred to as **deed in lieu** of foreclosure. In this process, the borrower negotiates with the lender to forgive the debt and simply take the property encumbered by it, instead of foreclosing. The borrower voluntarily signs a deed in favor of the lender who, if agreeing to accepting it, acquires title. By doing so, the borrower avoids the public knowledge of the action, as is the case in a foreclosure, and any stigma attached to it. The process is simple, and the lender avoids the time and cost involved in foreclosing, as discussed below in the "Foreclosure Process" in this chapter. However, it may not be as easy as it appears.

A common obstacle is the existence of junior liens against the property. Unlike a foreclosure action in which junior liens are extinguished, they remain attached to the property and become the responsibility of the lender accepting the deed. The lender won't consider accepting the deed with having to deal with these additional encumbrances, especially nonmortgage liens such as homeowners association assessments, judgments, and taxes.

Another problem arises when the lender is entitled to a deficiency judgment if and when it were to foreclose. A lender having acquired title to a property through a judicial foreclosure will usually sell it to another party. Not uncommonly, the price offered by a buyer and accepted by the lender is less than the full amount of the debt owed by the foreclosed-upon borrower. In such a case, the lender may return to court and obtain a judgment for the difference between the sales price and the balance of the debt, the deficiency for which the judgment is granted. Therefore, it's understandable why such a lender would be reluctant to accept a deed in lieu and, in the process, walk away from the possibility of eventually recovering the entire debt owed. Of course, the lender is faced with other issues, such as the borrower filing for bankruptcy protection. Attorneys on both sides may participate in negotiations for the deed in lieu to try to reach a mutually acceptable and legally enforceable agreement that may include "playing the bankruptcy" card.

■ FORECLOSURE PROCESS

As discussed in Chapter 5, lenders use one of two security (or debt) instruments: a deed of trust or a mortgage.

Lenders Using a Deed of Trust

Lenders that use deeds of trusts (trust deeds), such as in California, are called beneficiaries, and their borrowers are called **trustors**. A third party also exists, and this is the trustee, who performs services on behalf of the **beneficiary**. The **trustee** is usually a title company or an attorney on privately held (noninstitutional) loans. On institutional loans, the trustee is often a corporate subsidiary of the institutional lender but may also be a title company or law firm. Under a trust deed, the foreclosure process begins with the lender or its trustee merely filing and recording certain documents with the county recorder, and without having to go to court, and the process is called nonjudicial foreclosure.

Lenders Using a Mortgage (Mortgagee)

Lenders in 23 states (California is not one of them) customarily use **mortgages** instead of deeds of trust as their security agreement. The lender under a mortgage is called a **mortgagee** and the borrower is called a **mortgagor**. There is no third party, no trustee as in a deed of trust, involved in a mortgage. To foreclose under a mortgage, the lender must go to court to commence the process, called a judicial foreclosure.

The principal difference between the two processes is found in the loan documents and security instruments used. The deed of trust contains a provision by which the borrower conveys what is known as bare legal title accompanied by the power of sale to the lender. It is this clause under which the law allows the lender to foreclosure without a court action. The mortgage does not contain such a provision, and therefore court action is required.

Foreclosure Under a Deed of Trust

Three steps are involved in the foreclosure process under a deed of trust.

1. Notice of default

2. Notice of sale

3. Trustee's sale

Notice of Default   Technically, a borrower is in default if failing to make a payment the day after it is due, and the lender could begin the foreclosure process. In practice, however, most lenders do not commence foreclosure for months after the payment is first delinquent, sometimes after even years. In California, a lender under a deed of trust begins the foreclosure process by instructing the trustee to file and record a **notice of default** (NOD) in the county where the property is located, with a copy mailed within 10 business days after recording to all borrowers and to those who have requested such notice.

Pro-Tip: Escrow Holder's Role in Request for Notice of Default

An escrow holder may have an escrow in which a party, even one other than a principal to the transaction, has asked for a "request for notice of default" to be recorded on his or her behalf. Typically, for example, a junior mortgage lender will make such a request in order to have adequate time to explore options to protect its interest. A seller carrying back financing will certainly want such notice. If represented by a real estate licensee the seller will have had an addendum as required under the law delivered to him or her by the licensee that describes the terms of the carry back financing. Included in the addendum will be a Request for Notice of Default of a senior loan and lien. The addendum will become a part of the escrow documents, and a potentially critical part.

The mailing includes the lender's declaration that it has complied with all applicable federal and state laws before filing the notice of default, such as options for avoiding foreclosure. During the NOD term (by law, a minimum of three months), the borrower may reinstate the loan by making up all the delinquent payments plus any late charges and costs. If so, the NOD is cancelled and the borrower retains the property and the loan. If the borrower fails to cure the default, the trustee is instructed to file and record a notice of sale (NOS).

Notice of Sale

The **notice of sale** (NOS), which has a minimum term of 21 days, may actually be filed and recorded 85 days after filing the NOD, therefore before the end of the third month. The sale, however, cannot take place sooner than three months and twenty-one days after filing the NOD. The NOS indicates the date, time, and place of the upcoming trustee's sale. The notice must be posted, mailed to the borrowers and the others who have requested the notice of default, and published once a week for three consecutive weeks in a newspaper of general circulation. Up to five days before the trustee's sale, the borrower may still reinstate the loan by curing the default (reinstatement period), just as was possible during the NOD term, by making up the missed payments plus any allowable foreclosure costs. After the reinstatement period has expired, the borrower may only keep the property through redemption. Redemption involves paying the entire loan balance, plus interest and costs, before the bidding begins at the trustee's sale. It is important to understand that the lender may voluntarily allow the borrower to reinstate the loan at any time, even after the statutory reinstatement period has expired.

Trustee's Sale

On or after the 21st day of the sale period, but no sooner, the **trustee's sale** may commence. At this time, the property may be sold at public auction to the highest bidder, to whom title is then transferred. The sale may be held on any business day between the hours of 9:00 am and 5:00 pm and must take place at the location specified in the notice of sale. The trustee may require proof of the bidders' ability to pay their full bid amount. Anyone may bid at the sale, which must be made at public auction to the highest bidder. If necessary, the sale may be postponed by announcement at the time and location of the original foreclosure sale. For purchase-money trust deeds, lenders may not seek a deficiency judgment after a nonjudicial foreclosure sale and the borrower has no rights of redemption.

Trustee Sale Guarantee (TSG)

The title company becomes involved in facilitating title protection to the lender using a deed of trust through the **trustee sale guarantee** (TSG), a special title report for the foreclosing lender that provides all items pertaining to the ownership interests and encumbrances on a property in foreclosure. The TSG is issued at the start of the foreclosure. The fees increase with the liability amount, and rates are filed with each state insurance department. The TSG assures both the foreclosure attorney and the lender against losses suffered up to the loan balance as a result of errors in the TSG. It includes the legal description and vesting, liens on the property, property taxes, bankruptcies, and mailing addresses required for service. Also included is a list of all parties who recorded a special request to be notified if any NOD or NTS is filed against the particular trust deed in foreclosure. Furthermore it gives the trustee a list of all the local publications that qualify to advertise the notice of trustee's sale (once a week for three consecutive weeks). The TSG will provide an indemnification that protects the trustee and the beneficiary from the consequences of any title record error in the foreclosure proceeding.

■ CHAPTER 18 QUIZ

1. The Making Home Affordable Program, part of the Helping Families Save Their Homes Act of 2009, continues to offer assistance to homeowners in default through two other plans known as

   a. HARP and HAMP.

   b. HELP and HOPE.

   c. HARP and HOME.

   d. HELP and HAMP.

2. The short sale occurs at escrow closing when the seller's lender agrees to

   a. a short escrow.

   b. accept less for the loan payoff than what is due.

   c. both a and b.

   d. neither a nor b.

3. California foreclosure law under the California foreclosure time line provision applies to

   a. owner-occupied homes having one to four units.

   b. both owner-occupied and investment homes having one to four units.

   c. all residential properties, regardless of number of units.

   d. all real estate properties.

4. Regulated lending institutions include

   a. national banks, state-chartered banks, federal savings and loans, and federal credit unions.

   b. only national banks and federal savings and loans.

   c. only national banks, federal savings and loans, and federal credit unions.

   d. only those regulated by the U.S. Treasury.

5. Reserves of regulated lenders are required in a specified percentage of the outstanding loan balance of

    a. performing loans.

    b. nonperforming loans.

    c. REO properties.

    d. all of these.

6. The deed in lieu of foreclosure

    a. does not immediately release the borrower from most of the debt.

    b. requires a court filing and public disclosure.

    c. requires the indebtedness to be secured by the real estate transferred.

    d. is likely to impact the borrower's credit as severely as a foreclosure.

7. Lenders that use deeds of trusts (trust deeds) are called

    a. mortgagees.

    b. trustors.

    c. mortgagors.

    d. beneficiaries.

8. With a deed of trust, the lender begins the foreclosure process by instructing the trustee to file and record a notice of default in the county where the property is located and to mail a copy to all borrowers and to those who have requested such notice within

    a. 30 business days after recording.

    b. 20 business days after recording.

    c. 10 business days after recording.

    d. 5 business days after recording.

9. The title company becomes involved in facilitating title protection to the lender using a deed of trust through the

    a. trustee sale guarantee (TSG).

    b. trustor sale guarantee (TSG).

    c. trust-deed sale guarantee (TSG).

    d. trustee seller's guarantee (TSG).

10. The TSG provides an indemnification for the consequences of any title record error in the foreclosure proceeding and protects the

    a. the trustee and beneficiary from damages.

    b. the loan officer from damages.

    c. the borrower from damages.

    d. none of these.

QUIZ ANSWER KEY

Chapter 1

1. **c** California's property ownership concepts have their roots in English law. (p. 2)

2. **b** The character of property interests and private property rights in California can be traced back to the Spanish. (p. 2)

3. **c** Spanish missions began sprouting up along the California coast, known at the time as Alta California. (p. 2)

4. **a** Following the Mexican-American War, title to properties was established under the Treaty of Guadalupe of Hidalgo. (p. 2)

5. **a** Property is considered either real or personal. (p. 9)

6. **b** Estates in property are either freehold or less than freehold. (p. 11)

7. **a** Estate for years is a lease with a specified termination date. (p. 13)

8. **a** An estate at will has no specified term. (p. 13)

9. **c** Fee simple estates are inheritable. (p. 12)

10. **c** A common interest property is one with tenants in common. (p. 10)

Chapter 2

1. **c** California Civil Code Section 1000 specifies that property in the State of California may be acquired in one of five ways: occupancy, accession, transfer, will, and succession. (p. 18)

2. **a** Trust deeds transfer only dormant title. (p. 23)

3. **c** Probate is not required if title was held as joint tenants. (p. 19)

4. **a** Intestate succession applies to one who died without a will. (p. 19)

5. **a** Transfer of title to real property is called alienation. (p. 20)

6. **c** Recording a document provides constructive notice. (p. 20)

7. **a** To be valid, grant deeds must be in writing and must be signed by a competent grantee. (p. 21)

8. **d** Grant deed forms include joint tenancy grant deeds and interspousal grant deeds. (p. 22)

9. **c** A quitclaim deed conveys title from the grantor to the grantee with no guaranty. (p. 22)

10. **a** An all-inclusive deed-of-trust is a junior deed of trust. (p. 39)

Chapter 3

1. **a** A grant deposited by the grantor with a third person delivered on performance of a condition is called an escrow. (p. 53)

2. **d** Background checks are required of all escrow company personnel with no exceptions. (p. 56)

3. **b** The escrow office manager must have five years of experience. (pp. 62, 67)

4. **b** The escrow holder holds documents and money as a neutral depository for both principals. (p. 57)

5. **d** Title policies offer financial protection to the buyer who is financially damaged by the title company's faulty search. (p. 60)

6. **d** Escrow agents may never resolve disputes as impartial arbitrators. (p. 65)

7. **d** Escrow companies, except broker-owned, are regulated by the Department of Corporations. (p. 62)

8. **a** Independent escrow agents are required to possess liquid assets of $25,000. (p. 62)

9. **b** The escrow positions include the junior escrow officer. (p. 70)

10. **a** The principals direct the transaction, and the escrow holder is more reactive than proactive. (p. 65)

Chapter 4

1. **a** Title insurance protects the property against losses due to defects in title. (p. 79)

2. **c** The title insurer reimburses the property owner for covered losses up to the face amount of insurance plus legal expenses. (p. 79)

3. **d** The title company's primary facility that stores copies of all public records is the title plant. (p. 81)

4. **c** The chain of title lists the parties and the documents, such as a trust, grant deed, and recording dates. (p. 84)

5. **d** A patent deed transfers land from the federal or state government to a private individual. (p. 86)

6. **a** Using a statement of information (SI), the title searcher performs a "general index run." (p. 87)

7. **c** If the searcher discovers an error in spelling on a previously recorded deed, escrow may send a corrected deed to the grantor to sign and record. (p. 87)

8. **a** *Underwriting* is defined as "to write under or at the end" of something. (p. 88)

9. **b** The preliminary title report shows the conditions under which a title policy will be offered. (p. 89)

10. **c** Title policies are written on the basis of public records that impart constructive notice. (p. 90)

Chapter 5

1. **a** An ALTA extended coverage loan policy covers matters not of record. (p. 102)

2. **c** Defects such as no access to a public street are covered by an ALTA extended coverage policy. (p. 123)

3. **d** An ALTA policy will not cover liens created by the insured, known to the insured and not specified in writing or no loss incurred by the insured. (p. 124)

4. **c** The CLTA standard policy is the most frequently used. (p. 98)

5. **c** CLTA standard policies cover forgery and fraud. (p. 98)

6. **d** CLTA policies will not cover liens created by the insured, known to the insured but not specified to the underwriter or with no damage. (p. 101)

7. **d** ALTA policies cover matters disclosed by physical inspection, inquiries of the occupants, or by a recent survey. (p. 121)

8. **a** Encumbrances include taxes, assessments, liens, restrictions, easements, encroachments, and legal actions. (p. 127)

9. **c** Eminent domain is the power of condemnation by a public agency. (p. 130)

10. **b** Trust deeds are used almost exclusively in California. (p. 133)

Chapter 6

1. **a**   An express contract may be written or verbal. (p. 143)

2. **c**   A bilateral contract occurs when a promise to perform from a party is met by an equal promise. (p. 143)

3. **a**   A contract that is considered valid but unenforceable if rejected by one party is voidable. (p. 144)

4. **a**   A valid, effective, and enforceable contract includes mutual consent, capacity to contract, consideration, and a lawful object. (p. 144)

5. **d**   Under the statute of frauds, a real estate listing or purchase agreement must be in writing but not commission-sharing agreements. (p. 147)

6. **c**   Structural pest control reports include Section I and II. (p. 150)

7. **c**   A Natural Hazard Disclosure Statement is required only for one-to-four-unit properties. (p. 159)

8. **b**   A master insurance policy is obtained for condominium properties. (p. 156)

9. **a**   Regulation Z defines a creditor as one who extends credit secured by a dwelling more than five times a year. (p. 166)

10. **c**   The primary regulator for residential lending is the Department of Housing and Urban Development (HUD). (p. 163)

Chapter 7

1. **b**   Real estate brokers may not nominate the escrow holder as a condition of sale. (p. 176)

2. **d**   An applicant for a California real estate license must be 18 or older and cannot have been convicted of a crime. (p. 177)

3. **a**   Before taking the California real estate salesperson license exam, an applicant must complete three college-level courses as specified by DRE. (p. 177)

4. **a**   Members of the State Bar in California are exempt from the college course requirements. (p. 177)

5. **a**   California real estate broker exam applicants must have full-time licensed salesperson experience for two out of the last five years unless they have a college degree or are a member of the State Bar. (pp. 179, 180)

6. **b**   CAR purchase contracts calls for loan contingency removal in 17 days. (p. 182)

7. **a** Under TIL disclosure laws, a borrower's rate increase of 0.125% or greater requires waiting three more business days before signing loan documents. (p. 184)

8. **b** Buyer's Choice Act violators are subject to damages three times the escrow and title fees. (p. 189)

9. **b** A beneficiary who acquired a property through foreclosure is not exempt from disclosing defects. (p. 190)

10. **a** Federal law allows the buyer 10 days to inspect for lead-based paint. (p. 190)

Chapter 8

1. **b** If a CAR purchase contract is used, the escrow holder usually only prepares supplemental instructions. (p. 200)

2. **b** A For Sale by Owner without a sales contract requires that the escrow holder inform the parties to have one prepared. (p. 207)

3. **c** A statement of information or identity asks the buyer to provide information necessary for the title company's search. (p. 209)

4. **d** A statement of identity obtains liens, judgment, and bankruptcy information of the party. (p. 209)

5. **b** The take sheet is an orderly sequence of questions asked by escrow of the parties. (p. 211)

6. **d** Information for a complete and accurate escrow includes sales price and loans to be obtained, paid, or remain. (p. 211)

7. **c** The contingency removal term in a CAR contract is 17 days. (p. 212)

8. **a** Prorations may be based on a 30-day month or actual days. (p. 212)

9. **d** Standard hazard insurance doesn't cover floods or earthquakes. (p. 213)

10. **b** Southern California escrow custom is to prepare bilateral escrow instructions at opening. (p. 214)

Chapter 9

1. **d** The basic information in the escrow instructions includes legal description, street address, vesting, and title. (p. 222)

2. **c** The Southern California allocation of costs usually has the seller paying for the owner's title policy. (p. 224)

3. **a**   If a seller is a foreign person, the buyer must withhold and send 10% of the sales price from seller's proceeds to the IRS. (p. 232)

4. **a**   The documents an escrow holder may draw are limited under rule of the bar treaty. (p. 225)

5. **b**   If an acquired property has an HOA, the buyer and the lender will require it to provide an HOA certification report. (p. 227)

6. **c**   Releasing buyer's deposit funds to the seller could cause serious consequences if problems arise during escrow. (p. 231)

7. **b**   Under California withholding, if applicable, the buyer withholds and sends 3⅓% of the sales price from the seller's proceeds to FTB. (p. 234)

8. **a**   A declared homestead property, if sold and the proceeds reinvested within six months in a new home, may be selected as a declared homestead. (p. 236)

9. **c**   YSP is the yield spread premium paid to broker. (p. 225).

10. **a**   Signing an affidavit of occupancy warns the borrower of possible mortgage fraud. (p. 224)

Chapter 10

1. **d**   The preliminary title report indicates coverage and exclusions based on conditions discovered and items to be resolved. (p. 247)

2. **d**   Issuing a preliminary title report requires the property's legal description and current and prospective parties on title. (p. 247)

3. **d**   A title report shows dominant and servient tenements. (p. 248)

4. **c**   Covenant, conditions, and restrictions can apply to all real property. (p. 249)

5. **b**   The escrow officer orders a beneficiary statement from the lender for a buyer assuming a seller's loan. (p. 250)

6. **a**   An acceleration clause allows the lender to call the note due and payable if title is transferred. (p. 251)

7. **a**   Southern California escrow focuses on the loan aspect of a transaction, except for all-cash sales. (p. 254)

8. **b**   Southern California purchase escrow instructions are bilateral. (p. 254)

9. **a**   If only one party has signed escrow instructions, escrow is not considered open. (p. 254)

10. **c**   California's good funds law provides that wire transfer funds are good the same day received and cashier's checks are good the next business day. (p. 257)

Chapter 11

1. **a** The entity receiving the borrower's payments is called the loan servicer. (p. 265)

2. **c** MERS stands for Mortgage Electronic Registration System. (p. 265)

3. **d** MERS aids lenders with more rapid loan payoff, eliminates closing delays, and indicates who owns or services loan. (p. 265)

4. **a** The property tax year in California begins July 1. (p. 268)

5. **b** The first half of property taxes is due Nov. 1 and is delinquent if not paid by Dec. 10. (p. 268)

6. **a** Mechanics' liens claimants include contractors, laborers, subcontractors, and materialmen. (p. 269)

7. **d** TIL law requires that escrow not close for three days if the borrower's loan rate increases 0.125% or more than the amount first disclosed. (p. 272)

8. **c** Under the law, the escrow holder must retain general escrow instructions for five years. (p. 275)

9. **c** The Preliminary Change of Ownership Report (PCOR) gives the assessor information to value property and to determine if transfer eliminates the need to reassess the property. (p. 280)

10. **a** The PCOR establishes the base year value. (p. 280)

Chapter 12

1. **a** The closing statement reflects columns identified as "credits" and "debits." (p. 290)

2. **b** The buyer's consideration is shown as a debit on closing statement. (p. 291)

3. **d** The buyer's deposit, loan, and balance of funds due are shown as a credit on closing statement. (p. 292)

4. **d** The buyer's debits include appraisal and escrow and title fees. (p. 292)

5. **c** If the borrower's loan includes impounds, the closing statement shows 14 months' insurance. (p. 293)

6. **a** Property taxes in California become a lien on property at noon on January 1 each year. (p. 294)

7. **b** The second half of property taxes is due on February 1. (p. 294)

8. **c**   The documentary transfer tax is based on $0.55 per $500 of the cash and new loans obtained by the buyer. (p. 301)

9. **a**   To find the sales price, divide the transfer tax by $0.55 and multiply by $500. (p. 301)

10. **a**   Rental prorations are based on a 30-day month regardless of the actual number of days in the month. (p. 304)

Chapter 13

1. **a**   The National Housing Act of 1934 established the Federal Housing Administration (FHA). (p. 327)

2. **c**   HUD is the government agency responsible for promoting adequate and affordable housing, economic opportunity, and a suitable living environment free from discrimination. (p. 328)

3. **c**   The largest investor in the secondary mortgage market is Fannie Mae. (p. 329)

4. **b**   Mortgage insurance is required for all loans sold to Fannie Mae and Freddie Mac with LTVs greater than 80%. (p. 331)

5. **b**   Mortgage brokers in California must be licensed by either the Department of Real Estate or the Department of Corporations. (p. 333)

6. **a**   FHA requires impound accounts, regardless of LTV. (p. 336)

7. **d**   Borrowers of FHA loans cannot pay for the tax service. (p. 338)

8. **a**   A surplus added to the estimated buyer's funds for closing is called padding. (p. 347)

9. **c**   Loan conditions may include PTD, meaning prior to documents being drawn, and PTF, which means prior to funding. (p. 348)

10. **c**   It is the escrow officer who initiates the request for funding the loan. (p. 350)

Chapter 14

1. **a**   TIL requires disclosing before the borrower is obligated under the loan, creditor name, loan amount, finance charge and rate, APR, and payment schedule. (p. 357)

2. **d**   Truth-in-lending disclosures are made by delivering the good-faith estimate of settlement costs and the TIL statement. (p. 357)

3. **a**   Right of rescission applies to a refinance of primary residence. (p. 358)

4. **a**   RESPA requires the lender to give the borrower an information booklet prepared by HUD and a good-faith estimate of costs before close of escrow. (pp. 364, 365)

5. **c** The penalty for violation of RESPA is a $10,000 fine or not more than one year in prison, or both. (p. 365)

6. **d** RESPA applies to lenders making over $100,000 a year in real estate loans, those regulated by the Federal Reserve, and those regulated by VA or HUD. (p. 365)

7. **a** The Unruh Civil Rights Act prohibits businesses from discriminating. (p. 366)

8. **b** Zoning is an example of police power. (p. 367)

9. **a** The Subdivision Map Act applies to subdivisions of land into two or more parcels. (p. 367)

10. **a** Pink Paper refers to the preliminary approval of a subdivision; White Paper is the final approval. (p. 369)

Chapter 15

1. **d** The lender of a multifamily property requires the rent roll, copies of leases, and information regarding delinquent rents. (p. 377)

2. **b** Tenants verify rent terms to the lender on estoppel certificates provided by the lender. (p. 377)

3. **c** The lender's cash flow requirement factor is debt service coverage ratio (DSCR). (p. 378)

4. **d** An apartment LTV may be reduced by property age, condition, construction, cap rate, or unit mix. (p. 378)

5. **b** The IRS form that lists borrower's rental property income and expenses is Schedule E. (p. 379)

6. **a** The lender may allow funds to be held by escrow at closing for work required, referred to as a hold-back. (p. 386)

7. **d** The prepay penalty may be declining prepay, yield maintenance, and defeasance. (p. 387)

8. **a** *Like-kind* means properties of same nature or character even if they differ in quality. (p. 389)

9. **b** The 45-180 rule: Exchangor has 45 days from closing his property to identify a replacement and 180 days to close new property. (p. 391)

10. **a** A reverse exchange is buying a replacement property before selling the old property. (p. 391)

Chapter 16

1. **c**   Bulk sales laws are designed to prevent sellers from defrauding their creditors. (p. 398)

2. **c**   Escrow is required for a transaction involving a liquor license. (p. 398)

3. **a**   The purpose for notifying the state Board of Equalization under the bulk sale law is to obtain a tax clearance and a seller's permit. (p. 399)

4. **a**   A buyer who fails to comply with bulk sale notice requirements may be liable for damages in the amount of any claims against the seller. (p. 399)

5. **a**   A claim to be valid under bulk sale law must be filed within one year of the date of sale. (p. 399)

6. **c**   The document to be recorded as constructive notice for a security instrument for personal property is the California UCC-1. (p. 401)

7. **c**   An agreement that a seller of a business will not compete against the buyer is covenant not to compete. (p. 401)

8. **b**   The two categories of liquor licenses are new and previously issued. (p. 402)

9. **a**   Two groups of liquor licenses are on-sale and off-sale. (p. 403)

10. **a**   The escrow holder must obtain a written release from FTB, EDD, or the Board of Equalization for a buyer liable for taxes to any of them. (p. 403)

Chapter 17

1. **d**   True easements may consist of a right that may not be obvious, such as private utility lines and the right to receive air from an adjacent estate. (p. 416)

2. **c**   True easements must be created by the owner of the servient estate. (p. 417)

3. **a**   Open and notorious use of another's land or with the knowledge and acquiescence of the owner is required to create an easement by prescription. (p. 418)

4. **d**   An easement by condemnation is considered an easement in gross, has no dominant estate, and is created under the power of eminent domain. (p. 418)

5. **a**   Profit á prendre refers to the prohibition of rights to profits or proceeds from the servient estate. (p. 422)

6. **b**   A license expires with the death of the holder. (p. 423)

7. **b** Geographic coordinates refer to locating a point on the earth by the intersection of latitude and longitude. (p. 425)

8. **c** The U.S. rectangular survey system is the basis for the creation of townships and sections and established 42 initial beginning points. (p. 427)

9. **b** A township is six miles square. (p. 428)

10. **a** POB as used in a metes-and-bounds land description means point of beginning. (p. 430)

Chapter 18

1. **a** Under the Helping Families Save Their Homes Act of 2009, HARP refers to the Home Affordable Refinance Program and HAMP refers to the Home Affordable Modification Program. (p. 439)

2. **b** A short sale occurs at escrow closing when the seller's lender agrees to accept less for the loan payoff than the amount due. (p. 440)

3. **a** The California foreclosure time line applies to one-to-four-unit owner-occupied homes. (p. 441)

4. **a** Regulated lending institutions include national banks, state-chartered banks, federal savings banks, savings and loans, and federal credit unions. (p. 442)

5. **d** Regulated lenders are required to hold reserves in a specified percentage of the outstanding loan balance for both performing and nonperforming loans, as well as REO properties. (p. 442)

6. **c** The deed in lieu of foreclosure requires the indebtedness to be secured by the real estate transferred. (p. 443)

7. **d** The lender under a trust deed is referred to as the beneficiary. (p. 444)

8. **c** The trustee, after filing the NOD, must mail a copy to the borrower and all others who requested such a notice, within 10 days after recording it. (p. 445)

9. **a** A special title report used for lenders of foreclosed properties is the trustee sale guarantee (TSG). (p. 447)

10. **a** The TSG protects the trustee and the beneficiary from damages because of an error in any title in the foreclosure proceedings. (p. 447)

CALIFORNIA LAWS

The following are important regulations of the State of California that govern activities and procedures of the escrow holder with which the escrow and title professional should be familiar. These include California Escrow Law, which is contained in Division 6 of the California Financial Code of the California Code of Regulations, and which begins with Section 1700. Also included in this appendix is the California law governing the transfer of title of real property, Civil Code sections 1052–1059, and California law that regulates the recordation of documents, Civil Code sections 1213–1220.

(The material in Appendix I is quoted from Escrow Law, California Department of Corporations, www.corp.ca.gov/Laws/Escrow_Law/.)

■ CALIFORNIA ESCROW LAW

The Escrow Law protects members of the public who entrust their money or other assets to independent escrow agents in California. Escrow agents, joint control agents, and Internet escrow agents are subject to the provisions of the Escrow Law.

Persons or companies performing escrow services over the Internet in California, or performing escrow services over the Internet for consumers in California, are subject to the licensing requirements of the Escrow Law. See Press Release No. 00-13 on the Department's home page for information regarding the enforcement of these licensing requirements.

The definitions in the Escrow Law determine who is subject to the licensing requirements of the law.

The Escrow Law defines "escrow agent" as any person engaged in the business of receiving escrows for deposit or delivery. The Escrow Law defines

"Internet escrow agent" as any person engaged in the business of receiving escrows for deposit or delivery over the Internet.

"Joint control agent" is defined under the Escrow Law as any person engaged in the business of receiving money or other property for disbursal or use in payment of the cost of labor, material, services, permits, fees, or other items of expense incurred in the construction of improvements upon real property.

Finally, the Escrow Law defines "escrow" as "any transaction wherein one person, for the purpose of effecting the sale, transfer, encumbering, or leasing of real property to another person, delivers any written instrument, money, evidence of title to real or personal property, or other thing of value to a third person to be held by such third person until the happening of a specified event or the performance of a prescribed condition, when it is then to be delivered by such third person to a grantee, grantor, promisee, promisor, obligee, obligor, bailee, bailor, or any agent or employee of any of the latter."

The Escrow Law requires any person engaged in the escrow business or joint control business in this state to be a corporation organized for that purpose and to be licensed by the Commissioner.

The following persons are excluded from the licensure requirements of the Escrow Law:

Any person doing business under any law of this state or the United States relating to banks, trust companies, building and loan or savings and loan associations, or insurance companies.

Any person licensed to practice law in California who has a bona fide client attorney relationship with a principal in a real estate or personal property transaction and who is not actively engaged in the business of an escrow agent.

Any person whose principal business is that of preparing abstracts or making searches of title that are used as a basis for the issuance of a policy of title insurance by a company doing business under any law of this state relating to insurance companies.

Any real estate broker licensed by the Real Estate Commissioner while performing acts in the course of or incidental to a real estate transaction in which the broker is an agent or a party to the transaction and in which the broker is performing an act for which a real estate license is required.

The requirements for obtaining a license are as follows:

Payment of the application fee. Fees for filing an application are $625 for the first office or location and $425 for each additional office or location along with an investigation fee of $100 for each location. The fees are non-refundable.

Membership in Escrow Agents' Fidelity Corporation (EAFC). An escrow agent must be a member of EAFC if the escrow agent will be engaging in the following types of escrows as specified in Section 17312(c) of the California Financial Code:

Real property escrows, including, but not limited to, the sale, lease, exchange, or transfer of title, and loans or other obligations to be secured by a lien upon real property.

Bulk sale escrows, including, but not limited to, the sale or transfer of title to a business entity and the transfer of liquor licenses or other types of business licenses or permits.

Fund or joint control escrows, including, but not limited to, transactions specified in 17005.1 of the California Financial Code and contracts specified in Section 10263 of the Public Contract Code.

The sale, transfer of title, or refinance escrows for manufactured homes or mobile homes.

Reservation deposits required under Article 2 (commencing with Section 11010) of Chapter 1 or Part 2 of Division 4 of the Business and Professions Code or by regulation of the Department of Real Estate to be held in an escrow account.

Escrows for sale, transfer, modification, assignment, or hypothecation of promissory notes secured by deeds of trust.

Fidelity bonding. Each applicant must file with the Department a fidelity bond if the transactions processed are of the type not listed in Section 17312(c) (i.e., the transactions listed in paragraph 2 above). The fidelity bond must provide fidelity coverage on each officer, director, trustee and employee of not less than $125,000 for the purpose of indemnifying the escrow agent (or the escrow agent's successor in interest) for loss of trust obligations held by the escrow agent as a result of fraudulent or dishonest abstraction, misappropriation, or embezzlement of trust obligations by an officer, director, trustee, or employee of the escrow agent.

The fidelity bond may contain a deductible; however, the escrow shall deposit with the Commissioner a surety bond satisfactory to the Commissioner in the amount of the deductible. The amount of the surety bond shall always be maintained in the amount of the deductible of the fidelity bond. The surety bond shall run to the state for the use of the state to cover any loss of trust obligations that the escrow agent's fidelity bond does not cover due to the fidelity bond's deductible.

Minimum financial requirements. Financial requirements must be demonstrated through submission of audited financial statements that indicate that the company has liquid assets in excess of current liabilities of $25,000 and tangible assets in excess of total liabilities of $50,000. If branch offices are maintained by the escrow agent, the tangible net worth requirement increases by 50% of the requirement for the first branch office and 25% for each additional branch office. Any losses projected by the applicant during the first few months of operation as shown in the applicant's proposed budget must be taken into consideration when calculating the tangible net worth and liquid assets.

Surety bonding. Each escrow agent must file with the Commissioner a surety bond of at least $25,000. The bond is intended to be used to pay to the state or any person any amount that is due to the state or such person under the provisions of the Escrow Law. The amount of the bond required may increase up to a maximum of $50,000 depending on the escrow liability of the company. The bond must be increased by $5,000 for each additional licensed office. In lieu of the surety bond a licensee may deposit with the Commissioner a cash bond in the amount required. The cash bond may be represented by cash deposited in a bank, an industrial loan company or a savings and loan association. Such cash deposits or certificates must be assigned to the Commissioner and may not be included in the assets of the licensee for purposes of the tangible net worth and liquid asset requirements.

Background checks. All stockholders, officers, directors, managers and employees must have background checks performed by the Department. These background checks include, among other things, obtaining criminal history information through the Department of Justice and conducting civil court checks for activities that would indicate previous involvement in fraud, embezzlement, fraudulent conversion, or misappropriation of property. Each stockholder, officer, director, manager, and employee will be required to file fingerprints cards, which must be cleared through the Department of Justice. Applicants may use the Live Scan program to submit fingerprints electronically to the Department of Justice for clearance. The fee for each clearance is $10 plus any fee charged by the Department of Justice or the live scan operator.

Minimum experience. The Escrow Law requires a manager who possesses a minimum of five years of responsible escrow experience to be stationed at the licensed location during open office hours.

Signed affidavit. An applicant must provide a signed affidavit certifying that the applicant has read and is familiar with the Escrow Law and regulations.

Branch offices. An applicant must file a branch office application to establish additional business office locations.

■ TRANSFERRING TITLE—ESCROW HOLDER DUTIES

California Civil Code Sections 1052–1059:

1052. A transfer may be made without writing, in every case in which a writing is not expressly required by statute.

[1053.] Section Ten Hundred and Fifty-three. A transfer in writing is called a grant, or conveyance, or bill of sale. The term "grant," in this and the next two Articles, includes all these instruments, unless it is specially applied to real property.

1054. A grant takes effect, so as to vest the interest intended to be transferred, only upon its delivery by the grantor.

1055. A grant duly executed is presumed to have been delivered at its date.

1056. A grant cannot be delivered to the grantee conditionally. Delivery to him, or to his agent as such, is necessarily absolute, and the instrument takes effect thereupon, discharged of any condition on which the delivery was made.

1057. A grant may be deposited by the grantor with a third person, to be delivered on performance of a condition, and, on delivery by the depositary, it will take effect. While in the possession of the third person, and subject to condition, it is called an escrow.

1057.3. (a) It shall be the obligation of a buyer and seller who enter into a contract to purchase and sell real property to ensure that all funds deposited into an escrow account are returned to the person who deposited the funds or who is otherwise entitled to the funds under the contract, if the purchase of the property is not completed by the date set forth in the contract for the close of escrow or any duly executed extension thereof.

(b) Any buyer or seller who fails to execute any document required by the escrow holder to release funds on deposit in an escrow account as provided in subdivision (a) within 30 days following a written demand for the return of funds deposited in escrow by the other party shall be liable to the person making the deposit for all of the following:

(1) The amount of the funds deposited in escrow not held in good faith to resolve a good faith dispute.

(2) Damages of treble the amount of the funds deposited in escrow not held to resolve a good faith dispute, but liability under this paragraph shall not be less than one hundred dollars ($100) or more than one thousand dollars ($1,000).

(3) Reasonable attorney's fees incurred in any action to enforce this section.

(c) Notwithstanding subdivision (b), there shall be no cause of action under this section, and no party to a contract to purchase and sell real property shall be liable, for failure to return funds deposited in an escrow account by a buyer or seller, if the funds are withheld in order to resolve a good faith dispute between a buyer and seller. A party who is denied the return of the funds deposited in escrow is entitled to damages under this section only upon proving that there was no good faith dispute as to the right to the funds on deposit.

(d) Upon the filing of a cause of action pursuant to this section, the escrow holder shall deposit the sum in dispute, less any cancellation fee and charges incurred, with the court in which the action is filed and be discharged of further responsibility for the funds.

(e) Neither any document required by the escrow holder to release funds deposited in an escrow account nor the acceptance of funds released from escrow, by any principal to the escrow transaction, shall be deemed a cancellation or termination of the underlyingcontract to purchase and sell real property, unless the cancellation is specifically stated therein. If the escrow instructions constitute the only contract between the buyer and seller, no document required by the escrow holder to release funds deposited in an escrow account shall abrogate a cause of action for breach of a contractual obligation to purchase or sell real property, unless the cancellation is specifically stated therein.

(f) For purposes of this section:

(1) "Close of escrow" means the date, specified event, or performance of prescribed condition upon which the escrow agent is to deliver the subject of the escrow to the person specified in the buyer's instructions to the escrow agent.

(2) "Good faith dispute" means a dispute in which the trier of fact finds that the party refusing to return the deposited funds had a reasonable belief of his or her legal entitlement to withhold the deposited funds. The existence of a "good faith dispute" shall be determined by the trier of fact.

(3) "Property" means real property containing one to four residential units at least one of which at the time the escrow is created is to be occupied by

the buyer. The buyer's statement as to his or her intention to occupy one of the units is conclusive for the purposes of this section.

(g) Nothing in this section restricts the ability of an escrow holder to file an interpleader action in the event of a dispute as to the proper distribution of funds deposited in an escrow account.

1057.5. Except for the normal compensation of his own employees, no person acting as an escrow agent whether required to be licensed as such or not, shall pay over to any other person any commission, fee, or other consideration as compensation for referring, soliciting, handling, or servicing escrow customers or accounts.

> "No escrow agent shall enter into any arrangement, either of his own making or of a subsidiary nature, or through any other person having a dual capacity, or through any person having a direct or indirect interest in the escrow, or other device, permitting any fee, commission, or compensation which is contingent upon the performance of any act, condition, or instruction set forth in an escrow, to be drawn or paid, either in whole or in part, or in kind or its equivalent, prior to the actual closing and completion of the escrow. The provisions of this section shall not be deemed to supersede, negate, or modify any of the provisions of Section 12404 of the Insurance Code."

1057.6. In an escrow transaction for the purchase or simultaneous exchange of real property, where a policy of title insurance will not be issued to the buyer or to the parties to the exchange, the following notice shall be provided in a separate document to the buyer or parties exchanging real property, which shall be signed and acknowledged by them:

> "IMPORTANT: IN A PURCHASE OR EXCHANGE OF REAL PROPERTY, IT MAY BE ADVISABLE TO OBTAIN TITLE INSURANCE IN CONNECTION WITH THE CLOSE OF ESCROW SINCE THERE MAY BE PRIOR RECORDED LIENS AND ENCUMBRANCES WHICH AFFECT YOUR INTEREST IN THE PROPERTY BEING ACQUIRED. A NEW POLICY OF TITLE INSURANCE SHOULD BE OBTAINED IN ORDER TO ENSURE YOUR INTEREST IN THE PROPERTY THAT YOU ARE ACQUIRING."

1057.7. All written escrow instructions executed by a buyer or seller, whether prepared by a person subject to Division 6 (commencing with Section 17000) of the Financial Code, or by a person exempt from that division under Section 17006 of the Financial Code, shall contain a statement in not less than 10-point type which shall include the license name and the name of the department issuing the license or authority under which the person is operating. This section shall not apply to supplemental escrow instructions or modifications to escrow instructions. This section shall become operative on July 1, 1993.

1058. Redelivering a grant of real property to the grantor, or canceling it, does not operate to retransfer the title.

1058.5. (a) A notice of nonacceptance of a recorded deed executed by a holder of a security interest, which notice identifies the security interest, contains a legal description of the property, properly identifies the parties to the deed, the date of recordation of the deed, the county in which the project is located, and the county assessor's parcel number of the real property referenced in the deed, may be recorded in the office of the county recorder where the real property is located.

(b) Where a trustee's deed is invalidated by a pending bankruptcy or otherwise, recordation of a notice of rescission of the trustee's deed, which notice properly identifies the deed of trust, the identification numbers used by the recorder or the books and pages at which the trustee's deed and deed of trust are recorded, the names of all trustors and beneficiaries, the location of the property subject to the deed of trust, and the reason for rescission, shall restore the condition of record title to the real property described in the trustee's deed and the existence and priority of all lienholders to the status quo prior to the recordation of the trustee' s deed upon sale. Only the trustee or beneficiary who caused the trustee's deed to be recorded, or his or her successor in interest, may record a notice of rescission.

1059. Though a grant be not actually delivered into the possession of the grantee, it is yet to be deemed constructively delivered in the following cases: 1. Where the instrument is, by the agreement of the parties at the time of execution, understood to be delivered, and under such circumstances that the grantee is entitled to immediate delivery; or,

2. Where it is delivered to a stranger for the benefit of the grantee, and his assent is shown, or may be presumed.

■ CALIFORNIA RECORDATION LAWS

Civil Code Sections 1213–1220:

1213. Every conveyance of real property or an estate for years therein acknowledged or proved and certified and recorded as prescribed by law from the time it is filed with the recorder for record is constructive notice of the contents thereof to subsequent purchasers and mortgagees; and a certified copy of such a recorded conveyance may be recorded in any other county and when so recorded the record thereof shall have the same force and effect as though it was of the original conveyance and where the original conveyance has been recorded in any county wherein the property therein mentioned is not situated a certified copy of the recorded conveyance may be recorded in the county where such property is situated with the same force and effect as if the original conveyance had been recorded in that county.

1214. Every conveyance of real property or an estate for years therein, other than a lease for a term not exceeding one year, is void as against any subsequent purchaser or mortgagee of the same property, or any part thereof, in good faith and for a valuable consideration, whose conveyance is first duly recorded, and as against any judgment affecting the title, unless the conveyance shall have been duly recorded prior to the record of notice of action.

1215. The term "conveyance," as used in Sections 1213 and 1214, embraces every instrument in writing by which any estate or interest in real property is created, aliened, mortgaged, or encumbered, or by which the title to any real property may be affected, except wills.

1216. No power contained in an instrument to convey or execute instruments affecting real property which has been recorded is revoked by any act of the party by whom it was executed, unless the instrument containing such revocation is also acknowledged or proved, certified and recorded, in the same office in which the instrument containing the power was recorded.

1217. An unrecorded instrument is valid as between the parties thereto and those who have notice thereof.

1218. A certified copy of an instrument affecting the title to real property, once recorded, or a certified copy of the record of such instrument may be recorded in any other county, and, when so recorded, the record thereof has the same force and effect as though it was of the original instrument.

1219. Oil and gas leases may be acknowledged or proved, certified and recorded in like manner and with like effect, as grants of real property. However, an oil and gas lease may be recorded and constructive notice of the same and the contents of that lease given in the following manner: Any person may record in the office of county recorder of any county fictitious oil and gas leases. Those fictitious oil and gas leases need not be acknowledged, or proved, or certified, to be recorded or entitled to record. Oil and gas leases shall have noted upon the face thereof that they are fictitious. The county recorder shall index and record fictitious oil and gas leases in the same manner as other oil and gas leases are recorded, and shall note on all indices and records of the same that they are fictitious. Thereafter, any of the provisions of any recorded fictitious oil and gas lease may be included for any and all purposes in any oil and gas lease by reference therein to those provisions, without setting the same forth in full, if the fictitious oil and gas lease is of record in the county in which the oil and gas lease adopting or including by reference any of the provisions of the lease is recorded. The reference shall contain a statement, as to each county in which the oil and gas lease containing such a reference is recorded, of the date the fictitious oil and gas lease was recorded, the county recorder's office in which it is recorded, and the book or volume and the first page of the records or the recorder's instrument number in the recorder's office in which the fictitious oil and gas lease was recorded, and a statement by paragraph numbers or any other method that will definitely identify the same, of the specific provisions of any fictitious oil and gas lease that are being adopted and included therein. The recording of any oil and gas lease which has included any provisions by reference shall operate as constructive notice of the whole including the terms, as a part of the written contents of any oil and gas lease, of any provisions so included by reference as though the same were written in full therein. The parties bound or to be bound by provisions so adopted and included by reference shall be bound thereby in the same manner and with like effect for all purposes as though the provisions had been and were set forth in full in the oil and gas lease.

1220. Contracts for the purchase or sale of standing timber or trees, for severance or otherwise, and all instruments in writing by which any estate or interest in, or right to cut, standing timber or trees is created, aliened, mortgaged or encumbered or by which the title to any standing timber or trees may be affected, may be acknowledged or proved, certified and recorded in like manner and with like effect, as grants of real property, and all statutory provisions relating to the recordation or nonrecordation of conveyances of real property and to the effect thereof shall apply to such contracts and instruments with like effect. Any such contracts for purchase and sale or instruments in writing affecting the title to standing timber or trees, executed and delivered before the effective date of the amendment of this section at the 1959 Regular Session of the Legislature but unrecorded before such date, shall become subject to all statutory provisions relating to the recordation or nonrecordation of conveyances of real property and to the effect thereof one year from said effective date.

California Civil Code Sections 880.310–880.370

880.310. (a) If the time within which an interest in real property expires pursuant to this title depends upon recordation of a notice of intent to preserve the interest, a person may preserve the person's interest from expiration by **recording** a notice of intent to preserve the interest before the interest expires pursuant to this title. Recordation of a notice of intent to preserve an interest in real property after the interest has expired pursuant to this title does not preserve the interest.

(b) Recordation of a notice of intent to preserve an interest in real property does not preclude a court from determining that an interest has been abandoned or is otherwise unenforceable pursuant to other law, whether before or after the notice of intent to preserve the interest is recorded, and does not validate or make enforceable a claim or interest that is otherwise invalid or unenforceable. Recordation of a notice of intent to preserve an interest in real property creates a presumption affecting the burden of proof that the person who claims the interest has not abandoned and does not intend to abandon the interest.

880.320. A notice of intent to preserve an interest in real property may be recorded by any of the following persons:

(a) A person who claims the interest.

(b) Another person acting on behalf of a claimant if the person is authorized to act on behalf of the claimant or if the claimant is one of a class whose identity cannot be established or is uncertain at the time of **recording** the notice of intent to preserve the interest.

880.330. Subject to all statutory requirements for recorded documents:

(a) A notice of intent to preserve an interest in real property shall be in writing and signed and verified by or on behalf of the claimant. If the notice is made on behalf of a claimant, the notice shall include a statement of the authority of the person making the notice.

(b) The notice shall contain all of the following information:

(1) The name and mailing address of the claimant. If the notice is made by or on behalf of more than one claimant the notice shall contain the name and mailing address of each claimant.

(2) A statement of the character of interest claimed. The statement shall include a reference by record location to the recorded document that creates or evidences the interest in the claimant.

(3) A legal description of the real property in which the interest is claimed. The description may be the same as that contained in the recorded document that creates or evidences the interest in the claimant.

880.340. Subject to all statutory requirements for recorded documents, a notice of intent to preserve an interest in real property shall be in substantially the following form:

RECORDING INFORMATION
Recording requested by: FOR USE OF COUNTY RECORDER

After recording return to: Indexing instructions.
This notice must be indexed as follows:

Grantor and grantee index--each claimant is a grantor.

NOTICE OF INTENT TO PRESERVE INTEREST
This notice is intended to preserve an interest in real property from extinguishment pursuant to Title 5 (commencing with Section 880.020) of Part 2 of Division 2 of the Civil Code (Marketable Record Title).

Claimant Name:
Mailing address: (must be given for each claimant)
Interest Character (e.g., power of termination):
Record location of document creating or evidencing interest in claimant:

Real Property Legal description (may be same as in recorded document creating or evidencing interest in claimant):

I assert under penalty of perjury that this notice is not recorded for the purpose of slandering title to real property and I am informed and believe that the information contained in this notice is true. If this notice is made on behalf of a claimant, I assert under penalty of perjury that I am authorized to **act** on behalf of the claimant.

Signed: _____ Date: _____
(claimant)

_____
(person acting on behalf of claimant)

State of _____,
County of _____, ss.
On this _____ day of _____, in the year _____, before me (here insert name and quality of officer), personally appeared _____, personally known to me (or proved to me on the basis of satisfactory evi-

dence) to be the person whose name is subscribed to this instrument, and acknowledged that he (she or they) executed it.

Signed: _____ Official Seal:

Office: _____

880.350. (a) A notice of intent to preserve an interest in real property shall be recorded in the county in which the real property is situated.

(b) The county recorder shall index a notice of intent to preserve an interest in real property in the index of grantors and grantees. The index entry shall be for the grantor, and for the purpose of this index, the claimant under the notice shall be deemed to be the grantor. If a notice of intent to preserve is recorded by or on behalf of more than one claimant, each claimant shall be deemed to be a grantor and a separate index entry shall be made for each claimant.

880.360. A person shall not record a notice of intent to preserve an interest in real property for the purpose of slandering title to the real property. If the court in an action or proceeding to establish or quiet title determines that a person recorded a notice of intent to preserve an interest for the purpose of slandering title, the court shall award against the person the cost of the action or proceeding, including a reasonable attorney's fee, and the damages caused by the **recording**.

880.370. If the period prescribed by statute during which a notice of intent to preserve an interest in real property must be recorded expires before, on, or within five years after the operative date of the statute, the period is extended until five years after the operative date of the statute.

APPENDIX TWO

HOW TO READ A PRELIMINARY TITLE REPORT

The following pamphlet, reprinted with permission by and provided courtesy of Fidelity Title Insurance Company, provides a complete step-by-step explanation of the preliminary title report. It serves as a useful guide not only for title insurance, escrow, and real estate licensee professionals but also for the buyer or the seller of real property.

HOW TO READ A PRELIMINARY TITLE REPORT

A Preliminary Title Report (PR) is a report which shows the terms upon which the company may issue its policy. It does not constitute a policy nor a commitment to issue such a policy. Also set out in the PR are information items that will assist the customer in expediently closing the proposed transaction thus enabling Fidelity to issue its policy(ies) of title insurance.

The PR is issued after a thorough title search has been made on the real property and all the documents affecting said property have been examined to determine their effect on said property.

The title search is made of the public record, generally including the following offices:

The County Recorder of the county in which the real property is located.

The taxing authority(ies) that levies(y) taxes and assessments on real property.

The clerk of various courts of the State of California

The clerk of the United States District Court.

In addition to the above mentioned public records, certain types of policies to be issued by Fidelity require that we make a physical inspection of the property. This inspection may disclose additional encumbrances or rights of other parties in and to said property not disclosed by the public records.

Following is a brief explanation of some of the more common items shown in a PR together with an explanation of some of the preprinted items shown therein. The Preliminary Report provided herein is a sample of what a customer would receive shortly after placing the title order with Fidelity. The numbered items shown on the sample PR.

"Preliminary Report Top Sheet"
Help us stay on top of your transaction!
WILL ANY OF THESE SITUATIONS
AFFECT YOUR TRANSACTION?

- Are your principals exchanging this property?   _____Yes   _____No

- Will your principals be using a power of attorney?   _____Yes   _____No

- Are any of the parties in title deceased?   _____Yes   _____No

- Has there been a change in marital status?   _____Yes   _____No

- Will there be a new entity formed?
  ie., partnership or corporation.   _____Yes   _____No

- Are the sellers of this property non-residents
  of California?   _____Yes   _____No

If you answered "YES" to any of these questions,
please call your Escrow Officer.

- Do all parties signing document have valid
  photo I.D. or drivers license?   _____Yes   _____No

If "No", now is the time to apply for a valid I.D.

This is a "Quick List", call your Escrow Officer if you have additional information that you think may be important, or if you have any questions.

Thank you for choosing
Fidelity National Title Company

Fidelity National Title Company
OF CALIFORNIA

PRELIMINARY REPORT

1 In response to the application for a policy of title insurance referenced herein, **Fidelity National Title Company** hereby reports that it is prepared to issue, or cause to be issued, as of the date hereof, a Policy or Policies of Title Insurance describing the land and the estate or interest therein hereinafter set forth, insuring against loss which may be sustained by reason of any defect, lien or encumbrance not shown or referred to as an Exception herein or not excluded from coverage pursuant to the printed Schedules, Conditions and Stipulations of said Policy forms.

2 The printed Exceptions and Exclusions from the coverage and Limitations on Covered Risks of said Policy or Policies are set forth in Exhibit A attached. Limitations on Covered Risks applicable to the CLTA and ALTA Homeowner's Policies of Title Insurance which establish a Deductible Amount and a Maximum Dollar Limit of Liability for certain coverage are also set forth in Exhibit A. Copies of the Policy forms should be read. They are available from the office which issued this report.

3 This report (and any supplements or amendments hereto) is issued solely for the purpose of facilitating the issuance of a policy of title insurance and no liability is assumed hereby. If it is desired that liability be assumed prior to the issuance of a policy of title insurance, a Binder or Commitment should be requested.

The Policy(s) of title insurance to be issued hereunder will be policy(s) of Fidelity National Title Insurance Company, a California Corporation.

Please read the exceptions shown or referred to below and the exceptions and exclusions set forth in Exhibit A of this report carefully. The exceptions and exclusions are meant to provide you with notice of matters which are not covered under the terms of the title insurance policy and should be carefully considered.

It is important to note that this preliminary report is not a written representation as to the condition of title and may not list all liens, defects and encumbrances affecting title to the land.

Fidelity National Title Company

BY _____ President

ATTEST _____ Secretary

_____
Countersigned

SEAL

(Rev. 11/17/04)

1 This preprinted paragraph states as of the dated date of the Preliminary Report, that Fidelity is willing, as of said date, to issue a policy(ies) of title insurance showing the items listed in the PR.

2 This preprinted paragraph is a statement that in additional to the specific exceptions shown in the PR, the policy(ies), when issued, will contain certain standard preprinted exceptions and exclusions not shown in the PR. Exhibit "A" to which the PR is attached will set out what these exceptions and exclusions will be.

3 This preprinted paragraph makes the statement that the PR is not a policy, and therefore no liability is assumed as to its correctness. If liability is required when the order is opened, the costumer should request a Binder or a Commitment rather than a PR.

Fidelity National Title   **Explanation of a Preliminary Title Report**

Fidelity National Title Company

301 E. Vanderbilt Way, Suite #400 • San Bernardino, CA 92408
(909) 890-0601 • FAX

PRELIMINARY REPORT

4 ESCROW OFFICER: Jane Escrow
TITLE OFFICER: Joe Title

ORDER NO.: 999999 **6**
LOAN NO.:

5 TO: Any Reliable Escrow

ATTN: Jane Escrow
YOUR REFERENCE.:   1122-EO

SHORT TERM RATE: Yes

PROPERTY ADDRESS: 2536 Brandywine Avenue, Palm Springs, California

---

7 EFFECTIVE DATE: May 1, 2005, 07:30 A.M.

The form of Policy or Policies of title insurance contemplated by this report is:

8 California Land Title Association Standard Coverage Policy - 1990
American Land Title Association Loan Policy (10-17-92) with A.L.T.A. Form 1 Coverage

1.   THE ESTATE OR INTEREST IN THE LAND HEREINAFTER DESCRIBED OR REFERRED TO COVERED BY THIS REPORT IS:

9   A Fee

2.   TITLE TO SAID ESTATE OR INTEREST AT THE DATE HEREOF IS VESTED IN:
Robert M. Sellerperson and Mary K. Sellerperson, husband and wife as joint ten ants, at to an undivided 1/2 interest; and John Doe, as Trustee U.D.T. dated
10   January 15, 1980, as to an undivided 1/2 interest

3.   THE LAND REFERRED TO IN THIS REPORT IS SITUATED IN THE CITY OF PALM SPRINGS, IN THE COUNTY OF RIVERSIDE, STATE OF CALIFORNIA, AND IS DESCRIBED AS FOLLOWS:

11   SEE EXHIBIT "ONE" ATTACHED HERETO AND MADE A PART HEREOF

CLE\CLE 05/06/2005

1

(Rev. 11/17/04)

Order No. 999999

EXHIBIT "ONE"

11 Lot 25 of AP0LLO UNIT NO. 3, in the City of Palm Springs, County of Riverside, State of California, according to Map thereof No. 7979, filed in Book 123 page 45 of Maps, Records of Riverside County California.

2

(Rev. 11/17/04)

4 This is the name of the title officer responsible for processing the order. Any questions regarding any items shown in the PR should be directed tot his person. The telephone number of this peron can be found to the right of their name. Remember to refer to the order number when calling the Title Officer.

5 The information set out here is the name, address, reference number, and contact person of the customer who requested the PR from Fidelity. If a lender will be tying into the transaction, Fidelity will furnish that lender a copy of the PR also.

6 In this area, a number will appear. This will be the order number that Fidelity assigned to the transaction when the order was opened by the customer. When directing any questions or correspondence to us, please refer to the order number shown in this space. This will assist us to quickly respond to your inquiry.

7 This is the date and time to which the public records have been examined in compiling the PR. Any items or documents recorded on this date or after this date will be reported to the customer by means of a supplemental title report and/or an amended PR.

8 This item shows the type, or types of policy(ies) that Fidelity has been requested to issue one the transaction closes. It is important to remember that some policies, most notably the ALTA, will require that Fidelity physically inspect the property before issuing such policy(ies). If such a policy will be required, please inform your title officer as soon as it is known to you, preferably when the order is opened. This will enable us to make the inspections well in advance of the contemplated closing date of the transaction.

9 This item indicates the type of estate that the vested owner holds in the real property. In most instances it will be a fee estate, which means the vested owner owns the dirt and the structures, if any, attached thereto. Other types of estates that could be covered by a PR include "leasehold," "life estate" and easement."

10 This shows, as of the date of the PR, the name of the person(s) are entity(ies) who hold title to the estate shown in item "9" above. In most instances this item will show who owns the real property. Also included herein will be the status of the vestee (i.e. single, married, etc.) and the manner in which they hold title (i.e. joint tenants, community property, etc.)

11 On the next page.

Fidelity National Title   **Explanation of a Preliminary Title Report**

11 This is the legal description of the real property for which the PR was prepared. Fidelity requires that all documents to be recorded at the close of the transaction contains this exact legal description. Any discrepancy between the legal description in the PR and the documents to the recorded should be discussed with the Title Officer as soon as possible to avoid any delays in the closing of the transaction.

Order No. 999999

12 AT THE DATE HEREOF, ITEMS TO BE CONSIDERED AND EXCEPTIONS TO COVERAGE IN ADDITION TO THE PRINTED EXCEPTIONS AND EXCLUSIONS IN SAID POLICY FORM WOULD BE AS FOLLOWS:

13 1. Property taxes, which are a lien not yet due and payable, including any assessments collected with taxes to be levied for the fiscal year 2004-2005.

14 2. Said property has been declared tax defaulted for non-payment of delinquent taxes for the fiscal year 2004-2005.

APN:	230-110-023
Default No.:	
Default Date:	June 30, 2004

Amounts to redeem for the above stated fiscal year (and subsequent years, if any) are:

Amount:	$839.30
By	September 30, 2004
Amount:	$850.54
By:	October 31, 2004

15 3. Supplemental assessment for 2004-2005

Bill No.:	839-012-025-07
1st Installment:	$102.50 Unpaid
Must be paid by:	December 10, 2004
2nd Installment	$102.50 Unpaid
Must be paid by:	April 10, 2005

16 4. The lien of supplemental taxes, if any, assessed pursuant to the provisions of Chapter 3.5 (Commencing with Section 75) of the Revenue and Taxation code of the State of California.

17 5. Easement(s) for the purposes(s) shown below and rights incidental thereto as delineated or as offered for dedication, on the map of said tract.

Purpose:	planting and maintenance
Affects:	the Southwesterly 7 feet

18 6. Covenants, conditions and restrictions (deleting therefrom any restrictions indicating any preference, limitation or discrimination based on race, color, religion, sex, handicap, familial status or national origin) as set forth in the document

Recorded: January 15, 1974, Instrument No. 74-159206, of Official Records

Said covenants, conditions and restrictions provide that a violation thereof shall not defeat the lien of any mortgage or deed of trust made in good faith and for value.

NOTE: Section 12956.1 of the Government Code provides the following: If this document contains any restriction based on race, color, religion, sex familial status, marital status, disability, national origin, or ancestry, that restriction violates state and federal housing laws and is void. Any person holding an interest in this property may request that the county recorder remove the restrictive language pursuant to subdivision (c) of Section 12956.1 of the Government Code.

(Rev. 11/17/04)

12 Any matter that affects the real property will be shown following this paragraph. These matters, called encumbrances and liens, will also be shown in the policy(ies), to be issued, unless they are paid off and released, or otherwise eliminated, prior to or concurrently with the issuance of said policy(ies). The usual matters shown here would be taxes, easements, covenants, conditions, restrictions, deeds of trust, money liens and judgements.

13 Most real property is subject to property taxes assessed by the tax collector. The tax information will always be shown as the first item in the PR because taxes have priority over all other matters. This item means that the property taxes for the fiscal year of July 1st to the following June 30th actually become a lien on January 1st preceding the fiscal year even though the amount of the tax will not be available until the end of October of the fiscal year. This item will always be shown in any PR dated between January 1st and November 1st, the date the first installment of the tax is due and payable.

14 If the property taxes for al fiscal year are not paid by June 30th, the last day of the fiscal year, those property taxes are in default and the property is referred to as "tax defaulted property." Prior to September 11, 1984, tax defaulted property was referred to as "tax sale to the State." If the property taxes are in default for prior fiscal years, the amount necessary to redeem the property will be shown in this item.

15 The Legislature in 1983 passed a law providing for the prompt reassessment of real property anytime that property changed ownership or new construction has been completed thereon. Such reassessment will result in a supplemental tax bill for the additional tax amount. Supplemental tax bills will always be forthcoming if property has changed ownership or if new construction has been completed. However, they will not become a lien on the property until such time as they are posted in the records of the tax collector, which could be at a date after both the PR and the Title Policy(ies) are issued at the close of the transaction.

16 This item will always show in the PR and the Policy(ies) because of the aforementioned law passed in 1983. Supplemental tax bills will always be forthcoming if property has changed ownership or if new construction has been completed. However, they will not become a lien on the property until such time as they are posted in the records of the tax collector, which could be at a date after both the PR and the Title Policy(ies) are issued at the close of the transaction.

17 This item refers to an easement as disclosed by the recorded subdivision map. An easement is the limited right of someone other than the owner of the property to use the property for a specified purpose.

18 Covenants, conditions and restrictions (CC&R) are limitations or qualifications on the use of real property imposed by a former owner by a conveyance or other document within the chain of title. If requested, Fidelity will be happy to furnish the customer a copy of the document imposing the CC&Rs so that any party of the transaction will be aware of what those limitations are regarding the use of the property.

Fidelity National Title   **Explanation of a Preliminary Title Report**

ITEMS: (Continued)   Order No. 999999

19 7. Easement(s) for the purpose(s) shown below and rights incidental thereto as granted in a document.

Granted to: Southern California Edison Company
Purpose: public utilities
Recorded: July 13, 1974, Instrument/File No. 74-152681, of Official Records

Affects: the Northeasterly 6 feet

20 8. A deed of trust to secure an indebtedness in the amount shown below, and any other obligations secured thereby

Amount: $70,000.00
Dated: July 15, 1974
Trustor: Marvin Priorowner and Sally W. Priorowner
Trustee: Fidelity National Title
Beneficiary: Lake Mortgage Company
Address: 6000 Lake Avenue
                       Waterfront, CA 92111
Loan No.:   98765
Recorded: August 1, 1974, Instrument No. 74-160505, of Official Records

21   A Notice of Default under the terms of said deed of trust.

Executed by: Lake Mortgage Company
Recorded: January 4, 1993, Instrument No. 1993-0002163, of Official Records

22 9. An abstract of judgment for the amount shown below and any other amounts due:
Amount: $13,512.00
Debtor: Marvin Priorowner and Sally W. Priorowner
Creditor: Charles A. Winner
Date Entered: August 14, 2000
County: Riverside
Court: Municipal Court
Case No.:   567009
Returned to:
Name: Charles A. Winner
Address: 444 Winner Circle
                       Riverside , CA 92111
Recorded: August 14, 1999, Instrument No. 2000-0123879, of Official Records

An examination of said proceedings has been ordered. Upon completion the Company reserves the right to except additional items and/or make additional requirements.

23 10. A tax lien for the amount shown and any other amounts due, in favor of the United States of America, assessed by the District Director of Internal Revenue.
Federal
Serial No: 0031-2134673
Taxpayer: Robert M. Sellerperson
Amount: $5,850.00
Recorded: April 15, 2001, of Official Records

4

19 This item refers to an easement. Usually easements are for utility purposes, widening of streets and private driveway. It is important to remember that an easement shown in this part of the PR runs over the subject property and does not refer to an easement that benefits the property shown in the PR such as access. Easement(s) for access to the property would be shown in the PR as part of legal description.

20 A deed of trust is a conveyance in trust from the owner of the property to the trustee set out in the deed of trust for the purpose of securing repayment of a monetary debt or some other form of obligation. If this item is to be paid off concurrently with the close of the transaction, the beneficiary of record must be contacted in order to obtain a reconveyance of the deed of trust.

21 A notice of default is recorded as a result of the owner of the property failing to preform their obligation under the terms of the obligation secured by the deed of trust. Usually when recorded it means the property owner has failed to make the monthly payments due under the debt secured by the Deed of Trust. Immediate attention should be given to this item if it is shown in the PR.

22 An abstract of judgment is recorded as a result of a judicial determination as to the winner, called the creditor, and the loser, called the debtor, at the conclusion of a lawsuit. The debtor could be a former owner, the present owner or the proposed buyer of the property. Once again, immediate attention should be given to this item as the creditor must submit a demand and a satisfaction of judgment prior to or concurrent with the close of the transaction if this item is to be eliminated from the policy(ies).

23 A federal tax lien will be filed by the Internal Revenue Service as a result of taxpayer's failure to pay their income taxes. Like an abstract of judgment, this could be against the present/previous owner or the proposed buyer in the transaction. In order for this item not to show in the in the policy(ies) to be issued, the IRS will have to de contacted to get a demand and a release of the lien prior to or concurrent with the close of the transaction. Similar type liens may also be recorded by the State of California or the Tax Collector of the County for various reasons, such as failure to pay state income taxes or failure to pay unsecured property taxes.

Fidelity National Title   **Explanation of a Preliminary Title Report**

ITEMS: (Continued)   Order No. 999999

24 11.   A pending Court Action as disclosed by a recorded notice:

Plaintiff:	John I. Want and Sara Ann Want
Defendant:	Robert M. Sellerperson and Mary K. Sellerperson
County:	Riverside
Court:	Superior Court
Case No.:	235678
Nature of	
Action:	for specific performance
Attorney:	David S. Court
Address:	9988 Law Street
	Any Court, CA 95666
Recorded:	September 10, 2002, Instrument No. 2002-287901, of Official Records

25 12.   We find various Liens and Judgments, that are of record against persons with similar or the same name as that of our vestee(s) shown herein. In order to complete this report, this Company requires a Statement of Information to be provided for the following vestee(s), which may allow and assist elimination of some or all of said Liens and Judgments. After review of the requested Statement(s) of Information, the Company reserves the right to add additional items or make further requirements prior to the issuance of any Policy of Title Insurance.

   Vestee(s):   Robert M. Sellerperson and Mary K. Sellerperson

26 13.   We find various Liens and Judgments, that are of record against persons with similar or the same name as that of our vestee(s) shown herein. In order to complete this report, this Company requires a Statement of Information to be provided for the following vestee(s), which may allow and assist elimination of some or all of said Liens and Judgments. After review of the requested Statement(s) of Information, the Company reserves the right to add additional items or make further requirements prior to the issuance of any Policy of Title Insurance.

   Vestee(s):   John Doe

27 14.   Any invalidity or defect in the title of the vestees in the event that the trust referred to herein is invalid or fails to grant sufficient powers to the trustee(s) or in the event there is a lack of compliance with the terms and provisions of the trust instrument.

   If title is to be insured in the trustee(s) of a trust, (or if their act is to be insured), this Company will require a Trust Certification pursuant to California Probate Code Section 18100.5. The Company reserves the right to except additional items and/or make additional requirements after reviewing said documents.

28 15.   This company will require a statement of information from the parties named below in order to complete this report, based on the effect of documents, proceedings, liens, decrees, or other matters which do not specifically describe said land, but which, if any do exist, may affect the title or impose liens or encumbrances thereon. After review of the requested Statement(s) of Information the Company may have additional requirements before the issuance of any policy of title insurance.

   Parties: John Buyer and Mary Buyer

   (Note: The statement of information is necessary to complete the search and examination of title under this order. Any title search includes matters that are indexed by name only, and having a completed statement of information assists the Company in the elimination of certain matters which appear to involve the parties but in fact affect another party with the same or similar name. Be assured that the statement of information is essential and will be kept strictly confidential to this file).

(Rev. 11/17/04)

24 This item indicates that a lawsuit has been commenced in court that affects the title to real property. Reasons for which the lawsuit might be commenced include condemnation, foreclosure of a mechanic's lien or breach of contract. This item should always be cleared prior to the close of the transaction by obtaining a dismissal of the action. If not eliminated, the Buyer's title will be subject to the final outcome of the action. If the final outcome is unfavorable, the Buyer could lose title to the property.

25
26
28 These items indicate that when the title search was made, many items, such as tax liens, and abstracts of judgments, have been recorded against people having the same or a similar name of the parties to the transaction. In order for Fidelity to make a determination as to whether these items are against the parties to the transaction, we will need a Statement of Information from these parties. Make your Title Officer a happy person. Please try to get the Statements of Information to them as soon as possible. If one of the parties to the transaction is "John Smith," many, many documents will have to be examined to determine if our "John Smith" is the same "John Smith" shown on these documents. This can only be done after the Statements of Information have been received.

27 When reporting and insuring title where ownership is in a trustee of a trust, we request the customer supply us with a copy of the trust and all supplements and amendments to it, to confirm the legal existence of the trust, the identity of the trustee(s), and the sufficiency of their power under the trust to deal with real property in the manner contemplated by the proposed transaction. Trusts have come into increasing use for a variety of reasons, with this use we have seen reluctance to supply us with a complete copy of the Trust. We now have a way, provided under Probate Code Section 18100.5, for us to accept a Certification of Trust, in most cases, instead of the entire trust document.

Fidelity National Title   **Explanation of a Preliminary Title Report**

ITEMS: (Continued)   Order No. 999999

END OF ITEMS

29 Note 1. NOTE: The ALTA Homeowners Policy of Title Insurance (10-17-98) contains specific deductible amounts and specific liability maximums for Covered Risk numbers 14, 15, 16 and 18 of said policy that have been filed and approved by the various Departments of Insurance where the forms have been filed. Please consult with your escrow or title officer if you have questions regarding the policy.

30 Note 2. The Note shown below, which recites: "California Revenue and Taxation Code Section 18668, effective January 1, 1991, requires that the buyer in all sales of California Real Estate, wherein the Seller shows an out of State Address, withhold 3-1/3% of the total sales price as California State Income Tax, subject to the various provisions of the law as therein contained."

is hereby deleted and replaced with the following:

California Revenue and Taxation Code Section 18662, effective January 1, 1994 and by Amendment effective January 1, 2003, provides that the buyer in all sales of California Real Estate may be required to withhold 3 and 1/3% of the total sales price as California State Income Tax, subject to the various provisions of the law as herein obtained.

31 Note 3. None of the items shown in this report will cause the Company to decline to attach CLTA Endorsement Form 100 to an Extended Coverage Loan Policy, when issued.

31 Note 4. The Company is not aware of any matters which would cause it to decline to attach the CLTA Endorsement Form 116 indicating that there is located on said land Single Family Residence known as 2536 Brandywine Avenue, Palm Springs, CA to an Extended Coverage Loan Policy.

31 Note 5. There are NO deeds affecting said land, recorded within twenty-four (24) months of the date of this report.

32 Note 6. Wiring instructions for FIDELITY NATIONAL TITLE INSURANCE COMPANY, INLAND EMPIRE, California, are as follows:

Receiving Bank:	Bank of America
	1850 Gateway Blvd.
	Concord, CA 94520
Federal Routing No.:	121-000-358
Account Name:	Fidelity National Title Insurance Company
	Title Trust Account, Inland Empire
Account Number:	12356-19437
Title Order No.:	999999
TITLE OFFICER:	Joe Title

This information is to be included in the wire text.

(Rev. 11/17/04)

29 When the contemplated policy involves a sale transaction, this is where the buyers names are shown. Any discrepancies in the spelling of the names should be immediately brought to the Title Officer's attention, so the appropriate corrections can be made.

30 This paragraph relates to whether the property does or does not qualify for the automatic issuance of the 1987 ALTA-R Policy. If the property does not, Fidelity may have to physically inspect the property before a determination can be made. Any items disclosed by inspection will be disclosed by a supplemental report and/or an amended PR.

31 If a lender's ALTA policy has been requested Notes 3, 4 and 5 are shown to verify that the 100 endorsement can be issued and what type of improvements and the street address of the property in question is. It will also show any conveyances within 6 months from the date of the report.

32 This item will show whether Fidelity will bill the customer the full term rate premium or the short term rate premium once the policy(ies) is issued. The customer will be entitled to the short-term rate (80% of the full term rate) if any title company has insured the property within the last five years, excluding foreclosure guarantees and other types of guarantees.

Fidelity National Title   **Explanation of a Preliminary Title Report**

ITEMS: (Continued)   Order No. 999999

33 Note 7. Section 12413.1, California Insurance Code became effective January 1, 1990. This legislation deals with the disbursement of funds deposited with any title entity acting in an escrow or subescrow capacity. The law requires that all funds be deposited and collected by the title entity's escrow and/or subescrow account prior to disbursement of any funds. Some methods of funding may subject funds to a holding period which must expire before any funds may be disbursed. In order to avoid any such delays, all fundings should be done through wire transfer, certified check or checks drawn on California financial institutions.

34 Note 8. The charge where an order is cancelled after the issuance of the report of title, will be that amount which in the opinion of the Company is proper compensation for the services rendered or the purpose for which the report is used, but in no event shall said charge be less than the minimum amount required under Section 12404.1 of the Insurance Code of the State of California. If the report cannot be cancelled "no fee" pursuant to the provisions of said Insurance Code, then the minimum cancellation fee shall be that permitted by law.

35 Note 9. California Revenue and Taxation Code Section 18662, effective January 1, 1994 and by amendment effective January 1, 2003, provides that the buyer in all sales of California Real Estate may be required to withhold 3 and 1/3% of the total sales price as California State Income Tax, subject to the various provisions of the law as therein contained.

Fidelity National Title Company
OF CALIFORNIA

(Rev. 11/17/04)

33 The amount of the previous years property taxes when the current years taxes are not yet available. To the right of the amounts will be a notation indicating the current status of the tax such as "paid," "open" or "delinquent." If the tax such is delinquent the penalty amount will also be shown. Also shown is the value at which the County Assessor has assessed the real property for the previous year.

34 This item deals with Fidelity's policies regarding holding money at the close of escrow for the last payment of taxes and /or last monthly mortgage payment. All holds can be waived if we supplied with a copy of the cancelled check or other proof of payment.

35 Notes 9, 10 & 11 are informational notes regarding statutory requirements that need to be complied with at the time of closing or cancellation of the title transaction.

36 Accompanying each PR will be a map of the property showing its location (sample on next page).

Fidelity National Title   **Explanation of a Preliminary Title Report**

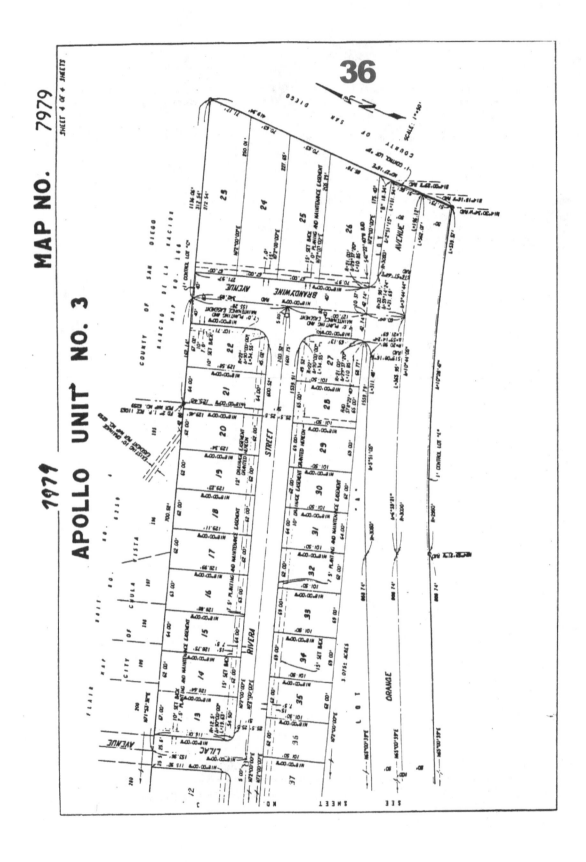

Notice

You may be entitled to receive a $20.00 discount on escrow services if you purchased, sold or refinanced residential property in California between May 19, 1995 and November 1, 2002. If you had more than one qualifying transaction, you may be entitled to multiple discounts.

If your previous transaction involved the same property that is the subject of your current transaction, you do not have to do anything; the Company will provide the discount, provided you are paying for escrow or title services in this transaction.

If your previous transaction involved property different from the property that is subject of your current transaction, you must inform the Company of the earlier transaction, provide the address of the property involved in the previous transaction, and the date or approximate date that the escrow closed to be eligible for the discount.

Unless you inform the Company of the prior transaction on property that is not the subject of this transaction, the Company has no obligation to conduct an investigation to determine if you qualify for a discount. If you provide the Company information concerning a prior transaction, the Company is required to determine if you qualify for a discount.

Effective through November 1, 2014

Fidelity National Title   **Explanation of a Preliminary Title Report**

<u>Fidelity National Financial Group of Companies' Privacy Statement</u>

July 1, 2001

We recognize and respect the privacy expectations of today's consumers and the requirements of applicable federal and state privacy laws. We believe that making you aware of how we use your non-public personal information (°Personal Information±), and to whom it is disclosed, will form the basis for a relationship of trust between us and the public that we serve. This Privacy Statement provides that explanation. We reserve the right to change this Privacy Statement from time to
time consistent with applicable privacy laws.

In the course of our business, we may collect Personal Information about you from the following sources:

> From applications or other forms we receive from you or your authorized representative;
> From your transactions with, or from the services being performed by, us, our affiliates, or others;
> From our internet web sites;
> From the public records maintained by governmental entities that we either obtain directly from those entities, or from our affiliates or others; and
> From consumer or other reporting agencies.

Our Policies Regarding the Protection of the Confidentiality and Security of Your Personal Information

We maintain physical, electronic and procedural safeguards to protect your Personal Information from unauthorized access or intrusion. We limit access to the Personal Information only to those employees who need such access in connection with providing products or services to you or for other legitimate business purposes.

Our Policies and Practices Regarding the Sharing of Your Personal Information

We may share your Personal Information with our affiliates, such as insurance companies, agents, and other real estate settlement service providers. We also may disclose your Personal Information:

> to agents, brokers or representatives to provide you with services you have requested;
> to third-party contractors or service providers who provide services or perform marketing or other functions on our behalf; and
> to others with whom we enter into joint marketing agreements for products or services that we believe you may find of interest.

In addition, we will disclose your Personal Information when you direct or give us permission, when we are required by law to do so, or when we suspect fraudulent or criminal activities. We also may disclose your Personal Information when otherwise permitted by applicable privacy laws such as, for example, when disclosure is needed to enforce our rights arising out of any agreement, transaction or relationship with you.

One of the important responsibilities of some of our affiliated companies is to record documents in the public domain. Such documents may contain your Personal Information.

Right to Access Your Personal Information and Ability to Correct Errors or Request Changes or Deletion

Certain states afford you the right to access your Personal Information and, under certain circumstances, to find out to whom your Personal Information has been disclosed. Also, certain states afford you the right to request correction, amendment or deletion of your Personal Information. We reserve the right, where permitted by law, to charge a reasonable fee to cover the costs incurred in responding to such requests.

All requests must be made in writing to the following address:

Privacy Compliance Officer
Fidelity National Financial, Inc.
601 Riverside Avenue
Jacksonville, FL 32204

Multiple Products or Services

If we provide you with more than one financial product or service, you may receive more than one privacy notice from us. We apologize for any inconvenience this may cause you.

2
EXHIBIT A
AMERICAN LAND TITLE ASSOCIATION
RESIDENTIAL TITLE INSURANCE POLICY 16-1-87) EXCLUSIONS

In addition to the Exclusions, you are not insured against loss, and the expenses resuiting from:

1. Any rights, interests or claims of parties in possession of the and not shown by the public records.
   - land use
   - improvements a the land
   - land division
   - environmental protection

   The exclusion does not apply to violations or the enforcement of these matters which appears in the public records at policy date.

   This exclusion does not limit the zoning coverage described in items 12 and 13 of Covered Title Risks.

2. The right to take the land by condemning it, useless:
   - a notice of exercising the right appears in the public data
   - the taking happened prior to the Policy Date and is binding

   on you if you brought the land without knowledge edge of the taking

3. Title Rules:
   - that are created, allowed or agreed to by you
   - that are known to you, but to us, on the Policy Data-useless

   they appeared in the public records
   - that results in no loss to you
   - that first affect you title after the Policy Date - this does not

   limit the labor and material lien coverage in item 8 of Covered Title Risks

4. Failure to pay value for your title.

5. Lack of a right:
   - to any land outside the area specifically described and referred to in item 3 of Schedule A

     or
   - in streets, alleys or waterways that touch your land.

     The exclusion does not limit the access coverage in item 5 of the Covered Title Risks.

SCHEDULE B
EXCEPTIONS

In addition to the Exclusions, you are not insured against loss, and the expenses from:

1. Any rights, interests or claims of parties in possession of the and not shown by the public records.

2. Any easements or liens not shown by the public records. The does not limit the lien coverage in item 8 of Covered Title Risks.

3. Any facts about the land which a correct survey would disclose and which are not shown by the public records. This dows not limit the forced removal coverage in item 12 or Covered Title Risks.

4. Any water rights or claims or title to water in or under the land, whether or not shown by the public records

CALIFORNIA LAND TITLE ASSOCIATION STANDARD COVERAGE POLICY -1990
EXCLUSIONS FROM COVERAGE

The following matters are expressly excluded from the coverage of this policy and the Company will not pay loss or damage, costs, attorney's fees or expenses which arise by reason of;

1. (a) Any law, ordinance or governmental regulation (including but not limited to building and zoning laws, ordinances, or regulations) restricting, prohibiting or relating to (i) the occupancy, use, or enjoyment of the land (ii) the character, dimensions or locations of any improvement now or hereafter erected on the land; (iii) a separation in ownership or a change in the dimensions or area of the land or any parcel of laws, enforcement thereof or a notice of a defect, lien or encumbrances resulting from a violation or (b) Any governmental policy power not excluded by (a) above, except to the extent that a notice of the exercise thereof or a notice of a defect, lien or encumbrance resulting from a violation or alleged violation affecting the land has been recorded in the public records at Date of Policy.

2. Rights of eminent domain unless notice of the exercise thereof has been recorded in the public records at Date of Policy, but not excluding from coverage amy taking, which has occurred prior to Date of Policy which would be binding on the rights of a purchaser for value without knowledge.

3. Defects, liens, encumbrances, adverse claims, or other matters:
   (a) created, suffered, assumed or agreed to by the insured claimant;

   (b) not know to the Company, not recorded in the public record at Date of Policy, but known to the insured claimant and not disclosed in writing to the Company by the insured claimant prior to the date the insured claimant become an insured under this policy;

   (c) resulting in no loss or damage to the insured claimant;

   (d) attaching or created subsequent to Date of Policy, or

   (e) resulting in loss or damage which would not have been sustained if the insured claimant had paid value for the estate or interest insured by this policy.

4. Unenforceability of the lien of the insured mortgage because of the inability or failure of the insured at Date of Policy, or the inability or failure of any subsequent owner of the indebtedness, to comply with the applicable doing business laws of the state in which the land is situated.

5. Invalidity or unenforceability of the lien of th insured mortgage, or claim thereof, which arises out of the transaction evidence by the insured mortgage and is based upon usury or any consumer credit protection or truth in lending law

6. Any claim, which arises our of the transaction vesting in the insured the estate or interest insured by this policy or the transaction creating the interest of the insured lender, by reason of the operation of federal bankruptcy, state insolvency or similar creditors' right laws.

SCHEDULE B
EXCEPTIONS FROM COVERAGE

This policy does not insure against loss or damage (and the Company will not pay costs, attorney's fees or expenses) which arise by reason of:

PART 1

1. Taxes or assessments which are not shown as existing liens by the records of any taxing authority that levies taxes or assessments on real property or by the public records. Proceedings by the public agency which may result in taxes or assessments, or notices or such proceedings, whether or not shown by the records of such agency or by the public records.

2. Any facts, rights, interests or claims which are not shown by the public records but which could be ascertained by an inspection of the land or which may be asserted by persons in possession thereof.

3. Easements, liens or encumbrances, or claims thereof, which are not shown by the public records.

4. Discrepancies, conflicts in boundary liens shortage in area, encroachments, or any other facts which a correct survey would disclose, and which are not shown by the public records.

5. (a) Unpatented mining claims; (b) reservations or exceptions in patents or in Acts authorizing the issuance thereof; (c) water rights, claims or title to water, whether or not the matters excepted under (a), (b), or (c) are shown by the public records.

2
EXHIBIT A
(CONTINUED)
AMERICAN LAND TITLE ASSOCIATION LOAN POLICY A(10-17-92)
WITH A.L.T.A. ENDORSEMENT-FORM 1 COVERAGE AND
AMERICAN LAND TITLE ASSOCIATION LEASEHOLD LOAN POLICY (10-17-92)
WITH A.L.T.A. ENDORSEMENT-FORM 1 COVERAGE
SCHEDULE OF EXCLUSIONS FROM COVERAGE

The following matters are expressly excluded from the coverage of this policy and the Company will not pay loss or damage, costs, attorney's fees or expenses which arise by reason of;

1. (a) Any law, ordinance or governmental regulation (including but not limited to building and zoning laws, ordinances, or regulations) restricting, prohibiting or relating to (i) the occupancy, use, or enjoyment of the land (ii) the character, dimensions or locations of any improvement now or hereafter erected on the land; (iii) a separation in ownership or a change in the dimensions or area of the land or any parcel of which the land is or was a part; or (iv) environmental protection, or the effect of any violation of these laws, ordinances or governmental regulations, except to the extent that a notice of the enforcement thereof or a notice of a defect, lien or encumbrance resulting from a violation or alleged violation affecting the land has been recorded in the public record at Date of Policy. (b) Any governmental police power not excluded by (a) above, except to the extent that a notice of the exercise thereof or a notice of a defect, lien or encumbrance resulting from a violation or alleged violation affecting the land has been recorded in the public records at Date of Policy.

2. Rights of eminent domain unless notice of the exercise thereof has been recorded in the public records at Date of Policy, but not excluding from coverage any taking, which has occurred prior to Date of Policy which would be binding on the rights of a purchaser for value without knowledge.

3. Defects, liens, encumbrances, adverse claims, or other matters:
   (a) created, suffered, assumed or agreed to by the insured claimant;
   (b) not know to the Company, not recorded in the public records at Date of Policy, but known to the insured claimant and not disclosed in writing to the Company by the insured claimant prior to the date the insured claimant become an insured under this policy;
   (c) resulting in no loss or damage to the insured claimant;
   (d) attaching or created subsequent to Date of Policy, or

(e) resulting in loss or damage which would not have been sustained if the insured claimant had paid value for the estate or interest insured by this policy.

4. Unenforceability of the lien of the insured mortgage because of the inability or failure of the insured at Date of Policy, or the inability or failure of any subsequent owner of the indebtedness, to comply with the applicable doing business laws of the state in which the land is situated.

5. Invalidity or unenforceability of the lien of th insured mortgage, or claim thereof, which arises out of the transaction evidence by the insured mortgage and is based upon usury or any consumer credit protection or truth in lending law

6. Any statutory lien for services, labor or materials (or the claim of priority or any statutory lien for services, labor or materials over the lien of the insured mortgage) arising from an improvement or work related tot he land which is contracted for and commenced subsequent to Date of Policy and is not financed in whole or in part by proceeds of the indebtedness secured by the insured mortgage which at Date of Policy the insured has advanced or is obligated to advance.

7. Any claim which arises out of the transaction creating the interest of the mortgagee insured by this policy, by reason of the operation of federal bankruptcy, state insolvency, or similar creditors' rights laws, that is based on;
   (i) the transaction creating the interest of the insured mortgage being deemed a fraudulent covenance or fraudulent transfer, or (ii) the subordination of the interest of the insured mortgagee as a result of the application of the doctrine of equitable subordination; or (iii) the transaction creating the interest of the insured mortgagee being deemed a preferential transfer except where the preferential transfer results from the failure:
   (a) to timely record the instrument of transfer, or
   (b) of such recordation to impart notice to a purchaser for value of a judgement or lien creditor.

AMERICAN LAND TITLE ASSOCIATION OWNER'S POLICY (1017-92) AND
AMERICAN LAND TITLE ASSOCIATION LEASEHOLD OWNER'S POLICY (10-17-92)
SCHEDULE OF EXCLUSIONS FROM COVERAGE

The following matters are expressly excluded from the coverage of this policy and the Company will not pay loss or damage, costs, attorney's fees or expenses which arise by reason of;

1. (a) Any law, ordinance or governmental regulation (including but not limited to building and zoning laws, the land; (ii) the character, dimensions or locations of any improvement now or hereafter erected on the land; (iii) a separation in ownership or a change in the dimensions or area of the land or any parcel of which the land is or was a part; (iv) environmental protection, of the effect of any violation of these laws, ordinances or governmental regulations, except to the extent that a notice of the enforcement thereof or a notice of a defect, lien or encumbrance resulting from a violation or alleged violation affecting the land has been recorded in the public records at Date of Policy. (b) Any governmental police power not excluded by (a) above, except to the extent that a notice of the exercise thereof or a notice of a defect, lien or encumbrance resulting from a violation or alleged violation affecting the land has been recorded in the public records at Date of Policy.

2. Rights of eminent domain unless notice of the exercise thereof has been recorded in the public records at Date of Policy, but not excluding from coverage any taking, which has occurred prior to Date of Policy which would be binding on the rights of a purchaser for value without knowledge.

3. Defects, liens, encumbrances, or other matters:

(a) created, suffered, assumed or agreed to by the insured claimant;
(b) not know to the Company, not recorded in the public records at Date of Policy, but known to the insured claimant and not disclosed in writing to the Company by the insured claimant prior to the date the insured claimant become an insured under this policy;
(c) resulting in no loss or damage to the insured claimant;
(d) attaching or created subsequent to Date of Policy, or
(e) resulting in loss or damage which would not have been sustained if the insured claimant had paid value for the estate or interest insured by this policy.

4. Any claim, which arises our of the transaction vesting in the insured the estate or interest insured by this policy, by reason of the operation of federal bankruptcy, state insolvency, or similar creditors' rights law, that is based on :
   (i) the transaction creating the estate or interest insured by this policy being deemed a fraudulent conveyance or fraudulent transfer, or
   (ii) the transaction creating the estate or interest insured by this policy being deemed a preferential transfer except where the preferential transfer results form the failure:
   (a) to timely record the instrument or transfer, or
   (b) of such recordation to impart notice to a purchaser for value or a judgement or lien creditor.

The above ALTA policy forms may be issued to afford either Standard Coverage or Extended Coverage or Extended Coverage. In addition to the above Exclusions from Coverage, the Exclusions from Coverage in a Standard Coverage policy will also include the following general Exceptions:

SCHEDULE B
EXCEPTIONS FROM COVERAGE

This policy does not insure against loss or damage (and the Company will not pay costs, attorney's fees or expenses) which arise by reason of:

1. Taxes or assessments which are not shown as existing liens by the records of any taxing authority that levies taxes or assessments on real property or by the public records. Proceedings by the public agency which may result in taxes or assessments, or notices or such proceedings, whether or not shown by the records of such agency or by the public records.

2. Any facts, rights, interests or claims which are not shown by the public records but which could be ascertained by an inspection of the land or which may be asserted by persons in possession thereof.

3. Easements, liens or encumbrances, or claims thereof, which are not shown by

the public records.

4. Discrepancies, conflicts in boundary liens shortage in area, encroachments, or any other facts which a correct survey would disclose, and which are not shown by the public records.

5. (a) Unpatented mining claims; (b) reservations or exceptions in patents or in Acts authorizing the issuance thereof; (c) water rights, claims or title to water, whether or not the matters excepted under (a), (b), or (c) are shown by the public records.

2
EXHIBIT A
(CONTINUED)
AMERICAN LAND TITLE ASSOCIATION
HOMEOWNER'S POLICY OF TITLE INSURANCE
FOR A ONE-TO-FOUR FAMILY RESIDENCE (10-17-98)

In addition to the Exclusions, you are not insured against loss, and the expenses resuiting from:

1. Governmental police power, and the existence of violation of any law, or government regulation. This includes ordinances, laws and regulations concerning:
   a. building
   b. zoning
   c. land use
   d. improvements on the land
   e. land division
   f. environmental protection
   This exclusion does not apply to violations or the enforcement of these matters which appears in the Public Records at Policy Date.
   This Exclusion does not limit the zoning coverage described in items 14, 15, 16, 17 or 24.
2. The failure of your existing structures, or any part of them, to be constructed in accordance with applicable building codes. This Exclusion does not apply to violations of building codes if notice of the violation appears in the Public Records at the Policy Date
3. The right to take the land by condemning it, useless:
   a. a notice of exercising the right appears in the Public Records at the Policy Date: or

   b. the taking happened before the Policy Date and is binding on you if you brought the land without knowledge edge of the taking
4. Risks:
   a. that are created, allowed or agreed to by you, whether or not they appear in the Pubic Records;
   b. that are known to you at the Policy Date, but to us, useless they appeared in the Public Records at the Policy DAte;
   c. that results in no loss to you; or
   d. that first occur after the Policy Date - this does not limit the coverage described in Coverage Risk 7, 8.d, 22, 23, 24, or 25.
5. Failure to pay value for your title.
6. Lack of a right:
   a. to any land outside the area specifically described and referred to in item 3 of Schedule A; and
   b. in streets, alleys or waterways that touch your land. The exclusion does not limit the access coverage described in Covered Risks 11 and 18..

RESIDENTIAL TITLE INSURANCE POLICY
ONE-TO-FOUR FAMILY RESIDENCE
ENHANCED VERSION (1997)

EXCLUSIONS

In addition to the Exclusions, you are not insured against loss, and the expenses resuiting from:

1. Governmental police power, and the existence of violation of any law, or government regulation. This includes ordinances, laws and regulations concerning:
   a. land use
   b. improvements on the land
   c. land division
   d. environmental protection
   This exclusion does not apply to violations or the enforcement of these matters which appears in the Public Records at Policy Date.
   This Exclusion does not limit the zoning coverage described in items 12.c, and d, 13 and 18 of the Covered Title Risks.
2. The right to take the land by condemning it, useless:
   a. a notice of exercising the right appears in the Public Records at the Policy Date: or
   b. the taking happened before the Policy Date and is binding on you if you brought the land without knowledge edge of the

   taking
3. Title Risks:
   • that are created, allowed or agreed to you by;
   • that are known to you, but to us, on the Policy Data-useless they appeared in the public records
   • that results in no loss to you; or
   • that first affect you title after the Policy Date - this does not limit the labor and material lien coverage described in item 3.b, 8, 17, and 19 of Covered Title Risks
4. Failure to pay value for your title.
5. Lack of a right: (a) to any land outside the area specifically described and referred to in item 3 of Schedule A or (b) in streets, alleys or waterways that touch your land.
   The exclusion does not limit the access coverage in item 5 and 12.a of the Covered Title Risks.

GLOSSARY

absolute ownership No restrictions on ownership rights to real property.

abstract of title Written report describing liens and other matters affecting title to real property.

accession Process of land being attached to another piece of real property.

accommodator A third party used to execute the exchange of property under the guidelines of the IRS Code, Section 1031.

acquisition of property Refers to the method of acquiring property under California Civil Code Section 1000.

actual notice Physical delivery of a document into the hands of the intended party.

Alcoholic Beverage Control The State of California Department of Alcoholic Beverage Control.

alienation clause The clause in a mortgage or deed of trust that entitles the mortgagee or beneficiary to accelerate the note's payoff date, requiring the borrower to pay the remaining debt in full.

all-inclusive trust deed (or deed of trust) Also referred to as a wrap-around deed of trust, the all-inclusive trust deed (AITD) is a junior debt instrument that includes a senior debt and lien typically for seller financing.

allocation of costs The division of closings costs between a buyer and a seller in a real estate sale.

ALTA extended policies A title insurance policy issued under the guidelines of the American Land Title Association offering additional protection coverage for the property owner.

ALTA lenders' policies A title insurance policy issued under the guidelines of the American Land Title Association offering concurrent protection for a property owner's lender and that carries more protection coverage for the lender than that of the owner's policy.

amendments Changes to original escrow instructions.

American Escrow Association A national organization offering membership to escrow professionals.

apartment buildings Refers to multifamily residential rental properties and usually those having five units or more.

apportionment of charges The allocation of closing costs divided between a buyer and a seller.

appurtenant In real property, that which belongs to something else or someone else, accompanies it, is attached to it, or is annexed to it.

assessor's parcel number The identification for a piece of land, as assigned by the county assessor, that refers to the book, section, and page number of the county's real property ownership records.

bankruptcy A legal process under federal law that enables a debtor to be released of debts or to enter into a repayment plan as authorized by the court.

Bar Treaty An agreement no longer in effect that once established certain documents that the escrow holder may prepare and those it may not as they relate to legal advice. The State Bar of California revoked the agreement in 1979.

base line In the public land survey system (PLSS), the base line is the east-west line that runs through the initial beginning point.

beneficiary The term used to describe the lender in a deed of trust.

beneficiary statement A statement issued by a mortgage lender and provided to the escrow holder that contains all unpaid balance and other financial details about a borrower's loan.

bilateral contracts A contract that must be performed by both parties.

bilateral instructions Escrow instructions prepared for both parties and under which both parties are bound.

bills of sale Evidence of a sale of personal property; also used to transfer an interest in a mobile home.

Board of Equalization The department for the State of California responsible for business taxes.

bulk sales law Bulk sales laws are designed to prevent sellers from defrauding creditors by either selling the business for less than the market price and not paying creditors in full or by not paying the creditors at all in the event an escrow is not used.

covenants, conditions, and restrictions (CC&Rs) CC&Rs are private rights established by prior owners of the land that impose limitations on the use and occupancy of the land, including any improvements on it.

CalHFA loan program The California Housing Finance Agency provides low down payment fixed-rate financing at below-market interest rates.

California good funds law The state law that specifies when funds deposited into escrow may be disbursed.

California Buyer's Choice Act Specifically prohibits a seller who as a beneficiary acquired title by foreclosing on the property to require the buyer to use a certain escrow holder or title insurer.

Civil Code Section 1057 Section 1057 states that "a grant may be deposited by the grantor with a third person, to be delivered on performance of a condition, and, on delivery by the depositary" (referring to the escrow holder), "it will take effect."

California Escrow Association An organization offering membership to escrow professionals in California.

California Recording Act An act providing that any instrument or documents affecting the title to or possession of real property may be recorded.

California property tax chart The chart used by escrow holders which shows the property taxes due from the buyer and seller respectively based on the escrow closing month.

California tax withholding California tax withholding similar to the basic guidelines of the federal FIRPTA.

CalVet loan program The California Department of Veterans Affairs, called CalVet, authorized by the Veterans Farm and Home Purchase Act of 1974, provides real estate loans for qualified veterans.

certificate of title The title to a manufactured home (considered personal property).

chain of title A history of all previous property owners in chronological order beginning with the present, then searching back in time for any matter that may affect title.

clear and marketable title The condition of title to real property that allows its titleholder to own, use, enjoy, and convey it to another or to encumber.

closing statement The settlement statement that accounts for all funds received and disbursed in accordance with the Real Estate Settlement Procedures Act (RESPA).

cloud on title Matters that could affect title or prevent the title from being transferred or encumbered.

CLTA (standard) policies The owner's policy, referred to as a standard policy, provides basic protection through insurance coverage for the policyholder but mostly limited to matters of public record.

CLTA extended coverage policies Policies with extra protection limited to items that are not recorded and that the title insurance underwriter would have no way of knowing without additional research or some sort of physical inspection of the property and that represent risks to the title insurance company.

commercial properties Generally defined as any type of property that is not intended for residential dwelling use.

commission instructions The commission agreement, including any fee split between the listing agent and selling agent, is contained in and is in addition to and separate from the instructions for and between the seller and the buyer in a purchase transaction.

condemnation The process employed by a government agency in executing its power of eminent domain.

construction draw In construction financing, a lender provides funds at various completion stages or phases called construction draws.

constructive notice Accomplished by recording a document with the county recorder's office, enables the "world at large" to learn that a recorded agreement exists because the matter is available to any person to see, being found in these recorded and, now public, documents.

Consumer Financial Protection Bureau Responsible for regulation of the Truth in Lending Act and RESPA.

contingency removal The contingency removal procedure allows a principal a certain number of days to perform, such as obtain a loan approval or perform inspections.

conventional loans Nongovernmental or non-government-backed loans.

covenant not to compete An agreement between the buyer and the seller that the seller will not compete against the buyer by reopening his business at another location within a specified distance, or by opening a new but similar business if the buyer's purchase of the property included buying the business.

credits Money received or a credit against monies owed by the party.

date down The process of searching the chain of title, a history of all previous property owners in chronological order, beginning with the present, then searching back in time for any matter that may affect title.

debits Money owed by the party.

debt service coverage ratio The ratio of the annual loan payment to an income property's net operating income (NOI). The ratio is calculated by dividing the NOI by the annual loan payment.

deed in lieu A deed granting title to real property to a lender who accepts title instead of foreclosing.

defects in title Matters clouding title to real property that may prevent conveying or encumbering it and therefore making it uninsurable by a title insurer.

deficiency judgment A court action in which a lender that has acquired title to a property through a judicial foreclosure obtains a money judgment against the borrower for the difference between the sales price the lender received upon resale and the remaining unpaid balance of the debt.

demand statement A statement from a mortgage lender indicating the amount required to pay off a loan.

depository A financial institution that accepts monetary deposits from customers such as a bank, savings or thrift institution, or credit union.

documentary transfer tax Also referred to as transfer stamps, a tax imposed on the seller and/or the buyer of real property by the state, county, and city in California. The tax is collected at the time of recording.

dominant estate In an easement, the land that is benefited is called the dominant estate.

due-on-sale clause A provision in a promissory note that gives the lender the ability to call the loan due and payable if the borrower transfers title, or any part of it (such as quitclaiming a partial interest to another person), and the loan is not paid off at the time of transfer of title and without the expressed approval of the lender.

easements The right to use the land of another for a particular use, such as utilities, ingress, and egress.

easements in gross Easements that are not appurtenant and that convey the right to use the land of another for some particular use and not necessarily for an adjoining land.

eminent domain The power of local, state, or federal government agencies to take private property for public use so long as the government pays just compensation.

encumbrances Encumbrances against a property consist of taxes, assessments, and liens, as well as building restrictions, encroachments, easements, and pending legal actions.

endorsements Additional protection coverage identified by other forms included with the policy and referred to as endorsements, which may include leaseholds, bankruptcies, eminent domain, Native American lands, tidelands, foreclosure probate, plus others.

Equal Credit Opportunity Act A federal law that prohibits discrimination in the extension of credit.

escrow The act of a grant "deposited by the grantor with a third person, to be delivered on performance of a condition, and, on delivery by the depositary, it will take effect. While in the possession of the third person, and subject to condition, it is called an escrow."

Escrow Law The Escrow Law under the California Financial Code is intended to protect members of the public who entrust their money or other assets to independent escrow agents in California.

essential elements of deeds Those items which must be present for a deed to be valid.

estates Refers to the degree or extent of one's interest in land.

estimated closing statement The statement prepared by the escrow holder that provides an accounting estimate of all monies, reflecting debit and credit columns as in standard bookkeeping practice, with columns headed "Seller," "Borrower," "Buyer," and "Lender."

estoppel certificates A statement prepared by the buyer's lender (or by the buyer paying "all cash") requesting each tenant to confirm the amount of the periodic rent payment, the security deposit paid, and any other special terms of the lease or rental agreement such as parking or concessions.

exchanges Refers to the IRS Code Section 1031, which allows for the tax-deferred disposition and acquisition of investment real estate in which any tax that may be otherwise due on gain (profit) may be deferred to a later date.

executory contracts A valid contract yet to be performed by one or more of the principals is said to be executory

express contracts An express contract is one that has been put into words, whether written or verbal.

Fair Housing Act A federal law prohibiting discrimination against any applicant for financial assistance for purchasing any housing accommodation.

Federal Fair Housing Amendments Act The amendments broadened protected classes to explicitly include families with children and those who have physical or mental disabilities.

Fannie Mae Those who buy loans in the secondary mortgage marketplace are called investors. The largest and best known investor is Fannie Mae, or Federal National Mortgage Association (FNMA), 79.9% of which is owned by the U.S. government; it was originally established in 1938 as a government agency and was privatized in 1968 but placed into government conservatorship in 2008.

Federal Housing Administration Established by the National Housing Act in 1934, the Federal Housing Administration (FHA) introduced the long-term mortgage, which continues to today.

fidelity bonds A sort of insurance protection that pays for losses to principals of monies held in trust for them by their fiduciary.

financing documents The borrower's note and trust deed documents provided by a lender for a loan.

financing statement A statement "filed" with the secretary of state of California serves as public notice that a debt or a security agreement exists with the specified personal property used and secured as collateral.

FIRPTA Short for Federal Investment of Real Property Tax Act, FIRPTA is a federal law that is intended to ensure that the U.S. Treasury receives income taxes that may be due and payable from a seller of real property who resides outside the United States.

FSBO Pronounced "fiz-boe" and short for "for sale by owner."

foreclosure A remedy available to a lender that has a security instrument filed against real property as collateral for a loan it provided to a borrower who is now in default.

foreclosure time line Refers to the length of time it takes for a lender to begin and complete the foreclosure process under the law.

franchise agreement The contract between the owner of a business "name," along with its products and services, referred to as the franchisor, and the buyer, licensee, or dealer, referred to as the franchisee.

Freddie Mac A government-sponsored investor in the secondary mortgage market, Freddie Mac (the Federal Home Loan Mortgage Corporation (FHLMC)), was created in 1970 as a nonprofit government agency under the supervision of the Federal Home Loan Bank as part of the government's economic recovery program following the recession of 1969. Privatized in 1989, Freddie Mac, along with Fannie Mae, was placed into government conservatorship in 2008 with the United States government acquiring 79.9% of its ownership.

good-faith estimate of costs   A requirement of the federal Truth in Lending Act, the good-faith estimate of costs, called GFE for short, must include the identity of the creditor, amount financed, finance charge (including interest and fees), annual percentage rate (APR), and payment schedule.

government lots   In the original government survey system, waterways and other natural elements created parcels of land that were less than a quarter-section in size (called government lots). Government lots also contain land lost as a result of adjustments made by correction lines.

grant deed   Real property is usually acquired through the use of a grant deed, a voluntary transfer of title conveying all the estate of the grantor and free of any encumbrance placed on it by the grantor. It may also be used to convey after-acquired title.

Housing and Urban Development (HUD)   A cabinet level department of the United States government, the Department of Housing and Urban Development (HUD) has the stated mission "to promote adequate and affordable housing, economic opportunity, and a suitable living environment free from discrimination." HUD administers the FHA program.

hazard insurance   Hazard insurance policies are commonly referred to as fire insurance but actually include more perils, including liability.

Health and Safety Code   California Health and Safety Code (HSC) Section 18035(a) requires that an escrow account be opened for dealer sales and leases of new or used manufactured homes subject to registration by HCD.

high fire hazard severity zone   An area designated as being a high fire hazard severity zone under Section 51178 or 51179 of the Government Code must be disclosed to the buyer.

HOA certificate   Completed by the homeowners association, the homeowners association certificate (HOA cert) is completed by the HOA and delivered to escrow with the HOA's information (bylaws, articles of incorporation, and insurance policy). The HOA cert provides a summary of the fundamental information regarding the HOA.

HOA dues   If the property has a homeowners association, such as a condominium or planned unit development, the dues are those typically paid by the property owner on a monthly basis for the maintenance of the property's common area.

Holden Credit Denial Act A state law imposing substantially the same requirements, with respect to notice to an applicant of a lender's decision to extend credit or not, as those imposed by the Equal Credit Opportunity Act and Regulation B.

homeowners associations Common interest developments (CID), which include property types such as condominiums, in California require a homeowners association. In California, the Davis-Stirling Act is the law that governs common interest developments.

Homestead Act The Homestead Act in California provides protection from the homeowner's property being seized by creditors and resold for repayment of a debt. While the protection is not absolute, it guarantees the homeowner that any equity up to the amount of the homestead equity exemption is protected and at the same time reduces the property taxes on the homestead amount.

Housing and Community Development The Mobile Homes-Manufactured Housing Act of 1980, Health and Safety Code Sections 18000 et seq. is the authority and law governing the sale and transfer of mobile homes in California and is enforced by the California Department of Housing and Community Development (HCD).

HUD-1 Department of Housing and Urban Development closing statement form.

implied contracts An implied contract is one that has not been verbalized or written but has been implied by the actions of the parties.

implied easements Created when an owner of a parcel of land uses one part of the land that benefits another part of the same land, not another's land, and constitutes an inherent and future easement.

impound accounts An impound or escrow account (not referring to the escrow company) must be established with funds in a specific amount forwarded to the lender at closing to be held in the borrowers' account and used to pay property taxes and hazard insurance when due each year.

installment note A promissory note, commonly called an installment note, is prepared by a borrower's lender and will show the exact terms of the loan. The note is the evidence of the debt, signed and dated but not notarized.

insuring clause The provision in the policy that obligates the title insurer to pay the insured, or defend the insured against, claims on or to the title by others.

IRS Section 1031 The section of the IRS Code that allows for the tax-deferred disposition and acquisition of investment real estate in which the any tax that may be otherwise due on gain (profit) may be deferred to a later date.

joint escrow instructions Instructions prepared on one form for both the buyer and the seller.

judgment liens Once an individual obtains a judgment against a debtor through the court, the person must obtain an abstract of judgment to have it enforceable through the court. Once recorded, it becomes a lien against all real property of the debtor in that county.

judgments Court actions by and in favor of creditors against defaulting debtors.

judicial survey Performed to provide professional evidence regarding the legal description, including boundaries of a property to be used in a court of law.

land descriptions Land may be described in several ways. The legal description may be a lot and tract number, a metes and bounds, or a section and township. Other descriptions, which are not considered legal descriptions, would include the street address and the assessor's parcel number.

land divisions Range from vast areas including townships to sections and fractional sections and individual lots.

latitude Latitude lines are horizontal and parallel to the equator, even sometimes called parallels.

ledger sheet Before accounting for all funds, payments, and credits, the escrow holder accounts for these monies on the ledger sheet, indicating individual receipts and disbursements that are then transferred to the settlement statement.

legal description The legal description may be a lot and tract number, a metes and bounds, or a section and township.

lender's demand Also called a beneficiary demand statement, it is provided by the seller's lender and indicates all the necessary information for determining the amount to deduct from the seller's proceeds for paying off the loan.

license A license is written permission for a personal and revocable right but does not convey any legal interest in the estate.

lien date Regarding property taxes, the date on which a lien of the tax attaches to the property each year is at noon on January 1 preceding the fiscal year for which the taxes are levied.

liens Matters recorded against the property that may prevent a transfer or insurability of title, such as loans, judgments, easements, and taxes.

like-kind In an exchange to meet the tax-deferred test, personal property must be exchanged for personal property and real property must be exchanged for real property.

liquidated damages In a real estate escrow, liquidated damages refers to an amount agreed to under the terms of the contract as damages in the event the transaction fails to be completed and if one of the parties would be responsible.

liquor license: on-sale or off-sale An on-sale license is required for an establishment where alcohol is consumed on premises. An off-sale license is required for an establishment that sells alcohol to be taken off premises, such as a liquor store.

loan contingencies A loan contingency refers to a buyer's responsibility to obtain financing as stated in and under the terms of the contract. If unable to do so the buyer will be required to either cancel the escrow to be free of any penalty or loss of deposit or to waive the contingency and proceed with the transaction.

loan correspondent Mortgage bankers may act as loan correspondents on behalf of lenders, approved by them to perform certain services as their authorized representative.

longitude Lines of longitude, called meridians, run vertically and are perpendicular to lines of latitude. Longitude lines extend from pole to pole. Each longitude line represents an equal portion of the 360 degrees that encompass the earth.

manufactured housing Homes that have been registered with the Department of Motor Vehicles for at least one year and are greater than 8 feet wide and 40 feet long may be sold by real estate agents licensed by the California Department of Real Estate. Any manufactured or mobile home that does not meet the requirements may only be sold by a manufactured housing or mobile home dealer.

manufacturer's certificate of origin Escrow instructions must provide for the placement of the original MCO into escrow on or before the close of escrow on all new manufactured home sales that are subject to registration with HCD. HSC § 18035.2(b)(1) requires the same on all new manufactured homes that will become a fixture of the underlying real estate.

mechanics' liens An individual, vendor, contractor, or provider of materials who has performed work or delivered material to the seller and who was not paid may have filed a mechanic's lien, the recourse available to them under the law to help ensure they will be paid. Called claimants, the law has divided them into four groups: contractors, subcontractors, laborers, and materialmen.

meridian and base line The line that extends from north to south and runs through the initial point is called the principal meridian. The principal meridian has what is called a base line, the east to west line that runs through the initial point.

MERS MERS (Mortgage Electronic Registration System) holds title technically as nominee for the true mortgagees and beneficiaries in its system, and, as transfers occur, they are recorded on MERS's computer in a book-entry system similar to the transfer of stocks.

metes and bounds Metes are measures of length, such as feet and yards. The boundaries of a land description are called bounds.

mobile homes Technically known as manufactured housing.

mortgage Lenders in 23 states (California is not one of them) customarily use mortgages instead of deeds of trust as their security agreement. The lender under a mortgage is called a mortgagee and the borrower is called a mortgagor.

mortgage bankers A mortgage banker is an entity that takes the borrower's loan application, performs the processing and underwriting, issues the loan approval, and funds the loan. After funding, the banker will assign (sell) the loan to another entity, such as a commercial bank, mortgage company, or more substantial mortgage banker.

mortgage brokers The mortgage or loan broker is a third-party agent, licensed by either the California Department of Real Estate or, less commonly, the California Department of Corporations. Mortgage brokers originate loans through the institutional sources, providing access to a variety of lenders for the borrower in an efficient and time-savings process.

mortgage insurance Mortgage insurance compensates the lender for all or part of any losses incurred in the event of the borrower's default and foreclosure.

Mortgage Loan Disclosure Statement A California-required disclosure provided to a borrower, with details regarding the loan and the lender's compensation.

mortgagee The lender under a mortgage is called a mortgagee.

mortgagor The borrower under a mortgage is called a mortgagor.

natural hazard reports The Natural Hazards Disclosure Act of California requires that sellers of real property and their agents must provide prospective buyers with a Natural Hazard Disclosure Statement when the property being sold lies within one or more state-mapped hazard areas.

natural rights Natural rights are inherent in and incidental to the right of ownership. They include the right to benefit from the path of a natural water course, the right to discharge surface water onto another's land that lies unobstructed in its path, and to have one's land supported by adjacent land. It also includes the right to have the air in the immediate vicinity of one's land as free as possible from annoying odors, noises, and contaminants. These rights are a matter of law and are defined as natural rights.

negative easements A negative easement is one that prohibits or prevents the owner of land subject to the easement from doing that, which if no easement existed, he would otherwise be entitled to do.

new home sellout When a builder begins to sell the new homes in a new subdivision, the process is referred to as the sellout.

notice of default A lender under a deed of trust begins the foreclosure process by instructing the trustee to file and record a notice of default (NOD) in the county where the property is located.

notice of sale The notice of sale (NOS), which has a minimum term of 21 days, may actually be filed and recorded 85 days after filing the NOD, therefore before the end of the third month. The NOS indicates the date, time, and place of the upcoming trustee's sale. The notice must be posted, mailed to the borrowers and the others who have requested the notice of default, and published once a week for three consecutive weeks in a newspaper of general circulation.

occupancy A manner of acquiring title, a person who has been occupying it without the permission of the owner of record may claim title on the basis of occupancy. Such possession is considered hostile. Title may be acquired after five years of the occupant's open and notorious use.

off-record matters Those issues that have not been recorded by the county and, therefore, are not of public record, such as zoning restrictions and proposed assessments, which are not considered encumbrances.

operating expenses The itemized expenses attributed to a rental property. The escrow holder may be requested to obtain them from the seller of income property and provide to the buyer.

ordinances City and county rules and regulations that restrict or limit the use of a property.

patents A patent, as defined within the context of land and conveyance of its title, is a deed transferring land from the federal or state government to a private individual, thereby making it private land.

PCOR A common term used to refer to the preliminary change of ownership report, it is required before closing and is prepared by the buyers of a sale transaction or completing the memorandum of a lease. The form provides essential information regarding the terms of the sale. Each county in California has its own form. Escrow delivers the completed copy at closing to the county.

per diem Daily; usually used to describe the daily fee assessed to a buyer or a seller, such as a $100 per diem penalty for failing to close escrow when scheduled.

Phase I inspection The standard nonintrusive environmental investigation, limited to visual inspections and historical data research, to assess various potential environmental concerns, or to ensure the environmental soundness of a property and its surroundings.

Phase II inspection Performed to obtain findings relating to the possible contamination of surface soils, subsurface soils, and groundwater and certain discovery methods The buyer and the seller must be made aware of the intrusive nature of the Phase II inspection, which may involve drilling into the property's exterior and/or interior.

Phase III work Remedial or removal work as indicated by Phase II report, depending on the site-specific goals and regulatory requirements.

point of beginning The fixed and clearly identifiable starting point in a land being surveyed and to prepare its description.

portfolio loans Loans that are retained by the lender after origination, with the lender receiving monthly payments from the borrower and retaining all the interest.

predatory lending Practices such as knowingly lending more money than a borrower can afford to repay, charging high interest rates to borrowers based on their race or national origin and not on their credit history, charging fees for unnecessary or nonexistent products and services, and pressuring borrowers to accept higher-risk loans such as balloon loans, interest-only payments, and steep prepayment penalties.

preliminary title report A written opinion of title prepared by the title officer is called a preliminary title report. The report indicates the conditions under which a title insurance policy will be offered to the buyer or the borrower, including any exceptions to coverage.

prepay penalties Penalties assessed to a borrower for paying off a loan earlier than allowed by its terms.

premium The rate an insurer charges for its protection coverage.

principal meridian The north-south line that runs through the initial point of the survey is a true (principal) meridian.

profit á prendre In easements, the right of a person to remove part of the earth on land belonging to another, or something growing in or on it.

property May be considered either real (immovable) or personal (capable of being moved).

prorations Refers to the financial calculations for the division of charges at closing, such as fees, taxes, and expenses between or among the buyer, the seller, or third parties (such as the interest payable by the buyer or the seller for their respective loans).

public land survey system Land surveying and the subdividing of properties are based on the public land survey system (PLSS), a rectangular system dating back to the original 13 colonies.

public lands Under the Treaty of Guadalupe Hidalgo all lands not specifically granted to individuals, rancho owners, and specific states became property of the United States and are identified as public lands.

qualified ownership Ownership of property with another person is considered to be qualified if the use of the property is limited or restricted. Qualified ownership, when owned with others, allows title to be held in several ways, such as joint tenancy, tenants in common, and community property.

quiet title action Used to submit a discrepancy in title to a court for the judge to make a ruling. Unless the issue is complex, the request to have it reconveyed will usually be granted.

quitclaim deed Conveys any possible interest of the grantor in the property. However, unlike a grant deed, a quitclaim deed, while valid, carries no warranties or guarantees of title protection.

range Range designations indicate the location east or west of the principal meridian. Township designations indicate the location north or south of a base line.

ratification The ratification process in escrow instructions is based on the completion of items promised to be performed or provided, such as receipt of payoff demands, title reports delivered, pest control work ascertained, and new loans approved.

real estate licensing The California Department of Real Estate (DRE) has established certain requirements that must be met in order for an individual to obtain a real estate salesperson license, including certain educational requirements and a written examination. Once the examination is passed, an application for the license must be submitted to and approved by DRE. A license may be obtained by a person who does not immediately intend to be employed by a broker, but a salesperson without an employing broker may not perform acts requiring a real estate license.

Real Estate Settlement Procedures Act Describes unfair or illegal settlement practices and provides an item-by-item explanation of closing costs and services. The act requires the escrow holder to provide a full and complete accounting of all costs paid and monies received by or on behalf of the parties.

reconveyance The process of removing a lender's lien from the title; the title company will facilitate the reconveyance process by sending the request for full reconveyance to the trustee and upon receipt will record the full reconveyance.

rectangular survey system The rectangular survey system was enacted into law by the Land Ordinance Act of 1785. (See public land survey system.)

regulated lender A lender may be a regulated lender, which is a financial institution that accepts and holds monetary deposits from customers and allows for the disbursement of their monies through a variety of instruments or means. They are by law regulated by federal and state governments.

release clauses Any lien of record on a subdivision must contain a partial release clause allowing the individual lots to be released subsequent to map filing.

rent roll A list indicating the names of all tenants in a rental property, along with the amount of their individual rents and security deposits. A rent roll is customarily among the documents the escrow holder will obtain from a seller of income property to deliver to the buyer.

RESPA Common term for the Real Estate Settlement Procedures Act, intended to provide purchasers of real property with information regarding the settlement (closing) process and assist purchasers in obtaining the best value in settlement services for the money spent.

right of redemption The right of a borrower who lost a property through the judicial foreclosure process for up to one year after the foreclosure sale to buy the property back from whoever purchased it from the lender, or from the foreclosing lender if it has not resold the property

right of rescission California law prohibits the borrowers' new loan from funding and closing for at least three business days following the date the borrowers' sign loan documents. Sundays and holidays are not included in the waiting term.

salable loans Loans that are intended to be sold to investors such as Fannie Mae and Freddie Mac in the secondary mortgage market place.

sales tax clearance Under the sales and use tax law, the state Board of Equalization must be notified before the sale of all or part of a business or the stock of goods of an enterprise engaged in selling tangible business personal property. The purpose of the notification is to obtain a certificate of tax clearance and a seller's permit.

secondary mortgage market Those who buy loans in the secondary mortgage market place are called investors. The largest and best known investor is Fannie Mae (Federal National Mortgage Association [FNMA]), which was originally established as a government agency in 1938 to buy FHA, and later VA, loans. Next to Fannie Mae in size is Freddie Mac, the Federal Home Loan Mortgage Corporation (FHLMC), established in 1970.

selection of escrow (AB957) Buyers and sellers may select any escrow holder or title insurer. California law, AB 957, specifically prohibits the seller, who as a beneficiary acquired title by foreclosing on the property, to require the buyer use a certain escrow holder or title insurer. There is no requirement that a buyer use a particular company selected by the seller.

seller financing If seller financing is part of the transaction, the real estate agent will be required under the law to provide the seller with a disclosure regarding recommended terms, conditions, and obligations of the parties when seller financing is involved. The Seller Financing Addendum (CAR form SFA) will be prepared with the seller by the agent and then will be delivered to the escrow holder for presentation to the buyer.

servient estate The land that is encumbered by the easement, that which gives up a right for the benefit of the dominant estate, is referred to as the servient estate.

Settlement Statement HUD-1 The form and format of the closing statement of all funds received and disbursed as required by the Housing and Urban Development Department for delivery to the principals.

short sale The short sale occurs at escrow closing when the lender agrees to accept less for the loan payoff than the total amount due.

smoke detectors State law requires that residential properties be equipped with smoke detectors, and local ordinances may impose more rigid requirements. The specific requirements may vary depending on the type of property, the number of units, and the number of stories of the property.

spurious title False or erroneously acquired, occasionally is discovered after escrow closing. It could be a prior claim to title from another party, such as through adverse possession, and calls into question who is the legitimate owner.

state lands As a result of the Treaty of Guadalupe Hidalgo, state lands were granted by the U.S. Congress to the State of California.

statement of identity This form gives escrow important information about the parties in preparing the escrow instruction. It also provides the title company the necessary information regarding the buyer's identity to ascertain the existence of any public records about the buyer, such as tax liens, judgments, paroles, incompetency, attorneys in fact, guardianship proceedings, bankruptcies, probates, and any other matter that could affect title.

statute of frauds The statute of frauds specifies which contracts must be in writing and signed.

Subdivided Lands Act This act was intended to protect the consumer from fraudulent marketing practices in the sale of subdivided parcels, including condominium projects. The Subdivided Lands Act requires DRE approval before sale of certain types of real estate interests. To get the approval, the prospective seller submits a lengthy application that describes the project in detail.

Subdivision Map Act If the sale involves new construction in a subdivision, it is regulated under the Subdivision Map Act. This act is the authority granting cities and counties the right to implement subdivision ordinances. It applies to all subdivisions of land into two or more parcels and is designed to coordinate lot design, street patterns, and easements for public utilities, and to assure that dedicated public areas (streets and alleys) are improved properly.

submerged lands Lands whose shoreward (against the land) boundaries coincide with the seaward (toward the sea) boundaries of tidelands.

succession Intestate succession (transfer of title to property of one who dies without a will) is specified in the manner indicated by the Civil Code.

supplemental instructions In a purchase transaction, the escrow holder usually prepares only instructions referred to as supplemental instructions if the purchase agreement used is one provided by the California Association of REALTORS® (CAR). The CAR form already includes joint escrow instructions (*joint* meaning instructions prepared on one form for both the buyer and the seller) and therefore do not need to be prepared again by the escrow holder.

supplemental tax bills State law requires the assessor's office to reappraise real property upon change in ownership or completion of new construction. The assessor's office must issue a supplemental assessment, which reflects the difference between the prior assessed value and the new assessment. This value is prorated based on the number of months remaining in the fiscal year (July 1 through June 30).

surety bonds An escrow agent must file a surety bond of at least $25,000 with the commissioner, intended to be used to pay to the state or any person any amount that is due to the state or such person under the provisions of the Escrow Law.

take sheet The initial worksheet of the escrow holder, it includes information regarding the property information, the buyer and the seller (marital status, address, vesting, and other personal information), the new loan of the buyer (amount, terms, rate, lender, and other details), prorating property taxes based on the anticipated closing date, identifying the title company (policy number, officer, and any special consideration, coverage, or exclusions), and information regarding any existing loans of the seller that will be paid off.

third-party instructions Occasionally, a party other than the principal who has a financial interest in the transaction may execute a third-party instruction to the escrow holder. A typical third-party instruction is when the broker entitled to a commission, as identified in the agreement, orders a separate instruction to the escrow holder to be paid at the closing.

tidelands Lands located between the ordinary high-water and ordinary low-water lines of tidal waters.

title plant Instead of visiting the county recorder's office to search public records, title companies have established their own facilities, called title plants, where they store copies of all public records they obtain from the county recorder's office. These plants contain vast computer databases of all public records from the county in which the property is located.

title search The title process begins with a thorough and diligent search of all title records and public documents related to both the property and the principals, reviewing matters that may affect title and risk to the title insurance company for claims.

transaction outline A basic outline of the transaction after obtaining the initial information from the parties. When the preliminary title report is received, the escrow officer will update the information, correcting anything that differs from what the parties provided (after confirming with them first that the preliminary title report is correct). Outlining the details of the transaction in narrative form helps establish the objective of the principals.

transfer Refers to conveying title to real property to another in one of several methods.

Treaty of Guadalupe Hidalgo An important part of California's real estate history, it marked the end of the Mexican-American War in 1848, led to California's statehood in 1850, and established the fundamental principles of title to property.

true easements The fundamental characteristic of a true easement is that it benefits another particular piece of land, referred to as the dominant estate. The land that is encumbered by the easement, that which gives up a right for the benefit of the dominant estate, is called the servient estate.

trust Trust monies are those that belong to someone else. Trust is placed in the escrow holder, who represents and is the closing agent for all principals in the transaction, which could be a buyer, a seller, a lender, a borrower, a lessee (tenant), a lessor (landlord), a vendee (a buyer under a land contract), or a vendor (a seller under a land contract).

trust deed A trust deed (or deed of trust) is a debt or security instrument used by a lender to identify and secure the collateral (real property) being pledged by a borrower for obtaining a loan.

trustee In a trust deed, the trustor transfers the "bare legal title" to the land to a trustee on behalf of a beneficiary (lender) in order to secure a debt using the property as collateral. The trustee serves to facilitate the reconveyance of the lender's lien against the title upon the satisfactory payoff of the borrower's loan. The trustee also processes a foreclosure action against the borrower on behalf of the lender.

trustee sale guarantee The trustee sale guarantee (TSG) report provides the foreclosing trustee with the information necessary to process the trustee's foreclosure and guarantees the correctness of that information.

trustee's sale The final process in foreclosure under a trust deed. The property may be sold at public auction by the trustee to the highest bidder, to whom title is then transferred.

trustor Term used to identify the borrower under a deed of trust.

Truth in Lending Act The federal Truth in Lending Act requires a mortgage lender to provide the borrower with certain information before the borrower becomes obligated to receive loan funds.

Truth in Lending Act (Regulation Z) Regulation Z, frequently called "Reg Z," requires real estate licensees acting as creditors to furnish truth-in-lending disclosures to consumers.

UCC-1 The financing statement for transfers of business property. It may serve as the security agreement, but usually a separate security agreement is prepared.

unenforceable contracts Some contracts are unenforceable even if they are not void or voidable. For example, perhaps the statute of limitations has expired, making an otherwise and previously enforceable contract now unenforceable.

Unilateral Contracts A contract in which one party to the contract promises to perform but the other party or parties do not.

Unruh Civil Rights Act A state law expressing a policy of nondiscrimination in very broad terms, applicable to all business establishments of any kind whatsoever, and prohibiting certain discrimination in the rendering of "services" without further specification.

Veterans' Affairs (VA) The U.S. Department of Veterans Affairs provides VA loans up to 100% financing and up to an amount based on the veteran's entitlement, presently $104,250. The maximum VA loan with no down payment requirement is four times the entitlement.

vesting The names and manner of the parties taking title, such as John James and Mary James, Husband and Wife as Joint Tenants. The exact spelling should be compared with the names as indicated on the purchase agreement.

void contracts A contract is void, doesn't exist at all, if all elements of the contract are present except consideration, or if it involves an illegal act.

voidable contracts The contract is valid but not enforceable if rejected by one of the parties, typically the party who stands to be damaged because the contract lacks essential elements.

warranty deed Usually only contain certain title covenants offering limited protection to the titleholder.

will Property owners may will their interest in it to another, transferring title upon their death.

INDEX

INDEX